TROUBLED TRANSIT
Asylum Seekers Stuck in Indonesia

The **ISEAS–Yusof Ishak Institute** (formerly Institute of Southeast Asian Studies) was established as an autonomous organization in 1968. It is a regional centre dedicated to the study of socio-political, security and economic trends and developments in Southeast Asia and its wider geostrategic and economic environment. The Institute's research programmes are the Regional Economic Studies (RES, including ASEAN and APEC), Regional Strategic and Political Studies (RSPS), and Regional Social and Cultural Studies (RSCS).

ISEAS Publishing, an established academic press, has issued more than 2,000 books and journals. It is the largest scholarly publisher of research about Southeast Asia from within the region. ISEAS Publishing works with many other academic and trade publishers and distributors to disseminate important research and analyses from and about Southeast Asia to the rest of the world.

TROUBLED TRANSIT

Asylum Seekers Stuck in Indonesia

ANTJE MISSBACH

ISEAS YUSOF ISHAK INSTITUTE

Gedanken über die Dauer des Exils
Schlage keinen Nagel in die Wand
Wirf den Rock auf den Stuhl.
Warum vorsorgen für vier Tage?
Du kehrst morgen zurück.
Lass den kleinen Baum ohne Wasser.
Wozu noch einen Baum pflanzen?
Bevor er so hoch wie eine Stufe ist
Gehst du fort von hier.
Zieh die Mütze ins Gesicht, wenn Leute vorbeigehn!
Wozu in fremden Grammatiken blättern?

— Bertolt Brecht

First published in Singapore in 2015 by ISEAS Publishing
ISEAS–Yusof Ishak Institute
30 Heng Mui Keng Terrace
Singapore 119614

E-mail: publish@iseas.edu.sg
Website: <http://bookshop.iseas.edu.sg>

ISEAS Library Cataloguing-in-Publication Data

Missbach, Antje.
    Troubled Transit : Asylum Seekers Stuck in Indonesia.
    1. Refugees—Australia.
    2. Boat people—Australia.
    3. Asylums—Government policy—Australia.
    4. Refugees—Indonesia.
    5. Boat people—Indonesia.
    6. Refugees, Somalis—Indonesia.
    I. Title.
HV640.4 A81M67   2015

ISBN 978-981-4620-56-7 (soft cover)
ISBN 978-981-4620-87-1 (e-book, PDF)

Typeset by Superskill Graphics Pte Ltd
Printed in Singapore by Markono Print Media Pte Ltd

CONTENTS

LIST OF TABLES

ACKNOWLEDGEMENTS

I am heavily indebted to Frieda Sinanu for supporting this project from its very infancy until today. Without Frieda, I might not have had such a smooth entry into the field and, without her as a co-author, a number of related publications would have never seen the light of day. I am also much obliged to a number of colleagues from the University of Melbourne, particularly the Centre for Indonesian Law, Islam and Society. In particular, I would like to thank Tim Lindsey for commenting on the early drafts and Melissa Crouch, with whom I have co-authored two related publications. I owe special thanks to friends and colleagues for supporting this project in many ways: Jemma Purdey, Vannessa Hearman, Dave McRae, Julian Millie, Kate McGregor, Jeremy Kingsley, Sara and Julia Dehm, Anne McNevin, Michelle Bunnell Miller and Tim Bunnell, Nik Tan and Marshall Clark. Thank you also to Anne Kallies, Lisa Capri, Helen Pausacker, Kathryn Taylor, Tessa Shaw, Rheny Pulungan, Cosima McRae, Anna Dziedzic and Dewi Apsari. I have greatly benefited from Louise Ellis and her editorial assistance as well as from Chandra Jayasuriya who equipped this book with a most useful map. Anne Looker has accompanied my work for many years and once again was of tremendous help with this project. Great thanks go to Rachel Salmond for being an eagle-eyed editor.

During fieldwork in Indonesia, I was incredibly fortunate to enjoy the help of many friends and colleagues. In particular, I would like to thank the Centre of Strategic and International Studies for hosting me twice. Lina Alexandra deserves special mention for her incredible support with my visa applications. Moreover, I am deeply indebted to Bob Hadiwinata at the University of Parahyangan, as well as Lintje Pellu from Universitas Kristen Artha Wacana for welcoming me as a visiting fellow. Furthermore, special thanks to Dina Afrianty from Universitas Islam Negeri Syarif Hidayatullah, Taufiq Almakmun from Universitas Sebelas Maret, as well as Ferdinand Andi Lolo and Tri Nuke Pudjiastuti from Universitas Indonesia. For her incredible help as research assistant I am very thankful to Fitrah Siska Marissa and to Mayolisia Ekayanti for checking numerous translations.

Without the many interlocutors who took their time to talk to me about their experiences as transit migrants in Indonesia, writing this book would not have been possible. On countless occasions, I have appreciated the kindness of people who themselves suffered dreadful experiences during their displacement. Although I might not always have succeeded in convincing them of what good it would do them to write a book about their experiences of life in transit, many nevertheless provided me with their incredible insights and shared parts of their life stories with me. For this I cannot be grateful enough. I wish I could thank you all in person, but I have promised to keep your names confidential.

During fieldwork in Indonesia, I have tried to gather a variety of viewpoints on the topic of transit migration. It was of great concern to me to include both the perspectives of Indonesian state authorities and law enforcement bodies as well as those of representatives of non-government organizations. Again, it would be a great delight to thank by name all those who have provided me with detailed understandings and at times also challenged my own views, but unfortunately I have to refrain from doing so for confidentiality reasons. The same need for restraint also applies to the staff members from the IOM, the UNHCR and its implementation partner, the CWS, whom I interviewed and learned from. Although many people have contributed generously to the preparation of this book, all errors and shortcomings in this book are solely my responsibility.

Given that fieldwork often takes longer than expected and turns out to be more costly than anticipated, I was glad of the financial support that I could rely on. Many thanks to the University of Melbourne for granting me the McKenzie Postdoctoral Fellowship, to the Melbourne Law School for providing me with a research grant and to the Fritz Thyssen Stiftung for equipping me with a special fieldwork grant.

My special thanks go to Annett Fleischer, Katrin Bosshard, Enrico Dähnert, Sofie Arjon Schütte, Gunnar Andersson, Ingrid Wessel, Luise Jäckel, Alex Flor, Simone Scheffler and Oskar, Kim van den Nouwelant and Rahadian Permadi, Anh Nguyen, Bea Viegas, Simone Schütz, Nicholas Geard, Patrick Stockwell, Thomas Flenady and Rachel Sztanski.

During the last four years I have published a number of shorter pieces on transit migration in Indonesia, both in print and online media, which often formed the basis for longer pieces and essentially for this book. Parts of the book chapters draw on material published previously: "Asylum Seekers in Indonesia: Don't Come, Don't Stay, Don't Go", *Indonesian Quarterly* 40, no. 3 (2012): 290–307; "Waiting on the Islands of 'Stuckedness': Managing Asylum Seekers in Island Detention Camps in Indonesia: Late 1970s to the Early 2000s", *Austrian Journal of South-East Asian Studies* 6, no. 2 (2013): 281–306; "Doors and Fences: Controlling Indonesia's Porous Borders and Policing Asylum Seekers", *Singapore Journal for Tropical Geography* 35, no. 2 (2014): 228–44; and "Making a 'Career' in People-Smuggling in Indonesia: Protracted Transit, Restricted Mobility and the Lack of Legal Work Rights", *SOJOURN: Journal of Social Issues in Southeast Asia* 30, no. 2 (2015): 423–54.

N

Jayapura

WEST PAPUA
(IRIAN JAYA)

Merauke

Pacific Ocean

PHILIPPINES

Moluccas I.

Ambon

I N D O N E S I A

AUSTRALIA

Timor Leste

Maumere

Flores

Rote Island
Sabu Island

Kupang

SULAWESI

Sumba

Ashmore
Reef

South China
Sea

SABAH

SARAWAK

KALIMANTAN

Balikpapan

Pontianak

Makassar

Situbondo
Surabaya
Semarang
Purwakerta
Solo

Bima
Labuan Bajo

Bali
Mataram
Lombok
Sumbawa

Trenggalek

VIETNAM

CAMBODIA

THAILAND

MALAYSIA

Laut I.

Natuna I.

Anambas I.

Singapore
Batam
Bintan
Galang I.
Tanjung Pinang

Kuala
Lumpur

Tanjung
Balai
Asahan

Medan

ACEH

Banda Aceh

Pekanbaru

SUMATRA
Padang

Lampung

Merak
Panaitan I.

Cibinong
Jakarta
Cipayung

JAVA
Bandung
Bogor
Pelabuhan Ratu
Sukabumi

Puncak
Cisarua

Christmas I.

Indian Ocean

0   400 km

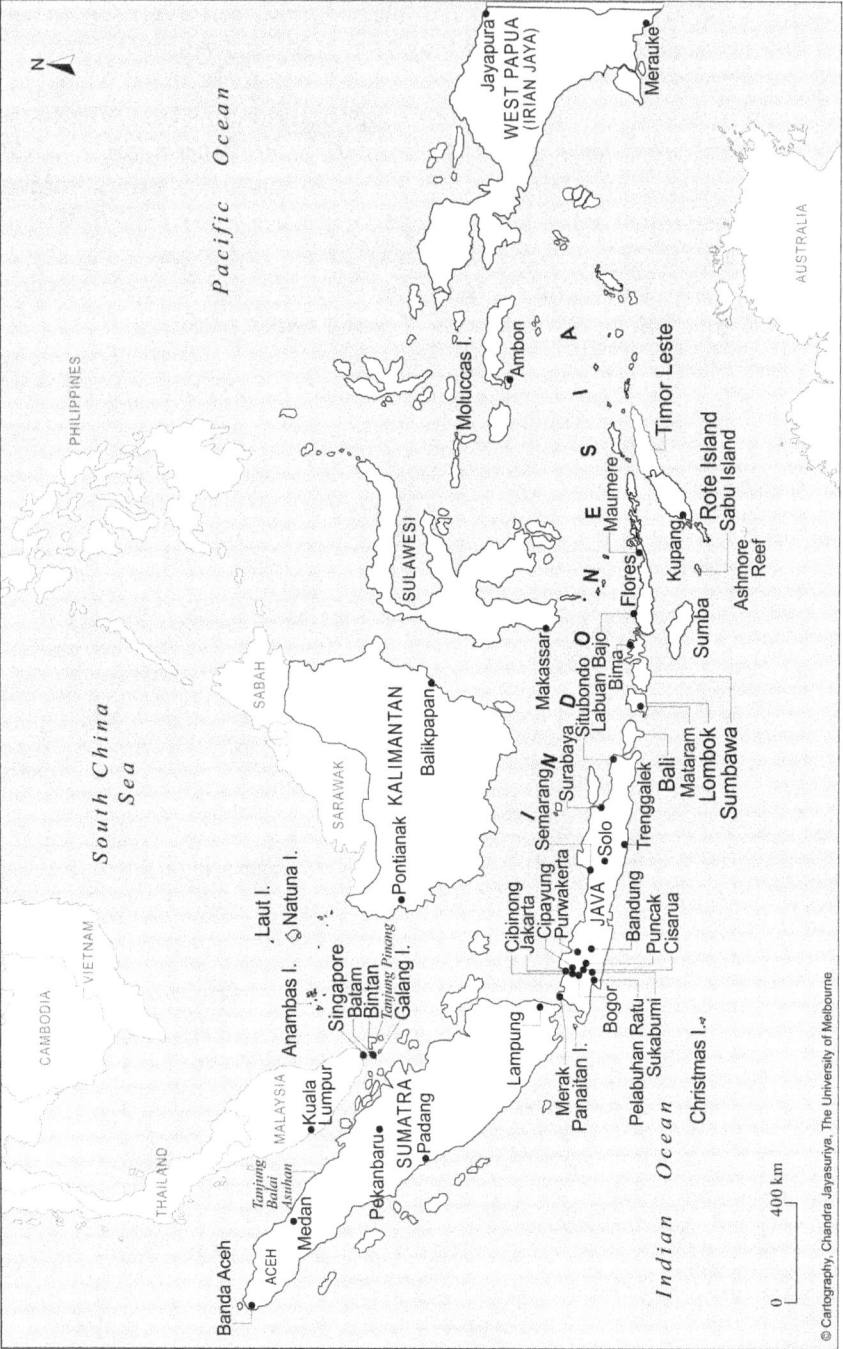

© Cartography, Chandra Jayasuriya, The University of Melbourne

ACRONYMS AND INITIALISMS

AFP	Australian Federal Police
AMSA	Australian Maritime Safety Authority
ASEAN	Association of Southeast Asian Nations
Baharkam	Badan Pemeliharaan Keamanan (Security Maintenance Agency of the National Police)
Bakorkamla	Badan Koordinasi Keamanan Laut (Maritime Security Coordination Board)
Basarnas	Badan SAR Nasional (National Search and Rescue Agency)
Bhabinkamtibmas	Bhayangkara Pembina Keamanan dan Ketertiban Masyarakat (Village Leadership for Social Security and Order [of the Police])
BNN	Badan Narkotika Nasional (National Narcotics Agency)
CAT	Convention against Torture and Other Cruel, Inhuman or Degrading Treatment or Punishment
CPA	Comprehensive Plan of Action
CWS	Church World Service
DIAC	Department of Immigration and Citizenship (Australian Federal Government)
FPI	Front Pembela Islam (Islamic Defenders Front)
Hizb-e Wahdat	Hizb-e Wahdat-e Islami Afghanistan (Islamic Unity Party of Afghanistan)
HRW	Human Rights Watch
ICCPR	International Covenant on Civil and Political Rights
ICEM	Intergovernmental Committee for Migration (predecessor of IOM)

INTERFET	International Force for East Timor
IOM	International Organization for Migration
jamkesmas	*jaminan kesehatan masyarakat* (community health insurance)
JCLEC	Jakarta Centre for Law Enforcement Cooperation
JRS	Jesuit Refugee Service
Komnas HAM	Komisi Nasional Hak Asasi Manusia (National Human Rights Commission)
LBH	Lembaga Bantuan Hukum (Legal Aid Institute)
LSAKK	Lembaga Studi Advokasi Keimigrasian dan Kewarganegaraan (Immigration and Citizenship Advocacy Study Institute)
LTTE	Liberation Tigers of Tamil Eelam (Tamil Tigers)
MCIIP	Management and Care of Irregular Immigrants Project
P3V	Panitia Pengelolaan Pengungsi Vietnam (Management Committee for Vietnamese Refugees) sometimes also translated as Penanggulangan dan Pengelolaan Pengungsi Vietnam (Prevention and Management of Vietnamese Refugees), Pusat Perlindungan Pengungsi Vietnam (Centre for the Protection of Vietnamese Refugees), or Pengamanan dan Perawatan Pengungsi Vietnam (Protection and Treatment for Vietnamese Refugees)
PMI	Palang Merah Indonesia, Indonesian Red Cross
Polres	Polisi Resor (district police)
Prolegnas	Program Legislasi Nasional (National Legislation Programme)
puskesmas	*pusat kesehatan masyarakat* (community health clinics)
RANHAM	Rencana Aksi Nasional Hak Asasi Manusia (National Action Plan for Human Rights)
RCA	Regional Cooperation Agreement Model (tripartite collaboration between IOM, the Government of Australia and the Government of Indonesia)

RELA	Ikatan Relawan Rakyat Malaysia (Volunteers of Malaysian People)
RMIM	Reinforcing Management of Irregular Migration (programme under IOM)
rudenim	*rumah detensi imigrasi* (immigration detention centre)
SATGAS	*satuan tugas* (taskforce)
SIEV	suspected irregular/illegal entry vessel
UNHCR	United Nations High Commissioner for Refugees
USAID	United States Agency for International Development

1

INTRODUCTION

> I am still alive; I have got near death.
> … our boat sank and split into two and the water
> got in and we all drank sea water, but we are still alive.
> (SMS from Ali, 15 April 2012)

"STRANGERS" IN "PARADISE"

In April 2012 a wooden boat with thirty-four Somalis on board was stranded on the tropical island of Sumbawa in the geographic heart of the Indonesian archipelago.[1] After two days of a disastrous journey headed for Australia that started on the island of Lombok, the boat had not moved very far from its initial point of departure. While other departure points for clandestine journeys to the "lucky country" have come under stricter border control in recent years, people smugglers have chosen Lombok as an alternative, despite the greater distance from Australia which makes the voyages even more dangerous. Not only are the boats that the asylum seekers use usually overcrowded, unseaworthy and crewed mostly by young and inexperienced Indonesians, but they sometimes even lack appropriate navigation equipment. The Somalis did not have good luck. On the very first day of the journey a storm hit and treated the boat — twelve metres long by three metres wide — like a nutshell in the ocean. After the engine and the pumps failed, people on board had to bail water to prevent the boat from going down. Unlike the many before them who had drowned on similarly dangerous passages,[2] the Somalis were lucky in one respect: a larger Indonesian ship discovered them and towed them back to the shore, where the police arrested them not long after.

Among these Somalis was a young man, Ali.[3] I had befriended Ali several months earlier when I spent time in Cisarua, a mountainous village in West Java that serves as a reception area for asylum seekers, recognized refugees and other undocumented migrants. While Ali's story is in many ways unique, it also represents the more common experiences of asylum seekers in transit in Indonesia. Thus, it is worth introducing Ali in detail.

After losing a lawsuit, a group of vigilantes from another clan killed Ali's father in his shop in Jowhar (central Somalia) and threatened the rest of the family. Ali's mother decided that it would be best if Ali left the country as soon as possible.[4] His brother had left earlier but went missing while trying to cross over to Yemen. A seemingly favourable opportunity arose for Ali when a Somali with Australian citizenship showed up and offered his services to take Ali to Australia, which was known to accept a higher percentage of those who applied for asylum than the percentage of applicants accepted in Europe. Ali's mother scraped together US$5,000 to pay for his services and Ali went with this man in early 2010. They travelled first to Djibouti and the United Arab Emirates. From Dubai they flew to Kuala Lumpur in Malaysia. Contrary to Ali's assumption that this man would take him all the way to Australia, he handed Ali over to another smuggler. After two weeks in the outskirts of Kuala Lumpur, Ali crossed over to Medan in North Sumatra by boat with seven Afghan men and then took a domestic flight to Jakarta. Although the seven Afghans were arrested at the Jakarta airport, Ali managed to slip through. Glad not to have been caught but now left entirely on his own, Ali had to find help quickly. After all, he was not even eighteen years old.[5]

After waiting several hours outside the terminal, he met an English-speaking Indonesian taxi driver who knew a number of Somali students and offered to take Ali to live with them on the outskirts of the city for a couple of days. The students provided Ali with food and shelter and advised him to register as an asylum seeker at the office of the United Nations High Commissioner for Refugees (UNHCR). Ali did so and soon moved into a shelter for underage, unaccompanied asylum seekers in Cisarua. Ali was the only Somali among dozens of teenagers from Afghanistan and Pakistan. Life in the shelter was bearable, but extremely boring. Ali longed to study but could not attend university as he had no high-school diploma, having been tutored mostly at home by his father until his father died. As an asylum seeker he was not allowed to attend school to catch up with the studies he had missed earlier in his life.

After about one year the UNHCR approved his claim for protection. Although recognized refugees can apply for resettlement to a third country, being a single young man with no formal education and no relatives in any Western resettlement country, Ali's chances were bleak and he was in for a long wait. When he turned eighteen he had to leave the shelter for underage refugees. A monthly payment of Rp1,200,000 (AU$120) from the UNHCR covered his daily expenses, such as housing, food and clothing. Renting a room in the house of an Indonesian family helped him quickly to become proficient in Indonesian. Despite some sports activities offered by a local non-government organization, Ali felt his life was on hold. There was nothing for him to do. Days, weeks, months drifted by. Ali volunteered as an interpreter for Arabic-speaking asylum seekers from Yemen, Somalia, and even Sudan, when they occasionally required his help, but that was not a very fulfilling activity. Rather than being thanked for his efforts, he was often blamed for misinterpretation or withholding information when people's expectations were not immediately met or when services delivered did not meet their demands. Since he could neither receive any proper education or vocational training nor work legally, he felt he was wasting his most valuable years doing nothing. For this reason — and against his better judgement, as he had learned of the dangers of boat trips to Australia — he eventually boarded a boat. Rather than having to find a smuggler, he was found by one.

One day, when visiting his former student friends in Jakarta, Ali witnessed a fight between some long-term stayers and a group of newcomers from Somalia.[6] The long-term stayers had offered to organize a boat and an Indonesian crew to take the newcomers to Australia, as they did not wish to join the queue at the UNHCR.[7] The discussion became heated when the newcomers found out that the man who organized the boat had charged them a much larger sum than he had then paid to the Indonesian people smugglers, among them a number of police officers from Lombok (Kusmayadi 2012).[8] Fearing that this self-enrichment might have negative consequences for the quality of the boat and the equipment on board, the newcomers wanted to talk directly to the Indonesian organizers to renegotiate the price. Unable to communicate with the smugglers themselves, the newcomers asked Ali to interpret for them and offered him a free passage. Even though he knew the risks of such journeys, Ali agreed. Given that Ali did not receive any remittances from his family back in Somalia that would allow him to pay for a trip to Australia, he thought that this would be a once-in-a-lifetime chance. A few days later, he found himself on a plane to Lombok.

Unlike hundreds of other asylum seekers who attempted to reach Australia by boat and lost their lives during these perilous journeys, everybody from Ali's boat survived. Once they were back on solid ground, this time on the island of Sumbawa, all of the passengers were promptly arrested. The Somalis were accommodated in a local hotel for a few nights while waiting for a decision as to which immigration detention centre this group would be sent. Knowing the bad fate that would await him in an Indonesian detention centre, Ali ran off with a friend who had managed to hide some cash from the police while being searched. Following their escape, they evaded the police who were chasing them; by night they slept in rice fields to avoid detection and by day they hitched rides from locals, took buses, making frequent transfers, and then a ferry back to Bali. After more than ten days, they finally arrived back at square one in Cisarua.

Even poorer, but happy to be alive, Ali reconsidered his options. While his friend decided to fly to Turkey to try to make his way into "fortress Europe", Ali applied for "voluntary" repatriation. When I first heard about this new plan, I was just as shocked as I was when he had told me about his boat trip. When I asked Ali what he planned to do in Somalia, he said he would try to get as quickly as possible to Kenya where, according to him, work opportunities for Somalis were plentiful. Having waited in Indonesia for more than two years, he had come to the conclusion that more waiting would get him nowhere. Contrary to the relatively quick repatriation processes for asylum seekers who have either not had their claims for protection recognized or have changed their minds and wished to return to their country of origin, Ali did not hear back from the UNHCR for months. He grew increasingly restless. Despite his bad experience on the boat, Ali then started thinking again about another boat trip, as he no longer wanted to "waste his youth" in Indonesia. As Michael Collyer (2007, p. 686) put it, Ali was "suffering [from a] senseless experience of travelling for years but never arriving". Yet Ali's story is far from over.

So far, Ali's story has clearly shown that people's searches for protection and a life worth living are often more staggered and less destination-oriented than is commonly assumed. Roaming refugees who determine their own mobility, however, might not conform to the omnipresent postulation of "the good refugee", who waits patiently in one place, allowing time to pass until help is finally delivered. Such wishful thinking is based on the idea that state or supranational bodies can effectively manage global refugee flows, but, given the growing numbers of displaced people worldwide, this idea seems to clash with reality more often than not (Georgi 2010). Displaced people, whether their claims for protection have been recognized or not, often have to move quickly and use whatever options are available to them at the time. Consequently, it is the exception rather than the rule for migratory plans to work out as they were first imagined; multiple changes occur along the way. Smugglers might abandon their clients halfway through, having taken all their money, which compels the abandoned clients to reconsider and reorient themselves. Longer and more fragmented journeys are a developing phenomenon around the globe, as the search for permanent protection often requires several separate journeys with detours around multiple obstacles on their way (Collyer 2007, p. 669). Many states consider uncontrolled mass mobility as a threat to their ability to decide who may enter their territory and who may not. According to Nicholas de Genova (2010, p. 39), "the sheer autonomy of migration, especially that of 'unauthorized' migration, remains a permanent and incorrigible affront to state sovereignty and the power of the state to manage its social space through law and the violence of law enforcement".

The mobility of transit migrants is often constrained by transit states and destination countries. They stagnate in transit because they are prevented from migrating to the countries they choose and from returning to where they came from as ongoing political unrest in those places seriously puts their lives at risk. While the control of unwanted immigration is high on the list of priorities of most countries, decision-makers tend to ignore the impact of transit migration on society as they assume that transit migrants will not become permanent members of society; despite the fact that, in reality, transit migrants can get stuck for many years in the same place before they are able to move onwards, if, indeed, they are ever able to do so. Even though they may be prevented from formally becoming naturalized and integrated, transit migrants assimilate into the host society, simply because they work, consume and mingle.

While the presence of the UNHCR and other migration organizations helps to cushion some of their hardship, asylum seekers, refugees and other migrants stuck in transit may still endure a prolonged time of waiting. Transit then becomes limbo, which although in its literal sense limbo means "on the border to hell", is in this context perhaps better understood as the suspension from the juridical-political existence of a person through the person's exclusion from mainstream society (Oelgemoller 2011, p. 419). The longer people live in limbo, the harder it seems to be for them to move on. No wonder that the promise of a boat trip to Australia, that promised land down under, becomes an appealing option to cut short the time in transit.

This book seeks to illustrate the variety of experiences of transit migrants in Indonesia, extending the view beyond their ubiquitous black-and-white projection, usually with a hallmark of either pity or security concerns. Since 2009 there has been widespread media interest in Australia in the arrival of asylum seekers, yet there has been astonishingly little investigation into what these people go through *before* entering Australian territory. Ignoring pre-arrival circumstances is a serious shortcoming (M. Phillips 2012), given that the increasing length of time refugee journeys are taking increases the severity of the impact on the people on the move and on their post-migration lives.

In writing this book I have tried to refrain from taking sides. I aim to present as impartially as possible my observations, the facts that I collected and the stories shared with me, even though it is very challenging to do so. Merging micro- and macro-perspectives into one description will, I hope, allow a balanced depiction of the situation of transit migrants in Indonesia. By applying a bottom-up perspective, which evolves directly from the narratives of transit migrants, in the first four chapters and then switching to a top-down perspective, which directs the focus to state perceptions of transit migrants, the resulting policy changes, and international cooperation regarding irregular migration, I hope to achieve some balance between the often conflicting perspectives.

TRIGGERS OF INTEREST

Although dozens of boats with asylum seekers on board had been intercepted in Australian and in Indonesian waters, the boat with Somali passengers aboard came as a novelty to many observers. Given that the asylum seekers usually hail from conflict countries in the Middle East, Central and South Asia, first and foremost from Afghanistan, Iraq, Iran and Sri Lanka, the question arises of why somebody from Somalia would choose to come to Indonesia, thousands of kilometres from their homeland, rather than to seek protection in Somalia's neighbouring countries, such as Kenya or Yemen. If these might not be considered safe enough, why, then, would they not try to seek asylum in Europe?

In order to answer these questions, a number of factors — accessibility of human rights protection and the nature of opportunities to reach safe territory, to name but two — need to be taken into consideration as they all have a significant impact on the choice of transit and destination countries. In addition to the push factors that cause people to leave their countries of origin more or less involuntarily, the pull factors in the potential country of final destination, such as immigration and asylum policies, living standards and average income, also need to be taken into consideration as they too influence the choice of transit countries.

Clearly, most displaced people in need of protection do not have Indonesia in mind as the ultimate country of final settlement. Rather, they view Indonesia as an intended way station and the final stepping stone on the journey to Australia. Australia has built a reputation as a safe and democratic country offering a fair go for everyone, and, more recently, as a rich country unaffected by the global economic crisis, with relatively low unemployment. Besides its economic advantages, which may be more relevant in the considerations of economic migrants than of asylum seekers, until 2013 Australia was known to have a higher refugee acceptance rate than European Union (EU) member states, especially in regard to irregular maritime arrivals (Koser 2010b, pp. 5–6, Phillips and Spinks 2013, p. 4). Whereas, for example, in 2011 only twelve per cent of about 240,000 applicants were granted refugee status in the first instance (Expert Panel 2012, pp. 105–7), acceptance rates for asylum seekers from Afghanistan, Iraq, Iran and Burma/Myanmar have reached up to ninety per cent and above between 2009 and 2012 (Australian Department of Immigration and Citizenship 2012a). Despite this, Australia is chosen by only a small number of refugees, both in absolute and relative numbers. One of the main reasons for choosing the path to Australia via Indonesia over Europe is the cost of the journey to Australia, which has been considerably lower than the cost of being smuggled to the EU or the United States (HRW 2002; Hoffman 2010a; UNODC 2011; Barker 2013, pp. 16–17).

Despite Australia's high annual intake of skilled migrants, wealthy migrants and migrants with family connections, it has reacted very adversely towards asylum seekers who arrive by boat and are generally perceived as bringing little economic benefit because they lack the desired financial or social capital. Aside from these socio-economic reasons,

Australia's migration policies appear to be driven by a subliminal invasion angst. Whereas in the past the angst focused on Chinese or Vietnamese arrivals, Muslims have now become the new target (Dunn, Klocker and Salabay 2007). The urge to shield the country and protect its many privileges goes hand-in-hand with the desire to externalize migration management and process asylum applications outside Australian territory. Indonesia, East Timor, Malaysia and, more recently, Nauru and Papua New Guinea, as well as Cambodia have been considered as potential asylum-seeker warehouses. The externalization of migration management is justified politically through the impact of maritime disasters involving asylum seekers and refugees. Their deaths at sea form the basis of policies that seek to "dissuade migrants from the perilous journey" to Australia (Gammeltoft-Hansen 2008, p. 23). In other words, externalized border controls, combined with protection screenings outside Australian territory, which, more often than not, lack the sophisticated appeal mechanisms usually available in Western countries, aim to circumvent not only the physical arrival of people but also their access to domestic legal systems that might offer more beneficial responses to their claims for protection. The reopening of offshore processing centres on Nauru and Manus Island in Papua New Guinea in August 2012 was intended as the principal deterrent of asylum seekers who are considering irregular boat journeys to Australia. However, given that the numbers of arrivals of asylum seekers by boat did not diminish following the implementation of the new policies, often also referred to as "Pacific Solution II", the Australian government's approach, under the two Labor prime ministers, Julia Gillard and Kevin Rudd, has been brought into question. With the change of Australian government in September 2013, the new prime minister, Tony Abbott, introduced Operation Sovereign Borders, a military-led border-control regime that has returned asylum seeker boats to neighbouring countries.

Australia's behaviour is, in fact, similar to that of other popular destination countries in the Northern Hemisphere, which have also seen a "recent surge to *externalise* or *extra-territorialise* both the regulation of migration control and the provision of refugee protection" (Gammeltoft-Hansen 2008, p. 12). Tony Kevin (2012, p. 124) has concluded, rather harshly, that "it appears that Australia is becoming part of a global process of moral desensitisation and brutalisation, taking place on the maritime border zones of rich Western countries that are readily accessible by sea to asylum seekers travelling from or through adjacent poor countries".

Other Australian commentators and human rights advocates criticized the new policies adopted by the respective Labor and Liberal governments as systematically undermining the 1951 International Convention relating to the Status of Refugees and its 1967 Protocol ("Refugee Convention") (Thom 2012; Taylor 2012). Against the fair-go rhetoric, Australian politicians tend to see the lives of refugees and asylum seekers as less valuable, and subject them to indefinite detention in the offshore processing centres. The national media in Australia have contributed equally to the demonization of asylum seekers who arrive by boat, labelling them as "queue-jumpers".[9] Claiming asylum is not illegal;[10] reaching a safe place, however, may involve the use of illegitimate methods of transportation and the illegal crossing of borders.

This book is not intended as yet another critical analysis of Australian asylum and immigration policies. Over the last decade, academics and political commentators have produced an enormous body of literature about the Australian immigration and asylum policies (Mares 2001; Marr and Wilkinson 2003; Magner 2004; Every and Augoustinos 2007; Hyndman and Mountz 2008; Grewcock 2007 and 2009; Crock and Ghezelbash 2010; Weber and Pickering 2011). Many more academics are currently researching these issues and protesting their implications on the lives of asylum seekers. Nonetheless, many of these significant contributions tend to be rather Australia-centric in their understanding of the matter, ignoring the larger socio-political context in asylum seekers' countries of origin and along the migratory routes, the pre-arrival experiences of asylum seekers in transit, and the perspectives of transit states towards people in transit. As scholars have not yet examined what it means to be stuck in transit in Indonesia, this book hopes to divert the hitherto Australia-centric gaze northwards.

So far little has been published on asylum seekers and refugees in Indonesia or on Indonesia as a transit country. Savitri Taylor and Brynna Rafferty-Brown (2010*a*, 2010*b*) have looked at some of the administrative procedures put in place to manage asylum seekers in search of temporary and permanent protection in Indonesia. The period of their investigation ended in 2009, and a number of circumstances have changed since. Other researchers also have spent short periods of time in Indonesia, but often limited their investigations to samples, sometimes rather small, of asylum seekers and refugees only.[11] Relying merely on the accounts of asylum seekers and refugees, without interviewing other actors, such as representatives of Indonesian state authorities, non-government organizations and the local population, who are involved to a significant extent in managing transit migrants, can produce a rather biased assessment. By excluding the views of Indonesian policymakers and state officials, the researcher runs the risk of portraying Indonesia only as a lush location in the tropics rather than as a real state with policies and political interests. Overlooking Indonesian domestic politics in regard to transit migration can lead to some rather incorrect statements, such as this one, by Mountz (2011a, p. 125): "Prime Minister Kevin Rudd increased detention capacity on Indonesian islands and moved recently intercepted migrants there".

Driven by the fascination of fragmented journeys and migratory experiences of individuals who are asylum seekers and refugees, this book cannot reconstruct entire journeys but seeks to highlight one particular point of the journeys — Indonesia, the last stepping stone. It aims to present the complexities of life in transit for more than one particular ethnic group or nationality and it seeks to make the transit country the centre of attention. Indonesia, a vast archipelago of more than 17,000 islands, is more than a location where people spend time in waiting; it is a state that interacts with transiting migrants and formulates policies that affect them. As the Indonesian state and its politics matter a great deal for transit migrants, the book tries to explain the complexities of transit migration from the perspective of the migrants when they are in Indonesia and before they arrive in Australia. As well as sharpening the focus on the perspectives of transit migrants and their decision-making, it encompasses the political challenges that Indonesia faces as a transit country. Taking Indonesian policies and policymaking into account gives Indonesia the attention it deserves, as a transit country and as an important partner in regional protection schemes and migration management. Even though, from a human rights perspective, some Indonesian policies appear less than favourable, and even reprehensible, Australian politicians, academics and activists would be well advised to pay more attention to Indonesia if they hope to alleviate some of the hardships suffered by asylum seekers in Indonesia.

In contrast to some studies of transnationalism that overemphasize deterritorialization tendencies (for example, Schiller, Basch and Blanc 1994; Sassen 1999), this book delves into unique incidents and collective narratives in order to re-emphasise real-place and real-time experiences. Migration flows not only have an impact on the countries of origin of migrants and the destination countries where they settle for good; they also influence transit countries. Research on transit migration in Africa, for example, has revealed how increased migration flows have revived ancient Sahara tracks and transformed desert cities from sleepy oases into vibrant commercial hubs (de Haas 2005, 2007; Kimball 2007; Bredeloup and Pliez 2011). Even though the scale of transit migration in Indonesia is not as great as the migratory flows in Northern Africa, initial adjustments to the presence of transit migrants, such as the emergence of certain types of food, clothing or services, can be observed in Indonesian communities where transit migrants have lived for a number of years.

No in-depth anthropological studies on transit migration in Indonesia have been undertaken so far, even though transit migration in other parts of the world has attracted academic attention over the last decade. Studies of migratory flows from South America via Central America into the United States and from Africa and the Middle East via the Mediterranean states into the EU dominate the literature (Adepoju 1995, 2004; Andreas 2000; Içduygu and Toktas 2002; Papadopoulou 2004, 2005; ICMPD 2004; Chatelard 2005; Baldwin-Edwards 2006; Dani 2006; Collyer 2006, 2007; Carling 2007; Kimball 2007; Papadopoulou-Kourkoula 2008). As Indonesia has become a significant transit location for asylum seekers and migrants from areas of conflict in Asia and even Africa, this book seeks to contribute to a deeper understanding of the situation of transit migrants in the Indonesian limbo. It does not simply elucidate how transit migration functions in Indonesia; it also seeks to explain the motivations behind transit migration.

This book seeks to identify the wide differences between the situation of transit migrants in Indonesia and that of transit migrants in other countries, such as Greece and Turkey. As a non-signatory to the Refugee Convention and its Protocol, Indonesia offers no formal rights to asylum seekers and refugees within its territory, but tolerates their presence as long as they are undergoing refugee-status determination under the UNHCR or have been referred to the services of the International Organization for Migration (IOM). Unlike in the European Union, which has adopted many political changes that seek to harmonize national legislation for protection procedures, assessment of claims and resettlement/integration across its territory, asylum seekers and refugee flows across the Asia-Pacific region are managed more on an ad hoc basis, as there is no regional cooperation framework. The socio-economic situation affecting transit migrants in Indonesia is also different. For example, whereas transit migrants in Libya can earn enough money in a manual job to finance the next leg of their journey, transit migrants in Indonesia face great difficulties in finding short-term employment because of the high levels of unemployment and underemployment in that country.

DEFINING TRANSIT MIGRATION

Before proceeding, the phrase "transit migration" calls for definition and my heavy use of it requires explanation. Although "transit migration" is not a new phenomenon, it did not find its way into public policy discussions as a category of migration until the EU expanded into Eastern Europe in the early 2000s. From its first uses in the public policy debate, "transit migration" was embedded in the discourse on "illegal immigration" and "asylum panic". A wide range of new EU policies sought to discourage people from entering the EU irregularly by directing more responsibility to neighbouring states to control migration flows more effectively and to deter the onward migration of "unwanted" migrants and asylum seekers. The IOM launched a number of studies on transit migration in the countries across the EU's borders, such as Poland (1994), the Czech Republic (1994), Ukraine (1994) and Turkey (1995), which supported the creation of stricter EU policies on asylum and migration.[12] Prime targets were the EU member countries known for their lax approach towards irregular migrants and their toleration of transit migration. From this point of view, in the European context, "transit country" was no longer merely a descriptive geographic entity but was re conceptionalized into a tool of governance (Oelgemoller 2011, p. 416).

Earlier definitions of transit migration by the IOM (1994, p. 2) were vague. Transit migration was understood to constitute "migratory movements to one or more countries, with the intention to migrate to yet another country of final destination. The intentions and plans can develop at any stage, from the outset to any time while in transit, a process that can take a few days or several years". Other supranational organizations, such as the United Nations Economic Commission for Europe (UN/ECE) (1993, p. 7), stressed in particular the aspect of illegality when trying to come to terms with the phenomenon: "migration in one country with the intention of seeking the possibility there to emigrate to another country as the country of final destination by means that are partially, if not fully, illegal".

Despite the proliferation of the concept and the terminology across Europe, none of the definitions available are commonly accepted, either in political or in academic spheres (Papadopoulou-Kourkoula 2008; Düvell 2012). The lack of an authoritative definition has diminished the term's applicability as a tool for analysis. Furthermore, the politicization of the term that connects it with irregularity and illegal means has had a negative impact on the study of the phenomenon.

Eurocentric Perceptions of Transit Migration

Because of its many politically charged associations, scholars have expressed their unease with the term rather more than politicians have (Düvell 2012; de Haas 2005). According to Franck Düvell (2012, p. 418), it was a "code for 'illegal immigration'" as it referred to people who "do not belong here". Equating transit migration with illegality made it easier for states to criminalize undocumented migration (Kimball 2007, p. 32). However, condemning transit migration solely for the fact that its accomplishment involves acts of irregularity and illegality obscures the bigger picture of this long-term migration process, which often includes both regular and irregular modes of entry and residence at different points. For example, a person might enter a country with a valid student or tourist visa and then overstay, thereby becoming an irregular migrant, or engage in work activities not allowed under the conditions of their visa. Khalid Koser (2010a, p. 183) notes that switching back and forth between regularity and irregularity may be attributed to lack of knowledge of administrative regulations, but it may also be a deliberate choice. The regularity and irregularity of migration modes should thus by no means become a defining criterion of transit migration, even though unlawful border crossing, criminality, smuggling or unlawful work activities might occur at some point during transit migration. As Christina Oelgemoller (2011, p. 417) points out, there is no use in condemning secondary movements or transit migration as "illegal", without asking questions about the sufficiency or appropriateness of the so-called de facto protection.

A second problem in defining transit migration seems to lie in its application to the case of "mixed flows", which combine voluntary and forced migrant streams, thus rendering the dichotomy between deserving and undeserving mobile people *ad absurdum*. Increasingly, economic migrants in search of better life prospects and asylum seekers in need of international protection head in the same directions, travel along the same paths, rely on the same modes of transport and are confronted by the same challenges during their journeys. Trying to make clear distinctions between voluntary labour migrants, whose mobility should be controlled and whose needs should be managed by the state, and involuntarily displaced people, who require protection and assistance from state or supranational institutions, is a challenge. After a person has left his or her home country more or less involuntarily, it is hard to determine what that person constitutes in terms of legal typologies, especially when that person has not yet been able to have his or her claims for protection properly assessed. Having multiple motivations for their movement does not make the definition of their status any easier. Moreover, human rights problems, persecution and discrimination of minorities often go hand in hand with poor social conditions and humanitarian problems (Papadopoulou 2005; Borjas and Crisp 2005). While asylum and "irregular" labour migration are different issues and concern different policy areas, they do overlap in certain circumstances, as they do, for example, when a rejected asylum seeker becomes an irregular migrant, or when an irregular migrant has decided to apply for international protection and uses the asylum system as a means of onward migration (Papadopoulou 2005; Schuster 2005*b*). Changes in migration status while in transit occur frequently; they are the rule rather than the exception.

As the developments in the EU have demonstrated over the last decade, the European restrictionism and securitization of migration have created a distorted situation. As long as economic migrants are instructed by their smugglers or others to apply for asylum as an alternative means of migration, and thus be tolerated at least temporarily, those in need of protection are often not serviced appropriately (Triandafyllidou and Maroukis 2012). Abuse of the asylum system overburdens and eventually blocks the system for more genuine applicants. Moreover, because the acceptance rates of EU member states differ considerably (Triandafyllidou and Maroukis 2012; European Commission 2013), asylum seekers in need of protection rely increasingly on people smugglers to reach countries with higher annual refugee intakes. For example, rather than applying for asylum in Italy or Greece, both of which are known to have very low acceptance rates, people prefer to move on to Germany or France. They remain undocumented in a transit country (or place of first asylum) only to move on to make their claim for asylum elsewhere. However, as this runs counter to the EU requirement to apply for protection in the very first place of asylum, they are, if detected, usually transferred back to the EU country that they entered first.

From an empirical point of view, the creation of strict categories of migration remains highly questionable, as the separation of deserving refugees and undeserving migrants becomes a tool of state power. From a protection-driven approach, however, treating refugees differently from other migrants is more convincing because states have more legal obligations towards the first group than towards the latter (Collyer, Düvell and de Haas 2012). Given the complex nature of the constantly shifting mixed flows, from an academic point of view it might be advisable to follow Papadopoulou's (2005, p. 2) suggestion to "unravel the complexity of this relationship by approaching irregular, 'transit' and asylum migration as a continuum in the experience of forced migration". The particular case of Indonesia introduces an additional layer of complexity, as the strict distinction between transiting asylum seekers and transiting economic migrants is of lesser relevance for their treatment by the state. Because it is not a signatory to the Refugee Convention, Indonesia has fewer obligations towards aliens seeking protection within its state territory, as will be explained in the following chapters.

Throughout this book I apply the term "transit migrant" to a wide range of people who are on the move, including undocumented migrants (who might or might not apply for international protection while in Indonesia), documented asylum seekers and recognized refugees, stranded return migrants and even accidental migrants who have been abandoned by their smugglers. Aware of its political implications in the European context, I hope to dissociate the phrase "transit migration" both from its Eurocentric application and from its politicized and value-laden connotations of "illegality" and apply it in a more neutral way to the context of Indonesia. Without doubt, the situation of transit migrants in Indonesia is defined no less politically than in the EU, but the defining political circumstances in Indonesia are different from the political circumstances of the EU. Transit migration in Indonesia has not been politicized to the extent it has been in Europe, although it may well become so in the future. To identify the parameters of a workable definition of transit migration, I turn to more academic treatises on the concept.

Conceptual Ambiguities

Scholars have not been able to precisely define "transit migration" or "migration in transit" either, or even to find any widely accepted definition

(Düvell 2006). Most commonly, the term "transit migration" is used to refer to the phenomenon of people coming to one country with the intention of going to and staying in another (Içduygu 2000; Papadopoulou 2004). This oversimplified theoretical conceptualization of transit migration has been criticized by a number of scholars (for example, Düvell 2006; Kimball 2007) because it does not encapsulate the inherent complexities of the migratory processes; it has triggered their inquiry into how transit migration should be classified and what the parameters of a definition should be. What, in other words, should be among the criteria for "transit" — the duration of stay in a transit place, the intention of onward migration, or the actual outcomes of the journeys?

Relying on temporal limitation to define "transit" and hence "transit migration" is problematic for a number of reasons. In contrast to identifying the beginning of a migration process, it is very hard to define the terminus of a journey, as that depends on many factors, such as the finality of a migration decision/desire and the feasibility of integration into a destination society. In fact, final integration or settlement might not be the *ne plus ultra* in the first place, given the more advanced and cheaper options for mobility that allow people nowadays to live transnational lives and to be at home in several places almost simultaneously. Not knowing which destination country will become the final host country makes it hard to define the end of transit migration. Expecting journeys to end, at least mid-term, reinforces an excessively deterministic understanding of transit migration that strengthens rather than overcomes the dichotomy between "origin" and "destination" (Collyer and de Haas 2012).

Theoretically, being "in transit" can be any period of time between a few days and several years, or even an entire lifetime. The indefinite period of time spent in transit is in question — when does temporary stop and permanent start? — and makes a time parameter comprehensible only a posteriori. Only a minority of irregular journeys proceed steadily and unhindered and lead to instant temporary or semi-permanent/permanent protection or integration in the very first country that migrants approach after their departure from their place of origin. If a transit country is unwelcoming, does not meet the migrants' need for such things as sustainable employment and appropriate living conditions, or if it cannot provide protection and durable solutions, people move on if they can (Papadopoulou-Kourkoula 2008; Düvell 2012). People can, in fact, be in a state of transit multiple times.

Conversely, the opposite scenario is conceivable as well. People's journeys might come to a permanent halt in a transit country, despite their desire to migrate onwards. For example, people get held up when their financial resources are depleted or when all their possessions are stolen; their onward journey may be interrupted by political unrest at the next station of their intended trip. While awaiting the chance to move on and earning enough money to do so, people might have to stay much longer than they would like. Even though migrants might wish to move onwards, their expectations might never be met and the desired outcome of their journey might be indefinitely unattainable. If onward migration is unaffordable, staying in the "second best" country and accepting partial integration and initial steps for settlement might be the only viable alternative (Collyer and de Haas 2012).

In fact, it is possible for people to become stuck in transit, despite pressure from transit countries' governments for them to leave, which complicates their lives in transit because they are deprived of basic needs, such as health care, free schooling and access to employment. If neither onwards migration nor integration into a transit country are viable options, transit migrants become second- or third-class inhabitants, deprived of basic rights because of restrictive policies of that transit country which seek to prevent their long-term integration into its society. Making people's intentions the basic parameter in defining transit migration is, therefore, not helpful, as it is often unclear how informed they are when they make decisions about their onward movements or even how much choice they have in making decisions in the first place, given that many of their decisions may result from their compliance with external circumstances imposed upon them. Michael Collyer and Hein de Haas (2012, p. 477) even argue that the idea of fixed intentions is "empirically naïve". It is not always the case that transit migrants have concrete plans to follow specific routes to reach a preselected destination. During my interviews with transit migrants in Indonesia, I often got the impression that many had left their homes with no specific destination in mind and with little useful information. Chances previously anticipated often disappear along the journey, while unanticipated ones materialize. Nevertheless, during the migration processes, people have to make rational calculations and revise earlier decisions. Despite their dependence on many external determinants shaped by the government in the transit country and other influential actors, transit migrants in Indonesia retained at least a small degree of agency; in making their own decisions they are not just "mobile actors" (Schuster 2005a, p. 757), but also actors of their own mobility.

Finally, it makes little sense to define transit migration according to its outcomes, as there is no fixed or foreseeable outcome. At best, transit migration can result in permanent resettlement in a desired destination country.[13] Among possible outcomes is also the return to the starting point of a journey, through both forced deportation and voluntary repatriation. At worst, transit migration becomes a stalemate of "permanent temporariness". The provisional character of transit migration and the unpredictability of its outcomes make it difficult not only to measure and quantify, but also to develop effective policy responses (Papadopoulou-Kourkoula 2008, p. 141). Given the various limitations in refining a practicable definition of transit migration as a migration category, it becomes first and foremost perceivable as a process, rather than a status. As Papadopoulou (2005, p. 21) expressed it: "Transit migration is not a different type of migration, but a phase in which both economic migrants and refugees find themselves. With regards to forced migrants in particular, transit migration is a result of the lack of opportunities for effective protection and durable solutions in the first asylum country." When resettlement, repatriation and integration are not options for a durable solution, people are stuck in transit. Ghassan Hage (2009, p. 97) even speaks of the condition of "stuckedness" as an even compacter formula of "permanent temporariness".

The time of waiting can be prolonged and uncertain, and often accompanied by constant anxiety. Lack of protection, uncertainty, ambiguity and contingency shape life in transit and make people vulnerable to many risks and threats. The emotions that arise from the experience of being trapped in limbo can be as influential on people's lives as legal restrictions and policy frameworks (Papadopoulou-Kourkoula 2008, pp. 6–7). Transit migrants often say that they feel their life has been put on hold. Waiting for life to continue, while being neither here nor there, often prevents people from interacting with their immediate environment on the assumption that they will not spend much time in that country, an assumption which very often turns out to be false. The absence of social contacts and support further aggravate their daily hardship, as explained later in greater detail. In short, poverty, insufficient protection, unemployment and social exclusion are the main characteristics of life "in transit", fostering a process of marginalization rather than integration (Papadopoulou-Kourkoula 2008, p. 88). Nevertheless, though transit migrants may be vulnerable, they are not passive and helpless.

METHODOLOGY, RESEARCH LIMITATIONS AND ETHICAL CONSIDERATIONS

Most studies of migratory experience rely on data and information collected after migrants have arrived in a destination country. The experience of arrival may seriously affect how the migratory process is remembered. Eventual success in reaching a destination country might mean that failed migration attempts and missed chances fade in their memory, which, in turn, may cause migrants and refugees to recount their journeys as having been more purposeful and cohesive than they actually were. Driven by a more or less subtle desire that their stories make sense, narrators might in retrospect add more linearity, forethought and purpose to the story of their journey than the actual experience really had. In order to understand migratory decision-making processes before they are tweaked, rectified or embellished by hindsight, it is important to observe and interview people when they are actually making decisions. By observing different stages of the migratory process, more clarity should be gained into the reasons why people opted for one opportunity over another. Although such observation avoids the hazards of recall bias, the immediacy of its encounters and narratives in and of transition is not without its problems.

Because they do not know what the future will bring and what the outcome of their journeys — resettlement, return, stagnation or even death — will be, people who are in the middle of a long and perilous journey cannot necessarily describe their decision-making openly and logically, as their immediate options may be rather limited for the time being. The implication for the observer is that he or she must rely only on snapshots from interlocutors situated in rapidly and constantly changing environments. Equally difficult is winning the trust of people encountered in the field. Telling the researcher too much might cause their plans to fail. While I was interviewing people in the field, there may indeed have been many restraints of which I was unaware that prevented people from talking about what they wanted to. Communicating in a language that was not their mother tongue limited the transit migrants' ability to express the nuances of their situation as they might have wished. Limited opportunities to speak freely affected not only transit migrants in detention, but also those living in the communities who needed to protect themselves from potential risk. When studying decision-making processes, these limitations need to be kept in mind. I hope that the information content of the ethnographic insights presented in this book prevail over the inherent methodical and methodological limitations of the study.

Because I had limited opportunities for triangulation of the stories I encountered, in order to find out whether somebody was telling the whole truth of their migration plans, I took a rather flexible approach towards authenticity. Concentrating more on the reasoning of intent rather than the immediate outcomes of their migration plans helped me to extract valuable information. The sporadic nature of many encounters with interlocutors, owing to their high mobility, meant that I often could not verify what somebody said he or she intended to do next. Equally problematic were the differences between what people said they intended to do and what they actually ended up doing. Therefore, it must be borne in mind that the limitations for triangulation of the stories has influenced the representativeness of the findings of this study. Rather than offering easily verifiable facts and representative figures, I intend instead to present a number of distinctive migration realities and strategies that promote an understanding of the complexity, unsteadiness and multi-directionality of many "migrational 'transit biographies'" (Hess 2012, p. 429). Actor-centred research reveals migrants' agency and subjectivity, which are often missing from the global debate on irregular migration and mobility. Against the victimization of transit migrants, I try as much as possible to see them as dynamic agents for their own lives without, however, downplaying structural limitations for their decision-making. I accepted their choice not to talk about certain issues and tried not to challenge any of their decisions. Furthermore, I acknowledge the active impact they had on the scope of my research, as it was them who decided what I could research and what I could not.

Fieldwork for this book was conducted mainly in three provinces: in West Java (Bogor, Cisarua, Sukabumi, Pelabuhan Ratu); in Nusa Tenggara Timor, mainly Kupang and Rote; and in the Riau Archipelago, mainly on Batam and Bintan. While the Riau Archipelago is a popular entry gate for clandestine migrants, the other two provinces are known to be hotspots for transit migrants trying to head to Australia by boat. Indonesian informants often referred to these areas as *pagar terakhir* (last fence) or *pintu terakhir* (last door), depending on whether they saw the sea borders as boundary or as gateway. I also spent considerable time in Jakarta, which allowed me to engage with national authorities and policymakers. Fieldwork encounters, between one and seven months at a time, took place at several intervals between March 2010 and March 2014. Over more than fourteen months in the field, I conducted about 180 formal and informal interviews with transit migrants inside and outside of immigration detention centres, representatives of the international organizations, such as the UNHCR and IOM, with Indonesian state officials from relevant ministries, and with law enforcement officers, including police officers, investigators, prosecutors and judges. Last but not least, I had the chance to talk to some convicted people smugglers, who had stayed on in Indonesia after being rejected as asylum seekers. Meeting all these different people offered a great variety of views and perspectives on transit migration and people-smuggling.

In order to recruit informants, I relied first and foremost on "snowballing" (asking interlocutors for additional sources and potential respondents). Some encounters were one-off, while other interlocutors I met and interviewed many times over the years. Some interlocutors, who have known me over a longer period of time, acted as gatekeepers and helped me to get in touch with informants. I asked a few asylum seekers to write down their stories in their own words for me. I still keep in touch with some of the transit migrants via Facebook, SMS, or email. Living near where many transit migrants resided gave me certain insights into the daily routines of their public lives, but, as I was not a part of their households, my knowledge of their more private lives was limited.

In most cases I encountered open and interested interlocutors; however, due to the topic of my research, some paths for accessing additional information were deliberately blocked by local authorities. For the sake of protecting the identities of some vulnerable interlocutors, I have given them pseudonyms. In some cases, I even refrain from revealing the time and location of a meeting or interview in order to minimize any risks for them. The majority of interviews and meetings took place in public spaces, inside or outside offices and in cafes. Although I did visit the temporary homes of some asylum seekers and refugees, for longer interviews I preferred to meet in quiet public spaces. During fieldwork, I had the chance to visit immigration detention centres, including in Makassar, Tanjung Pinang, Jakarta, Semarang, Pontianak and Kupang; prisons; shelters for unaccompanied minors; as well as temporary makeshift centres for arrested transit migrants in places such as schools and hotels. Additional materials presented in this book are open-source and non-classified, such as local newspapers, online fora and court documents.

Given that the main focus of my research was long-term transit migrants — people who have been living in Indonesia for at least three years — I was able to conduct most interviews in Indonesian, communicating in English to a lesser extent, depending on their national and educational background. Admittedly, the selection of interlocutors based on Indonesian language proficiency was a rather exclusive criterion, as it excluded people with more limited language options from being interviewed. The compromise, however, seemed inevitable, as I did not want to rely on interpreters, who were anyway hard to find in Indonesia for some languages. Younger transit migrants, in particular, managed to learn Indonesian easily, since some stayed with Indonesian families and others had local girlfriends. Consequently, migrants aged between eighteen and thirty-five years are overrepresented in this study. Generally, I found it easier to interview younger people, not only because our proximity in age helped me make contact with them, but also because their Indonesian language skills facilitated communication.

My status as researcher obstructed some encounters, as it was not in itself always a sufficient explanation of a request for an interview. Many found the fact that I was a German researcher who worked in Australia and came to Indonesia to do research rather puzzling. As people generally had certain expectations towards Westerners and their social roles — they are generally assumed to be from non-government organizations, the UNHCR/IOM or the staff of an embassy — I could not explain often enough why I was there and what the purpose of my questioning was. For some, writing a book appeared to be a good enough reason as they wanted their stories to be known to a larger, even though unknown, audience. Others made it clear to me that they wanted me to help them more directly to improve the particular situation in which they were ensnared. For example, detained asylum seekers hoped I would be able to facilitate their release from detention centres. Despite telling detention centre inmates that I was neither from an embassy nor from the UNHCR or IOM, they sometimes handed me letters or sneaked them into my bag. A few informants asked for money or other incentives, but, if that happened before the interview, I would usually cancel the meeting. If it happened during a meeting I would explain why I could not pay any money and ask if they wanted to continue. A few Indonesian government officials were also not free of expectation or speculation; some made it quite clear that they thought I was a foreign spy rather than a researcher. The fact that I was affiliated with an Australian university in no way allayed their suspicions. Given the sensitivity of the issue of asylum seekers to international migration organizations, it took time to win the trust of some staff members and have them talk openly with me about their daily concerns and difficulties in ways that went beyond their organizations' press releases. When talking to my interlocutors I tried to be as transparent as possible about my research agenda and as realistic, sensitive and responsible as possible about what they could expect from me in return for sharing their stories.

There may have been some jealousy of my many privileges as a Westerner, such as my freedom to travel back and forth between Germany, Indonesia and Australia, but it was never expressed in an aggressive or obstructive way. Opportunities to distance myself from the field and its psychological burdens were very important, especially at highly distressing times, such as when I learned that three young boys I had visited a number of times had drowned during an attempt to reach Australia. In order to maintain a healthy emotional distance from the transit migrants, many of whom were severely distressed or traumatized, I had to retreat from the field for periods of time in order to reflect on all these impressions and return later.

Aware of the context in which the encounters and information exchanges took place, I have to bear in mind the unavoidable interference and impact on situations arising from my mere presence in the field. When talking to me, transit migrants *might* have painted their lives in gloomier colours, in order to solicit my compassion, than they might have when, for example, talking to their friends back home from whom they might prefer to hide all misery and failure. Others might have deliberately kept quiet about certain negative experiences and hardships in order not to appear weak in my eyes. As people are not blank slates, having had many experiences along their journey, some good and some not, I had to be aware of unexpressed obstructions. For example, people who have been interviewed or questioned or interrogated many times before, by various entities and in various contexts, might find my simple request for an interview a rather uninviting call. As is the case in many ethnographic studies, situating what people narrate can only be achieved once the stiffness of interview situations is overcome. It is always better to encounter people in their daily lives, but that is not an option for people detained in detention centres.

Ethical dilemmas in the study of irregular migration arise not only during the data collection in the field, but also in presenting, writing, and publishing research findings (Düvell, Triandafyllidou and Vollmer 2010). Despite using pseudonyms and other means to ensure the anonymity of interlocutors, once something is published it may take on a life of its own that may run contrary to the author's intentions. Given the vulnerability of transit migrants, some concerned scholars have questioned the justification for studying irregular migration. After all, the potential for risk might increase for those living underground and may unintentionally bring negative impacts, such as more discrimination, regulation or interference when their otherwise concealed lives are exposed. Although the trade-off between protecting vulnerable people by not exposing them, on the one hand, and filling in gaps in order to produce a more comprehensive and in-depth knowledge, on the other, will never be finally or fully clarified, I hope this book helps eliminate misconceptions of Indonesia as a transit state and misperceptions surrounding transit migrants in Indonesia.

STRUCTURE OF THE BOOK

This book is divided into eight main chapters and a brief conclusion, each of which is driven by a leading research question and concentrates on one key issue that characterizes or shapes transit migration in Indonesia. Therefore, although cross-referenced and linked throughout the whole book, each chapter can be read on its own. It follows basic principles of grounded theory and applies a dialogical structure between each of the main stakeholders.

Chapter One has explained the methodological approaches and hurdles and laid the theoretical foundations of this book's main interest — the clarification of what it means to be in transit. It has introduced Ali, whose case has demonstrated the difficulty of living "in a world, in which it is increasingly more difficult and yet increasingly inevitable not to be where one does not belong" (Horn 2006, p. 249). Ali's experiences in Indonesia, as well as those of several other transit migrants, will accompany the reader throughout most of the following chapters, to deepen empathy for and understanding of transit migration.

The second chapter will shed light on what it means to be a transit migrant in Indonesia. By comparing the Indochinese boat people, who arrived in Indonesia between the late 1970s and the early 1990s, with the current flow of transit migrants, mostly from conflict areas in the Middle East, South Asia and East Africa, the chapter provides an historical overview of Indonesia's experiences as a transit country and provides up-to-date numbers of transiting populations. Special attention is given to the Indonesian government's deliberations and decision-making in regard to handling transit migrants on the island of Galang. Although the refugee camp on Galang, at least outside Indonesia, became a symbol of Indonesia's great hospitality offered to strangers, many Indonesians feel very uneasy when they are reminded of this historical episode, or even worse, of a potentially similar setup for transit migrants in the near future.

Chapter Three sheds light on modes of arrival and journeys within Indonesia in order to point out common characteristics of fragmented journeys into and within the country. As transit migrants' mobility is often impeded and onward migration obstructed, the chapter also provides a very detailed illustration of what life is like in limbo in Indonesia. It describes the policies of arrest and the living conditions of transit migrants in immigration detention centres. The praxis of indefinite detention of transit migrants in highly corrupt and at times dangerous environments adds to the de facto criminalization of transit migrants. The driving question behind this chapter seeks to scrutinize the logics of detention, which prioritize immigration law enforcement over refugee protection.

In Chapter Four registered transit migrants residing amongst Indonesian communities and undocumented transit migrants living "underground" are the focus. Unaccompanied underage asylum seekers and their plights receive special attention. By portraying a number of transit migrants and their daily hardships, characterized by the prohibition to work and earn a living, lack of education, xenophobic encounters and extortion, it becomes obvious why many transit migrants try to minimize the length of their stay in Indonesia and decide that the risk of crossing to Australia in a rickety boat is worth taking.

Switching from a bottom-up to a more top-down approach, Chapter Five examines the roles of the UNHCR and the IOM, both of which carry heavy responsibilities in managing transit migrants. It provides detailed information about resettlement options, voluntary return and deportations. By outlining the technicalities relevant to applying for protection and elucidating the limits of protection in transit, the chapter provides a basis for critically challenging the current approaches and politicking of the UNHCR and the IOM in Indonesia.

Indonesian state perspectives on transit migration are the focus of Chapter Six, the driving question of which is to determine the impacts that transit migration has on the transit country and its policies. Discussion of relevant existing laws and of persistent gaps in legal regulations for dealing with transit migration over a prolonged period of time will explain Indonesia's passivity hitherto. Given the higher influx of transit migrants into the archipelago, the chapter then outlines how Indonesia has become more assertive in controlling its borders and enforcing its new immigration laws and how it has become more active in maritime search-and-rescue operations while also pointing out a number of structural challenges and political problems resulting from the semi-permanent presence of transit migrants.

Chapter Seven explores the implications of transit migration for relationships between transit countries and their neighbouring potential destination countries. It includes a lengthy discussion of bilateral relations between Indonesia and Australia, which are overshadowed by issues of transit migration, people-smuggling and the extradition of people smugglers. Besides elaborating on a number of bilateral and multilateral approaches to curb transnational crime, including people-smuggling, the chapter mentions particularly contentious issues arising from differing domestic political scenarios in both countries.

A detailed investigation of people-smuggling dominates Chapter Eight, in which the main point of interest is the correlation between transit migration and the evolution of people-smuggling networks. The chapter shows how particular frustrations of prolonged transit have enabled foreign and local smuggling networks to flourish in Indonesia. By presenting three short case studies of rejected asylum seekers who have turned to people-smuggling as a way of making a living in transit, and their specific roles in the operations, the chapter demonstrates the resilience of people-smuggling networks in the face of anti-people-smuggling law enforcement activities. Unable to return to their conflict-ridden home countries and yet without options for resettlement to safe third countries, while at the same time being banned from legal work in the transit country, for the three men, entering the criminal networks and working as recruiters, middlemen and facilitators appeared almost as the last option left while stuck in transit. A brief conclusion summarizes the main themes of the book.

Notes

1. Although Somalia was the third most important source country of asylum seekers in 2009, falling to sixth place in 2010 (UNHCR 2011a), the numbers of Somalis in Indonesia remain very small. As of October 2012, forty-one Somali

women and eighty-one men were registered as refugees under the UNHCR in Indonesia, while another 241 Somalis (129 women and 111 men) awaited the outcome of their applications (UNHCR Indonesia 2012c). By March 2014, their numbers had increased to 292 refugees (133 women and 159 men) and 350 asylum seekers (250 men and 100 women) (UNHCR Indonesia 2014).

2. It has been estimated that more than 1,550 people lost their lives during voyages from Indonesia to Australia between 1998 and 2011 (Hutton 2013). Between 2001 and 2012, a total of 964 were confirmed to have either died or gone missing at sea (Expert Panel 2012, p. 75).

3. Not his real name. Names of asylum seekers who have shared their stories have been changed throughout this book for their protection.

4. Interview with Ali, 2 November 2011.

5. Interview with Ali, 28 February 2012.

6. Although a few Somalis have lived in Indonesia since the early 2000s, it was not until 2011 that Somalis started arriving there in more noticeable numbers. Most of them had lived for many years in Yemen to escape the violence of the civil war in Somalia. Thus the journey to Indonesia was a secondary movement necessitated when they were no longer safe in Yemen, following the deterioration of the security situation there once the events of the Arab Spring spilled over into Yemen in early 2011. Somalis were particularly affected.

7. Resettlement numbers for refugees in Indonesia are generally low, but the Somalis there seem to face even greater difficulties in being accepted by resettlement countries. Most of the Somali diaspora live in the United States, Canada, the United Kingdom, the Netherlands, Sweden, Norway, Denmark and Finland. No Somali refugees from Indonesia were accepted in Australia in 2012 or 2013 (UNHCR Indonesia 2012c and 2013d).

8. The court decisions show that there were other police officers involved in the people- smuggling operation who did not have to face the legal consequences of their involvement (District Court of Negeri Praya Decision No. 125/PID.B/2012/PN.PRA, 28 January 2013 [Burhanuddin]).

9. This derogatory phrase was introduced in the 1970s under the Fraser government, but became more frequent from the late 1990s during the Howard era. Despite the fact that there is no queue in which asylum seekers can line up to receive help, the phrase continues to enjoy widespread popularity, especially among conservative commentators and members of the Australian Liberal Party (see, for example, Nicholson and Dodd 2012).

10. Eva Horn (2006) and Didier Fassin (2013) show that the meaning of "asylum" has changed quite substantially over time. It can mean both place of refuge and place of confinement. The term asylum has both Greek (*asylon* "refuge", neuter noun from *asylos* "inviolable, safe from violence") and Latin (asylum "sanctuary") roots. Literally it means an "inviolable place" and was used in

the context of persons seeking protection. Over time it came to mean a safe and secure place in a more general sense. As mental institutions evolved in the eighteenth century, "asylum" came to be used for places that sheltered the outside world from those considered insane, violent or dangerous.

11. For example, Jessie Taylor (2009, 2010) has written on the situation in Indonesian detention centres and also produced the documentary, "Between the Devil and the Deep Blue Sea" (2012). One work that has attracted considerable attention is Robin de Crespigny's third-person account, *The People Smuggler* (2012). This book is based on the story of Ali Al Jenabi, a convicted people smuggler who operated within Indonesia in the early 2000s. It deals mostly with Al Jenabi's life in Iraq and Australia, with only one chapter devoted to his experiences in Indonesia. De Crespigny spent three years interviewing Al Jenabi about certain episodes of his life, an experience that may have engendered an enormous amount of trust between the two and enabled her to reconcile certain inconsistencies. Although her book does not claim to be a scholarly investigation, its reliance on Al Jenabi's account alone, without crosschecking it with other resources, leaves a number of issues unaddressed. In 2014, Paul Toohey, an Australian journalist, published a long essay on "Asylum seekers and the search for an Indonesian solution", in which he provides an up-to-date overview from an Australian perspective.

12. In the early to mid 1990s the UNHCR was not concerned with "transit migration", but rather concentrated on secondary movements (Papadopoulou 2005).

13. There is no formal right to resettlement. Many recognized refugees, who qualify under one or more UNHCR resettlement criteria, may not be resettled, mostly because of the limited capacity of resettlement countries to take more refugees. The eight global resettlement criteria include: (a) lack of legal or physical security for the refugees in the country of first asylum; (b) survivors of torture and violence; (c) persons with medical needs; (d) women and girls at risk; (e) children and adolescents; (f) elderly refugees; (g) family reunification after flight or displacement; and (h) when voluntary repatriation or local integration are not available or feasible in the foreseeable future (UNHCR 2010, p. 4).

2

TRANSITING INDONESIA: PAST AND PRESENT

> It is already clear that the Government of Indonesia cannot
> assist refugees to stay in Indonesia. Indonesia is only willing
> to help refugees to continue their journeys to a third country.
> From the perspective of humanitarianism we offer
> assistance when needed.
> (Indonesian Department of Information 1980, p. 2)

The transit of people through Indonesia is not a new phenomenon. Because of its geographic configuration and location, Indonesia, an archipelago with more than 17,000 islands linking Asia and Australia, has always attracted migratory movements. The impacts of foreign influence in the archipelago, some temporary, some permanent, are widely visible in its languages, customs, architecture and many other aspects of society.

This chapter investigates what it has meant to be a transit migrant in Indonesia in the recent past. First, attention is given to Indonesia's experiences with Indochinese (mainly Vietnamese) transit migrants between the late 1970s and the mid-1990s. By outlining the political constellations that led to the establishment of the refugee processing centre on Galang Island in 1979, the reasons why the Indonesian government agreed to receive transit migrants temporarily are explained. Shedding light on daily life on Galang Island helps clarify reasons for the use of island camps as a special tactic in migration control, or, in Alison Mountz's words, as a "broader enforcement archipelago of detention" (Mountz 2011a, p. 118).

Using official UNHCR reports, witness accounts and other sources, the chapter provides an overview of the general conditions on the island that became a temporary home for tens of thousands of Vietnamese, many of whom stayed there much longer than expected. Although hundreds of thousands of Vietnamese were resettled in the West, subsequent flows continued to crowd the regional refugee camps. Given the reluctance of Thailand, Malaysia, Singapore and Indonesia to become permanent settlement destinations, the international community, under the auspices of the UNHCR, agreed on the Comprehensive Plan of Action (CPA) in 1989. The CPA put an end to the outflow of people from Vietnam by implementing for the first time a new scheme for determining refugee status and by relying on both voluntary and forced repatriation of those who did not qualify as genuine refugees. Despite the forced returns, the CPA is still heralded as a great success in UNHCR-led international refugee cooperation (Betts 2006).

The second part of this chapter provides detailed information about more recent refugee and migrant streams, predominantly those emanating from the conflict zones in the Middle East and South Asia. Besides tracing trends and numbers, the chapter sets out to explain major differences in the modes of transportation used to reach Indonesia and in the reception of refugees and migrants in Indonesia. By comparing recent events with those from the 1970s to the 1990s, the persistence of successive Indonesian governments' hesitation in offering help to asylum seekers and refugees is explained. The twenty-year presence of Indochinese refugees in what were intended to be short-term processing transit centres had tested Indonesia's patience seriously, even though the reception of refugees was celebrated internationally as a great achievement for human rights and Association of Southeast Asian Nations (ASEAN) solidarity.

INDOCHINESE BOAT PEOPLE

Following the Communist victory and the fall of Saigon in April 1975, tens of thousands of Vietnamese who had supported the U.S. invasion, fearing retaliation, started to leave their home country. Economic hardship and political discrimination further increased the numbers fleeing by tens of thousands. Not only did Vietnamese and ethnic Chinese from South Vietnam leave, but thousands of Cambodians and Laotians chose to flee political unrest in their homelands too, either by trying to cross over to Thailand or by trying to reach Hong Kong, Malaysia, the Philippines or Indonesia by boat. Thousands perished in the South China Sea.

The first report of Vietnamese refugees coming to Indonesia appeared on 19 May 1975, when ninety-two people passed through the town of Tarempa (Riau Islands) on their way to Singapore (Fandik 2013). Only one week later, a Vietnamese boat landed on Pulau Laut, which is part of the Natuna Islands (Fandik 2013; Ismayawati 2013). From then on, Vietnamese refugees arrived, almost on a daily basis, at different islands, such as Batam, Bintan, Natuna and Kuku (Ismayawati 2013; Hasibuan 2007). Anambas Island soon had 4,000 people to feed and host (Fandik 2013). The United Nations (UN) General Assembly (1979) reported the presence of 43,000 "boat people" all over Indonesia by 30 June 1979, mostly Vietnamese and, to a lesser extent, Cambodians. Given the political circumstances of the Cold War, the Vietnamese refugees represented to the West welcome evidence of the Vietnamese Communist regime's arbitrariness. With no screening mechanisms for asylum seekers yet in place, all were automatically granted prima facie refugee status and some form of protection.

Despite the resettlement of about 200,000 Indochinese refugees in third countries in the West between 1975 and March 1979, it was the countries in Southeast Asia, in particular Thailand and Malaysia, that had to take care of more than 340,000 people stuck in camps. Refugee arrivals in Hong Kong and Southeast Asian countries for the first three months of 1979 are given in Table 2.1. By 30 June 1979, only 3,650 Vietnamese refugees had been resettled from Indonesia (United Nations General Assembly 1979). At first, the Indonesian government attributed the greatest responsibility for these refugees to the United States, not least because it was their intervention in Vietnam that had caused the flow of asylum seekers (Ismayawati 2013, p. 10); however, it soon accepted that the United States could not shoulder responsibility for the influx alone.

At the beginning of the Indochinese exodus in 1975, not a single country in Southeast Asia had acceded to the 1951 UN Refugee Convention or the 1967 Protocol, which meant that there was no domestic legal framework for the reception of refugees in any Southeast Asian country. To cope with the massive scale of the exodus, Southeast Asian countries had to appeal to

Table 2.1
Refugees from Indochina, 31 March 1979

Country of arrival	January 1979	February 1979	March 1979	Total (1975 to 31 March 1979)	People in camps as at 31 March 1979
Hong Kong	3,413	15	0	9,888	5,100
Indonesia	1,831	406	3,101	9,193	7,187
Malaysia	4,202	3,166	6,033	83,495	52,273
Philippines	199	797	254	5,819	2,150
Thailand	7,690	4,604	6,644	235,474	149,387

Source: Indonesian Department of Foreign Affairs 1979: Annexes.

the international community for assistance in managing the refugee flows. Unable to deal with the continuing inflow of refugees and with limited facilities to host them, Malaysia called for the burden to be shared among Southeast Asian states and for the establishment of regional processing centres for refugees.[1]

After a series of meetings among ASEAN member states and Western resettlement countries in Bangkok and Jakarta in early 1979, the governments of Indonesia and the Philippines each offered to allocate a sparsely populated island for holding those refugees who had already been accepted for resettlement by third countries. While the Philippines offered to host 7,000 refugees temporarily on Tara Island, located about 250 kilometres southwest of Manila,[2] the Indonesian government chose Galang Island in the Riau Archipelago to become the temporary home for up to 10,000 refugees at a time. The main reason for the choice of Galang for the accommodation (*penampungan*) of refugees awaiting resettlement, apart from its strategic location and the relatively easy access by air and sea, was to separate them from the local population and minimize active intermingling (Ismayawati 2013).[3] Although Galang was 8,706.25 hectares in size, only 200 Indonesians were living on the island in 1979.

It was never intended that refugees were to be permanently settled on Galang; it was intended as a location for preparing them, through education and language courses, for resettlement elsewhere (Ismayawati 2013). From the very beginning the Indonesian government made it clear that it would not receive refugees permanently, but that it was forced on humanitarian grounds to host transiting migrants temporarily and that it would actively support efforts to find permanent solutions elsewhere (Indonesian Department of Information 1980, p. 1).

The meeting of ASEAN Foreign Ministers in May 1979 issued a statement on refugees, which stipulated that "countries providing the site or island for the processing centre shall retain the sovereignty, administrative control and security responsibility over the island" (Indonesian Department of Foreign Affairs 1979, p. 5). All costs of establishing and running these centres, including the provision of food, education and health care, were to be covered by the UNHCR. The international community at the time widely welcomed this plan, with UN delegates promising that their governments would provide extra funding, amounting to about US$160 million in cash and kind, to the UNHCR to cover the costs of these centres (Robinson 2004; UN General Assembly 1979, Appendix). Yet, it remained unclear which of the hundreds of thousands in waiting would be admitted to the centres and whether long-term stayers would be given priority treatment.

Moreover, the decision to establish temporary processing centres was based on the condition that the Vietnamese government would stop further illegal departures and promote direct and orderly departures instead, to which Vietnam agreed (Robinson 2004). Starting on 12 June 1979 and on the initiative of the Ministry of Defence, the Indonesian Navy, Maritime Police and Customs launched Operasi Halilintar (Operation Lightning) in order to close Indonesian territorial waters and stem the arrival of Vietnamese refugees (Indonesian Department of Information 1980, p. 6; Fandik 2013, p. 168).

On 2 July 1979 the Ministry of Defence established the Panitia Pengelolaan Pengungsi Vietnam (P3V, Management Committee for Vietnamese Refugees). The Presidential Decree Number 38, dated 11 September 1979, confirmed this team under the Ministry of Defence, but also announced integrated and coordinated measures with the Ministry of Foreign Affairs and the Ministry of Interior Affairs for the handling of the "Indochinese refugee problem" (paragraphs 2–4). It was envisaged that the refugees would stay there only for a "reasonable period", estimated not to exceed three to five years. Indonesian government reluctance to spend any domestic resources on establishing and running the centre (Indonesian Department of Information 1980, p. 7) meant the UNHCR had to cover all costs, which were estimated to be about US$18,562,000 (Indonesian Department of Foreign Affairs 1979).

THE TEMPORARY REFUGEE PROCESSING CENTRE ON GALANG

The processing centre was established very quickly near Sijantung village on Galang Island between June and August 1979. At first, it was mainly refugees on nearby islands who were transferred there. In an attempt to avoid attracting direct arrivals and becoming a reception centre, only refugees who were already in the region were admitted to Galang. When Malaysia and Singapore started to prevent refugees from disembarking in their territory, Galang started to see more direct arrivals from Vietnam.

Inside the camp, people were housed in barracks, one containing up to a hundred people (Fandik 2013; Ismayawati 2013). Galang camp had water, sanitation, schools, a hospital and even a port. Compared to local standards, conditions in the camp were adequate but basic. The UNHCR provided about Rp400 (US$0.64) per person per day in rations, not in cash. The centre was supposed to assist refugees to improve their standards of health and fitness, as required by most resettlement countries. In preparation for resettlement, they received intensive language classes (English and French) and cultural instruction classes, often taught by volunteers, to ease their integration into the countries they were to be resettled in (Prasetyo 2010). Two non-governmental organizations (NGOs), Save the Children and Écoles Sans Frontières, opened schools in the camp (Ismayawati 2013).[4]

Since the Vietnamese refugees generally organized themselves well, before long they set up organizations for religious and cultural activities. Given that some refugees had brought with them cash and other valuables, they also started commercial activities inside the camp. Some, for example, built coffee shops, while others sold cigarettes and convenience goods. Over time, churches, temples, markets, bakeries, gardens and even gambling spots (dominoes), cinemas, video parlours and discotheques sprang up (Cohen 1993). There were even small jails in the camp to lock up drunkards or people who had been involved in fights. According to former inmates of the camp, the Indonesian security guards were rough (Fitzpatrick 2009a). Sexual violence and intimidation, by both fellow refugees and guards, were reported widely (Tran 1995, p. 486). Given that people died while awaiting resettlement, a cemetery had to be established.

Initially the local population on Galang welcomed the centre's establishment, as it offered temporary employment. Later, once there had been incidents of theft, public opinion towards the Vietnamese refugees shifted and social envy emerged. Sometimes camp inmates would leave the premises overnight to go to town. According to Indonesians who had worked in the camp, there were substantial business dealings between Vietnamese refugees and the Chinese community on nearby Bintan Island. The Red Cross provided assistance with money transfers, but some of the local businessmen also helped refugees with international financial transactions.[5] Although, in general, local businesses, traders and services did benefit from the presence of refugees, it was members of the military who profited most from the commercial and employment opportunities that arose with the establishment of the camp. Unlike the interaction between the camps and local populations in the Philippines,[6] interaction with local communities on Galang remained limited.

    In the early years of cooperative action (1979–80), the UNHCR tried to resettle an average of about 25,000 people per month in third countries from all Southeast Asian camps (UN General Assembly 1979). Between July 1979 and July 1982, about 623,800 Indochinese refugees were resettled from Southeast Asia in twenty resettlement countries, principally in the United States, France and Canada (UNHCR 2000). The logistics of resettlement were managed by the Intergovernmental Committee for Migration (ICEM), the predecessor of today's International Organization for Migration (IOM). From 1980 to 1986, resettlements from Galang outpaced new arrivals on the island (Robinson 2004), but from 1987 onwards, when more people from North Vietnam joined the exodus, the number of refugees arriving in Southeast Asia increased dramatically (Balfour 1993). Although conditions in the processing camps were far from ideal, the prospect of eventual resettlement was a strong pull factor. In order to deal with the rising numbers, a second camp for newly arrived refugees was installed on Galang. Operasi Halau (Operation Dispersal), a joint operation of the Air Force, Navy and Army to stop the flow of Vietnamese refugees, was also launched in May 1985 on Lanud Ranai (Natuna Island) (Indonesian Air Force 2009). The Operasi Halau mission was driven by Indonesian anxiety about Communist infiltration in the region (Conboy 2004). Joint patrols with Malaysia and Singapore aimed to prevent the arrival of more refugees (Fandik 2013, p. 168). However, this cooperation was overshadowed by Malaysia's unilateral "redirection policy", adopted in the late 1980s, which was responsible for pushing boat people back to sea (Tran 1995, p. 483; UNHCR 2000).[7] Malaysia prevented at least 5,600 refugees from landing on Bidong Island (Azam and Vatikiotis 1990), despite international protest.[8] Some deaths were reported, and many were not; most of those rejected by Malaysia decided to go to Indonesia (Betts 2006, p. 37). According to Yen Tran (1995, p. 475), Indonesian forces also fired on a refugee boat. In 1989 there were fewer than 2,000 people on Galang, but, owing to Malaysia's redirection policy, the number of inmates in the Galang camp increased to 16,500 in the following year, thereby overburdening Galang's facilities (Tran 1995).

GALANG UNDER THE COMPREHENSIVE PLAN OF ACTION (CPA)

Between 1975 and 1995, almost two million people from Indochina fled their home countries, about 800,000 of them on boats, looking for asylum and hoping for resettlement (Tran 1995, p. 466; UNHCR 2000). During this period, between 122,000 and 145,000 asylum seekers transited Indonesia (Fields 1992; Cohen 1993; McBeth 1994; UNHCR 2000; Ismayawati 2013).[9] Despite ongoing resettlement, mainly in the United States, Canada, Australia, France and several other European countries, in late 1989 there were still more than 200,000 Indochinese people in the refugee camps across Southeast Asia awaiting resettlement. On the one hand, the numbers of arrivals continued to rise, while on the other, waiting times for resettlement increased as compassion fatigue set in among the Western resettlement countries, making it necessary for the ASEAN countries to adopt strategies to discourage the Indochinese from coming (Tran 1995, p. 475). Consultations had begun in 1988 for what later came to be known as the Comprehensive Plan of Action for Indochinese refugees, subsequently celebrated as a model for regional refugee processing.

The International Conference on Indochinese Refugees, held in Geneva in June 1989, oversaw the beginning of a new era in managing large refugee flows, as it introduced for the first time a scheme for determining refugee status. Rather than recognizing all Indochinese as refugees prima facie and trying to resettle them in the West, the new scheme required people to provide evidence to support their cases for recognition as genuine refugees. If they could not provide evidence of individual persecution, they would be seen and treated as economic migrants. The CPA declared a cut-off date, after which every new arrival had to undergo a screening procedure to establish the grounds of their case for seeking protection. To prove a well-founded fear of persecution, it was no longer enough to cite previous maltreatment or discrimination; people had to show that their lives would be endangered if they returned to their country of origin.[10] Those who were found not to be in need of international protection and resettlement were to be returned to Vietnam (Helton 1990/91, 1993; Tran 1995; Betts 2006). The CPA's main purpose was to discourage departures from Vietnam, as it was believed that, although political persecution and discrimination drove some people to flee their homeland, the option for resettlement in the West had become a strong pull factor for many Vietnamese who were not suffering persecution and discrimination.[11] The CPA did not achieve its main purpose immediately, as 400,000 more people came to Southeast Asia while the CPA was in force (Robinson 2004), but, after the first repatriations to Vietnam, the annual exodus of Vietnamese slowed drastically. Whereas the number of refugees arriving in ASEAN countries during 1989 was still about 64,000, the number dropped to about 32,000 in 1990 and about 23,000 in 1991 (Bari 1992, p. 509).

In order to ensure fairness within the process of determining refugee status, the CPA sought to introduce uniform screening mechanisms across the region (Bari 1992). Countries with no domestic system in place to determine refugee status relied on the UNHCR as advisor, observer and sponsor. National officials in each of the countries were trained to assess refugee claims. In Indonesia, the aforementioned P3V — composed of army, navy, immigration and police personnel — was in charge of conducting the interviews and making decisions in the first instance (Bari 1992, p. 495). The cut-off date in Indonesia was 17 March 1989; everybody arriving after that date had to be screened. Screenings started in June 1989 and continued until September 1993. According to Arthur Helton, one of the most vocal critics from the NGO community and representative of the Lawyers' Committee for Human Rights in New York, the screening procedures in Indonesia "began disastrously" because the authorities relied on resettlement criteria instead of refugee status criteria (Helton 1990/91, p. 121).

Before their screening interview with P3V, UNHCR representatives provided applicants with weekly information sessions, during which they distributed leaflets explaining the status-adjudication process, but not the actual criteria for being granted asylum.[12] UNHCR legal representatives also assessed applicants prior to their interviews with P3V. These initial assessments, together with a recommendation on whether the request for asylum should be granted or not, were then forwarded to the Indonesian authorities. The UNHCR representatives were not present during the P3V screening interviews, which in many cases were extremely short, sometimes lasting only twenty minutes. In most cases, P3V accepted the recommendation of the UNHCR representatives (Helton 1993, p. 548), making a different judgment in only twenty-two cases (United States General Accounting Office 1996, p. 43).

Nonetheless, complaints about the arbitrariness of the process of determining refugee status were widespread among applicants (Betts 2006). The Indonesian fast-track version, which often consisted only of simple *yes* and *no* questions, was deemed to seriously compromise the fairness of the interviews (Helton 1993). Other obstacles to a fair screening included the choice of interpreters, who were often recruited from within the camp. Legal consultants were not provided with sufficient training and, more generally, understanding of the situation in Vietnam was rather inadequate (Robinson 2004). Although the military staff appeared competent (Helton 1990/91, p. 122), allegations of corruption, bribery and demands for sexual favours in return for confirmation of refugee status were widespread (Betts 2006; Robinson 2004; Tran 1995). A report to the Chairman of the Subcommittee on International Operations and Human Rights Committee on International Relations of the United States Congress House of Representatives, dated 21 October 1996, stated that:

> In fact, there is evidence that an undetermined number of nonmeritorious cases were also screened in by the Indonesian authorities. UNHCR recommended that these cases be screened out but did not challenge the authorities' decisions. Corruption in the Indonesian process likely contributed to undeserving cases gaining refugee status; however, it is unlikely that strong cases were denied refugee status due to unmet corruption demands. (United States General Accounting Office 1996, p. 8)[13]

By July 1992, three years after the introduction of the CPA, P3V had managed to screen about two-thirds of the people on Galang. The results of its screening process are given in Table 2.2.

Decisions were communicated to rejected asylum seekers in writing, but the reasons for the decision were often cursory. They could appeal within fifteen to thirty days to a special review committee in Jakarta, also consisting of P3V members, as well as officials from the Ministry of Foreign Affairs. The UNHCR did not provide any help in preparing appeals. On the contrary, rejected applicants had to undergo special counselling with

Table 2.2
P3V Interviews and Decisions on Galang, June 1989–July 1992

	Number of people	Number of cases
Number interviewed	10,253	7,423
Positive decisions	3,657	2,293
Negative decisions	7,382	5,263
Positive review decisions	165	112
Negative review decisions	1,815	1,409

Source: Helton 1993, p. 549.

the UNHCR about voluntary return before they could make their appeal. Unlike asylum seekers in Hong Kong, people on Galang did not have access to private lawyers (Bari 1992, p. 492). In fact, Indonesia and Malaysia did not tolerate NGO involvement in advocacy on status determination; the services of NGOs were strictly limited to educational purposes (United States General Accounting Office 1996). Given the lack of legal advice, many faced considerable difficulty with the bureaucratic mechanisms of screenings and appeals, as they did not know how to present their cases.[14] A total of 18,131 people, including about 1,000 unaccompanied minors, were screened in Indonesia under the CPA between March 1989 and September 1993 (Fields 1992).[15] Table 2.3 depicts the results of the refugee-status determination.

Most of those accepted as refugees were resettled in the United States, Canada and Australia. Usually, the UNHCR matched the resettlement criteria of potential resettlement countries with the refugees in the camps, and the IOM provided logistical support for resettlement (Betts 2006, p. 40). Generally, the longer people had stayed in Galang, the harder it was

Table 2.3
Refugee Status Determination in Indonesia, March 1989–September 1993

	Status approved	Status not approved	% approved
First instance screening	5,083	10,048	28
Appeal	2,759	9,463	22.5
Total	7,842	10,289	43.3

Source: United States General Accounting Office 1996, p. 13.

to find resettlement options for them (Ismayawati 2013, p. 91). Problems also arose for some people in particular circumstances, for example, for couples in de facto relationships. Family reunion often proved difficult, because legal marriages could not take place in the camps and informal marriages did not qualify couples for resettlement as a family unit, unless the couple had produced children.

In June 1996, the UNHCR funding for Indochinese refugees under CPA stopped throughout the region (Robinson 2004, p. 330). Although Indonesia and Thailand extended their involvement with the CPA for another ninety days, it was decided that all inmates remaining in the camps were to be returned. Following Hong Kong's example, already in October 1992, Indonesia, Thailand and the Philippines had signed an agreement with the UNHCR and Vietnam on a programme for the orderly return of rejected asylum seekers. Although Vietnam had promised to take its people back and reintegrate them without punishment or persecution, most were hesitant to return voluntarily. Despite being offered incentives to return, such as reintegration grants (Betts 2006, p. 38), only 3,911 of the rejected asylum seekers on Galang had accepted repatriation by September 1993 (Tran 1995).[16]

Aware that the option of voluntary repatriation would not be attractive to enough of the rejected asylum seekers, the UNHCR and IOM understood that involuntary repatriation would have to be used as a means of return as well, but neither organization wanted to be involved in organizing involuntary repatriation, as it was considered a violation of their constitutions. Consequently, the primary responsibility for repatriating those who did not want to be returned was left to the transit countries (Betts 2006, p. 36). More than 109,000 Vietnamese were repatriated during the CPA's eight-year period (UNHCR 2000). In contrast, between 1975 and 1995, a total of 1,311,183 Indochinese refugees were resettled in third countries (UNHCR 2000, p. 99), including at least 132,000 from Galang (McBeth 1994). The countries in which most Indochinese refugees were resettled were the United States (822,977), Australia (137,543), Canada (137,145) and France (95,671) (UNHCR 2000, p. 99).

Rejected asylum seekers on Galang did not accept their destiny without protest. Although the Indonesian authorities used several different media to foster homesickness and nostalgia among the camp population and even engaged journalists to travel Vietnam and produce a documentary on the current living conditions there in order to persuade them to return home (Hasibuan 2007, pp. 49, 63), many remained reluctant to do so. In

1994 in particular, there were hunger strikes, supported by more than 500 camp inmates, of whom seventy-nine had to be hospitalized, and riots, in which inmates attacked the Indonesian officials with homemade firebombs ("Hundreds of Vietnamese" 1994; Lander 1996). To protest against their rejection and their imminent repatriation, a number of people committed suicide, either by hanging or by self-immolation (Fields 1992; McBeth 1994; Ismayawati 2013). A few tried to escape from the camp and reach Australia on their own (Gilley 1996; Hasibuan 2007; Ismayawati 2013). If discovered, they were punished severely by the Indonesian authorities. In July 1994 a group of Vietnamese, who had been rejected as refugees on Galang, made it to Broome in Western Australia (Grewcock 2009, p. 129).[17] As the Indonesian government was determined to clear Galang as soon as possible so that it could implement plans to redevelop Galang as a special industrial zone, the Indonesian army assisted in the eventual return by sea and air of most of the remaining 8,500 Vietnamese, despite their protest and resistance (Cohen 1993; Hasibuan 2007).

Nowadays, almost twenty years after the last Vietnamese refugee left the island, the camps on Galang are in ruins, apart from a newly built Buddhist temple near the barracks and a number of renovated gravestones placed in the cemetery by former camp inmates or their relatives (Tran 2012). Some years ago, a museum was established to document life in the camp in enthusiastic terms. Recently, members of the Indonesian parliament proposed building a hotel in the grounds of the former camps to accommodate visitors and tourists (Pertiwi 2012). Under former President Soeharto (1965–98), Galang was even identified as a flagship of Indonesia's exemplary human rights record (Betts 2006, p. 38; Adam 2005). The brochure of the museum on Galang states: "Galang Island [is] a **Monument of Humanity** in the rescue of Vietnamese refugees stranded in the territory of Indonesia" (Museum Pulau Galang c.2010; bold in the original). The personal accounts of former inmates, however, differ substantially from Indonesian public representation.

In interviews, some Indonesian officials tended to perceive the refugee camp on Galang as an unpleasant, if not traumatic, experience that overstretched the country's capacity for hospitality.[18] Despite the fact that UNHCR funding spared Indonesia any financial burden for the refugees, Indonesian sources often note the indirect costs arising from the presence of the asylum seekers over almost two decades, which amounted to "rather substantial government expenditure" (Hasibuan 2007, p. 47). Now confronted with contemporary flows of asylum seekers and refugees from the Middle East, the idea of establishing another island camp for refugees in Indonesia, like that on Galang, has come up again, as will be discussed later.

NEW WAVES OF TRANSIT MIGRANTS

After the refugee flows from Indochina dried up, few transit migrants arrived in Indonesia, at least for a few years. Given Indonesia's instability in the late 1990s, the archipelago was no longer an attractive stopover for people from conflict areas. When the thirty-two-year authoritarian reign of President Soeharto came to an abrupt end in 1998, Indonesia slipped into a series of crises (Wanandi 2002). Besides dealing with the consequences of the Asian economic and financial crisis, such as high inflation and unemployment, successive post-authoritarian governments, led by Presidents Bacharuddin Jusuf Habibie, Megawati Sukarnoputri and Abdurrahman Wahid, had to cope with political unrest in some of the outer parts of the country that threatened the unity of the Indonesian state. The separation of East Timor (later Timor Leste) from Indonesia caused the displacement of more than 160,000 people in September 1999.[19] While most of those fleeing the violence in East Timor sought shelter in the Western part of Timor Island, about 2,000 East Timorese fled to Australia.[20] Conflict in the Moluccas (1999–2002), Central Kalimantan (2001) and Central Sulawesi (1998 and 2005) resulted in the involuntary displacement of 1.2 million altogether (McRae 2013; Bertrand 2002; Bräuchler 2010). Furthermore, separatist conflict in Aceh drove hundreds of thousands of Acehnese from their homes, many of whom became internally displaced people in the neighbouring province of Northern Sumatra or, if they could afford it, asylum seekers in nearby Malaysia (Missbach 2011). The armed struggle for independence in West Papua (at the time known as Irian Jaya) had since the 1960s sent thousands of refugees into neighbouring Papua New Guinea and, to a lesser extent, to Australia (Neumann and Taylor 2010). On the brink of breaking apart in the troubled years after 1998, Indonesia was not an attractive haven for transit migrants. Nevertheless, asylum seekers from the conflict-ridden Middle East started arriving in Indonesia in the mid-1990s.

The first five asylum seekers from Afghanistan and the first seven from Iran to apply for protection under the UNHCR in Indonesia were recorded in 1996. Their reasons for choosing to come to Indonesia were not only the poor political and economic conditions in their homelands, in particular the rise of the Taliban in 1995, accompanied by widespread discrimination against religious and ethnic minorities, but also the policy shifts in countries of first asylum that resulted in their secondary movements. For example, in the late 1990s, Pakistan took a harsher approach towards Afghan asylum seekers residing in Pakistani territory, many of whom had been there for more than twenty years, from the time of the Soviet occupation of Afghanistan. Following a similar path, Iran stopped tolerating Iraqi and Kurdish asylum seekers who had arrived during the Iran–Iraq War and the first Gulf War. Applying for protection at UNHCR offices in Iran and Pakistan was often difficult, as local security forces prevented physical access to the UNHCR offices (HRW 2002). Life for asylum seekers in these two countries was very tenuous, because of their lack of legal status, health care, education and housing, combined with severe restrictions on employment and movement, as well as the ever-present risk of arrest, detention and deportation.[21] Jordan and Syria, the only two states in the wider region that signed the refugee convention, in theory could have served as safe haven but, because neither country has domestic laws for refugee protection, neither is a viable alternative. This absence of any framework for protection spurred local smuggling networks to create new routes for those asylum seekers who could afford to move on, not just into Europe but also to Australia where asylum policies were deemed to be more favourable, offering higher refugee application approval rates and, at times, allowing for family reunion and extensive integration services (Mason 2001). Yet, Khalid Koser (2010*b*) concluded that push factors in the countries of origin and the countries of first asylum were more powerful in forcing people to leave than any pull factors in Australia.

Compared to the earlier refugee flows from Indochina, the modes of arrival and, consequently, the treatment of Middle Eastern transit migrants by the Indonesian authorities differed substantially. Table 2.4 indicates the number of new arrivals, which, in both absolute and relative numbers, were comparatively small.

Nevertheless, the arrival of asylum seekers from the Middle East triggered several problems for Indonesia in regard to administering, accommodating and resettling them. As there was neither a legal framework for the processing of asylum seekers nor any national legal guidelines or standard procedures for immigration officials on how to handle transit migrants, local immigration authorities often did not differentiate between asylum seekers in need of international protection, on the one hand, and

Table 2.4
Asylum Applicants in Indonesia by Origin, 1995–2004

Origin	1995	1996	1997	1998	1999	2000	2001	2002	2003	2004
Afghanistan	0	5	8	12	39	196	687	281	9	40
Iran	0	7	8	8	5	136	41	60	2	37
Iraq	0	0	0	6	2	353	433	297	122	56

Source: UNHCR 2007, p. 347.

irregular migrants, on the other, especially when those seeking protection had no valid travel documents.

Given that the management of refugees and asylum seekers had previously been the task of the special committee P3V and the military, Indonesian immigration officers were rather inexperienced and had no understanding of international refugee procedures or the work of the UNHCR.[22] Lacking the knowledge that it is the right of every asylum seeker to apply for protection under the UNHCR, in some cases immigration officials prevented arrested foreigners from contacting the UNHCR (Roberts c.2001, p. 54). Following the closure of the refugee-processing centre on Galang, Indonesia had only limited detention facilities (*karantina imigrasi*), which were not fit for hosting undocumented migrants for any length of time. Overwhelmed by its many serious domestic problems at the time, Indonesia had little capacity for handling foreigners, whose aim, after all, was to reach Australia. For this reason, it was hardly surprising that the Indonesian government did not welcome Australia's plan to open an asylum-seeker processing centre in Indonesia (Mason 2001). Peter Mares (2002, p. 239) quoted the Indonesian Minister for Justice and Human Rights, Yusril Ihza Mahendra, who asked "why doesn't Australia use one of her own islands [for such an asylum-seeker processing centre]? We already have a lot of problems in this country."

During the late 1990s and early 2000s, Indonesia chose to ignore as far as possible the presence of these transit migrants, assuming that they would not stay for the long term (Hoffman 2010b). Instead of enacting new laws for handling refugees or installing a domestic mechanism for assessing asylum claims, Indonesia preferred to rely on the services of the UNHCR in Jakarta for processing the applications of asylum seekers and their resettlement, not least because the Immigration Department lacked the funds to deport them or even to bring charges against them for breaching Indonesian immigration law (Lindsey 2002; Mason 2001).

Consequently, people seeking protection had to contact the UNHCR office in Jakarta in writing or in person. After an initial interview, they would be equipped with a letter of attestation, in English and Indonesian, which explained their status as asylum seekers. Possession of the letter was intended to minimize the risk of detention and forced deportation, but there was no legal guarantee that the holders of such letters would not be detained or deported. In a second, more thorough, interview with the asylum seekers, UNHCR staff would attempt to determine whether they qualified as refugees or not. Because there were so few staff and interpreters at the UNHCR in Jakarta, the decision-making process could take months, if not years. Processing for resettlement also proceeded very slowly. For example, between January 1999 and August 2001, the UNHCR in Jakarta recognized 476 refugees but was able to resettle only eighteen of them to safe third countries (Lindsey 2002; HRW 2002, p. 38).[23] If asylum claims were rejected, the applicant could appeal once. Meanwhile, asylum seekers in waiting had access to minimal health care through the Palang Merah (Indonesian Red Cross). In 2000, the UNHCR's local operational partner was Caritas Indonesia, which offered its clients counselling and even financial support in exceptional cases. Generally, asylum seekers were expected to be self-sufficient.[24]

Given the harsh conditions for asylum seekers and refugees, it is not surprising that many tried to leave Indonesia as soon as possible. The demand for irregular onward migration to Australia created a new smuggling industry, especially in Indonesia's impoverished Eastern provinces, such as Nusa Tenggara Timur (Balint 2005). People-smuggling from Indonesia to Australia peaked in 2001, when 5,516 asylum seekers arrived by boat (Phillips and Spinks 2013). In the first three weeks of August 2001 alone, 1,212 people arrived at Australian outposts (Howard 2003, p. 37). Altogether, more than 6,000 asylum seekers reached Australia by boat from Indonesia between 2000 and 2002 (Kneebone 2010, p. 354). Given the events of 9/11 and the fact that most asylum seekers were Muslims, their reception in Australia was less than hospitable (Kabir 2005; Mansouri 2006).

THE PACIFIC SOLUTION

The turning point in Australia's asylum-seeker reception policy came in September 2001, following the rescue by the Norwegian freighter, MV *Tampa*, of 438 people, mainly Hazaras, from a sinking Indonesian fishing vessel en route to Australia towards the end of August. At first, the *Tampa* was supposed to return to Merak in Indonesia, but the Indonesian government denied access to the port, even though it had initially agreed to grant access. Moreover, the rescued passengers pleaded with the Norwegian captain not to take them back to Indonesia (Marr and Wilkinson 2003). Even though some of the passengers were in need of medical treatment, the Australian Government under Prime Minister John Howard would not allow their disembarkation at the nearest port, which would have been on Christmas Island.[25] Spurred on by the looming diplomatic incident between Norway and Australia, by this time known as the Tampa Affair, and just weeks away from federal elections, Howard fast-tracked the establishment of an extraterritorial asylum-seeker processing system (Marr and Wilkinson 2003; Edwards 2003; HRW 2002; Metcalfe 2010). In late September 2001, the Australian Parliament passed seven bills to amend the 1958 Migration Act, and the new Border Protection Act. The new policies, which became known as the "Pacific Solution", validated not only the decision to reject the asylum seekers on the *Tampa*, but also allowed more generally for the interception of asylum seekers at sea.

Under the Pacific Solution policies, *Tampa* passengers were redirected to Nauru and Manus Island (Papua New Guinea), with whom the Australian Government quickly agreed on the establishment of detention facilities (officially called processing centres) to be managed by the IOM.[26] Through the amendments to the 1958 Migration Act, almost 4,000 islands were excised from Australia's migration zone, which meant that asylum seekers could no longer lodge their claims for protection when they arrived at one of these outposts (Edwards 2003; Kneebone 2010). Asylum seekers could apply only for temporary protection (introduced in 1999) and not for permanent protection visas. This deprived asylum seekers of the right to travel away from Australia and then re-enter the country, which was requested, for example, by those wanting to visit family members stranded in transit places. Under the new regulations, judicial review rights and the right to family reunion for asylum seekers were also abolished. Furthermore, in accordance with a 1992 regulation, new maritime arrivals faced indefinite mandatory detention.[27] The new regulations cemented a difference in standards of treatment and rights for those arriving by air and those coming by sea, which has attracted widespread criticism since 2001 as offshore processing leaves applicants with fewer rights than those who are processed onshore in Australia.

Aside from these legal changes, the Howard government also initiated Operation Relex to increase its border protection measures and deter "unauthorized" boats. Under this operation the Australian defence forces were allowed to intercept any suspected illegal entry vessel (SIEV) once within the vicinity of Australia's contiguous zone.[28] If the unauthorized boat crews ignored the warning given to them and continued into Australian waters, Australian forces would then proceed to board the vessel in order to turn it back to the high seas (Howard 2003). Under Operation Relex several boats containing asylum seekers were towed back to Indonesia without prior formal agreement with the Indonesian government and with no guarantee of their protection there (Howard 2003, p. 41; Crock and Ghezelbash 2010; HRW 2002). By forcibly returning these boats to Indonesia, Australia breached several of its obligations under human rights law and international maritime law.

Between October 2001 and December 2001, the Australian Navy intercepted four boats (SIEVs 5, 7, 11 and 12) and towed them back into Indonesian waters. SIEVs 7, 11 and 12 were taken close to Rote Island, but SIEV 12 ran aground near Rote Island. Previously, SIEV 5 had been returned to Indonesian waters after its passengers had spent seven days in the open in a lagoon at Ashmore Island. On board SIEV 5, a woman who had given birth during the interception was denied adequate medical treatment for the complications she experienced (HRW 2002, p. 41). Australian forces reacted to the protests of the passengers with force and deception. In order to discourage further resistance, men were separated from their wives and children and transported separately back to Indonesia. Australian forces confiscated surplus fuel supplies to prevent the asylum seekers from changing course at sea. It was estimated that the four returned SIEVs contained at least 500 people (Howard 2003) to be kept in Indonesia for an undetermined period of time (Hunter 2004; HRW 2002).

The Navy also attempted to turn back three other vessels (SIEVs 4, 6 and 10), but they sank during the course of interception (Metcalfe 2010; Taylor 2013). During the interception of SIEV 10 in November 2001, two female asylum seekers drowned near Ashmore Reef (Hope 2002). A boat that was not intercepted was SIEV X; it sank in October 2001 in international waters just south of Java and 353 of its passengers drowned (Kevin 2004). The last boat the Australian Navy escorted out of Australian waters into international waters near Indonesia was the *Minasa Bone* in November 2003 (Downer and Vanstone 2003; Weber 2006, p. 21).

The Pacific Solution can be judged to have met its stated targets, as the numbers of unauthorized boat arrivals from Indonesia to Australia reduced dramatically after the end of 2001. Nevertheless, the policy disregarded Australia's obligations under international human rights law, and the costs of its implementation, an estimated AU$1 billion, were exorbitant (Metcalfe 2010, p. 274).

One of the first acts of the newly elected Labor government under Prime Minister Kevin Rudd in late 2007 was to abolish the Pacific Solution, which formally ended on 8 February 2008, and to allow the resettlement of the recognized refugees remaining on Nauru and Manus in Australia (Phillips and Spinks 2013).[29] When numbers of maritime asylum seekers coming to Australia increased again from 2009 onwards, the Labor government under Prime Minister Julia Gillard revived the Pacific Solution in August 2012. However, before examining these developments, what happened to the people who were returned to Indonesia and to those who kept coming to Indonesia in the meantime needs to be investigated.

IN LIMBO IN LOMBOK

As conditions for the forcibly returned asylum seekers in West Timor (Rote Island and Kupang) were too harsh and the UNHCR could not access them there, they were taken in January 2002 to the provincial capital, Mataram, on Lombok, and accommodated in several hotels (HRW 2002; Hunter 2004; Gallagher 2005; Field and Edwards 2006; Taylor and Rafferty-Brown 2010a). The IOM covered the costs of their accommodation and medical services, as the Australian government in cooperation with the Indonesian government had contracted the organization to provide custodial care (Mountz 2011a, p. 125).[30] Most of these asylum seekers,

Table 2.5
Unauthorized Boats Arriving from Indonesia, 2001–8

	2001	2002	2003	2004	2005	2006	2007	2008
Boats	43	1	1	1	4	6	5	7
Passengers (excluding crew)	5,516	1	53	15	11	60	148	161

Source: Phillips and Spinks 2013.

mainly Iraqis, Afghans (Pashtun, Hazara, Baloch, Tajik and Uzbek) and Iranian Mandaens, became stranded in seemingly perpetual limbo, as they could not be deported to their home countries where political instability persisted and they did not have the funds to finance further attempts at onward migration with the help of people smugglers.

Once the asylum seekers were in Mataram, the UNHCR could access them. The process for determining their status was, however, widely criticized as inadequate. Not only were there not enough interpreters, but their partiality gave applicants cause to complain, as they were alleged to favour some ethnic groups over others or were not trained in all dialects spoken by the asylum seekers (Nassery 2004; Ghulam 2004). Other complaints about the UNHCR status-determination process concerned lack of access to legal advice, lack of preparatory assistance in addressing certain interview questions and in providing evidence to back up the asylum seekers claims, and a lack of time in the interviews to provide full accounts (Nassery 2004). The number of people who were accepted as refugees after the first assessment was relatively small, leading rejected asylum seekers to believe that the UNHCR status-determination process was merely a "lottery" that only could be won by those with relatives living overseas who were prepared to pay lawyers to assist them with their applications (Nassery 2004).

While they awaited the outcome of their assessments, the asylum seekers were visited by representatives of the Afghan and Iraqi embassies, who tried to convince people to return voluntarily and offered to provide them with travel documents. Of the 220 Afghan asylum seekers, about 142 accepted these offers (Nassery 2004). Iraqis were less inclined to return following the United States' invasion of Iraq in March 2003, because of which the UNHCR agreed to reassess them once more, even though some of them had already been rejected twice (Hunter 2004).

In October 2003, two years after their return to Indonesia, 146 people, including newborn babies, were still living in Mataram (Hunter 2004), most of them with little to do. Although the asylum seekers theoretically enjoyed freedom of movement, only those who still had some funds left or received remittances from friends and families overseas could make use of that right, and then only with the permission of the IOM. One Afghan took the initiative to teach children and adults English and to give computer lessons. For a short interval, there was a mixed soccer team of Iraqi and local Sasak players. A few men formed romantic relationships with Indonesian women, causing tension with the local communities (Roberts c.2001). Tension also arose from social jealousy, as many locals envied the asylum seekers for what they perceived as privileges, such as free accommodation and food (Hunter 2004). Interethnic differences among the Iraqis and the Iranians, mostly religious differences such as the Sunni–Shia divide, led to the redistribution of accommodation according to ethnic background. When the local population learned of the presence of Shiites, some of them threatened to burn down the hotels in which they were accommodated, thus requiring the police to guard them for several weeks (Hunter 2006).

News of a hunger strike by asylum seekers on Nauru in December 2003 (Metcalfe 2010, pp. 147ff.) reached asylum seekers in Mataram early in January 2004. They decided to organize one too to protest their continuing detention and the rejection of their asylum claims (Hunter 2004; Kneebone 2010). Afghans, seven of whom sewed their lips together, were among the hunger strikers (Ghulam 2004).[31] The hunger strike lasted one week and attracted considerable attention in Australia. Unlike the Galang detainees two decades earlier, the asylum seekers on Lombok were in regular contact with activists and advocates in Australia and, to a lesser extent, with friends and family in their homelands and desired countries of destination. The protesters ended their strike after meeting with a UNHCR protection officer who promised to review their cases in the light of the most up-to-date information about the situation in their home countries.

During the early 2000s, the Indonesian government insisted that all asylum seekers be accommodated outside Jakarta in relatively remote places. As well as Mataram, some asylum seekers were hosted in Situbondo, East Java. If asylum seekers tried to leave their designated places of accommodation, as some did in order to protest their situation outside the UNHCR Office in Jakarta, they were threatened with denial of further assistance and with detention if they refused to return (Field and Edwards 2006).

In October 2005, ninety-two Iraqis and Afghans were still in Lombok, the others having returned to their homelands, been resettled, or could not be traced (Refugee Action Collective 2005). In December 2007, after many attempts to persuade the Afghans to accept voluntary return in exchange for free travel and a AU$2,000 assistance payment, which the Afghans declined, nine men were separated from their wives and children and transferred to the detention centre in Makassar (on Sulawesi) (Mountz 2011a, p. 125;

Ashutosh and Mountz 2011, p. 33). The separation was intended to increase pressure on the asylum seekers to return "voluntarily" to Afghanistan and some of them eventually acquiesced, despite the unsafe conditions there.

Given the complicated and tense situation on Lombok, all remaining asylum seekers were eventually resettled in Cisarua, a village in the mountainous area near Bogor about sixty kilometres from Jakarta, where they continued to be under IOM care. Given the deteriorating political conditions in their countries of origin, the UNHCR in Jakarta, contrary to usual procedure, decided to reassess the rejected asylum seekers once more and some were eventually accepted in 2009, after their fourth assessment (Taylor and Rafferty-Brown 2010b). Resettlements on humanitarian visas to Canada, Australia and New Zealand took place until 2011.

CURRENT NUMBERS AND TRENDS

In 2011, the UNHCR counted more than 42 million forcibly displaced people worldwide, of whom 10.4 million were acknowledged to be refugees. The Asia-Pacific region hosted about one third of the global refugee population, which translates to 3.6 million people (UNHCR 2012a, p. 11). Compared to the large population of people of concern to the UNHCR in Thailand, with 136,499 refugees, 4,712 asylum seekers and 506,197 stateless persons in 2014 (UNHCR Thailand 2014) and in Malaysia, with 97,513 refugees, 43,039 asylum seekers and 40,000 stateless persons in 2014 (UNHCR Malaysia 2014), people of concern to the UNHCR in Indonesia were relatively small, as Table 2.6 indicates.[32]

Since 2009, not only has the number of asylum seekers coming to Indonesia increased, but the national backgrounds of the people of concern to the UNHCR have also become more diverse. Most of those seeking protection continue to be from Afghanistan, Iraq and Iran, but the number of asylum seekers from Myanmar and Sri Lanka has risen. Political instability in East and North Africa has driven Somali and Sudanese to seek asylum, choosing Indonesia as a transit country once routes into Europe were blocked following the Arab Spring of early 2011. The arrival of greater numbers of females and unaccompanied minors in recent years has altered the hitherto predominance of males among asylum seekers.

Once the number of asylum seekers arriving in Indonesia started to increase, the number of irregular passages to Australia also rose. Two events, in particular, attracted international attention. On 11 October 2009,

Table 2.6
Applications for Refugee Status in Indonesia, 2005–12

	Number of applications for refugee status	Positive decisions (convention status)	Positive decisions (complementary protection status)	Rejected	Otherwise closed
2012	7,199	1,218		58	2,994
2011	4,052	637		26	2,227
2010	3,905	632		27	2,948
2009	3,308	755		128	1,007
2008	385	177		13	53
2007	277	132		52	147
2006	423	106	7	27	76
2005	74	6	1	23	45

Source: UNHCR Statistical Online Population Database (data extracted 6 January 2014).

the boat *Jaya Lestari* with 255 Sri Lankans on board was intercepted in Indonesian waters by Indonesian forces and returned to the Indonesian port of Merak, as agreed jointly by the Australian prime minister, Kevin Rudd, and the Indonesian president, Susilo Bambang Yudhoyono. A six-month stand-off by the passengers followed, as they refused to leave their boat to set foot on Indonesian territory unless they were guaranteed resettlement by the UNHCR. Eventually they disembarked, without a resettlement guarantee, and were taken to the detention centre in nearby Tanjung Pinang and processed. All except five were found to qualify as genuine refugees. Over the next two years many of them were resettled, but seventy-eight were still awaiting resettlement in 2012 (Guest 2012).

Around the same time, another incident involving seventy-eight Sri Lankan asylum seekers sparked great interest. On 17 October 2009, a boat in distress in the Indonesian search-and-rescue zone was rescued by an Australian customs ship, *Oceanic Viking* (Kneebone 2010; Ford, Lyons and Palmer 2010). The initial intention was that the asylum seekers should disembark in Merak; however, because of the stand-off of the *Jaya Lestari* passengers, they disembarked on Bintan instead. Many of the passengers had lived in Indonesia and applied for protection there under the UNHCR before, but, frustrated with the lengthy resettlement process, they had chartered a boat to take them directly to Australia. The redirection of the *Oceanic Viking* resulted in a substantial diplomatic tiff between Indonesia and Australia about who was responsible for these asylum seekers. The local governor in Riau refused to allow the passengers to disembark in his province and the passengers refused to leave the boat. They were processed by Australian authorities instead of by the UNHCR. To persuade the passengers to leave the ship, Prime Minister Kevin Rudd promised that nobody would have to wait longer than twelve weeks for resettlement to a third country (Ford, Lyons and Palmer 2010). All seventy-eight were eventually resettled in Canada, the United States, Norway, New Zealand and Australia, although not within the promised time frame.

In October 2013 there were 2,718 refugees in Indonesia awaiting resettlement, having had their cases processed by the UNHCR in Jakarta, as detailed in Table 2.7.

Table 2.7
Recognized Refugees in Indonesia, October 2013

Country of origin	Female	Male	Total
Afghanistan	79	898	977
China	14	9	23
Congo	2	0	2
Côte d'Ivoire	0	1	1
Democratic Republic of Congo	2	0	2
Egypt	0	2	2
Ethiopia	6	10	16
Iran	74	101	175
Iraq	41	52	93
Kuwait	2	4	6
Myanmar	62	553	615
Pakistan	8	86	84
Palestine	47	61	108
Philippines	4	1	5
Somalia	131	159	290
Sri Lanka	53	217	270
Sudan	0	12	12
Syria	9	14	23
Ukraine	1	0	1
Yemen	0	1	1
Total	536	2,182	2,718

Source: UNHCR Indonesia 2013*d*.

Between September 2011, when Indonesia hosted 2,440 asylum seekers, and October 2013, there had been an almost fourfold increase in numbers, reaching 8,364 asylum seekers, as detailed in Table 2.8. The upward trend appears to continue.

Determining accurate numbers of asylum seekers and refugees is difficult, as they change daily but are only registered monthly. Official repatriations and resettlements are registered, but many asylum seekers abandon their claims and leave without a trace. The real number of transit migrants in Indonesia is most likely to be higher, for several reasons. Some transit migrants do not wish to register as asylum seekers with the UNHCR, either because they do not see much benefit in doing so or because they do not know how. Those who roam the country looking for possibilities for immediate departure do not appear in any statistics (HRW 2013) until they are arrested by Indonesian authorities and referred to the UNHCR or the IOM. Others, including the newly arrived and newly arrested, might not have had a chance to register with the UNHCR yet. Asylum seekers may wait for several months in detention for a UNHCR representative to visit. There are also inconsistencies in data shared amongst the UNHCR and other bodies, such as the IOM and the Indonesian Secretariat-General of Immigration. Every institution collects its own statistics in different ways. Numbers are generally considered incomplete; the Secretariat-General of Immigration, for example, only counts those transit migrants who are detained.[33] A new biometric-data-management system implemented in 2012 and funded by the IOM may provide more reliable tables in the future.

Indonesia is no more eager to host the transit migrants in its territory today than it was to host the earlier flows of refugees from Indochina, nor does it want to allow them to integrate into Indonesian society, which only a few asylum seekers want to do anyway (CWS 2013). Nonetheless, many people have ended up spending several years in transit in Indonesia, and their experience is described in greater detail in the following chapter.

SUMMARY

Indonesia's reception and handling of asylum seekers and refugees in its territory over the last thirty years was, first and foremost, characterized by an open aversion to hosting them for the long term. Despite its unsympathetic official rhetoric, Indonesia has allowed asylum seekers and refugees to remain in its territory, often for many years, not least because the UNHCR has covered all costs. In the spirit of regional cooperation

Table 2.8
Asylum Seekers in Indonesia, October 2013

Country of origin	Female	Male	Total
Afghanistan	369	3,058	3,427
Algeria	0	3	3
Bangladesh	1	94	95
Cameroon	0	10	10
Central African Republic	0	1	1
China	14	11	25
Congo	0	5	5
Côte d'Ivoire	2	2	4
Democratic Republic of Congo	4	9	13
Egypt	0	5	5
Eritrea	4	19	23
Ethiopia	3	12	15
Gabon	1	0	1
Gambia	0	1	1
Ghana	0	2	2
Haiti	0	1	1
India	2	4	6
Iran	434	807	1,241
Iraq	137	327	464
Jordan	1	0	1
Kuwait	1	0	1
Lebanon	1	3	4
Libya	0	1	1
Mali	0	3	3
Myanmar	238	594	832
Nepal	2	8	10
Pakistan	57	653	710
Palestine	110	135	245
Philippines	1	0	1
Saudi Arabia	1	1	2
Somalia	90	203	293
Sri Lanka	192	444	636
Sudan	3	206	209
Syria	14	35	49
Thailand	1	1	2
Tunisia	0	1	1
United Arab Emirates	0	1	1
Vietnam	1	3	4
Western Sahara	1	0	1
Yemen	3	12	15
Total	1,688	6,676	8,364

Source: UNHCR Indonesia 2013d.

and burden-sharing, Galang was Indonesia's contribution to the regional management of the Indochinese refugee flows. The camps on Galang served as the main reception point for asylum seekers in Indonesia, both under the 1979 Regional Agreement for the Indochinese Refugees and, later, the 1989 CPA.

Contained on a relatively remote island and managed by the military, the processing of asylum seekers proceeded steadily, but was, nevertheless, often marked by human tragedy, exploitation and other wrongdoing. It became a special site of exclusion in which Indonesia and the international community invested heavily to manage migratory flows from Indochina. While the presence of the asylum seekers in Indonesia was largely shielded from the Indonesian public, Galang became President Soeharto's showcase of exemplary human rights treatment to the international community (Betts 2006; Ismayawati 2013), which tended to be critical of Indonesia's human rights record, mostly because of the violent oppression in East Timor.

Despite international appreciation of Indonesia's successful refugee management on Galang, Indonesian officials show little enthusiasm to repeat this form of asylum-seeker management (Alford and Nathalia 2013*b*). Nonetheless, proposals for a similarly centralized island camp for refugees, that would shield asylum seekers and migrants from public attention and legal representation, frequently emerge in Indonesian public discourse and are warmly welcomed by Australia. After all, Australia has benefited greatly from the immobilization and warehousing of asylum seekers in Indonesia, which reduced the number of people reaching its shores. Yet, the "out-of-sight-out-of-mind approach" worked only for limited periods of time, as the riots on Galang and the strikes in Nauru and on Lombok attracted the public spotlight in the end. Even though refugee-related issues have never played a significant role within Indonesian media and politics, new information technologies have helped the asylum seekers to direct their protests to more attentive audiences elsewhere.

Finally, this chapter has directed attention to the most recent asylum-seeker flows into Indonesia, which constitute only a small proportion of the hundreds of thousands displaced by political unrest in the Middle East, South Asia and parts of Africa. Nonetheless, the presence of officially 11,082 asylum seekers and refugees in Indonesia in October 2013 has started to make the Indonesian government uneasy. The living conditions of the present flows of asylum seekers, refugees and undocumented migrants are the focus of the following chapter.

Notes

1. Tan Sri Zakaria bin Jahi Mohd Ali, the Malaysian government representative at the Meeting on the Establishment of a Processing Centre for Indochinese Refugees on 15 and 16 May 1979 in Jakarta, stated: "I would like however to emphasise the importance the countries of first transit like Malaysia attach to the commitment that we should not be left with any residual problem — that is to say that we need to be given the assurance that, in providing transit facilities, we would not in the end be left with unwanted refugees" (Indonesian Department of Foreign Affairs 1979).
2. Tara Island had a population of about a hundred families, mostly fishers or farmers. The total estimated cost of establishing and running the camp for two years was US$6,072,853.3. About 150 people were considered necessary to manage the processing centre (Indonesian Department of Foreign Affairs 1979).
3. Galang Island had served as a transit location for Japanese soldiers on their return to Japan in 1946 (Fandik 2013; Hasibuan 2007).
4. For photographs of and additional information on life in the camps on Galang, see <http://www.refugeecamps.net/GalangCamp.html> (accessed 12 November 2014).
5. Interview with former UNHCR staff, 10 February 2012, Pancawati.
6. Refugee camps in the Philippines enjoyed a better reputation. People were not locked away, but were free to find work and mingle with the locals; both adults and children also had to attend school. At first, locals saw the presence of refugees as economic stimulus for the region as it created jobs; over time, however, xenophobic animosity increased (Tran 1995, p. 493).
7. Vietnamese boat people were also pushed back by Thai officials at Khlong Yai port, assisted by Thai fishermen (Helton 1990/91, p. 114) and by Singaporean coastguards (Fitzpatrick 2009a).
8. Some of the strongest voices of protest came from the United States, although at the same time the United States government forcibly returned thousands of refugees fleeing Haiti by pushing their boats back into the Caribbean Sea (Tran 1995).
9. UNHCR figures for Vietnamese arrivals in Indonesia between 1975 and 1995, considered by some to be conservative, total 121,708 (1975–79, 51,156; 1980–84, 36,208; 1985–89, 19,070; 1990–95, 15,274) (UNHCR 2000, p. 98).
10. The *"sur place* principle" was especially relevant for people who had been involved in spreading propaganda against the Vietnamese government in the camps, even though they may not have been anti-communist when they fled Vietnam, as for them a return would not have been acceptable, even if they had previously been screened as unlikely to be discriminated against on their repatriation.

11. James Hathaway (1993, p. 689) criticized the inconsistent labelling of asylum seekers from Vietnam, stating that the "conceptual shift between the unbridled inclusion of Vietnamese asylum-seekers under the 1979 Accord and the presumption of economic motivation in the 1989 Plan is not explained by a substantive shift in the nature of the protection claims advanced", as basic civil and political rights, such as free speech, press and assembly, continued to be denied post-reform Vietnam, and practices, such as forced labour and relocation to areas known as "new economic zones", persisted.

12. According to Helton (1993), the UNHCR provided pictorial leaflets for illiterate people.

13. According to the same source, UNHCR officials acknowledged that no information was distributed in the camps urging residents to refrain from participating in corruption or to report any bribery solicitations. Similarly, no UNHCR notices were distributed to camp officials and no provision was made for residents to report their exposure and observation of corruption and bribery anonymously.

14. The percentage of applicants deemed not to be refugees was between 60 and 70 per cent across all of the Southeast Asian camps, which led to serious charges of procedural deficiencies; but it was only towards the end of the CPA that guidelines were provided to applicants on how to prepare a submission.

15. The majority of camp inmates tended to be young, with about 75–85 per cent under thirty (Fields 1992).

16. Between 1993 and 1995, the UNHCR spent US$34.4 million on economic and social reintegration projects for returnees in Vietnam. It also employed observers in Hanoi and Ho Chi Minh City to oversee the wellbeing of the returnees. The European Union contributed about US$135 million for the reintegration of returnees in Vietnam (Robinson 2004). For the first year of their repatriation, returnees received between US$240 and US$360 as assistance (Cohen 1993; Balfour 1993; UNHCR 2000).

17. Nearly two decades earlier, between 1976 and 1978, 2,087 Vietnamese asylum seekers had arrived in Australia on fifty-five boats (Kneebone 2010, p. 347).

18. Interviews with Deputy Head of the Transnational Crime Desk at the Coordinating Ministry for Politics, Legal and Security, 27 January 2012, and with Head of Section on Irregular Migrants and the Protection of Victims of Transnational Crime at the Directorate General of Immigration, 5 March 2012, Jakarta.

19. In 1999 there were 162,472 people from Timor Leste in Indonesia, while in the next three years, their numbers shrank to 122,202 (2000), 73,042 (2001) and 28,097 (2002) (UNHCR 2003, p. 343).

20. In September 1999, the Australian government offered temporary refuge to almost 2,000 East Timorese evacuees. There had been an earlier influx of East

Timorese to Australia after the Indonesian invasion of the former Portuguese colony. Between 1976 and 1981, 2,447 people arrived, of whom 1,940 were Timorese Chinese. Many more came after that under a special family reunion programme. The Dili massacre of November 1991 created further internal unrest, causing a further 1,650 refugees to flee to Australia between 1994 and 1996 (McCormack 2008). At the time of the 2001 Australian Census, there were 9,380 East Timor–born people in Australia, equalling 0.2 per cent of the overseas-born population (Australian Department of Immigration and Citizenship 2007).

21. Despite the deteriorating situation in countries of first asylum within the Middle East, the largest numbers of Afghan asylum seekers are in Pakistan (about 550,000), mainly in Quetta, and in Iran (roughly 1.1 million).

22. The 1992 Indonesian Immigration Law (UU 9/1992, Sections 8 and 24) governed who could enter the country lawfully, but had no provisions for asylum seekers or for granting them asylum or effective protection.

23. Resettlement countries were extremely reluctant to accept refugees from Indonesia, as they considered the caseload in Indonesia to be a direct outcome of Australia's refugee policy (HRW 2002). Most of those who were resettled went to New Zealand, Sweden, Norway and Canada, and only a few went to Australia.

24. Interestingly, an information leaflet, dated 6 September 2000, that UNHCR provided to asylum seekers in Indonesia, contained not only brief guidelines on the refugee-determination process, but also recommendations for affordable hostels in Jakarta, because the UNHCR did not run shelters or accommodation.

25. Although the *Tampa* was much closer to the harbour in Christmas Island than to the harbour in Merak, the Merak harbour had more appropriate facilities for large freighters to berth.

26. On 19 September, Peter Reith, Australian Minister for Defence, and the President of Nauru, Rene Harris, signed a Statement of Principles, in which Nauru agreed to host more than 500 intercepted asylum seekers until May 2002. In return Australia agreed to provide AU$20 million of assistance. In December 2001 the initial agreement was replaced by the "Memorandum of Understanding between the Republic of Nauru and the Commonwealth of Australia for Cooperation in the Administration of Asylum Seekers and Related Issues", which made no mention of an expiry date. In this MoU Nauru now pledged to host up to 1,200 asylum seekers and Australia pledged not only to cover all costs related to the accommodation of the asylum seekers, but also agreed to provide AU$10 million in development aid to Nauru. On 11 October 2001, Australia signed another MoU with Papua New Guinea, in which Papua New Guinea agreed to host intercepted asylum seekers. This agreement was extended a number of times. Unlike Nauru, Papua New

Guinea did not receive additional development funding. Although Papua New Guinea is party to the Refugee Convention, it has expressed many reservations regarding employment, housing, public education and freedom of movement of asylum seekers and refugees. It also lacks both a domestic mechanism for refugee determination and a legislative framework for refugee protection (Taylor 2005).

27. The introduction of this "culture of containment" (Grewcock 2009, p. 10) in 1992 was intended to discourage potential asylum seekers from Indochina and China.

28. Since its introduction into Australian administrative and political communications in the late 1990s, SIEV has been used as an acronym for both "suspected illegal entry vessel" and "suspected irregular entry vessel".

29. Between 2001 and February 2008, a total of 1,637 people were detained in the detention centres on Nauru and Manus, of whom 1,153 (70 per cent) were ultimately resettled in Australia and other countries (Phillips and Spinks 2013).

30. There were widespread allegations of corruption, especially against caretakers paid by IOM to provide food to asylum seekers, who provided cheap, low-quality food to the asylum seekers and pocketed the rest of the funds (Nassery 2004).

31. Hassan Ghulam visited the Afghans in Lombok twice in 2004, in February and again in March, and reported on their situation to the UNHCR in Jakarta and Geneva.

32. Given that each authority collects its own data, the numbers of refugees and asylum seekers differ, often quite substantially, between UNHCR, IOM and the Indonesian Immigration Department.

33. The annual statistics of the Indonesian Secretariat-General of Immigration, a part of the Ministry of Justice and Human Rights, only date back to 2010.

3

THE POLITICS OF DETENTION

> If you don't have money to pay your way out of [immigration]
> detention, you stay there for years. If you go mad, nobody cares.
> (Interview with Tariq, Cisarua, 17 January 2012)

TARIQ'S JOURNEY

In January 2012, in a mountainous village near Bogor, West Java, I met a
young man who had just turned eighteen, whom I will call Tariq. He had
just been released from immigration detention and was eager to share his
story with me. Unlike many other youngsters I had met before, Tariq's
English was almost faultless as he had studied it for almost three years in a
private language school in Quetta (Pakistan). Tariq's family were originally
Afghani Hazara, and his father's activities for the Hizb-e-Wahdat (Islamic
Unity Party of Afghanistan) compelled his father and then his entire
family to flee from Afghanistan and find shelter in Pakistan. Tariq had
spent about six of his eighteen years in Quetta and had had little formal
education, except for the English classes, which his parents considered an
indispensable investment for the family's future. The idea of migrating
overseas was therefore not entirely new, but several events had triggered
its premature realization.

In mid-2010, after witnessing some gruesome incidents targeting fellow
Hazaras near his home in Quetta, Tariq approached his father to ask his

permission to leave home for Australia, arguing that "if I can reach it, we all can be a bit safe".[1] Tariq's father did not try to stop him. His mother cried when she found out, but she had no part in the decision-making. Tariq's father contacted a smuggler to arrange his son's journey. To pay for his travels, the family took out a loan of US$7,500 from an acquaintance who charged them high interest rates, even though that is not permitted under Islam. Unable to fly to Australia on a direct commercial flight in order to launch his request for asylum there, Tariq had to accept a longer, more dangerous and much more expensive trip. Not long after Tariq left Quetta, his father had a heart attack and died, leaving his mother to repay the remaining debt of US$4,500 by taking in laundry.

Tariq's reasoning seemed to indicate that, for him, Australia was more an abstract idea promising a better, safer life than a real location. His geographical knowledge of the country was vague. His idea of going to Australia had developed to a large extent from what he had heard from other men who had tried to reach Europe but had ultimately failed; they told frightening stories about other transit places, especially Turkey. Tariq explained that "I hear about Turkey is a bad place for asylum seekers with a lot of bad people who just want money. They are thieves. They hound asylum seekers with dogs, they hit them and if their relatives do not pay ransom, they cut off their ears and fingers."[2]

For most of his journey to Indonesia, Tariq had no idea where he was heading next. He only learned about the route from the different associates of his smuggler as the journey was unfolding. First Tariq travelled twelve hours by car from Quetta to Karachi, where he was given a fake passport, which allowed him to board a plane to Bangkok. There he stayed in a safe house for two weeks, before flying to Kuala Lumpur, where he stayed in another safe house in Chow Kit, a suburb of Kuala Lumpur with a high density of migrants. He went to Penang by bus and from there took a plane to Banda Aceh in Indonesia and, finally, to Jakarta. At each airport he and his fellow travellers were handed over to a new contact person who assisted them with the immigration procedures and accompanied them to their new safe house. Tariq recollected in particular his first contact person, a Punjabi, who was very strict and "would not even allow them to order a tea on their own". After reaching Jakarta, they were once more picked up by a member of the smuggling network, who instructed them "to go to UN office for registration in order to be safe from police".[3]

While registered as an asylum seeker, Tariq made several attempts to leave Indonesia for Australia by boat, each of which failed for different reasons. Eventually, he was arrested and detained for several months in the immigration detention centre in Kupang, even though he was then still an unaccompanied minor (under the age of eighteen years) and should have been exempt from detention. Tariq recounted:

> [Four days after our arrest], they took us to the guest house — "Rudenim Ditensi Imigrasi Kupang". We were told it was camp, but instead we saw high walls, wires, and cells with twenty sad faces looking at us. We were taken one by one into the cells. [We were] twelve people in a small room that was big enough for just five persons. The cell was locked and it remained locked for ten days. On the eleventh day, the head of the immigration came and threatened us that they would send us to jail [where Indonesians are kept], if anybody would try to escape from here.

The process of determining Tariq's refugee status continued while he was detained. He was formally recognized as a genuine refugee by the UNHCR in Jakarta and was to be released from detention immediately, but, because he lacked the money to speed up the bureaucratic process in the Kupang detention centre, it was several months before he was transferred out of detention to a special shelter for unaccompanied minors. Free from detention, Tariq could leave the shelter during the daytime, join in activities offered by a NGO, meet other Afghani acquaintances and make new friends. His life improved immediately. But, because he was conscious that his mother had to repay the smuggler, Tariq longed to get to Australia as soon as possible, one way or another.

For some transit migrants, especially those who had spent extended periods in detention, conditions in transit in Indonesia were bad, sometimes even worse than what they had experienced in their home countries. However, any regrets they may have had about leaving their homes in the first place came too late as, for most transit migrants, returning home was no longer an option; they had to "keep going" (Triandafyllidou and Maroukis 2012). I met Tariq several times to hear more of his account of life as a refugee, but then lost contact with him until mid-April 2012 when he phoned me for the last time. When he called, he was on a boat. The call only lasted a few seconds before the connection was cut off. Judging from Tariq's screaming and that of others in the background, I could only assume that the boat was in distress. In the few seconds of that final call, Tariq had given me no information about his location. Several days after this call, an empty boat was washed ashore on the south coast of Lombok (Fitri 2012a). There was no trace of the passengers when locals reported the boat to the authorities. It remains unclear whether or not the locals assisted the passengers to continue their journey. It is also possible that the people smuggler sent another boat to pick up the passengers. Whatever their fate, I have not heard from Tariq since that last phone call.

It is generally considered that there are two defining moments of transit migration: the moment of departure from home, and the moment of arrival at what it is hoped could become a new home. In between departure and ultimate arrival, transit migrants spend substantial amounts of time in often more than one transit country. Although transit migrants can apply for protection in some of the transit countries along the way, many prefer to keep going and reach Australia, or at least Indonesia. International law does not mandate that asylum seekers seek protection in the first state that offers effective protection after they have left their country of origin.[4]

Until they reach a destination where they feel safe to launch their asylum claim, they tend to travel in a clandestine manner to elude authorities along the route (Mountz 2011a, p. 119). During their staggered journeys, transit migrants follow surprising, even unexpected, routes out of necessity. Law enforcement officials tend to see only the irregularity and clandestine nature of their mobility and movements, overlooking what these staggered journeys really depict — the search for safety and protection. Although asylum seekers should be exempt from immigration detention when trying to reach safe ground, in many countries they are often arrested and detained for arbitrary periods of time before they have had a chance to launch an asylum claim. Once they have been arrested and detained, their journeys to protection are brought to an abrupt halt. Immigration detention is thus understood as one effective means to "rendering undesirable people immobile" (Schuster and Majidi 2013, p. 222). This chapter analyses how movements of transit migrants in and through Indonesia have been obstructed and how people on the move have faced criminalization rather than being offered protection.

Mechanisms of disruption and interception impede transit migrants' mobility, particularly at borders and in border zones. Bearing in mind Indonesia's geographic dimensions of almost two million square kilometres and a coastline more than 80,000 kilometres long, it is not difficult to accept that controlling the borders of the archipelago is an enormous challenge for which Indonesia lacks both the financial and human resources, rendering much of its border rather porous. Because of the limited resources, Indonesian border control is concentrated on a number of hotspots along certain smuggling and trafficking routes. Although border control cannot be exercised evenly and unremittingly, there is a striking geographic imbalance in its implementation. Statistics of arrests of irregular migrants have indicated that borders in the north, particularly along the coastlines of Sumatra, the Riau Archipelago and Kalimantan, which migrants cross when they enter the country, are much less strictly controlled than Indonesia's southern borders, which they typically cross when they are leaving Indonesia (Missbach 2014a). Consequently, many transit migrants who come to Indonesia are not arrested immediately upon their arrival but at some time further into their journey through Indonesia, mostly at transport hubs such as airports, ferry ports and bus terminals along the most travelled routes. Other places where they are frequently arrested are living areas, hotels and apartment complexes that are popular among transit migrants, as surveillance and raiding of these places by national and local police and immigration officers have increased substantially since 2010.

This chapter has three objectives. Firstly it offers insights into general and specific characteristics of fragmented journeys into and within Indonesia. As entry and arrival modes have such a strong impact on the subsequent experiences of transit in Indonesia, it is necessary to describe the variety of entry modes used by different transit migrant cohorts. The second part of this chapter presents statistics of arrests of transit migrants in Indonesia and compares them with field observations relating to the arrest and detention of transit migrants, which often contradict the statistics. Inconsistency in immigration law enforcement reveals Indonesia's weakness in controlling its borders and, more importantly, its overall reluctance to serve as the last bulwark for irregular migration flows to Australia. In the third part of this chapter, attention is directed to the realities and politics of immigration detention. Although detention of immigration offenders is not mandatory, many asylum seekers, refugees and other undocumented transit migrants are kept in Indonesia's immigration detention system, often for unspecified periods of time. By providing an insight into everyday life in detention and by describing a few extraordinary events, such as escape attempts, riots, physical abuse, acts of resistance and solidarity among the detainees, this part of the chapter reveals the human cost of the deterrence of irregular migration flows.

ARRIVAL MODES

Transit migrants have chosen both regular and irregular modes of arrival, which makes it difficult to generalize their entry into Indonesia. Over the last ten years, modes of arrival have changed and adapted in response to successive changes in border control and immigration law enforcement. Whether transit migrants come to Indonesia clandestinely or carrying authentic or fraudulent travel documents and visas depends on the options available to them. Given the limited options for receiving a visa on arrival, only a small percentage of transit migrants arrive directly from their home country at one of the twenty international airports in Indonesia and make use of short-term visitor visas. Citizens of most European countries, the United States, Japan and Australia can purchase a visa on arrival for US$25, if they have a valid return ticket. Until mid-2013, Iranians were eligible to get a visa on arrival in Indonesia and many made use of it.[5] During the first four months of 2013 more than 4,000 thirty-day visas were issued to Iranians on their arrival in Indonesia (Alford 2013c). Simultaneously, the number of Iranians arriving irregularly in Australia by boat increased as well. Responding to Australian government pressure on the Indonesian government, the Indonesian Minister for Justice and Human Rights, Amir Syamsuddin, signed a decree in July 2013 to terminate arrangements for Iranians to be granted visas on their arrival in Indonesia. The effectiveness of the new regulation remains in question, as Iranians still enjoy up to three months of visa-free travel to neighbouring Malaysia (Malaysian Immigration Department 2013).[6] Approximately sixty per cent of the asylum seekers have entered Indonesia from Malaysia, as of October 2013 (Morrison, Campbell and Lancaster 2013).

Citizens of conflict-ridden countries such as Iraq, Afghanistan and Sri Lanka are not eligible for visas on arrival and must apply for other categories of visas (for example, social, business or student visas) when planning to come to Indonesia. Acquiring these involves a more bureaucratic process that requires invitations, sponsorship and even guarantees by third persons or institutions in Indonesia. Student and business visas were especially popular among Somali and Sudanese transit migrants.[7] Lacking the time and inclination to rely on the rather uncertain outcomes of these lengthy and costly processes, many transit migrants purchase fraudulent passports for travel to Indonesia and to other transit countries close to Indonesia. For example, before 2013 many Afghans arrested in Indonesia were found to hold Iranian passports ("Immigration Detains Four" 2010).

The majority of transit migrants travel in fragmented journeys, having had multiple stopovers at one or more countries en route to Indonesia. It is not uncommon for some to have been abandoned by their smugglers halfway. Getting precise information about selected routes from transit migrants, when they were still in Indonesia, proved difficult. They often wished to keep this information to themselves, fearing that it could be used by law enforcement agencies seeking to prevent future travellers from entering Indonesia. Instead of providing authentic details, they chose to give rather general information about routes that were already known, some of which had even been stamped out. The actual pathways and entry points were only revealed when I interviewed some of them again once they had been resettled and, therefore, felt less exposed to risk.

Many transit migrants use travel documents for only one leg of the journey. For example, they rely on fake passports to enter and exit Dubai, Kuala Lumpur or Bangkok, but then return these travel documents to their smugglers to be recycled for use by other clients in the future. Cities such as Quetta and Teheran have earned a reputation as hotspots for delivering fake travel documents to affluent customers. Some Afghan informants also claimed that they were channelled around passport controls at airports as certain immigration officers collaborated with the smuggling networks and took them through back doors instead of the official gateways. According to Iraqi informants, one way of gaining entry to Indonesia, Malaysia or Thailand with poorly counterfeited travel documents was to bribe immigration officials with "green notes" (dollar bills).[8] Payment of bribes to officials in Indonesia has been mentioned in several Australian court documents relating to people-smuggling trials (Barker 2013). Increased awareness of irregular migration and of criminal activity among immigration officials and border guards, together with upgraded technical facilities for the inspection of travel documents at Indonesian airports, have reduced the chances of entering Indonesia with fraudulent papers (Wilson and Weber 2008). It can be assumed that among those arriving at an Indonesian border control point with fraudulent documents are many who intend to apply for international protection, but, instead of being allowed into the country to launch their registration at the UNHCR office in Jakarta, they are denied entry. If they arrived by plane, they are usually returned to where they came from, with the help of the transportation company that brought them to Indonesia. Getting information about the number of people refused entry into Indonesia proved difficult, as immigration officers generally denied the possibility that there may have been potential asylum seekers among those forcibly returned at the point of their arrival. According to Lembaga Bantuan Hukum (LBH, Legal Aid Institute) in Jakarta, there were two confirmed cases of Iranian men arriving at the Jakarta airport in 2013 with fraudulent papers; both men were denied entry even though they stated their wish to contact the UNHCR.[9]

Indonesian passport and visa controls could be avoided if the migrants stopped over in Malaysia and continued the journey to Indonesia by ferry, preferably to one of the many less strictly controlled seaports, or by charter boat to a point on the Indonesian coast that was not an official point of entry (Hoffman 2010a, p. 225). Some interviewees explained that they had disposed of their fake identity documents before taking a boat to Indonesia, so that if they were intercepted they could not be deported immediately. Others had held on to their papers and not disposed of them until they were aboard a boat to Australia, their final destination country.

The fact that transit migrants can apply for international protection under the UNHCR in both Thailand and Malaysia gives rise to the question of why many of them opt to come to Indonesia when doing so exposes them to further risk of arrest and physical danger, especially when taking boats. The reasons that come to mind are both obvious and obscure. The UNHCR regional offices in Thailand and Malaysia are both overloaded with cases. In January 2013, the UNHCR office in Kuala Lumpur was handling 90,185 refugees and 11,650 asylum seekers and the UNHCR office in Bangkok 84,479 refugees and 14,580 asylum seekers (UNHCR 2013a and 2013b). In contrast, the number of accumulated cases at the UNHCR in Jakarta was barely one-tenth of the number of cases handled by its neighbouring countries. Another incentive (*daya tarik*) are the services provided by the UNHCR and the IOM in Indonesia, which help to cushion some of the hardships of transit migrants and are deemed to be of much higher quality than services provided in Malaysia.[10] Tired of waiting in Malaysia, some people cross over into Indonesia clandestinely, even though they have been granted refugee status by the UNHCR in Malaysia and were already waiting for resettlement. These secondary migration movements feed into further smuggling, but do not accelerate their recognition and resettlement process at all, as the UNHCR in Indonesia has to verify their status all over again.[11]

For Muslim transit migrants, Malaysia and Indonesia at least hold the promise of some kind of Muslim solidarity, as opposed to Thailand with its majority Buddhist population. Furthermore, Indonesia is considered to be one step closer to Australia and, psychologically, this seems to have a big impact on transit migrants. Living expenses in Indonesia are also deemed to be lower, general living conditions more favourable and immigration law enforcement generally weaker. Although Malaysia is lenient in controlling entry, the Malaysian government takes a harsh approach towards irregular (labour) migrants, who are stigmatized as "illegal migrants" (*pendatang haram*). Crackdowns on irregular migrants take place frequently and paramilitary corps, such as Ikatan Relawan Rakyat Malaysia (RELA), readily assist state immigration authorities (Missbach 2011). Not only are there frequent raids, but offences against immigration laws in Malaysia carry severe punishments, including physical punishments such as caning (Hedman 2009). Last but not least, in the past Malaysia has deported registered asylum seekers and refugees.

For these reasons, transit migrants preferred to stay in Malaysia for as short a time as possible and leave for Indonesia as soon as they could. According to informants, the cost in 2010 for short-term shelter in Malaysia and passage from Malaysia to Indonesia was between US$500 and US$1,000. Boat departures were often from makeshift harbours along the Malaysian west coast, for example near Johor or Port Klang, to Batam in the Riau Archipelago. In some cases, transit migrants relied on the same boats used by Indonesian workers who have overstayed in Malaysia and were returning without valid documents (IOM Indonesia 2010*d*, p. iv). The Riau Archipelago, near Singapore, and the approximately 1,700-kilometre-long Sumatran coast offered plenty of provisional and temporary harbours (*pelabuhan tikus*) to serve as irregular entry points. Entry into Kalimantan via the adjacent East Malaysian provinces of Sabah and Sarawak was not unknown, but a road relatively less travelled.

Once in Indonesia, either on the Riau Archipelago or the Sumatran mainland, transit migrants who avoided arrest at their point of entry made their way to the nearest large city, such as Banda Aceh, Medan or Padang, in order to fly to Jakarta. Air tickets are usually bought through middlemen and sometimes under Indonesian names, as some domestic airlines do not check the identity of their passengers. Those wanting to avoid being caught at one of the strictly monitored airports chose to travel to Jakarta overland by bus. However, places like Lampung, the main harbour town on Sumatra from which ferries depart for Java, have come under stricter surveillance recently ("Lampung menjadi jalur" 2012). Jakarta remains the main stopover point, not only because the UNHCR headquarters are there, which is relevant for those who wish to register as asylum seekers, but also because in cosmopolitan Jakarta transit migrants can blend in more easily and have more opportunity to identify others of the same ethnicity who can supply information on smugglers.

The last mode of arrival mentioned here is the direct journey by boat to Indonesia, often relied upon by transit migrants from Myanmar and Sri Lanka, some of whom are stateless people, such as the Rohingyas, who faced widespread discrimination in Myanmar and were generally barred from possessing legal documents. Following further deterioration of their security in Myanmar in 2012, the Rohingyas started leaving in greater numbers (UNHCR 2013d). Given the presence of more than 23,386 Rohingyan refugees in Malaysia, many of those leaving Myanmar intended to reach Malaysia (UNHCR Malaysia 2013), but bad weather and a lack of navigation equipment meant that a number of their boats were washed ashore in Indonesia or rescued by Indonesian fishermen. Reports of last-minute rescues at sea appeared regularly in 2012 and 2013 (Hasan 2013a; Simanjuntak 2012; "Boats Carrying" 2013). Moreover, because law enforcement is stricter in Malaysia, Rohingyas have increasingly had to make secondary journeys from Malaysia to Indonesia (Alford 2013b; Hasan 2013b).

Ongoing violence and discrimination after the end of the Sri Lankan government's war against the separatist Liberation Tigers of Tamil Eelam (LTTE) caused a spike in the number of people fleeing Sri Lanka. Although Tamil transit migrants often tried to reach Australia's outposts — such as the Cocos Islands or Christmas Island — in one voyage, they occasionally had to stop in Indonesia for new supplies. Bad weather conditions have forced some Tamil boats ashore, while others have been intercepted in Indonesian waters (Fardah 2011).

From these observations it is clear that one cannot generalize about entry modes into Indonesia as they are, in fact, quite diverse. Different ethnic groups rely on different strategies for travel and entry into the archipelago, which depend on the options available to them in the first place. Although the paths of different ethnic groups may sometimes cross and overlap, transit migrants usually travel in the company of their fellow countrymen and choose, if possible, a smuggler from the same ethnic or national background. Once transit migrants reach Indonesia, they continue to exploit links with members of their ethnic or national community already living in Indonesia, which in turn foster relationships based on patronage between newly arrived transit migrants and their more established fellow countrymen (CWS 2013, p. 31).

CAT-AND-MOUSE GAMES: ARREST, ESCAPE AND RE-ARREST OF TRANSIT MIGRANTS

While Indonesian immigration law enforcement officials have in the past chosen either to look the other way or exercise a laissez-faire attitude whenever they encountered transit migrants, interceptions, arrests and detentions of transit migrants have increased nationwide since 2010. The police can arrest people who violate immigration regulations. Asylum seekers and refugees are neither exempt from arrest nor afforded special treatment. As Table 3.1 depicts, state authorities in Indonesia do not differentiate between undocumented migrants and asylum seekers in search of protection; as Komnas HAM (2012, p. 6) critically remarked, "they are put in the same category with illegal immigrants who commit administrative violations of immigration regulations".

Arrests are commonly made at transport hubs, along beaches and in hotels. As a result of many campaigns to raise awareness of people-smuggling and irregular migration among law enforcement personnel and ordinary citizens in regional hotspots, the police can now rely to a great extent on information provided by ordinary people. Rather than using many officers and large amounts of financial resources on patrolling hubs and hotspots, the police generally act once they have been called in by other people. In fact, the special people-smuggling taskforce (SATGAS) and its sixteen regional units (SATGASDA), initiated in 2009 in reaction to the increasing numbers of transit migrants being channelled through

Table 3.1
Migrant Arrests by Indonesian Authorities and Police, 2008–13

	2008	2009	2010	2011	2012	2013 (Jan–Sep)
Number of arrests	116	1,014	2,352	2,470	4,525	8,265

Source: Interview with director of Investigation and Immigration Enforcement at Criminal Investigation Police Headquarters, 13 November 2013, Jakarta.

Indonesia, have succeeded in building an extensive and penetrating informal network of civilian informants to monitor migrants' movements locally (Missbach 2014a). The Head of the SATGAS Anti-Penyelundupan Manusia in Bandung, claimed that along the route between Bogor and Pelabuhan Ratu, one of the departure points most frequently used by boats to Australia, "rickshaw drivers, village people, kiosk owners and moped taxi chauffeurs along the road keep an eye out for passing cars with asylum seekers" while waiting for customers. If they see something suspicious, they call us."[12] This form of state–civilian collaboration allows for targeted and cost-effective operations.

Indonesian authorities also rely on information about suspected irregular migrant movements from overseas intelligence sources, such as the Australian Federal Police (AFP), and maritime rescue authorities, such as the Australian Maritime Safety Authority (AMSA) and Indonesia's search-and-rescue agency, Badan SAR Nasional (Basarnas). Because of constraints of manpower, vehicles and operational funding, the police cannot always make arrests, even if irregular movements are brought to their attention. Although the IOM often reimburses the costs of petrol and vehicle rental incurred in police raids and subsequent arrests, some of these costs must be met before an operation is launched. If a police officer does not volunteer in advance of an operation to cover its costs from his or her own pocket, it can be impeded. Some arrests require substantial police numbers because of the large number of transit migrants involved; if they resist apprehension by fleeing or fighting back, police numbers need to match the size of the migrant group.[13]

Although Komnas HAM (2012, p. 6) reported a lack of coordination among law enforcement agencies in handling asylum seekers, refugees and undocumented migrants caught in Indonesia, many local officers and units have now developed an operational routine that incorporates collaboration with other agencies. Once arrested, transit migrants are usually checked for identity documents and registered. The police then inform the local immigration office so that they can perform the administrative tasks for which they are responsible and start to organize transfer of those arrested to an immigration detention centre. Local and national IOM contact-people are also informed, not least because they need to reimburse costs accumulated in the arrest of transit migrants, such as for temporary accommodation in hotels, schools and mosques; food; and additional security staff and night guards.[14] The IOM usually bears all expenses until those arrested have been transferred to an immigration detention centre,[15] a process that may take several weeks because of overcrowding in most immigration detention centres.

While awaiting final transfer to a detention centre, many transit migrants try to escape, by either bribing the guards or running away. When I visited temporary accommodation for newly arrested transit migrants in Sukabumi, which turned out to be a hotel used quite regularly for this purpose, I met Naim, a young Hazara man. Naim's ankle was wrapped in a dirty bandage, so I asked what had happened. He told me that, lacking the money to bribe his way out of the guarded hotel and figuring that he was taller and stronger than most of the Indonesian guards, he had tried to escape. He thought his chances of making a run for it were good, but when he jumped from the third floor and injured his ankle, his attempt had failed. While his two friends managed to run away into the dark night, he could not move and was taken back inside. Naim said the guards beat him up to teach him a lesson. Altogether twenty-five people escaped from Naim's group of forty-seven people ("47 imigran gelap ditangkap" 2012). Naim claimed that the guards did not fix a price to enable their escape and that they were open to negotiation. However, the longer the arrested people waited to attempt their escape, the more the guards demanded in bribes.[16]

Guards neglect their responsibilities for various reasons. Some might feel sympathy for the arrested transit migrants and allow them to get away. However, in my interviews with off-duty guards, they revealed that their negligence arose more often from a sense of frustration about the ineffectiveness of their jobs. They felt that if those arrested really wanted to escape from the temporary shelters, they would more often than not succeed anyway. Guards face disciplinary measures if they do not carry out their jobs properly, but they can at least benefit financially by making money from the escaping migrants. Payment of bribes in an escape attempt does not, however, guarantee its success. Some transit migrants complained that they paid a bribe, but were immediately re-arrested by other guards. Strategies to prevent escapes used by guards included confiscating shoes, glasses, cash and mobile phones, the last of which prevented transit migrants from calling their smugglers for help. There was a welcome side income for the guards in the sale of personal property they confiscated from arrested transit migrants. A number of those arrested also complained that guards had taken the UNHCR registration cards that proved their status as asylum seekers. Despite having been promised their belongings would be returned when they are released from detention, many of those released leave detention empty-handed.

Arrested transit migrants who do hold valid travel documents are usually sent to an Indonesian immigration detention centre, regardless of whether they are undocumented migrants, registered asylum seekers, or even recognized refugees. Although illegal entry into and exit from Indonesia are not criminal offences and should, under Indonesian Law on Immigration (6/2011, Paragraph 113), incur a sentence of only one year in prison and/or a fine of up to Rp100 million (AU$10,000), arrested transit migrants may face a lengthy period in detention. Irregular migrants awaiting deportation can be detained for a maximum period of ten years (Paragraph 85[2]). Although the Indonesian Law on Immigration does not specifically mention asylum seekers and refugees, Article 86 rules that victims of human trafficking or people-smuggling should be treated differently from general offenders against immigration law. Article 87, in fact, states that "victims of human trafficking and people smuggling who are in Indonesia should be placed in the immigration detention centre or elsewhere specified". Even though detention centres are not considered to be institutions for law enforcement and placement there is supposed to be "temporary", in practice arrested and detained transit migrants are treated as criminals as they are detained without judicial review or bail, often for an unspecified period of time. In this regard, the objective of the law is, as Weber and Pickering (2011, p. 17) have put it, to "immobilize illegalized travellers". Being placed in detention without individual judicial decision or recourse to judicial review, and for an unknown period, makes their confinement arbitrary, which is prohibited under international law (HRW 2013, p. 28; Yursal 2012). Even though Indonesia is not a signatory to the 1951 Refugee Convention, which states that detention violates the right of freedom of movement of people seeking protection,[17] Indonesia acceded in 2006 to the International Covenant on Civil and Political Rights (ICCPR), which forbids arbitrary confinement.

From the perspective of the Indonesian state authorities, the temporary placement of transit migrants in immigration detention centres is not seen as punishment but rather as a "means of protection":

> In principle and from the government point of view, putting them into a detention centre is a form of protection (*bagian dari perlindungan*). Only there can we make sure that they are safe and sound (*tempat yang jelas*

dan aman). By giving access to the international organisations whose job is to take care of them, it is also ensured that they have access to health care and to some extent also have access to education for their children. Outside of detention centres we cannot guarantee that.[18]

The statement above exemplifies official responses to accusations of arbitrary detention and the denial of comparisons of immigration detention centres with prisons. The following sections of this chapter, however, scrutinize the perspective of Indonesian state authorities by describing in detail conditions in immigration detention which make transit migrants vulnerable to additional risk. To date, the regulation of the handling of detainees has been limited to Regulation of the Director-General of Immigration Number IMI-1489.UM.08.05 of 2010 on the Processing of Illegal Migrants. Because they are not subject to the nationally applicable standard operating procedure, the head of each detention centre has far-reaching discretionary authority in handling inmates, which explains the wide variation in conditions across Indonesia's detention centres (Komnas HAM 2012, p. 14).

LIFE IN DETENTION

Until 2004, Indonesia only had very limited quarantine facilities (*karantina*) to accommodate criminal foreigners awaiting punishment or deportation. Conditions in the *karantina* and Indonesian police cells were below international standards during the first influx of Middle Eastern asylum seekers in the early 2000s (Field 2006, p. 123). Most detention centres were built and enlarged after 2004 as the numbers of transit migrants coming to Indonesia grew.[19]

In 2012, there were thirteen immigration detention centres (*rumah detensi imigrasi*, or rudenim) in use in Indonesia, with a combined capacity to host 1,488 detainees, as shown in Table 3.2.[20] Although conditions in detention centres have been improved over the last decade, thanks to Australian funding channelled mainly through the IOM,[21] various reports indicate that the general conditions in Indonesian detention centres remain poor by Western standards (HRW 2013; Taylor 2009). The list of deficiencies and defects in detention centres is long, ranging from the lack of medical attention, low-quality housing and nutrition, to corporal punishment, physical abuse and torture.

Immigration detention centres have been regularly required to house more inmates than they have the capacity for. For example, the Kupang detention centre, built to house ninety people, had to shelter up to 240 people at times in 2010.[22] Table 3.2 gives an overview of the capacity of the detention centres and indicates which were over and under capacity for selected months in 2012 and 2013.

Seemingly unaware of frequent overcrowding in some centres, Minister for Justice and Human Rights, Patrialis Akbar, announced in 2011 that the existing immigration detention centres were sufficient to accommodate the illegal immigrants in Indonesia and that there was no need to increase their capacity at that time, describing the detention centre conditions as very good ("Rumah detensi imigrasi" 2011). Despite the minister's positive assessment in 2011, the frequent overcrowding caused many problems. For example, flooding of cells during the monsoon season, combined with deficient hygiene standards and a lack of clean water, caused diseases such as gastroenteritis and dermatitis (Meliala et al. 2011).

Inmates in immigration detention centres are generally segregated by gender. Single adult men, by far the largest cohort of transit migrants, are

Table 3.2
Detainees in Indonesian Immigration Detention Centres 2012–13

Detention centre	Capacity	Jan 2012	Feb 2012	Nov 2012	June 2013
Tj. Pinang	600	362	343	320	276
Surabaya	60	72	73	69	132
Semarang	0	1	1	11	n.a.
Pontianak	100	109	79	23	111
Pekanbaru	80	137	134	151	154
Medan	120	167	166	238	118
Manado	100	128	135	94	134
Makassar	80	113	134	92	56
Kupang	90	27	113	149	197
Jayapura	8	0	0	n.a.	n.a.
Jakarta	103	80	110	73	109
Denpasar	80	18	52	78	108
Balikpapan	10	18	10	n.a.	n.a.
TOTAL	1,488	1,232	1,350	1,298	1,395

Source: Compiled from unpublished data supplied by the Indonesian Directorate General of Immigration in March 2012 and IOM Indonesia (2012a and 2013a).

housed in different detention blocks from women with children; frequently, fathers and older male children are also separated from the rest of their family (HRW 2013, p. 28). Despite UNHCR (2012b) recommendations that families of arrested transit migrants be exempt from detention and housed instead in monitored community housing schemes, during my visits to immigration detention centres I saw many detained families and children and some unaccompanied minors. However, in some detention centres, such as the Kupang centre, facilities have been extended with extra family rooms to accommodate detained families, although the risk of physical and sexual assault from other inmates has often meant that families have been locked all day in a small cell with barred metal windows to prevent them from mingling with the other detainees in the yard or in the common rooms. Unaccompanied minors were usually hosted in the same facilities as adult men, thereby exposing them to the risk of abuse. Conversely, detainees who were unlikely to escape or who rendered certain services to the security guards enjoyed special privileges. In the detention centre in Makassar, for example, a Vietnamese inmate had a local wife in the nearby village whom he was allowed to visit regularly.[23]

Detainees often complained in interviews about the bad quality and insufficient quantity of food. For example, detainees found insects, metal and other items in their food (HRW 2013, p. 58). Maintenance and sustenance of immigration detention centres, as well as staff expenses, are met from the Indonesian central government budget. According to Asep Kurnia (2011, p. 58), detention centres allocate Rp15,000 (US$1.50) per person per day for food. As this amount is often insufficient to cater for adequate meals, especially in the outer islands where food is generally more expensive, IOM provides another Rp45,000 per day per person for food.[24] This extra allowance is only provided to people already registered under the UNHCR, and not to migrants who are still undocumented or other detainees, such as "illegal" fishermen, who are usually also kept in immigration detention centres until their deportation. Given the discrepancy in food provision and other services, those who do not receive the extra allowance are jealous of those who do and theft occurs (Komnas HAM 2012, p. 12).

Although the total of Rp60,000 could be considered sufficient by Indonesian standards to provide detainees with decent meals three times a day, complaints about meals were widespread in the detention centres I visited, as some of the funds allocated for detainees registered under the

UNHCR are embezzled and misappropriated. Opportunities for abuse of food provision are rife. For example, while the detention centre in Kupang at first employed a chef to cook Middle Eastern dishes for the detainees, a newly appointed head of the centre outsourced the provision of meals to a catering company owned by his wife and the quality of food declined.[25] Other ways of self-enrichment by falsely attributing costs to the inmates of detention centres include overcharging the IOM for its services. According to IOM staff in Kupang, bills for drinking water that they receive from the detention centre for reimbursement are so high that every inmate must drink an average of 200 litres every day.[26] The flow of generous funding from the IOM has given rise to other forms of embezzlement; for example, there seems to be an inexplicably frequent exchange of inmates between some detention centres. Because of the regular overcrowding, a head of a detention centre can request the transfer of inmates to another, less crowded detention centre. However, after they have been transferred, the head of a detention centre would then offer spaces that were allegedly available to other overcrowded detention centres. The IOM fully funds the travel of inmates and their escorts (prison guards or officers from the provincial immigration department), whose airfares are paid for and who receive a generous daily allowance. At times irregularities in their travel occur, as, for example, when security escorts travel a day before or after the detainees travel or they travel on a different aeroplane.[27]

The entrenchment of a culture of embezzlement, extortion and self-enrichment among detention centre staff gives rise to many problems. If transit migrants have not already lost their belongings to the police during arrest, they are exposed to the confiscation of their mobile phones, money and other valuables in detention centres, which, according to transit migrants, are rarely returned upon release (Seo 2010). At the beginning of their stay in detention, the detainees are given a set of clothes, consisting of a pair of trousers, T-shirts, socks and a pair of shoes. Once a month, the IOM also provides the detainees with shampoo, detergent, toothpaste, soap, toothbrush, sugar and tea. According to former inmates, however, these services often arrived late and sometimes not until complaints had been made to the central IOM office in Jakarta.[28] Detainees also complained that guards expected to be handed over a share of the goods provided by the IOM.

Of greater concern, however, was the general level of security in some immigration detention centres. Many detainees generally seemed to become aware from hearsay of the reputations of certain centres and their heads before being sent there. In particular, Pontianak and Medan had very bad reputations, and arrested transit migrants tried as hard as they could to avoid being transferred there. While in detention, detainees were physically and psychologically mistreated by fellow inmates and security guards. Kicking, punching and slapping have been reported widely (HRW 2013, p. 3) and detainees have been forced to watch when their fellow inmates were beaten and abused. Detained children and teenagers were even intimidated by having to witness guards as they carried out corporal punishment.[29]

The first death of an asylum seeker in custody made public was that of Taqi Nekoyee, a young man from Afghanistan who died on 28 February 2012 in the Pontianak immigration detention centre. Together with five fellow detainees, Taqi had escaped from the detention centre but was later recaptured by the police (Missbach and Sinanu 2013). A medical report made upon their arrival in the detention centre stated they were all in good health. During the night that followed, Taqi and the two other recaptured detainees were mistreated by a group of ten guards (Komnas HAM 2012, pp. 20–22). Taqi was severely injured and, because the guards failed to get medical assistance in time, he died the next morning. Taqi's autopsy revealed massive wounds and cigarette burns, which indicated he had been severely beaten and tortured.[30]

Another violent incident that was the focus of widespread media attention was a three-hour brawl between Muslim and Buddhist detainees in the Belawan immigration detention centre; it caused the death of eight detainees from Myanmar in April 2013 (Gunawan 2013; UNHCR 2013e). The police investigation indicated that a group of Rohingya men attacked the Buddhist men in retaliation for alleged sexual harassment of Rohingya female refugees. The detention centre was understaffed at the time, so the guards present that night did not intervene while the detainees attacked one another with metal and wood from broken chairs (Missbach and Sinanu 2013). Tension and deep animosity had been building in the centre between the Burmese Muslims and Buddhists, yet no precautions had been taken to prevent violence between them. The two groups had even been detained in the same rooms.

Given that immigration detention centres were generally understaffed, breakouts from centres were widespread and frequent, and fatalities occurred in some of them ("16 imigran kabur" 2011). Methods of breaking out varied; some escapees cut the iron bars of their windows, others used ropes or sheets and sarongs for abseiling, and some even dug tunnels ("55 imigran kabur" 2012; Kistyarini 2011a; Brown 2012). Some detainees planned their escape well and had arranged for cars to pick them up outside the detention facility, while others who lacked the financial means to organize outside support just hoped to get away on their own.

It differed from case to case whether the security guards were paid for their silent complicity or whether they were simply caught by surprise and outnumbered. In just one month (June 2013), for example, 140 people escaped from the makeshift detention facility in Kupang, of whom roughly half were later recaptured (IOM Indonesia 2013b). Some of the tunnels and holes in the wall, allegedly used for their escape, were too small for a person to fit through, suggesting that the guards had consented, at least tacitly, to their escape. The inadequacy of the tunnels and holes, intended as evidence of a clandestine escape strategy, raised the suspicion that the guards may have willingly escorted them out of the detention centre. To protect the guards from disciplinary action, the escapees had prepared the false evidence to excuse the guards from any claims of negligence they might face.

When re-arrested, escapees were often beaten by the prison guards and, occasionally, also by civilians involved in their recapture ("55 imigran kabur" 2012).[31] Back in detention, detainees usually faced one to two weeks of solitary confinement.[32] Tariq, the young man introduced at the beginning of this chapter, also experienced escape from detention, re-arrest and isolation. For weeks Tariq and three friends had planned to escape during a regular recreational activity at a shopping mall. With the assistance of an acquaintance outside the detention centre, they had organized a car to pick them up. Unable to run quickly enough from the guards, their attempt failed and they were rounded up with the help of bystanders who kicked and slapped them. Back in the detention centre, Tariq was separated from his friends and put in solitary confinement. After one week on his own, Tariq said he became seriously unwell.[33]

Although vulnerable to numerous risks, transit migrants in detention are not completely helpless. Through acts of solidarity, collective protest and bribery, they have been at times able to improve their conditions or, at least, find some relief. The strongest displays of solidarity were apparent among relatives; Friedrich Heckmann (2004, p. 1117) has written of an "obligation of solidarity" among kin in migratory contexts. However, although detainees often preferred to align themselves with other detainees from the same ethnic background, inter-ethnic solidarity was also evident at times. Tariq described a situation in the detention centre in Kupang while he was held there. A young Iranian couple's request for a more nutritious diet, because the wife was eight months pregnant, was initially denied by the detention centre staff. Even though racial tension between Afghan and Iranian inmates had erupted into fighting not long before their request, almost everybody decided to put aside their animosity and support the expectant couple. A group of detainees made a special claim to the IOM on the couple's behalf. The collective protest proved successful and the woman received extra rations and special care. Tariq explained:

> We used to discuss every problem. We used to discuss what we need, how to ask from IOM, and how to deal with the Immigration [officers]. So we used to say that here in the detention there is no Irani[an] and no Afghani. We are all detainees. Nationality, colour, language, it doesn't matter. We are all refugees; we have left our country for a safe life. So here we should not be fighting, we should not be arguing with each other. Rather [we have] to be united, and ask the Immigration or IOM for what we needed.[34]

Other forms of resistance inside detention centres included protests (*berunjuk rasa*), hunger strikes and suicide attempts. There were many protests against the long waiting times in detention and the slow processing of asylum applications by the UNHCR. For example, in late July 2011, 250 detainees in Tanjung Pinang urged the UNHCR to come to the detention centre in order to start the refugee-determination process for those who had not been interviewed and to speed up the decision-making process on applications already submitted (Mohari 2011; Kistyarini 2011*b*). For those who had had their refugee status confirmed but remained in detention, the protesters demanded their immediate release into community housing. Posters and shouting were the dominant means of protest.

Hunger strikes have occurred in a number of detention centres and for various reasons. For example, in May 2012 more than 160 detainees in Tanjung Pinang detention centre went on hunger strike to protest against their imprisonment — some had been detained for almost two years — and the long processing times at the UNHCR, echoing protests made the previous year ("Imigran Afghanistan" 2012; "160 Afghan Asylum Seekers" 2012). Lacking any response from the UNHCR, the hunger strike went on for over two weeks and more than forty people had to be treated in nearby hospitals. In response to the Belawan detention centre guards' failure to render assistance in the clash between Buddhist and Muslim detainees in April 2013, described above, eighty detainees went on a hunger strike to protest against their lack of safety in the centre ("80 orang pengungsi" 2013). Hunger strikes were also launched for petty reasons, as in Kupang in February 2012 when the head of the detention centre employed a new catering company, also described above.[35]

Staff at detention centres appeared at times rather callous and uncaring in their attitude to the problems of detainees. For example, the head of the Kalideres detention centre said disparagingly, "most hunger strikes only last two days because after that the detainees would simply be too hungry". After a long period of detention and not knowing what the future held for them, many detainees suffered from depression. According to staff members in the detention centres in Kupang, Kalideres and Tanjung Pinang, detainees in those establishments have attempted suicide, by cutting their wrists or inflicting electric shocks, for example, but they did not succeed ("Depresi" 2012). The head of the Kalideres detention centre was also insensitive to threats of suicide, saying that he did not take them seriously, as he thought they were only trying to give him a shock (*hanya untuk menakuti*). He claimed that his standard response was: "just go ahead and kill yourself that leaves us with less work".[36] Proper psychological counselling was rare; most detainees relied on strong sedatives instead, provided by the detention centre's medical unit.[37] In some detention centres, the IOM offered language classes to divert detainees and to help them fill in time. In other centres, the Jesuit Refugee Service (JRS) organized aerobics sessions to help detainees release their stress, but some centres terminated these activities because breakouts had been attempted during sports and recreational activities (JRS 2011; Komnas HAM 2012, p. 20).

Some detainees found temporary relief by giving in to the widespread culture of bribery. For example, although detention centre inmates are not officially allowed to leave the premises, some, if they can afford to pay a small fee to the guards and are unlikely to abscond, can leave for an afternoon on their own.[38] A detainee I met inside Kupang detention centre admitted that he took advantage of centre guards who wanted to earn extra income on the side. Whenever he needed to go to a shopping centre in Kupang to buy new clothes, use the Internet or collect money his relatives had wired him, he had to pay to rent a car, invite the guards for a meal at Kentucky Fried Chicken or McDonalds, buy them a T-shirt, or give them a minimum of Rp50,000 (AU$5) in cash.[39] From interviews with other detainees it became obvious that many guards expected tips from detainees for all sorts of favours to improve their daily supplies, such as extra food or cigarettes. Detainees stated that guards threatened them not to mention the bribes to outsiders. Those who could not afford to engage in bribery found life very difficult indeed.

A special kind of bribery is the one-off payment known as "exit fee" (*uang keluar*) or "thank-you money" (*uang terima kasih*), which detention centre staff expect in exchange for faster processing of the papers of detainees about to be released or transferred, or even for processing their papers at all. The amount of the payment is not necessarily fixed, but depends on the financial circumstances of the individual. Iranians, for example, are considered to be generally better off and always have to pay more than Afghans. Prices usually start at US$100, but could be as high as US$500.[40] Those who do not pay face further delays, such as the four additional months Tariq spent in the Kupang detention centre, even though he was still a minor and should not have been detained in the first place.

One of the main problems of immigration detention centres in Indonesia has been their general lack of regulation and the extent of the discretionary powers of centre staff. For example, the decisions at the discretion of detention centre heads include whether inmates can telephone their families or receive guests. In the course of implementing the Rencana Aksi Nasional Hak Asasi Manusia Indonesia (RANHAM, National Action Plan for Human Rights in Indonesia), Indonesia has become more aware of the need to uphold the human rights of immigration detention centre inmates. This awareness has led to development and delivery of training programmes for detention centre staff and to the publication by the Ministry of Justice and Human Rights (Kementerian Hukum dan HAM) of a guidebook on the human rights of the inmates of immigration detention centres. Nevertheless, the many instructions given in the guidebook continue to be ignored. For example, the guidebook specifically mentions that detainees are entitled to contact their national consulates or embassies and their families to inform them of their detention and that they are allowed to receive or reject assistance from their national consulates. Furthermore, they are entitled to receive visits from family members, sponsors, legal counsellors, spiritual leaders, doctors and state representatives. However, lawyers and even members of the National Human Rights Commission

(Komnas HAM) have repeatedly been refused entry to visit the inmates of detention centres.[41]

Not only has there been no independent complaints mechanism for detainees to access, but there has also been no system in place to check whether detention centre staff have adhered to the regulations outlined in the guidebook. Staff who have been found responsible for human rights abuses against their wards have generally faced fairly lenient penalties, as in the case of the ten guards who beat Taqi Nekoyee to death and were sentenced to only ten months in prison before resuming employment with the local department of immigration.[42]

Based on its investigations concerning the treatment of asylum seekers and refugees in immigration detention centres, the commissioners of the National Human Rights Commission stated that: "The placement of refugees and asylum seekers in prison-like detention centres breeds negative consequences, both for the mental health of refugees and asylum seekers as well as for respecting and upholding the rights of asylum seekers and refugees" (Komnas HAM 2012, p. 25). Currently, the minimum political demand is to improve the performance of immigration detention staff by developing binding standard operating procedures. Having clear, nationally applicable, standard operating procedures for immigration detention might help prevent the detention of vulnerable migrants and asylum seekers, establish benchmarks for acceptable conditions of confinement, and give those detained access to an effective complaints procedure about immigration staff conduct. The National Human Rights Commission also made more far-reaching political demands, urging the Indonesian government to sign the Refugee Convention, design a national strategy for the handling of asylum seekers and establish alternative shelters for asylum seekers (Komnas HAM 2012, p. 25). Possible alternatives include, for example, reception centres where, instead of being incarcerated, asylum seekers are provided with the basic necessities and remain free to leave.

Although the Indonesian government bears the responsibility for the appalling treatment of detainees in the immigration detention centres, Australian government pressure on Indonesia to detain transit migrants and, therefore, act as a bulwark in its own agenda of deterrence cannot be overlooked. It has been in the political interests of Australia as the final destination country to encourage the development and fund the expansion of the Indonesian immigration detention system (Nethery, Rafferty-Brown and Taylor 2013).

Given that the Indonesian government prioritizes immigration law enforcement over refugee protection, improving living standards in Indonesian immigration detention centres would represent a counterproductive tactic. If political relations with Australia are taken into account, improving conditions in immigration detention centres in Indonesia would reduce levels of deterrence to people entering Indonesia and, if they were treated more humanely in detention centres, many fewer detainees might be convinced to accept assisted voluntary return, opting instead for onward migration.

SUMMARY

This chapter has shown that transit migrants of different nationalities choose different travel modes and entry points, depending on the exit modes from their home countries, the accessibility and availability of their travel documents, visa restrictions on them when travelling to Indonesia, and budgetary considerations. Those who enter Indonesia with a valid visa and proper travel documents enjoy a regular status, at least for a short time. Only when they decide to overstay their visa or leave Indonesia from a port other than an official port of embarkation does their presence become irregular. Possessing valid papers also allows them more time to register as asylum seekers and/or to organize the next leg of their journey. In contrast, those without any valid documents face arrest and detention from the minute they enter the archipelago, not least because surveillance operations and arrests by enforcement officers have sporadically increased due to better incentives and amenities. Arrests, in particular, provide enforcement officers with opportunities for bribery, extortion and corruption, as they are in a position to abuse the weakness of transit migrants for their own benefit. Given the frequency of arrests, escapes and re-arrests, it becomes questionable whether the cat-and-mouse games between transit migrants and state officials serve any purpose other than to milk the migrants of whatever resources they may still have access to.

Extortion is also prevalent in detention, where detained transit migrants suffer from curtailed rights, isolation and uncertainty. Conditions and standards vary widely among Indonesia's thirteen official immigration detention centres, because there is no binding regulation of the management of centres and their responsibilities towards detainees. Poorly managed resources and funds, inadequately trained staff, and the general lack of accountability in cases of maltreatment and abuse exacerbate the poor conditions of the detention facilities, in which exploitation appears to be widespread and to lead to what Weber and Pickering (2011, p. 8) have called a "routinization of harm". The detention of asylum seekers and refugees as a punitive or disciplinary measure for illegal entry or presence in a country, or as part of a wider policy to deter the onward mobility of asylum seekers, contradicts the norms of refugee law (UNHCR 2012*b*). In fact, indefinite detention has been likened to "a form of social death" (Weber and Pickering 2011, p. 116). It is not enough, therefore, to demand that the living conditions of transit migrants in detention facilities be improved. The ultimate political demand must be that asylum seekers are not confined in immigration detention centres at all. In response to the chronic overcrowding in some immigration detention facilities, the Indonesian government has begun to tolerate other forms of accommodation, as will be discussed in the next chapter.

Notes

1. Interview with Tariq, 17 January 2012, Cisarua.
2. Other Hazaras gave similar accounts when I interviewed them in Cisarua in June 2010 and Sukabumi in June 2012. Triandafyllidou and Maroukis (2012) reported on the dangers for asylum seekers passing through Turkey, referring in particular to mafia-like kidnappers and widespread extortion.
3. Interview with Tariq, 29 March 2012, Cisarua.
4. "Effective protection means that: there is no likelihood of persecution, of *refoulement* or of torture or other cruel and degrading treatment; there is no other real risk to the life of the person[s] concerned; there is a genuine prospect of an accessible durable solution in or from the asylum country, within a reasonable timeframe; pending a durable solution, stay is permitted under conditions which protect against arbitrary expulsion and deprivation of liberty and which provide for adequate and dignified means of subsistence; the unity and integrity of the family is ensured; and the specific protection needs of the affected persons, including those deriving from age and gender, are able to be identified and respected" (UNHCR Canberra 2004).
5. Theoretically, transit migrants from Iran could have organized the trip to Indonesia on their own, as they did not necessarily require the services of people smugglers for the initial part of the journey. However, many of them made contact with smuggling networks to procure information or arrange for their reception in Indonesia (interview with Iranian interpreter, 26 May 2013, Melbourne).

6. In the early 2000s, Malaysia did not require citizens from most Islamic countries to have visas and about 80 per cent of all Middle Eastern asylum seekers passed through Malaysia at that time (HRW 2002, p. 33). After the events of 11 September 2001, Malaysia tightened some of its visa policies too.

7. A colleague from a university in Central Java reported that, within a year, his university received about 200 applications from Libyans, of whom ninety were accepted. However, given the great interest from Libya at a time when Libya experienced conflict, the university administration introduced stricter rules for overseas students. Future students had to demonstrate English proficiency and agree to a six-month compulsory language course for Indonesian before they began their studies. Consequently, in the following year, no Libyan students were accepted into the university's programmes (interview, 30 October 2013, Solo).

8. Interview with Iraqi refugee, 18 May 2013, Sydney.

9. Interview with Director of LBH, 14 November 2013, Jakarta. Relatives of the two men already residing in Indonesia had informed LBH of these cases.

10. Interview with Head of the sub-division for law enforcement at District Maritime Police, 22 March 2012, Sekupang.

11. Interview with UNHCR staff, 19 April 2012, Mataram.

12. Interview with Head of the Anti-People-Smuggling Taskforce of the Provincial Police in West Java, 11 June 2012, Bandung.

13. Interviews with Head of the Police Intelligence Section, 6 February 2012, Pelabuhan Ratu, and interview with Head of District Police in Rote Ndao, 30 April 2012, Rote.

14. Interview with staff members of the Immigration Department in Kupang, 26 April 2012, Kupang.

15. Interview with IOM field staff, 12 June 2012, Sukabumi.

16. Interview with Hazara asylum seekers, 12 June 2012, Sukabumi.

17. The 1951 Refugee Convention notes, regarding refugees unlawfully in a country of refuge, that: "1) The Contracting States shall not impose penalties, on account of their illegal entry or presence, on refugees who, coming directly from a territory where their life or freedom was threatened in the sense of article 1, enter or are present in their territory without authorization, provided they present themselves without delay to the authorities and show good cause for their illegal entry or presence; and 2) The Contracting States shall not apply to the movements of such refugees restrictions other than those which are necessary and such restrictions shall only be applied until their status in the country is regularized or they obtain admission into another country. The Contracting States shall allow such refugees a reasonable period and the necessary facilities to obtain admission into another country." (UNHCR 1951, Paragraph 31).

18. Interview with Deputy Director of Humanitarian Affairs at the Ministry of Foreign Affairs, 4 April 2012, Jakarta.

19. Decree of the Minister of Justice and Human Rights of the Republic of Indonesia No. M.01.PR.07.04 on the Organisation and Work Procedures of Immigration Detention Centres (2004); see also Regulation of Minister of Justice and Human Rights of the Republic of Indonesia No. M.HH-11.OT.01.01 on the Organisation and Administration of Immigration Detention Centres (2009).

20. All immigration detention centres are subordinate to the Directorate-General for Immigration of the Ministry for Justice and Human Rights.

21. According to Spinks et al. (2011), Australian contributions to the cost of managing irregular migrants in Indonesia leapt from AU$3 million in 2010–11 to AU$7.9 million in 2011–12, while Regional Cooperation and Capacity Building in Indonesia expenditure increased from AU$32.2 million in 2010–11 to AU$47.2 million in 2011–12.

22. Interview with Head of the Registration and Reporting Section at the detention centre in Kupang, 16 November 2011, Kupang.

23. Interview with Tamil detainee, 4 July 2010, Makassar.

24. Interview with IOM staff, 24 April 2012, Kupang.

25. Interview with IOM staff, 2 May 2012, Kupang.

26. Interview with IOM staff, 2 May 2012, Kupang.

27. Interview with IOM staff, 2 May 2012, Kupang.

28. Interview with Tariq, 17 January 2012, Cisarua.

29. While waiting in the reception area for an appointment with staff members of the Kupang immigration detention centre, I witnessed the following scene on 25 April 2012: an Egyptian family with two children, who had been apprehended a few days earlier and forced to live for the time being in a very small cell at the back of the detention centre, was invited by the guards to watch TV with them in the reception area. The film they watched was very brutal. The opening scene showed how a number of Mexicans tried to cross the United States–Mexican border and how vigilantes captured, mistreated and finally killed them. The guards were making jokes about these killings among themselves, and they also tried to address the Egyptian mother in broken English in order to pass on a warning about attempting escape.

30. Documents from the local District Court of Mempawah refer to the autopsy report in detail. See District Court of Mempawah No. 92/Pid.B/2012/PN.MPW, 30 August 2012 (Andy Hermawan et al.); District Court of Mempawah No. 93/Pid.B/2012/PN.MPW, 30 August 2012 (Rio Ojahan et al.); District Court of Mempawah No. 94/Pid.B/2012/PN.MPW, 30 August 2012 (Muhammad).

31. Interview with eyewitness, 19 March 2012, Tanjung Pinang. The eyewitness described how he saw a young foreigner eating noodle soup at a food stall, when, all of a sudden, he had to run from approaching police. Bystanders

helped the police to capture the man, who was beaten quite severely even after he had fallen. An image of the man showing his facial injuries appeared in the local press the next day.

32. Interview with Head of the Registration and Reporting Section at the detention centre in Kupang, 16 November 2011, Kupang, and interview with Head of the Tanjung Pinang immigration detention centre, 19 March 2012, Tanjung Pinang.
33. Interview with Tariq, 28 February 2012, Cisarua.
34. Interview with Tariq, 29 February 2012, Cisarua.
35. Interviews with two inmates in Kupang, April 2012. The Head of the detention centre in Kupang confirmed that the hunger strike had taken place.
36. Interview with Head of the Kalideres detention centre, 5 June 2012, Jakarta.
37. Personal observation in Kupang immigration detention centre.
38. Interviews with detainees in Makassar and Kupang and former detainees in Cipayung, June 2010 and November 2011.
39. Interview with Hazara asylum seeker, 24 April 2012, Kupang.
40. Interviews with JRS staff members, 29 June 2010, Yogyakarta and with Tariq, 29 March 2012, Cisarua.
41. Radio interview with Febi Yonesta, Director of LBH, Jakarta, 26 March 2013 (Carrick 2013), and interview with Head of the Research Section for International Law and Regulations, Komnas HAM, 21 June 2012, Jakarta.
42. District Court of Mempawah Decision No. 92/Pid.B/2012/PN.MPW, 30 August 2012 (Andy Hermawan et al.); District Court of Mempawah Decision No. 93/Pid.B/2012/PN.MPW, 30 August 2012 (Rio Ojahan et al.); District Court of Mempawah Decision No. 94/Pid.B/2012/PN.MPW, 30 August 2012 (Muhammad). Interview with staff member in immigration detention centre, 24 October 2012, Pontianak.

4

LIFE ON HOLD

What makes waiting so difficult is not the weeks and months,
but it is waiting for the days and hours to pass.
(Interview with Tamil refugee in Indonesia, 15 June 2010, Cipayung)

While in transit in Indonesia, transit migrants generally view the ability to move on as one of their most important resources, being at a standstill uses up time and money, and the tedium of an indefinite wait gives rise to downheartedness. In her study of transit migrants stuck in North Africa on their way to Europe, Aspasia Papadopoulou-Kourkoula (2008, p. 14) found that "the time spent in transit is frequently time being wasted with the rebuilding of the migrant's life put on hold". Similarly, Ghassan Hage (2009, p. 97) equates waiting with "stuckedness" and calls it a "sense of existential immobility". As mentioned earlier, transit migrants in Indonesia often spend several years in limbo before moving on. Waiting, which may result from any of a number of factors, such as lack of regulation and law enforcement, slow processing of refugee applications, and limited resettlement options, is a means to an end.

The lynchpin of this chapter is the "politics of waiting" and their role in deterring other potential transit migrants. The chapter examines the nature of the time transit migrants spend waiting, often indefinitely, for registration as asylum seekers, for the outcome of the process of determining refugee status and for resettlement. Waiting for these outcomes puts them under great stress, and some threaten to harm themselves or commit suicide if their applications are rejected.

This chapter portrays the experience of transit migrants whose lives are put on hold. Based on the fundamental principle that "being in transit is a condition of increased vulnerability, characterized by poverty, insufficient protection, insecurity and social exclusion" (Papadopoulou-Kourkoula 2008, p. 142), the main foci of inquiry are the housing, income generation, access to health services and education of transit migrants. The chapter takes into consideration the ethnic background, class and gender of transit migrants and examines the extent to which these factors determine the length and the conditions of their time in transit. It does not, however, analyse particular ethnic groups of transit migrants and their experiences in transit, even though the experiences of different ethnic groups do vary in regard to housing, income generation, onward migration and prices for people-smuggling. Instead the chapter utilises examples from the experience of different ethnic groups to depict the wide spectrum of experiences of life in transit in Indonesia. Special attention is directed to the lot of unaccompanied minors in transit, as their situation, in many respects, is even more arduous than that of most transit migrants.

Unwilling to take on responsibility for foreign asylum seekers and refugees and dedicate substantial amounts of money to their care, the Indonesian government relies heavily on collaboration with the UNHCR and the IOM, whose roles are described in greater detail in Chapter 5. Given that Indonesia is not a social vacuum, the chapter pays attention to relations between transit migrants and Indonesian citizens and local authorities in the communities where transit migrants are allowed to reside if they are not detained. Arrangements to accommodate transit migrants are made on an ad hoc basis, and this has given rise over time to a number of problems between host communities (whether or not they are recognizable and coherent communities) and transit migrants. Indonesia, like other "involuntary" transit countries, generally lacks proper state regulations for the protection of non-citizens and, consequently, oscillates between sporadic immigration law enforcement and de facto toleration, while insisting that it cannot offer a long-term solution for non-citizens in need of protection. My observations, derived from the analysis of my fieldwork notes and interview transcripts from Indonesia, suggest that the lack of political will, together with the very limited capacity to handle increasing numbers of transit migrants, have resulted in great confusion in the communities where transit migrants are located, as well as extensive wheeling and dealing among transit migrants and state authorities.

From a more theoretical perspective, this chapter sets out to contribute to academic debates on mobility and immobility. There is widespread academic fascination with mobility; indeed, many scholars perceive mobility as the defining feature of globalization (Nyers and Rygiel 2012). In the academic context, mobility, movements and flows are perhaps overemphasized, whereas involuntary immobility, stagnation and stasis tend to be overlooked. In much the same way as geopolitical forces displace people from their homelands, political forces dislocate them from their desired destinations (Mountz 2011a), forcing them to remain in transit and preventing them from moving on. The politics that prevail in the country where transit migrants are caught in an immobile state and in the countries to which they might hope to be resettled do, therefore, matter.

LIFE IN COMMUNITIES

Because Indonesian immigration detention centres have been filled beyond their capacity, more transit migrants have been hosted outside Indonesia's immigration detention system than within it. For example, of the 9,656 people registered with the UNHCR at the end of March 2013, "only" 1,046 asylum seekers and 311 refugees were detained (including 163 women and 270 minors) (UNHCR Indonesia 2013b). Some transit migrants who have not registered with the UNHCR and have evaded arrest by the police also live in local communities. Indonesian authorities consider the most cost-effective option for handling transit migrants is for them to live in monitored communities.

Unregistered asylum seekers living in local communities do not have access to special housing but have to find and pay for their own accommodation, whereas transit migrants who had previously been arrested and detained and who are considered vulnerable, especially minors, women and children, as well as those who are recognized as refugees, are referred to special community housing schemes and shelters for unaccompanied minors (people under the age of eighteen), because their protection cannot be guaranteed in immigration detention centres. The community housing schemes in Medan and Yogyakarta under IOM management are examples of alternatives to immigration detention to which they can be referred. In June 2013, a total of 3,549 people were under the care of the IOM, of whom 1,510 (42.55 per cent) were living in detention and 2,039 (57.45 per cent) were in IOM community housing (IOM Indonesia 2013*a*). A number of transit migrants, most of whom had been released from immigration detention, were accommodated provisionally in rented hotels in Makassar (Sulawesi), Surabaya and Bogor.[1] Although transit migrants are generally concentrated in certain locations so that they can be monitored, their housing bears no resemblance to refugee camps, which are usually characterized by their complete isolation from local communities.

Undocumented transit migrants who have evaded arrest and detention in Indonesia prefer to live in larger cities, such as Jakarta, Medan and Surabaya, rather than in rural areas, which are generally deemed less secure and as offering fewer chances for self-reliance. However, the availability of "protective spaces" in large cities is not guaranteed given the millions of Indonesian rural-to-urban migrants competing with the transit migrants for the limited space available. Moving into the often-overcrowded suburbs with poorer population groups also means living in environments that are spatially and socially very complex. Rented accommodation, costing on average Rp850,000 (AU$85) per month (CWS 2013, p. 70), is often of poor quality and there is little room for negotiation with landlords. Cramped and overpriced housing conditions give rise to tension with neighbours. As will be described in greater detail later in this chapter, interactions with members of the host society stimulate many different reactions, ranging from compassion and solidarity to mistrust, misunderstanding and competition for resources.

As their movement and activities are heavily restricted, transit migrants who are not in detention depend to a great extent on developing social networks and functional relationships to rebuild their livelihoods. Generally, newly arrived transit migrants seek out people of the same ethnic or national background in order to appeal to them for help and orientation, although single men occasionally share accommodation with transit migrants from a different ethnic background. In this respect, transit migrants in Indonesia are no different from those in Turkey, described by Daniş (2006), who has shown that the survival of individuals in that transit country depends more often than not on solidarity with co-ethnics, as family networks alone cannot provide medical care, legal assistance and practical help. Co-ethnics with more experience in Indonesia can offer help in overcoming cultural barriers and bureaucratic hurdles, and in finding affordable accommodation. Relationships along ethnic lines offer many advantages, but they also carry the risk of abusive patron–client relations and exploitation of newcomers by the long-term stayers (CWS 2013, p. 31).

One area particularly popular among transit migrants, and thus serves as a prominent example throughout this chapter, is the mountainous Puncak area, about sixty kilometres from Jakarta (Batoor and Belford 2013; Belford 2013). Cipayung and Cisarua, in particular, hosted at least 2,000 transit migrants in 2012 (Wulandari 2012). Although both places are villages, they are not really rural in comparison with other village settlements in West Java. Puncak is a popular holiday destination for weekend tourists from Jakarta and for international tourists (especially from Saudi Arabia) and, therefore, has good transport connections to Jakarta and Bogor, a well-developed infrastructure, plenty of relatively cheap accommodation options, and even stores stocked with Middle Eastern food. Situated among picturesque lush green hills that are often obscured by its high rainfall and mist, the Puncak area offers transit migrants a slightly cooler climate and less noise compared with the cities. Over about ten years Puncak became the temporary home for documented and undocumented transit migrants, the latter often living in the shadow of their registered counterparts. The presence of so many foreigners in Puncak gave a huge impetus to local business (Krismantari 2010). Whereas rents in Puncak used to be noticeably cheaper than in Jakarta, they began to rise considerably as demand for accommodation increased from 2009 onwards, enabling some Cipayung landlords to send their children to study in Malaysia and elsewhere.[2] Providers of other services, including many people smugglers, were attracted to Puncak to offer their help, also benefiting financially from the transit migrants' presence there.

Transit migrants who live among local communities are better off in many ways than those in immigration detention centres, as they have more freedom of movement, albeit within a limited radius. Documented asylum seekers and refugees are, nevertheless, required to report their presence regularly to the local authorities, most often to the village police (*polres*). Transit migrants found outside their assigned residential area can be re-arrested and returned to detention (Missbach and Sinanu 2011, pp. 71–72).[3]

The rise in the number of new transit migrants coming to Puncak coincided with an increased number of sweepings and dawn raids by local police and local immigration officials (Wulandari 2012; HRW 2013, p. 68;

"Imigrasi perketat pengawasan" 2012). While documented refugees and people possessing UNHCR letters (*"surat sakti"*) attesting that they have applied for international protection are usually left alone, the authorities tend to target those who only hold a slip for an interview appointment with the UNHCR.[4] Given that in 2012 it was taking between six and nine months to get an appointment for an initial interview with the UNHCR in Jakarta and, thereby, to get the refugee-determination process started, transit migrants who do not have a proper UNHCR letter are exposed to the risk of arrest and extortion for a long period.

Quite apart from the compulsory reporting requirement, there are many other limitations and challenges for those living outside immigration detention. The longer transit migrants live in the local communities, the more likely they are to achieve some level of integration into these communities, albeit temporary and mostly rather involuntary. Nonetheless, neither temporary settlement nor the achievement of any level of social and economic integration can be understood as "the opposite of being in transit" (Hess 2012, p. 435). Hess goes on to propose that "rather, the meaning of being in transit is extended to pending, suspended forms of transit-existence; or, to put it the other way round, to precarious, provisional forms of settlement".

As mentioned earlier, a substantial number of transit migrants are unregistered and, therefore, unrecorded by the UNHCR, the IOM or the Indonesian immigration system. Estimates of the number of undocumented transit migrants roaming Indonesia vary from two to five times the official numbers.[5] The local authorities in Puncak soon learned of the presence of unregistered transit migrants and intensified their raids and surveillance. Petty criminals also started to take advantage of these vulnerable transit migrants in Puncak, and blackmail became common. For example, transit migrants reported that they were visited in the middle of the night by people they did not know who asked to see their legal documents. If the transit migrants could not comply, they demanded money (US$200–500), threatening to report them to the police or even arrest them. Extortion took many forms and produced odd alliances. For example, one undocumented Afghan man told me that he was visited late at night by an Indonesian woman accompanied by two Pakistani men.[6] While the woman negotiated the protection fee, the two Pakistani men served as her bodyguards. Other victims of extortion explained that they were visited by an Indonesian, not in uniform, who, nonetheless, was using a staff car of the local immigration authorities.[7] Controllers rarely wore uniforms during dawn raids, making it difficult to verify whether the people who demanded protection fees were pretending to be immigration officers or whether they were in fact corrupt members (*oknum*) of the local authorities trying to make money on the side.

In addition, documented asylum seekers reported that they had to pay bribes of between Rp2.5 and 5 million (AU$250–500) to avoid arrest, despite holding valid documentation from the UNHCR.[8] Again, prices were not fixed, with amounts demanded even depending on the appearance of a person; for example, the more fashionable a transit migrant appeared in the eyes of an extortionist, the more she or he had to pay. The extortionists' expectation of immediate payment often compelled transit migrants to telephone friends to acquire the cash to avoid arrest, although sometimes mobile phones were accepted as payment as well. According to a poll of asylum seekers and refugees in Jakarta, trust in the Indonesian authorities was generally low, especially in the police and its ability to ensure law and order (CWS 2013, p. 111). The fact that many transit migrants feared the police prevented them from seeking help, even when they were robbed or maltreated by others. One Afghan woman, for example, told of how her clothes had been stolen several times from the clothesline, while a Tamil woman mentioned the theft of her mobile phone on a public mini bus.[9] Contact with local police was seen to increase the risk of arrest and detention or exploitation.

ACCESSING HEALTH SERVICES AND EDUCATION

Transit migrants in Indonesia are generally disadvantaged in terms of access to public services, such as health care and education. Unlike poor citizens in Indonesia, refugees cannot access community health insurance (*jamkesmas*), as they are not entitled to it (CWS 2013, p. 22). Transit migrants under the care of the UNHCR and the IOM usually enjoy a level of basic health care paid for by the two international organizations. When they require minor treatment at a hospital or a local government-run community health clinic (*puskesmas*), transit migrants have to pay upfront and are subsequently reimbursed by whichever organization is caring for them, while the organization pays upfront for more expensive treatments.

Contrary to the widespread fear that transit migrants introduce disease into the host communities, most of them catch diseases during their long stays in transit (Koser 2010*a*, p. 190). Diseases are frequently caused by poor water quality and unhygienic conditions; others are airborne or insect-borne, such as dengue fever. Given that Puncak has a very vibrant sex industry and is a generally more permissive society, sexually transmitted diseases are on the rise. Young male transit migrants suffer from them especially, owing to lack of protection and sex education. Syphilis is rife among young transit migrants.[10] An NGO working in Indonesia, Church World Service (CWS), used to distribute condoms and has occasionally organized workshops to raise awareness among the youngsters and explain how they can protect themselves. Feelings of shame and fear of stigmatization prevent many from seeking medical treatment in the early stages of sexually transmitted diseases.

Besides treatment for physical illnesses, many transit migrants are also in dire need of psychological treatment. Sue Hoffman (2010*a*, p. 282) found that asylum seekers in Indonesia "experienced high levels of depression and hopelessness over and above their fears and anxieties". Their manifold worries include concern for their own future and for the relatives they have left behind. In the words of a young Afghan: "I worry so much about my mother who is on her own and I pray to God that I can see her just one more time."[11] A Tamil woman who had lived in Puncak for more than three years exemplified the persistent high levels of stress experienced by transit migrants. She suffered frequent dizziness (*pusing*), headaches (*sakit kepala*), insomnia and hair loss, because of "too much worrying" (*kebanyakan pikir*), and, with no other effective treatment options, relied mainly on sedatives.[12] Abuse of sleeping pills seems to be widespread. Although the UNHCR arranges psychological counselling in Puncak twice a week, transit migrants have to book appointments up to five weeks in advance, as only ten appointments are available each week.

School attendance levels among transit migrants are extremely low, as the CWS confirmed in its study on urban refugees in Jakarta, which found that only eleven per cent of its clientele attended school (CWS 2013, p. 83). There are many reasons for poor school attendance, of which first and foremost is the unclear legal status of transit migrants, which prevents them from enrolling. Although CWS had negotiated an agreement with the regional education department for its clients to attend local public schools in the Bogor and Jakarta area, teachers and headmasters often do not know how to handle transit migrants' requests or whether they have the authority to accept foreign students. In 2012, across Indonesia, only seven schools (six in Bogor and one in Jakarta) took in refugee children and offered them free education (Maulia 2012). A second main obstacle to school attendance is lack of proficiency in the Indonesian language among transit migrants. Generally, transit migrants base their decisions on the assumption that they will spend such a short time in Indonesia that it is not worth the effort to learn the language or to enrol their children in schools; many find that this assumption is proved wrong. In addition, some parents consider the Indonesian school system to be poor and inferior to what they were accustomed to, and are, consequently, reluctant to place their children in that system. Attitudes to school attendance differ substantially from one ethnic group to another; while Afghans, Tamils and Somalis show more interest in formal schooling, there is widespread disinterest among Iranians (CWS 2013, p. 89).

Unlike the children of recognized refugees, children of asylum seekers are not entitled to attend public schools. Although some concerned parents have managed to negotiate with the head of a school and to enrol their children, the majority are left without access to formal education. To compensate for this lack of access, NGOs, such as CWS and Jesuit Refugee Service (JRS), organize afternoon classes on their premises and provide informal education in English, Indonesian and mathematics. For example, twice a week a local Indonesian teacher would come to the CWS office in Cipayung and offer language lessons. In other cases, skilled transit migrants volunteered to teach the children mathematics or computing. In my observation, however, there was little continuity in these efforts and the classes were insufficient to meet the educational needs of the children.

Above anything else, most transit migrants are interested in learning English and improving their proficiency in that language, as they consider it to be very useful for their future, especially if they are to reach an English-speaking final destination country. In an attempt to meet this demand, the UNHCR allocates extra funds for recognized refugees in Puncak under the age of eighteen to attend classes at a private language school in Bogor. Both their tuition fees and transport costs are covered. Those over eighteen do not attend these classes, as they would have to pay their own fees. Although some UNHCR representatives are of the opinion that transit migrants should acquire skills in order to increase their chances of acceptance by a potential resettlement country (*cari nilai plus*), the UNHCR has only supported formal education for minors. Those above the age of eighteen who are keen to learn some vocational skills can neither afford any training nor be accepted as apprentices anywhere. A rare exception was when two Afghan asylum seekers were offered scholarships in 2013 for humanitarian reasons to study agriculture and IT by the Sam Ratulangi University in Manado. The two siblings had managed to complete their schooling during the two years they lived inside a North Sulawesi immigration detention centre (Roberts 2013*a*).

MAKING ENDS MEET: INCOME GENERATION

The greatest financial constraints to asylum seekers and refugees in Indonesia are imposed by the fact that they do not have the right to work and the very limited work options. Unlike in North Africa and Central America, where transit migrants en route to Europe and the United States respectively often interrupt their journeys in order to earn money as casual workers (Papadopoulou 2005; Collyer 2007; Kimball 2007), there is very little opportunity for transit migrants to work in Indonesia, which has an oversupply of domestic casual workers. Even if there were opportunities, Indonesian law prohibits transit migrants from working.[13] This legal constraint results in a high level of reliance on organizations such as the UNHCR and the IOM. Household incomes vary widely, depending on what constitutes the main source of their income.

In mid-2012 the standard monthly allowance paid by the UNHCR to recognized refugees was Rp1.3 million (AU$130) per family, which had to cover rent, food and all other expenses. In comparison to the average household income in Indonesia, this amount was low. The UNHCR acknowledged that it was not sufficient to meet basic needs, but lacked the means to increase it (CWS 2013, p. 20). Asylum seekers who had not been recognized as refugees did not receive a monthly allowance unless they were considered to be highly vulnerable. For example, in mid-2012 single mothers under UNHCR care, before they had been recognized as refugees, were entitled to a monthly subsistence allowance of at least Rp1.2 million (AU$120). Because of a shortfall in funding for the UNHCR in Indonesia in late 2013 and the continuing increase in the number of asylum seekers arriving in Indonesia, the UNHCR has had to cease making monthly payments to refugees; financial support is now only granted in cases of exceptional need.[14]

In late 2011 former detainees under the auspices of the IOM received a monthly allowance of Rp1.25 million (AU$125) per person, whether or not they were yet recognized as refugees.[15] This amount was considerably higher than that which refugees were to receive from the UNHCR during 2012, not only because the IOM allowance was per person rather than per family, but also because transit migrants under the care of the IOM were provided with rent-free housing. Payment of the IOM allowance stopped after ten years, as this was considered the maximum period of time a migrant would be in transit in Indonesia. After that they were supposed to take care of themselves.[16] There were, however, a number of asylum seekers whose applications for refugee status or resettlement were rejected more than once but who remained in Indonesia with no means of providing for themselves. During my fieldwork, I met a Cambodian transit migrant whose sight was affected by cataracts. He and his Indonesian wife, who was due to give birth within ten days, had just lost their financial support from the IOM and faced eviction from their house, once the IOM stopped paying their rent.[17]

While Western scholars and observers have criticized the inadequacy of services and the slow provision of help to which transit migrants are entitled (Taylor 2009, 2010; Taylor and Rafferty-Brown 2010a, 2010b), Indonesian commentators have often blamed the existence and generosity of services of the UNHCR and the IOM as being a lure (*daya tarik*) that attracts transit migrants en route to Australia to Indonesia in the first place (Sitohang 2002, p. 55).

Members of local communities hosting transit migrants, especially those whose incomes were below the average monthly income of those communities, became jealous of the migrants' access to the monthly allowance. The perception among Indonesians that transit migrants were rich people grew from the fact that many of them had had the money to come to Indonesia and to pay the high costs the smugglers charged to take them to Australia. Observing that the refugees did not have to work but were still able to consume, fuelled the misconception among local Indonesians that the migrants enjoyed the *dolce vita* and had access to endless financial resources. A senior police officer who had dealt with a number of transit migrants conveyed his observations:

> From what I know, most of them are actually quite well off and most of the youngsters received money from their parents to cross over. Whenever they run out of money, all they have to do is to ring their parents.... Should they really run out of money, well then there still is the IOM to take care [of them].[18]

But the reality of the transit migrants' lives was nowhere near as "sweet" as some Indonesians imagined it to be. The majority of asylum seekers did not receive any financial support or housing. Aware of the lack of assistance and the financial needs of asylum seekers, the JRS in 2009 initiated a scheme of basic livelihood support and health care to some of the most vulnerable asylum seekers living in the community in Cisarua, but the scheme only had the resources to provide support to a maximum of sixty people.[19] In order to survive, transit migrants had to live very frugally and share costs. Prohibited from working legally, they were left with few options. First, they lived on whatever savings and resources they had arrived with; for example, women had to sell their jewellery piece by piece to pay rent and buy food.[20] Transit migrants who made it as far as Indonesia were, generally, not the poorest of the poor in their country of origin. Some had already sold their possessions back in their homeland in order to pay the fare that people smugglers charged to get them to Indonesia; others still had some saleable assets at hand. Second, some could rely on remittances from friends and family members back in their home countries and elsewhere to cover their expenses in Indonesia. Thus, it was not surprising to find many Western Union offices in those areas with larger numbers of transit migrants (Missbach 2012). Savings, exchangeable articles of value and remittances usually did not last very long and, sooner or later, support from friends and kin ran out.

The last option was to earn money despite the prohibition on work. Given the high rates of unemployment and underemployment in Indonesia, unskilled and semi-skilled transit migrants faced many challenges finding work, as they were competing with millions of locals. The only chance for them to generate some income was in the informal economy. In Cisarua, for example, some Afghan families baked bread for their compatriots in transit and catered for nearby Middle-Eastern restaurants. Other transit migrants briefly tried to find casual employment as motorbike taxi drivers (*tukang ojek*), which was one of the main employment options for local young men. Given the tough competition, these attempts failed outright.

In order to provide documented refugees with some sort of activity and also with income, the CWS, the NGO that delivered services on behalf of UNHCR, leased a garden of about 8,000 square metres in Puncak. Only a few refugees took up the offer of using the garden to grow vegetables for themselves, but those who did were able to provide for their families and to sell the surplus to fellow refugees or vendors at the traditional market, thereby earning between Rp800,000 and Rp1 million (AU$80–100) a month (Adamrah 2011). Despite the prohibition on work, the CWS and other NGOs encouraged the entrepreneurial initiatives of their clients, as long as they were not conducted in public and did not become too well known (Suminar 2011). For example, a Somali woman who sold cookies — one kilogram of cookies sold for Rp40,000 (AU$4) — in her neighbourhood in Jakarta had up to twelve orders a week. The CWS especially supported and provided the facilities for women to tailor clothes and produce handicrafts and sell them at events, such as World Refugee Day. In public and outside the sphere of the NGO, the local police did not tolerate any business activities by transit migrants and occasionally made an example by arresting some of them ("Jual roti" 2010).

One way of escaping the gaze of the authorities was to collaborate with other locals. Exemplifying such collaboration was a Burmese long-term refugee who had made friends with two Indonesian men he trusted and provided the funds to open a kiosk, in which his friends sold convenience goods. However, this was a very rare example of an entrepreneurial endeavour and the income from his kiosk was rather meagre, causing him to continuously delay his marriage plans.[21] Aside from such small-scale sales activities, a number of young men and minors started to work as hustlers in nightclubs catering for both heterosexual (often elderly) women (*tante-tante*) and homosexual men. Some young Iranians, especially those who were tall and had very light complexions, found regular customers ("sugar mamas") who paid their expenses and even gave them motorbikes to facilitate their presence at their sometimes nightly rendezvous. Prostitution was an open secret among their peers. Whenever they showed up with a new mobile phone, new flash clothes or a haircut, they were at once admired for their entrepreneurial talent, envied for their consumer goods, and scorned for their moral looseness.

The frustrations that resulted from the prohibition on work and from poverty encouraged some transit migrants to become involved in criminal activities. Given that their homelands were two of the world's main producers of opiates, Afghan and Iranian transit migrants could easily become involved in drug trafficking.[22] For example, Interpol issued a warrant for the arrest of Said Mir Bahrami, an Afghan refugee who had lived in Indonesia for eleven years. During his extended stay in Indonesia, Said not only tried to open a carpet import business but also became involved in drug trafficking and, allegedly, in people-smuggling (Interpol Indonesia

2011). He was eventually arrested in Malaysia and served a prison term there, while the Australian government tried to extradite him to Australia to face people-smuggling charges ("Malaysia to Extradite" 2012).

Transit migrants from Myanmar, one of the world's largest producers of synthetic drugs, had similar potential for making an income from drug trafficking, but I have not encountered any reports of their involvement in the trade so far. Besides trafficking drugs and, thereby, risking arrest and tough sentences, the cultivation of stimulants was an alternative way of making money on the side. In early 2013 the Badan Narkotika Nasional (BNN, National Narcotics Agency) discovered *khat* fields near Bogor (Arnaz 2013*a*). *Khat* chewing is especially popular among Somali transit migrants, whose numbers increased noticeably from 2010 on. Unlike drug trafficking, more evidence was available about transit migrants who became involved in people-smuggling. As will be described in Chapter 8, a number of long-term stayers and repeatedly rejected asylum seekers managed to build substantial people-smuggling networks all around Indonesia (Crouch and Missbach 2013; Missbach and Crouch 2013).

While they were barred from working legally, transit migrants with special skills often could not keep up with developments in their field of expertise, which caused their skill levels to decline. Unemployment during the many years they spent in transit resulted not only in socio-economic marginalization but also in social exclusion. Because of the migrants limited access to the formal economy in both urban and semi-urban environments, interaction between transit migrants and Indonesians was minimal, and the lack of interaction gave rise to interethnic discord.

MUSLIM SOLIDARITY?

Combining the fact that Indonesia has the world's largest Muslim population with the fact that the majority of transit migrants in Indonesia are Muslims would seem to justify any assumption of Muslim solidarity between Indonesians and their migrant visitors.[23] On closer inspection, however, the differences in perceptions of Muslim solidarity between Indonesians and transit migrants could not be greater. Indonesians generally stress the shared religion, assuming that coming to Indonesia "must be heaven for all these Afghanis [*sic*] and Iranians".[24] The Indonesian officials and scholars I interviewed generally gave the impression that they were ignorant of the Sunni–Shia division. To them, being Muslim appeared to be sufficient for Indonesians to demonstrate a greater readiness to accept the foreigners and provide them with assistance ("jadi karena sama-sama Muslim, lalu mereka diterima"). For example, a police officer explained that when Indonesian people received foreigners who shared the same religion with them, such as Afghans, Pakistanis and Iranians, "it quickly led to some sense of proximity".[25]

In contrast to the Indonesian perception that they were warmly welcomed, transit migrants lamented the lack of sympathy and assistance, especially when it came to renting houses and accessing services, as local Indonesians would generally demand inflated prices for these commodities. The lack of empathy became particularly apparent when it came to burying transit migrants who had died in Puncak, for example, in traffic accidents or from disease. According to Islamic custom the body of anyone who dies needs to be buried within one day, but because some local Muslim clerics staunchly denied space for foreigners in cemeteries, it sometimes took several days for NGO staff to find alternative locations for their funerals.[26]

Once it became more widely known among the local communities in Puncak that many transit migrants were in fact Shia Muslims, their freedom to practise their religious beliefs began to be further limited. For example, Shia Muslims did not want to pray amongst Sunni Muslims, as they feared discrimination because the position of their bodies in prayer was different. Although the IOM had previously made available a small building in Cipayung to be used as a house of prayer (*musholah*), it eventually had to withdraw the offer of the building fearing negative sentiment from the local community.[27] Moreover, Afghan and Iranian Shia Muslims in Cisarua were no longer allowed to celebrate Ashura (the tenth day of Muharram, the first month in the Muslim calendar), under the pretext that this religious celebration would not only attract too large a crowd from the surrounding villages but would also offer an opportunity for alcohol consumption.[28]

If there was a sense of Muslim solidarity at all, it materialized only in short-lived actions and concerned only certain transit migrants, such as the Rohingya, who had been victims of religious persecution in their homeland and received some help, including financial contributions. For example, after a group of Rohingya arrived in Aceh in February 2009, students and members of a computer club collected donations from motorists in the streets of East Aceh and handed over Rp5.1 million (AU$510) ("Indonesia: Aceh Embraces" 2009). Every year around the Muslim Day of Sacrifice

(Idul Adha), I noticed posters in Jakarta urging Indonesian Muslims to donate to the Rohingya, but to those living outside of Indonesia rather than Rohingya asylum seekers in Indonesia. Long-term support for the stranded transit migrants was, in general, conspicuous by its absence. A less positive and more worrying form of Muslim solidarity became apparent when Muslim extremists started to bomb Buddhist temples and the Myanmar Embassy in Jakarta in retaliation for the persecution of Muslim Rohingya in Myanmar ("Buddhist vihara" 2013).

HOSTILE HOSPITALITY: INTERACTIONS WITH THE LOCALS

Many Indonesian observers have, like Asep Kurnia, come to conclude that "within Indonesia, the presence of illegal immigrants has started to upset the local society" (Kurnia 2011, p. vii). This, however, has not always been the case. In the early 2000s, friendly curiosity prevailed, but, as the years progressed, the majority of the Indonesian public, if aware of transit migrants at all, have tended to see them as unwanted guests (*tamu tak diundang*) (*Tempo* 2012, p. 29). General awareness of the rights of asylum seekers and refugees amongst the Indonesian host society was minimal (CWS 2013, p. 29). Instead of seeing them as asylum seekers or refugees, locals tended to know little about their backgrounds and movements and simply thought of transit migrants as strangers, sometimes even confusing them with rich tourists (HRW 2002, p. 50). In the areas where the presence of transit migrants was more visible, responses and reactions tended to be more intense.

Daily interaction with Indonesians was severely limited by language differences and consequent communication problems. Transit migrants described their rare interactions as "superficial, fleeting and polite" (CWS 2013, p. 21). In the same breath, they often expressed little interest in learning the language of or making friends with Indonesians, assuming that this was unnecessary given their intention to stay only for a short time. Lack of interaction and communication gave way readily to social alienation and even disorientation, and enhanced the mutual mistrust between Indonesian hosts and transit migrants (CWS 2013, p. 31). Friendship and mutual help was the exception rather than the rule. For example, only a few of the female transit migrants who had lived several years in Puncak and could speak Indonesian well enough to communicate were able to provide illustrations of their positive neighbourly relations with Indonesians. One woman mentioned that she had been invited three or four times to attend weddings in the kampung, and another described how her neighbours drove her sick child to the hospital at night.[29]

In the eyes of the locals, transit migrants were merely risks to the community, as potential transmitters of disease, troublemakers and criminals. The fact that many transit migrants had been incarcerated in detention centres only served to substantiate their unfavourable perceptions of them. Conversely, the debilitating experiences of transit migrants in detention engendered mistrust on their part towards their local hosts.

Over the years of my fieldwork in Indonesia, I have witnessed the extremely rapid deterioration in relationships between transit migrants and their host communities. In 2010, I had the impression that the local residents in Puncak were well accustomed to the presence of foreigners and that daily interactions between them usually ran relatively smoothly, not least because some locals earned money by providing all sorts of services to the transit migrants. Two years later I found that relations between transit migrants and some segments of the local community had soured. Xenophobia was on the rise, often stemming from the accumulation of minor cultural misunderstandings, for which there was no mechanism for resolution, and from transit migrants' outright disrespect for local customs and religious sensitivities. Frequent matters of complaint were the migrants' parties, their consumption of alcohol, and their failure to fast during Ramadan.[30] The biggest bone of contention was unregistered marriage (*kawin sirih*), which not only caused social panic in the Puncak area but also had quite severe consequences for transit migrants.

Single male transit migrants who had spent many months or years in Puncak often befriended local women. Although they were not legally allowed to marry their girlfriends, as they did not have legitimate residence status under Indonesian civil law, many of the migrants formed long-term de facto relationships and lived with their Indonesian partners, some even establishing families with them. An Iraqi man, who had lived in Bogor for eleven years and raised a child with his Indonesian partner, even stated that he had no objections to staying on in Indonesia and taking out Indonesian citizenship, if that were an option available to him.[31] Although *kawin sirih* is accepted under Islamic law, public views of such alliances often went hand in hand with perceptions of promiscuity and even prostitution, partly because short-term affairs were equally common. Moreover, Puncak's public view of *kawin sirih* was influenced by the thriving sex industry in the region, which catered for Indonesian and Saudi Arabian tourists, who also relied on short-term marital contracts, often only valid for a few hours or days. Collective resistance towards transit migrants who were in the habit of hanging out with local women (*bergaul dengan wanita*) was on the rise. A number of local public figures stirred up moral panic as they exploited this issue for other purposes.

Prior to 2012 the response to the exposure of intimate affairs between transit migrants and Indonesian women was usually limited to uproar in the neighbourhood; from early 2012 the response escalated. For example, local residents marched into a house where they suspected a couple were engaged in a tête-à-tête and dragged them out. Although the man tried to escape, bystanders caught him and beat him up.[32] In cases where it was thought that a local woman was an involuntary participant in a sexual encounter, mass violence (*amuk masa*) occurred (Prima 2012). Following the sexual harassment of an elderly Indonesian woman in a public toilet in Cisarua, local residents complained to the local government about the presence of foreigners in their area and demanded that the responsible authorities relocate them elsewhere ("Warga Cisarua" 2012).

The issue of relocating all transit migrants from Puncak was magnified once members of the Front Pembela Islam (FPI, Islamic Defenders Front), which is generally thought of as an assembly of thugs under a religious banner, became involved ("4.000 imigran" 2012). According to one of the local FPI heads in Cisarua, the anger of the local community had arisen because their villages were no longer just "temporary shelters but had become permanent" and because the foreigners had failed to integrate and adopt local customs.[33] Not only did the FPI and its allies demonstrate for several days in front of the Mayor's office, but they also petitioned the local authorities to demand that the national authorities in Jakarta find alternative housing options for transit migrants.[34] The angry mob demanded an impossible timeframe of only thirty days for the relocation, threatening to conduct raids if relocation was not achieved within that time.[35]

Although the FPI masterminded the protests, Indonesian policymakers, including the Deputy Head of the Desk for the Handling of People-Smuggling, Refugees and Asylum Seekers (P2MP2S), insisted that the protests enjoyed the full support of the local community in Cisarua in their effort to "reject the presence of the foreigners". Of their objections to the presence of the transit migrants, he went on to explain:

> The reason for this is that there already is deep disquiet in the community due to their behaviour (*perilaku mereka-mereka*) that disturbs the habits and customs of the local community. For example, with their daily activities they turn night into day and day into night. At night they disturb the peacefulness in their neighbourhoods. Also on Fridays, when all the villagers go to the mosque (*jumatan*), they keep walking around and do all sorts of things (*mereka lalu-lalang dan lain sebagainya*).[36]

The first response to the community uproar was that of a number of local hotel owners who had for years been profiting from renting out their facilities. Assuming that the whole uproar was only an expression of social jealousy between those who had been making money from the transit migrants and those who had not, some of the hotel owners handed out cash amounts of up to Rp50 million (AU$5,000) to the leaders of the protest in an attempt to silence them.[37] Their response came too late, as indicated by a member of the local administration in Bogor who commented: "obviously emotion has become so intense that the local communities just want these foreigners evicted".[38]

Following these demonstrations and vehement protests, the caretaker organizations urged all transit migrants in Puncak to refrain from spending much time outside their houses. Fearing physical attack, some asylum seekers did not dare leave their houses for a week. The national authorities could not find an appropriate alternative housing area within the thirty-day timeframe the protest leaders insisted on, but the first of the relocations did take place in early 2013. While some transit migrants from Puncak decided to leave Indonesia altogether by boat, most people were transferred back to Jakarta, including dozens of unaccompanied minors, who had been living in four shelters in Puncak (Cassrels 2013).

By late August 2013, most transit migrants had left Puncak. Those under the care of CWS had to find their own accommodation in Jakarta, which is significantly more expensive than in Puncak.[39] Those under the care of the IOM were transferred to Jakarta and Medan, where they either lived in boarding houses or in community housing. Nevertheless, a small number of undocumented transit migrants remained in Puncak, but, while they continue to live there, they cannot have their needs assessed by any of the organizations that previously provided services to asylum seekers, as those organizations have left Puncak as well. In November 2013, a Pakistani transit migrant was beaten to death by an angry mob after he had gone on an alcohol-infused rampage in a mosque ("Imigran mabok di masjid" 2013). The case received no attention beyond Puncak. In 2014 I heard about more beatings of transit migrants in Puncak, but no punishment of perpetrators was reported.

When I visited Cisarua again in March 2014, there were still about 800 transit migrants left, most of them were newcomers to Indonesia. As neither the CWS nor the IOM operated any longer in Puncak, they were mainly left to themselves. Unable to receive financial support from these caretaker organizations in order to rent houses and buy basic supplies, many of them faced homelessness, as they had run out of their own resources. While in previous years transit migrants had tried hard to avoid arrest and detention by Indonesian authorities, they now started to surrender themselves to the authorities in order to be given basic services in detention. At the same time, the local authorities were discussing plans for further raids and evictions in Puncak, but given the overcrowding in detention centres and the lack of options for community accommodation, these plans were put on hold for the time being.

UNACCOMPANIED MINORS

Academics, policymakers and NGOs often tended to treat female transit migrants and children as passive migrants. Given that 1,178 unaccompanied children were among transit migrants residing in Indonesia in 2012 (HRW 2013, p. 2), this tendency was seriously short-sighted. Most of the unaccompanied children were male. During my fieldwork, I came to know of only two female unaccompanied asylum seekers under the age of eighteen, one from Somalia and one from Afghanistan. Unaccompanied girls were at particularly great risk of abuse and exploitation. Exemplifying exposure to such risk was the case of an Afghan girl who had been raped several times by an Afghan man who kept her locked up after promising to take her to Australia.[40]

Young male transit migrants played an extraordinary role in the migration aspirations of families, as their parents often sent them ahead, investing heavily in their journey and, thus, in the future of the families, as they hoped that their children's resettlement would enable family reunion one lucky day (Schuster and Majidi 2013). One such young male was a seventeen-year-old Hazara boy who told me that he had never attended school in Quetta, but had private English tuition, paid for by his aunt who considered proficiency in the English language a crucial skill for the migration plans the family had made for the boy.[41] Many boys, some of them only thirteen or fourteen years old, ended up in Indonesia, even though it had not been their intended destination. Another Hazara boy from Afghanistan said that his family originally only intended to send him to live in Pakistan, but a few days after his arrival in Quetta he witnessed a gruesome target killing. He noticed that a number of people around him were preparing to leave for Australia, so he decided spontaneously to join them.[42] In order to stop parents from sending their underage children to Indonesia on their own, Australia has adopted the strategy of not providing special treatment or fast-track resettlement for these children (O'Brien 2013). Consequently, they face the same hardships and challenges that adults face while waiting in Indonesia.

Although Indonesia signed the UN Convention on the Rights of the Child, it has not been meeting its obligations under Article 22(1) of the convention (Gultom 2013, p. 6); many unaccompanied minors have been kept in immigration detention centres instead of in special shelters (HRW 2013, p. 20). In the detention centres they lacked access to any form of legal representation or guardianship to help them with their asylum applications. The few existing shelters for unaccompanied minors in Indonesia, organized by the UNHCR and the CWS, had the capacity to accommodate only 225 minors — less than one-fifth of the total number of unaccompanied children in Indonesia in 2012.[43] Some of the occupants in the shelters looked significantly older than they claimed to be and some UNHCR staff members referred to them as the "grey-haired minors". Presumably some transit migrants pretended to be younger than they actually were in order to access the weekly payments and other forms of help. It is also indeed possible that the extraordinary strains they have been placed under during their childhood, youth and the migration process have accelerated their aging. Although the number of minors arriving in Indonesia has kept on increasing as many underage detention centre inmates were referred to Puncak, there have been only two social workers, both overworked, looking after all of them.

Minors who lived in the shelters received Rp150,000 (AU$15) per week. If they failed to report on the day that allowances were paid, they lost their entitlement.[44] Housing, water, electricity and gas were provided, but they had to cook their own food. In my observation, daily life in the shelters was quite organized and many possessions, such as clothes, were used communally. Shelter occupants took turns to cook and wash the dishes.

Although some of them had become used to earning their own living in their homeland, as, for example, carpenters or tailors, none of them worked in the occupation they had previously been engaged in. They spent their time in front of the computers at the CWS office getting the latest news from their homeland and from Australia and communicating with family members they had left behind.[45] As mentioned earlier, some of the minors improved their financial situation through prostitution.

Members of local communities objected even more strongly to the shelters for minors than to other forms of migrant accommodation. Trouble with neighbours arose frequently when their peace was disturbed at night. Because of several incidents resulting in injury, shelters had to adopt stricter rules over time. For example, occupants who were not back at their shelter by 10 p.m. would be refused entry. Nonetheless, trouble in the neighbourhood continued. CWS staff members reported physical fights among the minors and locals. When, for example, a young man received news that his immediate family had died, he got very drunk and went on a rampage, hitting everybody who crossed his path.[46] Village people and CWS staff rushed to end the tumult. To restore peace, the CWS slaughtered a goat at the next village festivity, but efforts at reconciliation and greater understanding were in vain when a minor was suspected of involvement in a rape (CWS 2013, p. 21). The owners of the building used for the shelter in Cisarua did not extend the annual rental agreements and it became almost impossible to find new houses in Puncak for use as shelters. In the process of relocating all transit migrants from Puncak, all shelters were closed and the minors were taken to Jakarta, although some of them escaped in order to find a smuggler to take them to Australia.

Unaccompanied minors are at great risk when pursuing boat trips, as the story of Ismail's stressful circumstances illustrates. Ismail could be any age between sixteen and twenty-one. On the one hand he seemed youthful, adventurous, while on the other his face was marked by a severity that made him seem much older. Ismail came to Indonesia in mid-2010; he was arrested by the police several times and spent some time in Indonesian immigration detention camps. Ismail is one of the few survivors from an overcrowded boat that sank on 17 December 2011 about fifty-five nautical miles from Java in bad weather typical of the rainy season (Harsaputra 2011). Indonesian fishermen rescued Ismail after he had been in the sea for almost two nights and three days. Although the exact number of passengers is not known, it is estimated that about 250 people, mostly from Iran, Afghanistan and Iraq, were on board. More than 200 drowned or went missing. During the very first day, Indonesian fishermen rescued thirty-four people, but the storm hampered further search-and-rescue missions. According to Ismail's account, after the vessel sank about 150 were still alive. After the first night, there were about eighty people left, and after the second night only thirty-five, of whom only thirteen survived. Ismail watched many people drowning, including one of his closest friends. From afar, he saw sharks circling the bodies. In the long hours of fear, hunger, thirst and sleep deprivation, he saw several boats passing by, none of which came to help them.

I met Ismail about four weeks after the tragedy in a shelter for unaccompanied and underage asylum seekers.[47] He told me that it had been his third attempt to escape from Indonesia and reach Australia. He was determined to try again:

> We are compelled to risk our lives. I will try to go again, I don't care about the season and the danger. I have seen hunger and thirst in Pakistan, so I must go. I am not shocked of what I have seen in the water. I have seen many [more gruesome] incidents back home. Resulting from bombs, such as [detached] hands, arms, fingers, open lungs. I am not shocked by this [boat accident]. It is nothing for me!

As I listened to him speak of his family background, of the way his father was killed, of the debts his mother back home had accumulated to pay for his hazardous journey to Indonesia, and of the tough experiences he had had while in Indonesia, it became clear why Ismail refused to stay in Indonesia for much longer. As he put it in direct and dramatic terms, tinged with youthful insolence: "The smuggling won't be stopped. We are all poor now; we all want to have money. If Australia doesn't take us we will all become *chokra* [recruiter for a smuggler]. I suggest to Australia to process my case quickly, otherwise I will become a *chokra*".

SUMMARY

This chapter has attempted to illustrate why mobility is so important for transit migrants in order to identify durable solutions. While the "politics of mobility" rely on a connection between being mobile and having rights, the "politics of waiting" are shaped by the absence of guaranteed rights and a lack of clarity regarding the legal status of the transit migrants. Although the presence of documented asylum seekers and refugees in Indonesia is temporarily tolerated, the Indonesian hospitality can, at times, be quite hostile. Therefore, as the chapter has demonstrated, transit migrants do not see staying in transit for any length of time as a viable option in their migration plans. Even if they are not in immigration detention, they face many challenges in their daily life, whether in finding housing or in accessing health services and education. The prohibition on work and the consequent reliance solely on savings, remittances and the services of the IOM and UNHCR leaves them in dire straits. Widespread fear of arrest and harassment by the police and others encourages them to isolate themselves and deters them from interacting with the community they are in. Given the negative influences that transit migrants are purported to have on local host communities and the deterioration of relationships between transit migrants and host communities, most immigration officials favour immigration detention (*sebaiknya mereka terkurung saja*).[48] As the previous chapter has already substantiated, immigration detention for all of the asylum seekers present in Indonesia is not a viable option either. Welcoming transit migrants with open arms has never been Indonesia's intention; as an Indonesian academic has put it bluntly, "if we treat the smuggled people too nicely, they won't stop coming".[49]

While they wait and long for a better future, I gained the impression that many transit migrants idealise a distant future and the potential resettlement country of that future. For example, they make plans about what they would study, the occupation they would take up and the house they would live in. Engaging in what are often wildly exaggerated fantasies is one way of making the present more bearable. Unable to live with full rights in Indonesia, transit migrants are left with the options of either legal or illegal onward migration or of the backward movement of repatriation or deportation. Although their chances of being selected for resettlement are much better for refugees currently based in Indonesia than those based elsewhere, the process usually takes many years. In many cases, those who tire of the waiting game that might or might not reward them with resettlement, set off by boat for Australia. Although aware of the risks involved in crossing the sea, many are not deterred by the knowledge that others before them have perished on the perilous journeys. For them, as for asylum seekers trying to cross the Mediterranean Sea, it is "either cross, or die" (Papadopoulou-Kourkoula 2008, p. 106). Those asylum seekers and refugees whose patience has worn out and have set off for Australia are, however, punished by mandatory detention in Australian immigration detention centres and, from 2012, by transfer to other Pacific states for offshore detention and processing.

Notes

1. On a number of occasions, people under IOM care raised allegations of embezzlement against IOM staff members, who allegedly received kickbacks from the owners of the hotels used regularly to accommodate intercepted transit migrants.
2. Group interview with JRS staff members, 27 June 2012, Jakarta.
3. According to Regulation IMI-1489.UM.08.05 promulgated by the Immigration Director-General in 2010 concerning "the treatment of illegal immigrants", transit migrants outside detention have to sign a declaration of compliance. First, they are to stay in the area designated by the Immigration Directorate-General only. Second, they are prohibited from airport or seaport areas unless accompanied by immigration officers. Third, they are required to comply fully with Indonesian laws, including not working or engaging in income-generating activities, driving without a licence and upholding order in their neighbourhood.
4. Group interview with JRS staff members, 27 June 2012, Jakarta.
5. Interviews with Head of Section on Irregular Migrants and the Protection of Victims of Transnational Crime at the Directorate General of Immigration, 5 March 2012, Jakarta; and Deputy Director of Humanitarian Affairs at the Ministry of Foreign Affairs, 4 April 2012.
6. Interview with Afghan man, 28 June 2012, Cisarua.
7. Interview with two Afghan minors, 29 March 2012, Cisarua.
8. Interview with Tariq, 29 March 2012, Cisarua.
9. Interview with Tamil woman, 15 June 2010; and Afghan woman, 16 June 2010, Cisarua.
10. Interview with CWS staff member, 29 March 2012, Cipayung.
11. Interview with young Afghan, 24 April 2012, Kupang.
12. Interview with Tamil woman, 15 June 2010, Cipayung.
13. Immigration Director-General Regulation Number IMI-1489.UM.08.05 Year 2010.
14. Interview with UNHCR staff member, 12 March 2014.
15. Interview with IOM staff member, 7 November 2011, Jakarta.
16. Interview with IOM staff member, 22 June 2012, Jakarta.

17. Interview, 28 June 2012, Cisarua.
18. Interview with Director of Investigation and Immigration Enforcement at Criminal Investigation Police Headquarters, 10 February 2012, Jakarta.
19. Interview with JRS staff member, 13 November 2011, Yogyakarta.
20. Interview with Afghan asylum seeker, 23 June 2010, Cisarua.
21. Interview with Burmese refugee, 12 March 2012, Cisarua.
22. Interview with Director of Investigation and Immigration Enforcement at Criminal Investigation Police Headquarters, 10 February 2012, Jakarta.
23. For general interpretations of Muslim solidarity with refugees, see Zaat (2007) and Al-Wafa (2011).
24. Interview with Criminologist at the Universitas Indonesia, 11 January 2012, Depok.
25. Interview with Director of Investigation and Immigration Enforcement at Criminal Investigation Police Headquarters, 10 February 2012, Jakarta.
26. Interview with CWS staff, 20 October 2012, Cipayung.
27. Interview with Iraqi refugee, 3 October 2011, Sydney.
28. Information provided by an intelligence officer, 19 April 2012.
29. Interviews with Tamil and Afghan asylum seekers, 15 June 2010, Cisarua.
30. Interviews with intelligence officer, 14 April 2012, Mataram.
31. Interview, 4 November 2011, Bogor.
32. Interview with CWS staff member, 29 March 2012, Cisarua.
33. Interview with Head of the FPI section in Cisarua, 30 October 2012, Cisarua.
34. Interview with Deputy Head of the Transnational Crime Desk at the Coordinating Ministry for Politics, Law and Security, 3 November 2012, Jakarta.
35. Interview with Head of the FPI in Cisarua, 30 October 2012, Cisarua. Additional information provided at the Joint Seminar on "Optimizing the Handling of Human Trafficking, Refugees and Asylum Seekers", 21 November 2012, Jakarta.
36. Interview with Deputy Head of the Transnational Crime Desk at the Coordinating Ministry for Politics, Legal and Security, 3 November 2012, Jakarta.
37. Interview with CWS staff, 30 October 2012, Cisarua.
38. Interview with Deputy Head of the Surveillance Section, Office for National Unity and Internal Affairs, 30 October 2012, Bogor.
39. Unlike in Puncak, where the rental market had adjusted to transit migrants and rent was paid on a monthly basis, houses in Jakarta, which are usually unfurnished, are rented out on a six- or twelve-month basis.
40. Interview with CWS staff member, 1 November 2011, Cisarua. The author was also able to read the police report on the victim's case.
41. Interview, 9 May 2012, Cipayung.
42. Interview, 24 April 2012, Kupang.
43. Interview with CWS staff member, 8 May 2012, Cisarua.

44. Interview with CWS staff member, 8 May 2012, Cisarua.
45. Group interview in one of the shelters, 1 November 2011, Cipayung.
46. Interview with CWS staff member, 1 November 2011, Cisarua.
47. Interview, 13 January 2012, Cipayung.
48. Interview with staff members from Immigration Department, 26 April 2012, Kupang.
49. Interview with Criminologist at the Universitas Indonesia, 11 January 2012, Depok.

5

THE LIMITS OF PROTECTION

Our soul (*nyawa*) is in their [IOM and UNHCR] hands.
(Interview with Rohingya refugee, 24 June 2010, Cipayung)

DISSIPATED PROTESTS?

In early November 2012, I was sitting in the ground-floor cafeteria of the building where the UNHCR registration office in Jakarta is located. Suddenly, half a dozen minibuses stopped next to the building. Out of the buses climbed a group of Somalis to stage a protest. On their posters were slogans such as "We need resettlement", "Stop empty promises and empty hopes", "We suffered in Somalia and yet we are suffering in Indonesia", "We need durable solution not words", and "Look at us, Listen to us, Don't ignore us, We are Somalian refugees". Among the protesters was Ali, whose story is told in Chapter 1.

While they were getting ready for the protest, I had a quick chat with Ali. He told me that this protest action had been inspired by another Somali demonstration in Makassar, where a small group of refugees had gathered in front of the local UNHCR premises and complained about UNHCR and Australian discrimination against them (Abdurrahman 2012). The Makassar protesters, most of whom had lived there since 2010, criticized the fact that there were no Somalis among the refugees resettled in Australia. They had concluded that their exclusion from resettlement was a deliberate decision by the UNHCR and the resettlement countries; they demanded that they be resettled too. Driven by similar suspicions, the Somali protesters in Jakarta demanded a meeting with the chief UNHCR representatives to explain their frustrations. They were not granted a meeting and left the area less than two hours later. Their protest attracted neither an official response from the UNHCR nor any debate, other than minimal coverage in some local and national newspapers ("Heartbreaking Protest" 2012; Leribun 2012).

A few weeks later I visited Ali to bid him farewell before I returned to Melbourne. We discussed a number of things, including the protest in Jakarta. Even though he did not consider the action a success, he was glad that the Somali community in Puncak had been able to express their frustrations. The simple fact that they had managed to organize their travel from Puncak to Jakarta, to raise the money to rent vehicles, and to prepare posters indicated both the sincerity of their complaints and the strong cohesion within the Somali community. To Ali, group cohesion amongst his fellow Somalis meant a great deal.

On that day Ali was in a good mood; at our previous meetings he was mostly depressed. The reason for his good mood was that he had finally received news from his mother, living on her own back in Somalia. She was often sick and had difficulty supporting herself. Unlike others in transit, Ali did not receive remittances from his extended family back in Somalia. The fact that Ali could not help his mother, who had paid for the first part of his journey, weighed heavily on him. During the preceding months when he could not find out his mother's whereabouts, Ali had slept badly and had little appetite. When I was about to say goodbye, Ali said, "Next time, I will meet you in Australia. I can no longer wait for the UNHCR to help me." His announcement left me puzzled, but I did not feel like quizzing him about it, even though I could guess what his next moves would be.

While the analysis has hitherto concentrated on the "stuckedness" of transit migrants in Indonesia and the difficulties people face both inside and outside immigration detention, this chapter sheds light on the options for regular onward migration. In particular, the roles of international organizations, such as the UNHCR and the IOM, in onward migration processes are examined. The meaning of "onward migration" is not necessarily restricted to resettlement in a third country; it can also mean to turn back, either to the country of origin or in "the direction they came from" (Kimball 2007, p. 3).

Unwilling to accept responsibility for asylum seekers and refugees or dedicate substantial amounts of money to their care, the Indonesian government relies to a great extent on collaboration with the UNHCR and the IOM, despite the fact that Indonesia is neither a party to the Geneva Refugee Convention nor a member state of the IOM, in which it holds only observer status. The UNHCR and the IOM are the two international organizations primarily concerned with handling transit migrants in Indonesia and with managing their regular onward migration. This chapter discusses general aspects of the work of these two organizations in Indonesia and their working relations with the Indonesian government. Although the Indonesian government remains distant from the day-to-day involvement with transit migrants, it needs to be informed of the work of the UNHCR and IOM, so that it can develop the policies required to support their programmes.

This chapter first describes some of the caretaker roles of the UNHCR and the IOM and then points out a number of their inadequacies. Both organizations have operated in Indonesia since 1979, when it became a place of temporary refuge for Indochinese asylum seekers (as outlined in Chapter 2). Whereas the UNHCR is mainly concerned with the protection and status determination of asylum seekers, the IOM is involved in a variety of tasks, some of which are antithetic to others, as will be described in greater detail. Of the many high-priority tasks that both organizations perform, this chapter concentrates on resettlement and repatriation — the two most relevant to the onward migration of transit migrants in Indonesia. Although the two organizations have different mandates and perform very different functions in regard to asylum seekers, refugees and undocumented migrants, both organizations are discussed in conjunction. This chapter is focused on the *direct* influence of these international bodies on transit migrants through their regular onward migration options, and on their *indirect* influence on the irregular onward migration of the many transit migrants who prefer not to make use of UNHCR or IOM services and organize their onward migration on their own terms, usually with the help of smugglers (whose activities are the focus of Chapter 8).

The driving question of this chapter concerns the limits of protection in transit in Indonesia. Although protection is one of the key provisions of the Refugee Convention, neither the convention nor the protocol defines what constitutes protection of asylum seekers and refugees. Generally, protection is understood as "all activities aimed at obtaining full respect of the rights of the individual in accordance with the letter and the spirit of the relevant bodies of law, namely human rights law, international humanitarian law and refugee law" (definition endorsed by the Inter-Agency Standing Committee).[1] In international law, protection is based on a mandate that is conferred by treaty or custom, which then authorizes an organization to ensure the respect of rights by states. The most important aspect of protection in the context of Indonesia is the prevention of the forced return (*refoulement*) of asylum seekers and refugees to their home country or any other country, where they could face persecution or dangers to their lives and freedom. In the light of the customary obligation of non-*refoulement*, this chapter then raises questions about the practical experiences of so-called voluntary repatriation that the UNHCR and the IOM widely support.

Because of structural and political shortcomings that hinder the provision of the greatest possible level of protection, I prefer to refer to what is provided to transit migrants in Indonesia as semi-protection. One reason why transit migrants do not enjoy the protection they should be receiving is that they are often perceived as receivers of services instead of as a political population with rights (Moulin and Nyers 2007; Mountz 2011a; Fassin 2013). Such a perception has significant implications for the people concerned. Once the understanding of the concept of "people with rights" has been manipulated into "people receiving services", both protection and resettlement become the materialization of pity and not the exercise of rights. The ambiguity of protection delivery in transit gives rise to the question of whether or not short-term services aimed at "cushioning the hardship" do, in fact, downgrade any right to protection to mere semi-protection.

THE UNHCR

As has been stressed several times in earlier chapters, Indonesia is not a party to the 1951 Convention relating to the Status of Refugees or to the 1967 Protocol, and it does not have any legislative framework for the protection of asylum seekers and refugees. In the absence of national refugee legislation and procedures, the UNHCR fulfils the role of primary provider of protection and assistance to refugees and asylum seekers.

As this book cannot give a comprehensive overview of the history of the relationship between the UNHCR in Jakarta and the Indonesian government, a few milestones must serve as a general orientation. In June 1979, the UNHCR established an office in Jakarta and signed an agreement with the Ministry of Foreign Affairs to formalize its relationship and define its responsibilities. The responsibilities included verification of the identity of refugees and asylum seekers for the purposes of the registration and the issuance of individual documentation, the registration of claims for international protection, the determination of refugee status and the search for durable outcomes. An additional agreement for cooperation between the UNHCR and the Government of Indonesia, signed in August 1996, reinforced the collaboration (Jordão 2012).

The UNHCR in Jakarta collaborates closely with the Ministry for Foreign Affairs and Ministry of Justice and Human Rights, in which the Directorate-General of Immigration and the Directorate-General for Human Rights are based. In cooperation with these government partners, the UNHCR has provided numerous training workshops for members of the Indonesian police on the role of the UNHCR and the rights of asylum seekers and refugees coming to Indonesia. As a mark of confidence, the UNHCR provides the responsible Indonesian authorities with monthly updates on asylum seekers and refugees. The UNHCR has criticized the conditions in immigration detention centres in Indonesia, actively promoting community housing schemes instead as they allow more freedom of movement (UNHCR 2012b). Knowing that the Indonesian government will persist for the foreseeable future with its policies of detaining irregular migrants in immigration detention centres, the UNHCR has been calling for binding standard operational procedures (SOPs) for these immigration detention centres (Jordão 2012). In order to improve the existing collaboration with Indonesian government bodies, the UNHCR has requested more frequent and regular meetings and exchanges of information with responsible partner institutions. Given that the relationship between the UNHCR in Indonesia and the Indonesian government has not always been trouble-free, UNHCR representatives are generally cautious in expressing any criticism, as they wish to avoid further tension in that relationship that might have a negative effect on their presence in Indonesia more generally.[2]

One of the key tasks of the UNHCR in Indonesia has been to encourage Indonesia's accession to the 1951 Refugee Convention and the 1967 Protocol.

In May 2006, when Indonesia was elected as a member of the United Nations Human Rights Council, it pledged to ratify the 1951 Convention and its 1967 Protocol by 2009 (UNHCR 2007). In 2007, the UNHCR drafted a 10-Point Plan of Action in Addressing Refugee Protection and Mixed Migration, which offered support for developing a mechanism to address effectively the problems relating to the protection of refugees and mixed migration flows with the aim of overseeing the country's transition towards becoming a signatory to the 1951 Convention (Türk 2013; UNHCR 2011b). Indonesia reiterated its intention to sign the Refugee Convention, listing it in the 2005–9 National Legislation Program (Prolegnas) (Indonesian Government 2005) of all the laws that the parliament planned to pass or revise in that five-year period, but nothing has happened so far. Despite the repeated assertions that the Refugee Convention would be ratified, the Prolegnas for 2010–14 made no further mention of any intention to do so. The National Action Plan for Human Rights (Rencana Aksi Nasional, RANHAM), implemented in 2011 and intended to cover the following three years, stated its objectives of supporting the respect, promotion, fulfilment, protection and enforcement of human rights in Indonesia. It explicitly mentioned the Refugee Convention and the need to ratify it (Presidential Decree 23/2011). However, this did not happen and the likelihood of ratification under the new government of President Joko Widodo, elected in July 2014, remains minimal. The predicted high cost of installing a domestic refugee processing mechanism is the main disincentive.[3] Perhaps of greater significance is the fact that, with a functioning domestic asylum system in place, Australia could then designate Indonesia as a safe first country and return people there, which Indonesia wants to avoid more than anything else. Indonesian state representatives insist that temporary protection for asylum seekers in Indonesia is already sufficient because "even without becoming a party of the Refugee Convention, in principle, we are already respecting and applying it, because we are committed by a number of other conventions" that Indonesia has already ratified.[4]

Outside its core tasks, the UNHCR is a key player in deliberations about irregular migration within Southeast Asia. For example, since 2001 the UNHCR has been participating as an observer in activities connected to the Bali Process, becoming a full member in 2007 and, in the same year, a full participant in the Bali Process Steering Group together with Australia, Indonesia, New Zealand, Thailand and the IOM.[5] Furthermore, since the Fourth Regional Ministerial Bali Meeting in March 2011, the

UNHCR has been working closely with the Ministry for Foreign Affairs to implement decisions made at that summit, especially to develop a Regional Cooperation Framework in order "to overcome the problems associated with regional experience of irregular movement and the movement of refugees" (UNHCR Indonesia 2011).[6] One crucial outcome of that collaboration was the sharing of a burden and the establishment of a regional support function for returning people who are not found to be in need of international protection to their countries of origin. This outcome, as will be demonstrated below, has severe implications for the repatriation of transit migrants.

As well as working with government bodies, the UNHCR works closely with its implementing partner to provide assistance to the refugees and the most vulnerable among the asylum seeker population (Chapter 4). In the past, the main partners were the humanitarian organization Yayasan Pulih and the Indonesian Red Cross (Palang Merah, PMI) (PMI 2005), but the main partner organization is now the Church World Service (CWS). Joint initiatives of the UNHCR and its implementing partners include the establishment and maintenance of programmes that enable asylum seekers and refugees to support themselves through gardening and other activities, the provision of counselling and home visits, and the facilitation of self-help group activities (Chapter 4), all of which aim to ensure that psychosocial needs of refugees and others of concern are met. Services provided to asylum seekers and refugees by the UNHCR and its partners are free of charge (UNHCR Indonesia 2012a). However, because of a shortage of funds, several UNHCR and CWS services, such as English lessons, football and swimming, were cut back or temporarily suspended in 2012, to the great regret of many transit migrants I spoke with. More generally speaking, UNHCR services received very diverse evaluations from their recipients. One refugee, who had been waiting for resettlement for more than five years, said "the UNHCR is a soft killer", whereas an Afghan youngster, newly released from immigration detention following the intervention of the UNHCR, said "from the deep bottom of my heart I really thank the people of UNHCR".[7]

One of the main non-government partners of the UNHCR in Indonesia is the IOM, especially regarding detention issues, community housing programmes and travel arrangements for resettlement, voluntary repatriation of refugees and assisted voluntary return of asylum seekers and others of concern. The relationship between the two international organizations has been complicated, not only in Indonesia, but also in other parts of the world. Given the many areas of overlap in their activities, the working relationship between the IOM and the UNHCR has a long history "marked by both close cooperation and bitter competition" (Betts, Loescher and Milner 2012, p. 122). Fabian Georgi (2010, p. 54) has also noted the long history of rivalry, in their work and their world view, between the two bodies. Although the IOM has no refugee mandate, it has increasingly become involved in handling activities that affect refugees and (rejected) asylum seekers, as in Indonesia. Consequently, competition for refugee-related funding has intensified between the two players. While the UNHCR in Indonesia constantly faces funding and staff shortages, the IOM is in a very privileged financial position.

The UNHCR in Indonesia operates on a limited budget and with a limited number of staff. In 2013, the UNHCR had its main presence in Jakarta and maintained regional offices in Kupang, Makassar, Medan, Pontianak, Surabaya and Tanjung Pinang, employing sixty-one staff altogether, including thirty-five national, international and affiliated staff (UNHCR Indonesia 2013c). In 2012, the UNHCR office in Indonesia operated on an annual budget of US$5,911,688; in 2013, the annual budget was increased to US$7,866,834 (UNHCR 2013c). The largest donors have been Australia and Norway. Despite its heavy reliance on the work of the UNHCR, the Indonesian government did not financially support the UNHCR between 2001 and 2011. From 2012 onwards, however, it has contributed US$50,000 per year to the UNHCR (UNHCR 2014). Given the limited resources, application processes and status determination can take many months, sometimes years. In late 2012, Manuel Jordão, UNHCR Country Representative in Indonesia, emphasized that "we [UNHCR in Indonesia] need more resources as the problem grows 'every minute'" (Jordão 2012). In 2013, the Australian government and the UNHCR in Geneva signed a partnership agreement, in which the Australian government pledged to provide unallocated contributions, totalling AU$93 million, to the UNHCR's annual budget for 2013–16 (Australian Government and UNHCR 2013). The agreement gives special emphasis to encouraging "local integration and voluntary return opportunities as well as international efforts to provide durable solutions to refugees and displaced persons in the region" (Australian Government and UNHCR 2013, p. 4). How much of that funding will be directed to Indonesia remains to be seen. According to the Houston report (Expert Panel 2012, p. 113), the UNHCR in Indonesia is working to build national capacity to take on more asylum-seeker responsibilities, but this may be the expression of wishful thinking on the part of the Australian government.

The next three sections examine the core tasks of the UNHCR carried out in Indonesia: determination of refugee status, resettlement and repatriation. Through the elucidation of some of the difficulties and weaknesses in these processes, I seek to demonstrate my supposition that transit migrants in Indonesia are afforded only semi-protection.

Determination of Refugee Status

One of the most significant tasks performed by the UNHCR is determining the status of asylum seekers seeking protection, for which Indonesia relies entirely on the UNHCR. Once asylum seekers have contacted the UNHCR in Jakarta or its staff members when they visit immigration detention centres elsewhere in Indonesia, they can initiate an application for international protection. The first step in the process by the UNHCR to determine the applicant's refugee status is verification of the applicant's identity. After verification, people can officially register and receive temporary documentation in English and Bahasa Indonesia, the official language of Indonesia, stating their status as asylum seekers. This asylum-seeker certificate contains a photograph of the asylum seeker, gives basic details such as name and date of birth and, more recently, expressly states that the bearer is a "person of concern to the Office of the United Nations High Commissioner for Refugees and should, in particular, be protected from forcible return to a country where s/he would face threats to her/his life or freedom, pending the final decision on her/his refugee status" (Taylor and Rafferty-Brown 2010b). This temporary documentation must be renewed every two to three months, to confirm that applicants are still in Indonesia and have not already moved on.[8]

In 2011, applicants could register at the UNHCR office in Jakarta on only three days per week and no more than twenty applications were accepted each day. Queues outside the UNHCR office in Jalan Kebun Sirih tended to be long and some people spent the night in front of the office to make sure they were at the front of the line. New registrations were limited, not only because of the shortage of staff but also because the UNHCR in Indonesia did not want to acquire a reputation for fast-track processing, as that might have attracted more asylum seekers to cross from Malaysia.[9]

However, because of the continuing influx of asylum seekers to Indonesia, during 2012 the UNHCR office in Jakarta offered registration on four days per week and increased the daily registration limit to thirty (UNHCR Indonesia 2013*a*). It also moved its entrance to the back of its compound, so that the queues were less exposed to unwanted attention of passers-by.

Except for those deemed particularly vulnerable, asylum seekers are not entitled to financial support from the UNHCR. Nevertheless, holding documents that certify the bearer's status as an applicant for international protection can make a huge difference by, for example, eliminating the risk of immediate deportation when arrested by the police. Although UNHCR papers for asylum seekers are no legal substitute for missing passports and residency permits, the police in Indonesia generally accept these documents.[10] Although holding asylum-seeker documents could spare them from deportation, they did not spare them from arrest and detention in immigration detention centres (as explained in Chapter 3). All registered asylum seekers must sign a code of ethics acknowledging their compliance with Indonesian laws.[11]

Usually many months pass between the initial registration with the UNHCR and the first interview in the process to determine refugee status, when claims for international protection are examined and substantiated. In 2012, the average waiting time between registration and the first interview was eight to ten months.[12] During the interview to determine refugee status, each asylum seeker has the right to be interviewed in his/her own language by a UNHCR officer assisted by a qualified interpreter. Given the lack of qualified interpreters for certain languages in Indonesia, interpreters and translators, many of them former refugees, are often flown in from Australia.[13] The UNHCR officer then assesses the merits of the claim for protection, taking many more months to determine refugee status. In 2012, the average time between the interview and the communication of its outcome to the asylum seeker was five to eight months; in rare cases it could take up to two years (Taylor and Rafferty-Brown 2010*b*). The asylum seeker is provided with a reasoned decision on whether refugee status is granted or not.[14] Generally, acceptance rates in the process to determine refugee status in Indonesia are fairly high, as Table 5.1 indicates for the year 2011.

The UNHCR-issued documentation proving refugee status, known as the "refugee card", has to be renewed every twelve months. The UNHCR provides monthly support for some recognized refugees (as described in

Table 5.1
Asylum Seekers Determined to be Refugees in Indonesia, 2011

	Number of decisions	Acceptance rate
Afghans	1,676	97%
Iranians	275	94%
Iraqis	461	89%
Sri Lankans	145	98%
Total	2,890	96%

Source: UNHCR 2012a.

Chapter 4) and works to arrange one of three possible durable solutions: resettlement in a third country, voluntary repatriation to the country of origin, or local integration. Given that local integration is not a viable option for recognized refugees in Indonesia because Indonesian legislation prevents it (see Chapter 7), resettlement in safe third countries is the option preferred among refugees (CWS 2013, pp. 113, 118).[15] The resettlement process is very time-consuming and has no guarantee of success. The UNHCR in Jakarta estimates about half of the people who register as asylum seekers "disappear" during the lengthy process. For example, in the first six months of 2013, the files of 1,173 individuals were closed because they had abandoned their claims (UNHCR Indonesia 2013c). It is safe to assume that at least some of these people have crossed the sea to Australia with the help of people smugglers, although not all of them may have survived the journey.

For a variety of reasons, some asylum seekers may not "qualify" as genuine refugees. When a claim for protection is rejected, the process of determination of refugee status allows for the asylum seeker to appeal against the decision within thirty days. What makes launching an appeal in Indonesia particularly difficult is the lack of advocacy and legal aid available to asylum seekers. Unlike in Australia, where asylum seekers whose claims for refugee status have been rejected have access to free legal aid from a variety of NGOs, only one Indonesian NGO, Lembaga Bantuan Hukum (LBH), has begun to look into asylum seeker issues.[16] Moreover, hardly any Indonesian lawyers specialize in international refugee law.[17] Given that many asylum seekers lack formal education, they face difficulty in expressing their claims or appeals within a highly bureaucratic and formal context. Once an appeal is submitted to the UNHCR, it is handled by a different, often more senior, case officer to guarantee an impartial review. Table 5.2 gives an overview of interviews and decisions made in the process of determining refugee status in Indonesia between 2011 and mid-2013.

Despite the high recognition rates of asylum seekers in Indonesia, Taylor and Rafferty-Brown judged that UNHCR procedures to determine refugee status there "do not meet the standards required for reliable determinations, such as the use of qualified interpreters, provision of detailed reasons for negative decisions and *independent* review of such decisions" (Taylor and Rafferty-Brown 2010*a*, p. 576).

Resettlement

The UNHCR in Jakarta has acknowledged that in "the Indonesian context, resettlement plays a particular strategic function in view of its relevance to the preservation of the "protection space" that the authorities grant to newly arrived asylum-seekers and refugees" (UNHCR Indonesia 2012*a*). During fieldwork, I often encountered a sense of entitlement to resettlement among transit migrants. Many were convinced that they deserved to be resettled and granted a better life, after suffering so much for so long, and were deeply disappointed to learn that there was no such thing as a right to resettlement. Resettlement to a safe third country is not a right, because there is no international obligation for states to accept refugees who are temporarily in transit elsewhere. Resettlement of transit migrants recognized as refugees depends, therefore, on the goodwill of the countries receiving refugees.

Because there is such a limited number of countries that regularly receive refugees and because the annual intake of refugees across the globe is relatively small, there is always a huge shortage of resettlement options. For example, in 2012, a total of 88,578 refugees were admitted by twenty-two resettlement countries (Refugee Council of Australia 2013). Given that there were 10.4 million recognized refugees worldwide in 2012, the resettlement number is very low. Stephen Castles (2012) calculated that, at the 2011 rate of global resettlement, it would take seventy years to resettle the 7.1 million refugees who have waited for five years or more and have little prospect of returning to a safe home. His calculation, however, excludes the refugees who will require protection in the years to come.

There is little cause for optimism among recognized refugees lingering in transit in Indonesia. According to tables from the IOM, between

Table 5.2
Refugee Status Determination Interviews and Decisions, 2011–July 2013

	July 2013		January–July 2013		2012		2011	
	Number of cases	Number of individuals	Number of cases	Number of individuals	Number of cases	Number of individuals	Number of cases	Number of individuals
Interviews								
First instance	151	202	995	1,286	1,004	1343	1,000	1,139
Appeal	6	8	40	53	40	71	60	69
Total (interviews)	157	210	1,035	1,339	1,047	1,414	1,060	1,208
Decisions								
Recognition (first instance)	111	121	610	776	850	1,193	517	585
Rejection (first instance)	11	18	71	121	185	264	197	243
Recognition (appeal)	0	0	28	42	42	54	14	29
Rejection (appeal)	3	7	28	48	54	77	24	26
Recognised after reopening	0	0	3	0	0	0	0	0
Total (decisions)	125	146	740	990	1,131	1,588	752	883

Source: UNHCR Indonesia 2013c.

December 1999 and June 2013, a total of 2,541 refugees in Indonesia were resettled to third countries (IOM Indonesia 2013*a*). Australia took in by far the greatest number of those refugees. Among other countries accepting refugees from Indonesia in the early 2000s were Canada, New Zealand, Sweden, Norway and the United States (Taylor and Rafferty-Brown 2010*b*, p. 28), but their willingness to resettle refugees from Indonesia diminished in the late 2000s. According to Susan Kneebone (2006, p. 60), refugees awaiting resettlement in Indonesia face the problem that other resettlement countries consider them to be Australia's responsibility and are, therefore, generally reluctant to accept them. For recognized refugees waiting in Indonesia, however, Australia is not necessarily the number one choice for resettlement. Unless they have family members already living overseas, most refugees have no specific preference, caring only about being resettled in a safe country as quickly as possible so that they can get on with their lives.

Between January 2010 and December 2011, 911 cases were submitted to Australia for resettlement, of which only 532 were accepted. In comparison, during the same period, 13 cases were submitted to Canada, of which 7 were accepted. The United States accepted 13 and Norway 3 (UNHCR Indonesia 2012*b*). According to information issued by the IOM (IOM Indonesia 2014, p. 5), in 2010, 147 refugees were resettled from Indonesia, 445 in 2011, 257 in 2012, and 900 in 2013. Table 5.3 shows which countries these refugees were resettled in.

As already noted, refugees usually have to wait several years for resettlement. The UNHCR tries to find faster resettlement options only for vulnerable refugees, such as women and children (Taylor and Rafferty-Brown 2010*a*). In order to determine the most suitable destination country for the refugees, the UNHCR partner organization, CWS, conducts interviews to find out about relatives living overseas who might help the refugees integrate into the host country. Once they have been accepted by a country, refugees undergo medical and security checks to ensure that they do not pose a health or security risk to that country.[18] Given that the results of medical check-ups are only valid for up to six months and that departures are often delayed because the results of security checks have not come through, refugees who are otherwise ready to depart for their new country frequently have to repeat the checks. For example, I met a Hazara woman who had undergone the medical and security checks three times, but was still waiting to be resettled. She had arrived in Indonesia in

Table 5.3
Resettlement of Refugees from Indonesia, 2000–February 2014

Destination	January and February 2014	Total for 2013	Total for 2012	Total 2000– February 2014
Australia	88	815	189	2,044
Canada			1	256
Denmark				31
Finland				13
France				4
New Zealand		78	53	160
Norway				120
Sweden		7	9	237
UK				17
USA	10		5	83
Romania				44
Philippines				13
Total	98	900	257	3,022

Source: IOM 2014.

2001 with her husband, who was in prison in Malaysia at the time of our encounter. Five of their eight children had been born in Indonesia. After three failed attempts to leave Indonesia by boat, the family applied for protection through the UNHCR. In 2008 they were recognized as genuine refugees. From that time the family, clearly expecting to be resettled soon, had lived with a suitcase containing the most essential items in their living room. The family's resettlement was rejected by Canada, New Zealand and Australia for different reasons.[19] While the family waited for another resettlement option from the UNHCR, the imprisoned husband was extradited to Australia in late 2012 to face trial for alleged people-smuggling. Seeking eventual reunion with her husband, the woman decided to pursue the irregular option of taking her eight children to Australia by boat in early 2013 and succeeded.[20]

Assisted "Voluntary" Repatriation

Applicants whose claims for international protection have been rejected twice by the UNHCR are supposed to leave Indonesia. They no longer enjoy the special concessions of asylum seekers who are in the process of determining refugee status. As rejected asylum seekers, the Indonesian authorities perceive them as "illegals" and they face the risk of deportation. Indonesia has carried out deportations, but because of their high cost there are usually only twenty to thirty deportations each year,[21] which is much fewer than the number of twice-rejected asylum seekers. For the Indonesian government, therefore, voluntary repatriation is the most desirable solution for rejected asylum seekers and other unwanted residents, because it is significantly cheaper than deportation (IOM Indonesia 2012b, p. 75).

If it is to succeed, voluntary repatriation must have the full support and commitment of the country to which the refugees are returning to ensure their safe reintegration. For a variety of reasons, voluntary repatriation is often not feasible for rejected refugees; many of their countries of origin are not only unable to guarantee the safety and security of returnees, especially if conflicts persist in those countries, but are also not eager to welcome them back. In order to be "deportable", rejected asylum seekers require valid documents, which many lack. If the embassies of their homelands in Indonesia are unwilling to provide valid documents, rejected asylum seekers linger on in Indonesia. Unable to be resettled and, at the same time, unable or unwilling to return to their country of origin, the rejected asylum seekers find themselves in a very difficult position. Occasionally, the UNHCR has reopened the cases of asylum seekers who have been rejected twice, especially of those from countries where the security situation has deteriorated dramatically or of those who have been able to produce new evidence to support their claim (Taylor and Rafferty-Brown 2010b). Such cases have, however, been the exception rather than the rule.

For the UNHCR, voluntary repatriation is the most preferable of the three options for a durable solution (Barnett and Finnemore 2004). For those who have grown tired of living in limbo and have, therefore, shown an interest in voluntary repatriation, the UNHCR in Jakarta offers counselling that is intended to ensure that their choice to return is informed and that repatriation proceeds on a strictly voluntary basis. However, unbiased and detailed information is often not available and there is much justifiable scepticism about how "voluntary" voluntary repatriations really are. For rejected asylum seekers in Indonesia, their only choice is between "voluntary" repatriation on the one hand, or imprisonment and destitution, as a result of losing basic support and accommodation and being prohibited from working, on the other (Webber 2011; Georgi and Schatral 2012). For those held in Indonesian immigration detention centres, in particular, "voluntary" repatriation may be the only alternative to indefinite detention. Even for transit migrants outside detention, the extent to which repatriation is truly voluntary is highly questionable, especially if the "volunteer" has no legal basis for staying permanently in the host country (Webber 2011, p. 104). The example of twenty-four-year-old Jafar Badri shows how transit migrants, having experienced the hardship of being stuck in transit in Indonesia, can be left without any viable options. During his nine months' stay in Indonesia from late December 2012, Jafar was jailed in an immigration detention centre after trying unsuccessfully to board a boat to Christmas Island, was robbed and beaten several times by locals in the streets of Cisarua on his release, and lost more than twenty kilograms through illness and malnutrition. Although he remarked that "there will be trouble for me in Iran", his preference is to return to Iran and face the difficulties there rather than stay on in Indonesia, because "the way we have been treated here has broken my heart" (Alford and Maley 2013b). His acceptance of repatriation, like that of many others, is only voluntary in the sense that he has no other real option to build a new life. Many such "voluntary" repatriations are really the result of direct or indirect coercion.

Although the UNHCR supports the voluntary repatriation of its former clients, it does not handle the formalities and practicalities of repatriation, which are managed by its operational partner, the IOM. It is the IOM that organizes travel documents, books flights, provides cash grants for use in their country of origin, and arranges an escort to the airport in the transit country and a pick-up at the destination. According to IOM statements (IOM 2012a, p. 43):

> return and reintegration assistance to help stranded irregular migrants returning to and reintegrating in their countries of origin is one of IOM's key areas of intervention in the region. These activities complement the Organization's activities in other areas of work, such as information campaigns to prevent irregular migration, combating migrant smuggling and trafficking, and cooperation with States in the fields of labour migration and border management.

For those registered through the UNHCR, their voluntary repatriation must be cleared by the UNHCR. Voluntary repatriation is also available to those who have been intercepted by Indonesian authorities and who may not have had the chance to register with the UNHCR. I interviewed several newly intercepted people who informed me that IOM staff had tried to convince them not to apply for international protection through the UNHCR but to accept repatriation offers instead.[22] Others were told by IOM officials that if they did not accept the assisted return offers they would face criminal charges for illegal entry (HRW 2002). IOM in Jakarta has rejected such allegations.

According to IOM statistics, about 3,200 people accepted voluntary repatriation between December 1999 and June 2013 (IOM Indonesia 2013a) and were returned to Afghanistan, Iraq, Iran, Sri Lanka, Pakistan, Bangladesh and Myanmar.[23] Table 5.4 shows the countries that received returnees from Indonesia.

From the little information that is available about returns, it would appear that some repatriations took place prematurely, as the countries of origin were not sufficiently safe and returnees faced physical harm and further displacement (HRW 2003; Corlett 2005). Tragically, some were killed upon return (Schuster and Majidi 2013).

Repatriation is, therefore, not simply a return; it often turns out to be a new beginning and a departure to an unknown future. Even if the security situation in their country of origin allows for a permanent return, transit migrants are often reluctant to be repatriated. If they have accumulated debts for the journeys they have made so far, they will have to repay their creditors. If they have sold their land, their house and all other assets in order to embark on their journey to Indonesia, they have nothing to return to (*Tempo* 2012, p. 60). As repatriation or return might be seen by their kin, neighbours, and friends as evidence of failure to reach their desired destination, shame can also influence their decision not to opt for return (Schuster and Majidi 2013). Although "voluntary" repatriation to some countries has been "rewarded" with a lump sum of up to AU$2,000 per person, handed out upon arrival by the IOM (Taylor and Rafferty-Brown 2010a), the amount is not enough for recipients to rebuild their lives easily. Some returnees use the money to make a down payment for another migration attempt (Schuster and Majidi 2013). Frequent reference to the IOM in this chapter already calls for a more systematic analysis of the organisation's role in Indonesia. The next section sheds light on a number of IOM programmes that are now playing out in the regulation of migrants, including those in transit.

THE IOM

Indonesia is not a member state of the IOM, but it has had formal observer status in the IOM Council since 1991. In order to operate in Indonesia, the

Table 5.4
Assisted Voluntary Returns from Indonesia, 2000–February 2014

Destination	January and February 2014	Total for 2013	Total for 2012	Total 2000–February 2014
Afghanistan	5	49	171	1,474
Angola				4
Bangladesh	40	197	7	232
Cambodia	1	37	36	92
Egypt				1
India		8	11	30
Iran	38	363	70	781
Iraq	10	21	65	308
Jordan				20
Morocco				3
Nepal		3	4	22
Pakistan	7	84	81	303
Saudi Arabia				2
Sierra Leone				5
Somalia				1
Sri Lanka	15	109	76	343
Syria				4
Thailand		1		2
Sudan	4	7		7
United Arab Emirates				2
Vietnam	1	12	50	218
Yemen				3
France				1
Myanmar	1	82	26	124
Uzbekistan		1	1	14
Columbia			4	4
Congo			4	4
Mauritius		1		1
Cameroon	1			4
Total	123	975	606	4,009

Source: IOM 2014.

IOM has to renew its contract with the Indonesian government every six months. Nonetheless, the IOM plays an extraordinary role in Indonesia. With its fourteen sub-offices from the eastern end of the archipelago to the west, IOM Indonesia is currently one of IOM's largest missions worldwide (IOM 2011a).[24] By its mandate the IOM can only act for the national governments that comprise its membership, but it has become increasingly proactive in recent years in helping states that are not members and those that are candidates for membership to set up programmes to combat irregular migration, primarily aimed at preventing the departure of irregular migrants from transit countries (Düvell 2012). The IOM is not part of the United Nations system; it has merely been granted a role as permanent observer of principal organs of the United Nations (agreed in 1996). Under international law, the IOM has no formal mandate to monitor human rights abuse or to protect the rights of migrants, asylum seekers or refugees. Nevertheless, the IOM increasingly interferes in refugee protection and provides assistance to asylum seekers who are referred by the UNHCR, and, consequently, has an impact on their lives. As this section will show, the IOM prioritizes migration management over the protection of rights.

Governments around the globe employ the IOM, making use of its services to carry out a range of migration-related tasks that governments themselves are unwilling or unable, because of political and legal restrictions, to undertake. Having signed an Arrangement on Migration Cooperation with the Indonesian government in October 2000, the IOM claims that it operates in Indonesia on behalf of the Indonesian government. In its own words, the IOM "helps the government in developing and implementing policies, legislation and administrative mechanisms for migration, both by means of technical support and training for government officials and helping the migrants themselves" (Hayaze 2012).

The IOM's activities in Indonesia concentrate mainly on labour migration from Indonesia, human trafficking and emergency response to natural disasters. Of greater significance for the present analysis is IOM's involvement at the forefront of capacity-building for state migration control, technical cooperation and operative migration and border control, as well as international migration policymaking to combat irregular migration. The IOM's multilevel involvement in Indonesia and the wide variety of services it delivers even encompass police training and the running of workshops on border security. Besides "ordering" migration flows and "managing" irregular migration, the IOM engages in various other fields, which Fabian Georgi (2010, p. 47) has summarized as a "contradictory variety of activities". Many scholars have accused IOM activities in many different parts of the world of violating the rights of migrants (Georgi 2010;

Düvell 2003; Georgi and Schatral 2012). According to Fabian Georgi (2010, p. 62), the IOM "appears to serve the hegemonic forces in industrialised countries in creating the bitter reality of migration controls characterised by thousandfold deaths at Western borders, by the mass illegalisation of workers, and a world of detention camps and deportations". Rutvica Andrijasevic and William Walters (2010, p. 979) have criticized particularly the fact that the IOM is working as a "major source of intelligence, assessment, advice and technical assistance in connection with national and regional border policies and practices". The close interaction of IOM staff members with asylum seekers during and after interceptions provides them with very specific knowledge about smuggling networks, which they might share with Indonesian and Australian authorities or use to develop new programmes and initiatives that, in turn, might help to secure future employment options for the IOM as a very important stakeholder within the global migration industry.

According to Ishan Ashutosh and Alison Mountz (2011, pp. 21, 28), the IOM is acting on behalf of nation states using the language of international human rights and humanitarianism, but some of the IOM's "assistance" puts migrants at greater risk and increases their vulnerability. The IOM's participation in the delivery of humanitarian aid also means that it competes with other long-established organizations, which feel the consequences of the IOM's engagement in a decline in funding for their work (Georgi and Schatral 2012).

Reliable data on the IOM's budget in Indonesia is very difficult to find. The last annual report that contained budget information was published in 2010. For the 2009 financial year, the IOM received funding from twenty-two different donors, of which the most generous by far was the Australian Department of Immigration and Citizenship (DIAC), contributing US$21,407,194, followed by the European Commission (US$17,631,483) and the United States Agency for International Development (USAID) (US$10,602,042) (IOM Indonesia 2010a, p. 103). Since Australia is the country with the greatest interest in keeping asylum seekers in Indonesia at bay, further contributions to the IOM were made by the Australian Customs (US$668,869) and the Australian Federal Police (AFP) (US$183,887) (IOM Indonesia 2010a, p. 103). Australia contributed US$781,825 towards the IOM's 2012 administrative budget, and US$56.3 million in allocated voluntary contributions towards IOM's domestic, regional and global projects in 2011 (Expert Panel 2012, p. 104). According to the IOM's annual global *Programme and Budget for 2013*, funds of US$19,797,300 were allocated for Indonesia's migration management systems, in particular for the delivery of social services for migrants and "travel assistance to countries of origin for irregular migrants stranded in Indonesia" (IOM 2012*b*, p. 110), and another US$9,579,900 to

> contribute to the efforts of the Government of Indonesia to address irregular migration and ensure suitable treatment of irregular migrants, by setting up a network of monitoring and coordination offices to help build national institutional capacity to deal with irregular migration, combat smuggling and provide improved assistance to irregular migrants. (IOM 2012*b*, p. 117)

Setting aside the difficulty of getting reliable and complete information about IOM Indonesia's operational budget, informal talks with IOM staff left me with the impression that, unlike many other organizations, including the UNHCR, shortage of funds has never been a problem. Some IOM staff members even joked about their "unlimited funding". Another common joke about IOM's abundance was that IOM stood for 10M (*sepuluh miliar* or ten billion). The apparent generosity of donor countries gives rise in any detailed analysis of IOM Indonesia's activities to the important question: who benefits the most?

Regional Cooperation Agreement (RCA)

As an intergovernmental organization, IOM signed a tripartite Regional Cooperation Agreement (RCA) with the Government of Australia and the Government of Indonesia in October 2001. Under the RCA, the IOM took on several responsibilities for the care of "stranded irregular migrants" (IOM Indonesia 2012*c*, p. 161), including most of the detained and rejected asylum seekers. After they have been referred to the IOM from the Indonesian immigration authorities or the UNHCR, IOM Indonesia provides them with basic accommodation, medical care, allowances for food, and counselling by IOM field staff (as described in Chapter 4).

In the early days of the RCA, the IOM's operations in Indonesia were almost wholly funded by Australia. According to a report by Human Rights Watch (2002), the IOM received an estimated US$250,000 per month, eighty per cent of which was spent on direct assistance, including accommodation, for asylum seekers or for people deemed not to be in need of international protection but who could not be repatriated. In the Australian government's budget for 2011 (Australian Government 2011), AU$23.8 million was allocated over three years to support the IOM under the RCA in providing accommodation, food and emergency medical assistance to irregular migrants intercepted in Indonesia, and for the agency's work in voluntary repatriation. In November 2012, the IOM carried responsibility for 1,368 transit migrants in detention and 1,513 transit migrants in generally more cost-efficient community housing (IOM Indonesia 2012*a*). Monthly support for transit migrants from the IOM is higher than the amount refugees receive from the UNHCR, which has given rise to resentment among different groups of transit migrants.

Reinforcing Management of Irregular Migration

Since 2007, the IOM has been implementing the Reinforcing Management of Irregular Migration (RMIM) project, with the aim of complementing and strengthening the RCA. The project includes the detection and monitoring of patterns of irregular migration flow in Indonesia, raising awareness of irregular migration through information campaigns targeting both relevant government officials and local communities, and providing training to the relevant law enforcement officials at local and provincial levels (Expert Panel 2012, p. 114). Training workshops and community socialization activities are held throughout Indonesia in locations determined by recent and frequent people-smuggling activity. The first phase of the RMIM was from July 2007 to June 2009 and had a budget of AU$2.6 million; the second followed in July 2009 and lasted until June 2013, with an overall budget of AU$7.9 million. Between 2007 and October 2012, the IOM organized 112 three-day training workshops attended by more than 7,000 participants from Indonesian law enforcement authorities. While initially targeting the capacity-building programmes of the uniformed police (Baharkam), the IOM has more recently also trained more frontline officers from the community police (Bhabinkamtibmas) in an attempt to extend its reach to district, sub-district and village levels of the national policing structure (IOM Indonesia 2013*b*).

IOM training workshops were usually held in upmarket hotels and attended by invited audiences (IOM Indonesia 2011; 2012*e*). Keynote speakers included very prominent tables from the immigration authorities, the national and provincial police, high-ranking representatives from the marine, community and air police and the People Smuggling Task Force, as well as the Australian Federal Police (IOM 2011*b*). Between 2007 and 2012, the IOM also organized 283 one-day workshops attended by 16,058 participants from the wider community and local authorities. In 2013, IOM provided training to 31,343 members of the police, immigration, local governments, army, prosecution and local communities.

The training and workshops have had a much greater influence than one might expect of the provision of mere technical assistance in a rather limited aspect of engagement. Rutvica Andrijasevic and William Walters (2010, p. 995) have argued that:

> [t]hrough projects that often take the mundane form of training seminars, via the promotion of manuals and texts such as handbooks on migration and border management which appear dull and technical, and through the embedding of these devices in networks of aid, regional development, and schemes of regional and national stabilization, the states of these borderlands are encouraged to take up the work of rebordering themselves.

Along with training workshops and awareness-raising seminars, the IOM in Indonesia has produced many printed materials and guidebooks for Indonesian law enforcement and immigration officers, such as the user guide for officers (IOM Indonesia 2009) and its 2012 revision (IOM Indonesia 2012*c*).[25] Additional guidebooks, pocketbooks and booklets relating to handling people-smuggling cases are also being prepared for the police, the prosecutors and the courts with the IOM's financial and technical support (IOM Indonesia 2012*b*, 2012*d*). Given the IOM's involvement in producing these and other publications, a closer look at some specific publications might help to understand further the nature of the IOM's engagement in terms of border control and the immobilization of transit migrants.

Public Information Campaigns

In order to increase awareness of people-smuggling among the Indonesian people, especially among fishermen and boat owners and builders, but also more generally among coastal populations, the IOM has engaged in intensive public information campaigns (PICs). The main aim of the campaigns is to prevent the involvement of vulnerable inhabitants of coastal areas in people-smuggling (Hayaze 2012; IOM Indonesia 2010*b*). The five localities that the PICs focused on particularly — Tanjung Balai Asuhan,

Lampung, Pelabuhan Ratu, Kupang and Labuan Bajo — were selected by Indonesian immigration authorities in consultation with Australian customs and border authorities (IOM Indonesia 2010*b*). In late November 2009, the Australian Customs and Border Protection Service engaged the IOM to design and deliver a PIC in Indonesia, entitled *Aku Tau Penyelundupan Imigran Illegal Itu Salah* (I know smuggling illegal immigrants is wrong). This PIC, costing AU$810,000, revolved around a series of events and activities conducted from March to July 2010 (IOM Indonesia 2010*e*; Australian Senate Standing Committee 2012). The IOM organized poster campaigns, film screenings, radio announcements and other forms of awareness raising about people-smuggling, which reached several thousand people. T-shirts, stickers and other tokens with anti-people-smuggling messages were distributed. Videos were produced in collaboration with the Indonesian police and the immigration authorities with titles such as *Aku Tau* (I know) or *Jangan Terlibat* (Don't get involved) (IOM Indonesia 2010*d*). Generally between fifteen and twenty minutes long, they carried three core messages about people-smuggling: helping illegal migrants is an offence against the law; it is destructive for the self-confidence of the offender; and it is a sin against God. Rather than offering any explanation of why foreigners might be approaching fishermen for help to go by boat to Australia, the films simply depicted the foreigners as "illegals", making no mention of their right to seek asylum or their need to find protection elsewhere (Missbach and McNevin 2014).

Other means of reaching out to the local inhabitants included the preparation of sermon books for both Muslim and Christian audiences. The IOM invited religious leaders in the five target localities to write six sermons per village that condemned people-smuggling. It then published these sermons in a booklet and distributed copies among other target groups. The author of one of these sermons, which were often rather short and poorly composed, began with the story of Judas who betrayed Jesus for thirty pieces of silver (IOM Indonesia *c*.2010, p. 20), and continued as follows: "The lesson we learn from this is that the Bible tells us not to do anything which is forbidden by our religion or the state (*negara*) only because we are lured by the money. One of these [temptations] includes helping illegal migrants." Linking Judas' betrayal of Jesus with the act of helping asylum seekers, the author concluded: "Let us not become like Judas who was looking for his personal gain over the wellbeing of common interest.... Remember that helping to smuggle illegal migrants is wrong.

God bless. Amen." Sermons like this one have proved highly effective in raising awareness, because the religious leaders enjoy the widespread respect of the often poorly educated members of their communities. However, these sermons and other elements of the PIC have also had some negative side effects for the target audience, especially for fishermen. For example, when encountering asylum seekers in an emergency at sea, fishermen had second thoughts about whether to rescue them or not, as they feared they might face legal consequences if they rendered assistance.[26]

According to the IOM evaluation of the PIC, the "most striking success is the radical shift in public opinion regarding the social and economic impact of the people smuggling during the course of the campaign, from one of general acceptance/tolerance or ignorance, to one of virtually unanimous rejection of people smuggling" (IOM Indonesia 2010*d*, p. ii). Because the Australian donors were also very satisfied with the outcome of the first round of the PIC, in November 2013 the Australian Department of Immigration and Border Protection provided AU$5 million for another round of PICs in Indonesian villages (Australian Senate 2014).

Database Project

Another of the IOM's highly influential projects is a database project for identifying and administering (*mengelola*) "illegal immigrants in all corners (*seluruh pelosok*) of Indonesia" (Hayaze 2012). With the frequency of breakouts and escapes from immigration detention centres and temporary shelters and of re-arrests, Indonesian authorities can no longer rely on the manual data collection methods they have used previously. As the capture of biometric identification of asylum seekers has become increasingly common in other parts of the world (Wilson 2006, p. 98), the IOM has helped install a new registration system for transit migrants in Indonesia that allows for data-sharing with other government authorities by providing fingerprint scanners and computer software. In early 2014, however, the new system was still not working, as data was not being entered regularly into the system as it became available.

Reimbursing Operational Costs of Interceptions

The impact of the IOM in Indonesia has gone beyond the funding of training sessions, workshops and databases, thus indirectly strengthening border control. Because of the chronic shortage of funds for the Indonesian police and other law enforcement agencies, the IOM has also covered operational expenses incurred in the interception and arrest of transit migrants, such as truck rental and fuel purchases for the police and the hire of nightwatchmen to guard the arrested migrants in their temporary shelters. Members of the police or immigration authorities who kept receipts for interception-related spending could claim reimbursement (*ganti rugi*) from the IOM.[27] Some police officers, however, for various reasons, including the difficulty of getting proper receipts, have missed out on reimbursements from the IOM and have carried a grudge ever since.[28] Given the frequent engagement of IOM staff members after interceptions, many IOM staff members have found themselves to be overworked. When talking about their routine work they would often quip with word play, for example, equalling migrants (*migran*) with migraine (*migren*). In using such Indonesian-language puns, they often conveyed their general lack of sympathy for transit migrants.

Management and Care of Irregular Immigrants Project

The Management and Care of Irregular Immigrants Project (MCIIP) began in 2007 and sought to enhance the capacity of the Indonesian Directorate General for Immigration to manage irregular migration through the development of standard operating procedures (SOPs) incorporating human rights instruments, enhancement of the repatriation process and the refurbishment and renovation of two detention centres (IOM Indonesia 2010*b*, p. 64). During the project's first phase (2007–9), the IOM contributed to the renovation of the immigration detention centre in Tanjung Pinang to make it the central immigration detention centre in Indonesia, and to the partial upgrade and refurbishment of the Kalideres detention centre in Jakarta. During the second phase (2009–11), the immigration detention centres in Balikpapan, Semarang and Batam, which hosted irregular migrants with families, and other women and children, were renovated. Australian funding to the IOM for the MCIIP totalled AU$19.9 million (Australian Department of Immigration and Citizenship 2012*c*).

During these two phases the IOM was pushing through the development and implementation of a SOP for immigration detention centres.[29] The SOP spells out the rights and duties of detainees, especially regarding nutrition, health care, communication, grievances and religion, and displays an overall understanding of human rights that is rather technocratic. Although the IOM had adopted "rights jargon", as is evident in many of its publications, the organization had not developed a standard for accountability when rights violations occurred during its operations (HRW 2003). Despite a number of staff training programmes for several of Indonesia's immigration detention centres, the essence of detainee rights protection has still not trickled down, as independent studies and reports have made apparent (HRW 2013). Aware of the often bad conditions of the immigration detention centres funded by the IOM, Human Rights Watch and other organizations have accused the IOM of violating the rights of those it claims to assist in Indonesia, Nauru and Papua New Guinea, and of involvement in the breach of international laws, such as the UN's Body of Principles for the Protection of All Persons under Any Form of Detention or Imprisonment (1988) (HRW 2002; Taylor 2009; Metcalfe 2010).

The IOM has widely ignored the human rights dimensions of migration and has focused narrowly on managed migration flows characterized by increasing securitization, border controls, expansion of immigration detention systems and questionable repatriation schemes. Some of the IOM projects designed to securitize Indonesia's borders and prevent irregular migration have denied — in part or in full — the rights of the very people it claims it assists.

SUMMARY

The allegations made by the Somali protesters, whose story began this chapter, of deliberate discrimination by the UNHCR towards them when it came to their resettlement to safe third countries could not be substantiated. It was the shortage of resettlement offers from potential resettlement countries that limited the options the UNHCR could offer the Somalis and other recognized refugees. While the UNHCR in Jakarta, faced with persistent funding shortages, has provided minimal services to the people under its care in Indonesia, UNHCR protection has its limits, as this chapter has shown. The UNHCR has, in Indonesia and other countries where it operates, shifted its focus from legal protection to material assistance, which is symptomatic of a significant change in the culture of the organization (Stevens 2013, p. 10). Observations in Indonesia have shown that the scarcity of resettlement options has placed inevitable pressure on transit migrants to accept voluntary repatriation.

Although resettlement quotas permit a limited and carefully selected group of refugees to reach Australia regularly, they also ensure that the majority do not reach the country, and cause the persistence of the "containment of refugees in the region" (Schuster 2005*b*, p. 17). The preference of most Western governments is "to select refugees from abroad for resettlement instead of welcoming spontaneous arrivals, as it leaves them to make selections according to their population needs" (Mountz 2011*a*, p. 382). Unsurprisingly, these governments draw on assistance from nongovernment and inter-government organisations. Rutvica Andrijasevic and William Walters (2010, p. 982) and others have argued that the IOM, in particular, seeks to align the migration policies of the global south to the needs, norms and aspirations of the global north. As illustrations and examples from Indonesia in this chapter have indicated, the "IOM manages migration for the benefit of only some" (Georgi 2010, p. 68). The IOM's services encompass a very wide range of activities, stretching across the arrangement of movements (both resettlement and repatriation), capacity-building of state migration control, operative migration control (such as mass information campaigns), and involvement in public debate and policymaking on asylum seekers (Georgi and Schatral 2012). It is clear that transit migrants are not the main beneficiaries of these services; rather, it is the donors and member state governments that are the main beneficiaries of IOM programmes (Georgi and Schatral 2012, p. 198). Moreover, the dominance of the IOM, with its benefactor-driven, rather than beneficiary-driven agenda, has weakened and compromised the role of the UNHCR.

By temporarily cushioning the hardship of some of the transit migrants, especially those excluded from UNHCR care, the IOM reduces their protection to semi-protection, particularly by taking advantage of transit migrants' lack of knowledge and by persuading them to accept assisted voluntary repatriation instead of pursuing their claims for international protection.

Some Australian commentators have proposed Australian screenings and processes to determine refugee status under Australian auspices in Indonesia as a possible solution to the inadequate protection of transit migrants in Indonesia. They maintain that Australian-run processing centres could not only speed up the processes and reduce waiting times, but also reduce the risk of people boarding boats heading for Australia. Extraterritorial protection schemes are not entirely new, and it seems that the European Union, in its search for extraterritorial solutions, has learned from Australia's Pacific Solution (Schuster 2005*b*). The UNHCR has actively promoted them in other parts of the world, as long as they do not become substitutes for proper protection provided by the resettlement countries (Papadopoulou-Kourkoula 2008, p. 43). The main risk of establishing regional protection areas in transit countries is their use by destination countries, such as Australia, as a means of shedding their responsibilities by arguing that asylum seekers and refugees can find de facto permanent protection in the transit country. This would be particularly problematic in a transit country such as Indonesia, where inadequacies in conditions for asylum seekers and refugees have placed them in limbo, as it would only serve to extend their plight even further.

While on the one hand, the Indonesian government has not been enthusiastic about Australian processing centres and regional protection zones within its national territory, as it perceives such initiatives as a form of external interference that would threaten its national sovereignty, on the other hand, it appears to have no interest in developing a domestic asylum system to provide more comprehensive protection to asylum seekers. Regional protection would require a number of changes on the part of the Indonesian government. Considering that Indonesia has no asylum systems and legislation, it would require the full commitment and political will of the Indonesian government to pursue a domestic asylum policy and provide the legal framework for a domestic refugee-status determination mechanism. It would require large-scale capacity-building to put a process in place, to receive and protect asylum seekers, to establish a registration scheme and, last but not least, to assist refugees to make their own living and integrate into the transit country. The next chapter sheds light on the prevailing conditions and debates in Indonesia relating to its status as a transit country and elaborates on the current political settings, which look anything but benevolent towards the installation of a domestic or regional protection scheme for asylum seekers in Indonesia. On the contrary, there are clear indications that Indonesia favours the securitization of migration over the protection of migrants.

Notes

1. It was not until 1994 that the UN General Assembly produced a definition of protection: "International protection thus begins with securing admission, asylum, and respect for basic human rights, including the principle of non-

refoulement, without which the safety and even survival of the refugee is in jeopardy; it ends only with the attainment of a durable solution, ideally through the restoration of protection by the refugee's own country. It includes promoting the conclusion and supervising the application of international conventions for the protection of refugees at the global and regional level, promoting legislation and other measures at the national — and increasingly, regional — level to ensure that refugees are identified and accorded an appropriate status and standard of treatment in their countries of asylum, and ensuring, with and through the national authorities, the safety and wellbeing of specific refugee groups and individuals in asylum countries" (UN General Assembly 1994).

2. It is very unlikely that a UN body like the UNHCR would be banned from operating in Indonesia. Any fear of "expulsion" expressed in interviews with UNHCR staff members probably referred more to the risk that visas of foreign UNHCR staff would not be renewed.

3. Interview with staff member of Directorate of Human Rights and Humanitarian Affairs, Ministry of Foreign Affairs, 26 January 2011, Jakarta.

4. Interview with Deputy Director of Humanitarian Affairs, Ministry of Foreign Affairs, 4 April 2012, Jakarta.

5. The Bali Process on People Smuggling, Trafficking in Persons and Related Transnational Crime (http://www.baliprocess.net/membership).

6. For a comprehensive overview of all the decisions made, see Fourth Bali Regional Ministerial Conference on People Smuggling, Trafficking in Persons and Related Transnational Crime (2011).

7. Interviews with Iraqi refugee, 18 May 2013, Sydney, and with Afghan minor, 23 June 2010, Cisarua.

8. Interview with UNHCR staff, 19 April 2012, Mataram.

9. Interview with UNHCR staff, 19 April 2012, Mataram.

10. For the period people spend waiting just to register with the UNHCR and begin the verification process, the UNHCR provides them with a simple note, which looks less official than the document that states that they are already awaiting an interview with the UNHCR on a specific date. Sometimes police officers do not recognize these notes.

11. Interview with UNHCR staff, 19 April 2012, Mataram.

12. Interview with UNHCR staff, 25 April 2012, Jakarta.

13. Among the Indonesian intelligence community, there were suspicions that some of the interpreters could use their access to detainees to facilitate contacts with certain people smugglers.

14. For more legal insights into the process, see also Taylor and Rafferty-Brown (2010*b*).

15. According to the study undertaken by the CWS (2013), a small number of male asylum seekers and refugees who had been living in Indonesia for a long time

and had formed families with Indonesian wives stated that they would like to live in Indonesia if proper integration and naturalization were available to them. In contrast, for female asylum seekers and refugees, integration was not a desirable alternative at all.

16. Interview with Director of LBH, 13 November 2011, Jakarta.
17. Interview with Head of the Immigration Division at the Regional Office of the Ministry for Justice and Human Rights in Sulawesi Tenggara and Director of the Immigration and Citizenship Advocacy Study Institute (Lembaga Studi Advokasi Keimigrasiandan Kewarganegaraan, LSAKK), 6 April 2012, Jakarta.
18. Visa applications from refugees with diseases or disabilities may be rejected if their treatment requires a permanent and significant cost to the taxpayers of a resettlement country (Taylor 2006, p. 579).
19. Interview, 28 June 2012, Cisarua.
20. Interview, 16 June 2013, Melbourne.
21. Interview with Head of Section on Irregular Migrants and the Protection of Victims of Transnational Crime, Directorate General of Immigration, 5 March 2012, Jakarta.
22. There have been reports of IOM staff in other transit countries, for example Malta (Mainwaring 2012), trying to dissuade those who have commenced their claims for international protection from pursuing them.
23. In 2010, 527 people were repatriated, 297 in 2011, 606 in 2012, and 975 in 2013.
24. The three countries with the most IOM offices are Colombia, Indonesia and Sudan (Ashutosh and Mountz 2011); for a concise overview of the IOM's development, see Georgi (2010) and Düvell (2003).
25. The 2012 revision was funded by the Australian Customs and Border Protection Service and has been distributed to 40,000 officers countrywide.
26. Interviews with fishermen in Pelabuhan Ratu, 22 September 2014.
27. Interviews with Head of the Intelligence Section of the Police, 6 February 2012, Pelabuhan Ratu; Head of District Police, 30 April 2012, Rote; and Head of the Operational Section at Provincial Maritime Police, 18 June 2012, Kupang.
28. Interview with members of the District Police, 22 May 2012, Kupang.
29. It was hoped that the SOP for immigration detention centres would become a supplement to the Law on Immigration (No. 6/2011).

6

INDONESIA AS A TRANSIT STATE: OBLIGATIONS, POLICIES, AND PRACTICE

> All expenses related to residence and living costs of
> illegal immigrants while undergoing status determination process
> or being under the protection of the UNHCR, are not the
> responsibility of the Immigration Office, Regional Office Ministry of
> Justice and Human Rights, or the Directorate General of Immigration.
> (Regulation of the Director General of Immigration No. IMI-1489.
> UM.08.05 2010: §6)

Amongst transit migrants I spoke with, the level of their prior knowledge about Indonesia and the conditions that awaited them there seemed to be low. One young man said he had never heard of Indonesia until a potential smuggler explained to him the advantages of going through Indonesia to reach Australia. In hindsight, he realized that much of what the smuggler had told him was either half-true or entirely wrong. Having to make impromptu decisions about why and where to go, in the midst of political turmoil in their homelands where they lack access to reliable information, means that many transit migrants are surprised by the environment and circumstances they face once they reach Indonesia. Unsurprisingly, they are not well prepared for their stay in transit, which is often much longer than anticipated. Many transit migrants I conversed with seemed astonished on their arrival in Indonesia by everything from the climatic conditions to the archipelago's geographical configuration. For Tariq, who was introduced in Chapter 3, "[i]t was my first time in countries like Thailand, Malaysia or Indonesia and I worried a lot because I did not know anything about those countries". All that Tariq knew about Indonesia came from a documentary about Bali he had once watched on TV. While he was "pleasantly surprised" on his travels through Thailand and Malaysia, Tariq's disappointment with Indonesia and its visible poverty led him to comment, "I thought there were only beggars in Pakistan and India".[1]

One of the migrants' most significant misapprehensions is the belief that Indonesia does not care much about transit migrants and allows them to travel through to Australia unhindered. Although that was the case in the early 2000s, Indonesia has since strengthened its efforts to control the movement of transit migrants into and out of the country and to restrict the operations of people-smuggling networks. This does not mean, however, that intensified law enforcement measures have been entirely successful in stopping an increase in the flows through Indonesia. The Indonesian reaction to the presence of *tamu [yang] tak diundang* (uninvited guests), as transiting asylum seekers are often referred to, is typical of most transit countries. While asylum seekers and refugees are not a popular topic in Indonesia, combatting irregular migration certainly is. As some observers have argued, the Indonesian government shows more concern about border protection than human protection.[2] A focus on limiting movement into and out of Indonesia, however, ignores the destinies of those already in the country. Indonesian policymakers do not view transit migrants as a target group in their policymaking, because they assume that these people do not participate in the society in which they are temporarily residing. As Düvell (2006, p. 7) has argued, the opposite of this assumption is true, because transit migrants work, spend, consume, learn the language and have medical and educational needs. Sooner or later, Indonesia must clarify its position on asylum and react to demands for the protection of transit migrants.

The implications of transit migration on the transit country are the main interest of this chapter. Recent policy changes that seek to regulate transit migration and the political incentive to enforce these changes receive particular attention. As well as retracing the most recent policy changes, which have tended to emphasize border and migration control and the prevention of people-smuggling rather than the provision of greater protection for transiting asylum seekers, this chapter asks how policy changes have been put into practice so far. First, it discusses Indonesia's obligations to provide protection and some legal shortcomings that undermine the provision of full protection to transit migrants. It then introduces a number of new initiatives that serve to increase border and migration control and the enforcement of anti-people-smuggling provisions. Finally, by shedding light on the Indonesian National Search and Rescue Agency (Badan SAR Nasional, Basarnas) and its recent operations to rescue transit migrants from maritime emergencies, the chapter draws attention to the conflicting principles of rescue and border control and the subsequent challenges for maritime transit states such as Indonesia.

From a theoretical perspective, Indonesia's approach to transit migration is typical of those of most transit states. However, when the most recent developments in Indonesia are compared with developments in states on transit routes to EU countries before their accession to the Schengen Agreement, a number of significant differences between Indonesia and the European transit states become obvious. To allow for meaningful comparison, the meaning of "transit state" needs to be made clear.

DEFINING THE TRANSIT STATE

In her study of transit states, Ann Kimball compares the situations of transit migrants in Mexico and Morocco, and uses four determinants — geography, migration, function and state response — to help define the transit state (Kimball 2007, p. 12). According to Kimball, for a country to be a typical transit state, it must first share a border with a fully developed country.[3] Second, it must have high emigration rates and low immigration rates. Third, it has to serve as a primary staging ground for migrants planning a clandestine entrance to a destination country whose borders are guarded, often heavily. Fourth, countries deemed transit states implement restrictive immigration policies and activities, more often than not with encouragement and financial assistance from the neighbouring country that is the intended destination country of transit migrants.

When the situation of Indonesia as a transit country for migrants on the way to Australia is examined against Kimball's four determinants, it becomes apparent that socio-political, legal, and even geographic conditions in Indonesia differ from those in other typical transit states, such as Mexico,

Morocco and Libya, each of which has been the subject of intensive study (Baldwin-Edwards 2006; Kimball 2007; Dowd 2008; Collyer 2007). In some ways Indonesia does fit Kimball's characterization of a typical transit state, but is notably exceptional in others. Indonesia does not share a direct land border with Australia, but is, nevertheless, an immediate neighbour of Australia, albeit across the sea that surrounds them both. The sea serves as a natural border for both countries, but to the seafaring peoples of the region the sea is a means of communication and transport, as the plentiful evidence of lively economic and social exchange, be it through the *trepang* trade or intermarriage, between Northern Australia and the Indonesian archipelago over many centuries attests (Lloyd et al. 2010). As this chapter will outline, Indonesia's maritime borders have long been porous. Lately, however, Indonesian authorities have made a greater effort to monitor and police certain borders and border areas in order to stop the clandestine movement of transit migrants (Missbach 2014*a*). Given that the entire length of Indonesia's border is twice as long as the equator, achieving effective border control is an enormous task (Indonesian Ministry of Maritime Affairs and Fisheries 2008).

With regard to the second of Kimball's determinants, migration flow, Indonesian migration rates clearly show an emigration surplus. The net migration rate in 2012 was estimated to be –1.08 migrant(s)/1,000 population, so more people are emigrating from Indonesia than immigrating to Indonesia (Index Mundi 2013). According to Ann Kimball (2007, p. 23), a typical transit state sits between the First and the Third World and, therefore, marks the "frontier of poverty", a term promoted by Roland Freudenstein (2000). Although it is undeniable that Australia is wealthier than Indonesia, where approximately thirty-two million, or about thirteen per cent of the total population, still live below the poverty line (World Bank 2014), Indonesians rarely seek to migrate to Australia for economic reasons. Instead, millions of Indonesians migrate for temporary employment to neighbouring Malaysia, Singapore, Hong Kong and to the Middle East (IOM Indonesia 2010*c*). The Indonesian government is committed to implementing policy changes to improve the rights of the more than two million Indonesian citizens working overseas, mostly in deplorable conditions and with dismal future prospects. Some of the policy changes intended to improve the plight of Indonesian citizens have also had an impact on non-Indonesian transit migrants, especially those related to irregular transportation.

Unlike Mexicans and Moroccans from the two transit countries studied by Kimball, large numbers of whom have joined the migration trail to find employment in the wealthy North, Indonesians have not sought to cross the "frontier of poverty" into Australia. One reason, but definitely not the most significant, might be Australia's rigid visa regulations which offer no special temporary working scheme to unskilled or low-skilled Indonesians, as they do for Pacific Islanders (Ball, Beacroft and Lindley 2011). Unlike those Indonesians who have the means to invest in the Australian property market, average Indonesians see few incentives in migrating to Australia. Even the numbers of Indonesian international students studying in Australia are currently stagnating (Australian Department of Immigration and Border Protection 2013). Although in mid-2012 Prime Minister Julia Gillard announced that Australia was to increase the number of work and holiday visas available to Indonesians from 100 to 1,000 places per year, only 176 Indonesians made use of this offer in 2012–13 (Australian Department of Immigration and Border Protection 2013).

Indonesia meets Kimball's third criterion in that it serves as a main staging ground for transit migrants who plan to reach Australia by boat. They either depart from an Indonesian exit point or cross through the Indonesian archipelago. Asylum seekers who have the means to enter Australia by air usually do not come via Indonesia, but fly straight from their countries of origin or a neighbouring country. In 2011–12, the largest numbers of onshore asylum applicants in Australia hailed from China, India, Pakistan, Iran and Egypt (Australian Department of Immigration and Citizenship 2012b, p. 7; Masanauskas 2011). Before 2012, the number of asylum seekers who arrived in Australia by boat was substantially smaller than the number who flew into the country and applied for asylum onshore. Between 2007 and 2008 only sixteen per cent of all onshore asylum applications were made by so-called "irregular maritime arrivals", whereas between 2009 and 2010 about forty-seven per cent of the applications for protection were made by "irregular maritime arrivals" (Phillips 2011, p. 6). Between January 2012 and June 2013, 30,310 people arrived in Australia by boat (Phillips and Spinks 2013), the majority of whom began their journeys in Afghanistan, Iran and Sri Lanka and staged their boat journeys from Indonesia.

Kimball's fourth determinant, relating to the implementation of restrictive immigration policies and activities, is especially noteworthy in the case of Indonesia and will therefore receive the lion's share of attention in this chapter. To date, Indonesia has had no functioning asylum system. Like other transit states, Indonesia prefers to discourage potential newcomers and restrict their entry rather than to improve the protection of asylum seekers, thus undermining the international asylum and protection system. According to Kimball (2007, p. 15), although some transit states simply enforce existing immigration policies, most transit states draft new policies. Political and diplomatic pressure from nearby destination countries leads transit states to employ existing and new migration policies and to intensify law enforcement in cracking down on clandestine border entry and exit. They also implement more rigorous controls within their territory to limit the movement of transit migrants. In this regard transit states are not just places that let "migrants travel through" (Kimball 2007, p. 11). As the chapter will later discuss in great detail, Indonesia's new Law on Immigration (2011) and the newly enforced mobility restrictions for asylum seekers reveal a level of Australian interference. In comparison with levels of foreign interference in hotspots for transit migration elsewhere, Australia's level of interference in the implementation of restrictions in Indonesia is significantly different than that of the EU.

In her studies on transit countries in east-central and southeastern Europe that served as "buffer zones" for the Schengen Area before they joined the EU, Milada Vachudova (2000, p. 153) notes that transit states face a unique challenge. On the one hand they are not interested in keeping transit migrants in their territory for long (which is also consistent with the intentions of most transit migrants). On the other hand, as they need to keep good relations with powerful neighbours, they must prevent transit migrants from crossing or even reaching the EU border. Despite the many negative impacts on those transit states of having to implement asylum procedures, to accept rejected asylum seekers from EU members and engage in readmission negotiations with other neighbouring states further away from the Schengen Area, many transit states that were candidates for EU membership complied with demands aimed at harmonizing border controls and visa requirements (Green 2006). The main incentive for their compliance, quite apart from the large amounts of EU funding they received, was their eventual acceptance as members of the EU and the concomitant promise of economic prosperity and political stability. In comparison to the lucrative incentives that place the EU in a position of power over transit countries, Australia has little to offer Indonesia in return for Indonesian compliance with Australia's request that it become a final barrier in stemming the flow of boats. Despite the many readily accepted Australian aid contributions to the Indonesian police and other law enforcement bodies, Indonesia has only partially fulfilled Australia's requests to serve as a buffer zone. Given Indonesia's significance in the region and its economic purchasing power, it is clear that Australia needs Indonesia more than Indonesia needs Australia (Roggeveen 2013; White 2013; Sen 2013). In this regard Indonesia emerges as an exception, as it demonstrates that not all transit states have a need to submit to the demands of wealthy neighbours.

Although she does not list it as a determinant of a transit state, Ann Kimball (2007, p. 150) mentions the tendency of transit countries to have a poor human rights record, which merits discussion in the Indonesian context. Despite only paying lip service in its unfulfilled proposal to sign the Refugee Convention and showing no sincere interest in implementing a domestic asylum mechanism, Indonesia tends to be very concerned about its international reputation and its human rights image, which it has tried to improve since *Reformasi* (the 1998 reform era). Enny Soeprapto, former UNHCR protection officer and one of Indonesia's leading scholars of international refugee law, has long advocated that Indonesia should accede to the 1951 Refugee Convention and its 1967 Protocol, claiming that to do so would "boost Indonesia's image as a nation committed to promoting respect for human rights, including the most basic human rights of refugees" (Soeprapto 2001). Because Indonesia is the most populous and potentially powerful member of ASEAN and because it nurtures a claim to be a regional leader (McRae 2014), it is sensitive to criticism of human rights violations in Indonesian territory. This sensitivity has increased since 2011, when Indonesia became Chair of ASEAN and announced that it would make human rights a top priority for ASEAN (Nugroho 2011; Nabbs-Keller 2010). As Asep Kurnia (2011, p. vii) has claimed, "the issue of illegal immigrants also brought negative impacts for the relations between Indonesia and other countries as well as for the image of Indonesia in the international world". Under the pressure of the scrutiny of recent reports, such as the Human Rights Watch report on the treatment of children in immigration detention in Indonesia (HRW 2013), Indonesian politicians and government officials are now compelled to deal with transit migration. Thus, Indonesia's sensitivity to international criticism of its human rights record might become a useful focus for those who are lobbying for better protection of asylum seekers passing through its borders.

LEGAL PROVISIONS AND REGULATION CONCERNING TRANSIT MIGRANTS

Because it is not a signatory to the 1951 United Nations Convention Relating to the Status of Refugees and the 1967 Protocol, Indonesia lacks a legislative framework for the protection of refugees and asylum seekers. Other international conventions to which Indonesia is party to, such as the Convention against Torture and Other Cruel, Inhuman or Degrading Treatment or Punishment (CAT) and the International Convention on Civil and Political Rights (ICCPR), should guarantee asylum seekers minimum protection by the Indonesian state. While the rights of asylum seekers and refugees are not formally acknowledged in Indonesia, except in a rather rudimentary way, Indonesia has recently extended its immigration regulations. Although new laws and regulations contain provisions that affect asylum seekers and refugees, who are not referred to as asylum seekers and refugees in the legislation, the key stipulations concentrate on the criminalization of people-smuggling rather than on the protection of those seeking asylum. A selection of relevant laws and regulations is offered here to give an overview of how Indonesia regulates requests for asylum.

Asylum Seeker Protection — The Legislative Gap

Indonesian legislation includes at least three laws with provisions that relate to applying for asylum. First, the second amendment to the 1945 National Constitution stipulates that "everyone has the right for political asylum in other countries". This stipulation was never translated into law, as will be outlined below. The very first regulation that explicitly mentioned political refugees was a Circular Letter of the Prime Minister on Political Refugees (No. 11/R.I./dated 7 September 1956). The Circular Letter provided some instructions, albeit non-binding and provisional:

> In view of the entry of persons of non-Indonesian nationality into the territory of the Republic of Indonesia who, after provisional investigation, could be considered as political refugees, it is deemed necessary to set the following guidelines:

> Article 1: Political refugees who entered into or are in the Indonesian territory will be granted protection on the basis of human rights and fundamental freedom in accordance with international customary law.

A number of issues arose relating to the definition of exactly who qualifies as a political refugee, because Article 2 states that having committed a political crime is a precondition: "A political refugee is defined as a foreigner who entered into or is in the Indonesian territory for having committed a political crime."[4] The decision on whether or not a claimant will receive protection as a political refugee in Indonesia is a joint decision delegated in Article 5 to the Minister of Justice, the Minister for Foreign Affairs and the Minister of Home Affairs. The Circular Letter was issued just one year after the Bandung Conference, which engendered the Non-Aligned Movement. Indonesia was open to several countries that were engaged in armed decolonization processes, including Algeria, whose Front de Libération Nationale (FLN, National Liberation Front) even had an office in Jakarta. It remains unclear whether any politically persecuted person used the provisions of the Circular Letter in the 1950s and 1960s to legalize their presence in Indonesia.[5]

De facto temporary asylum accorded to Indochinese asylum seekers in Indonesia from 1975 until 1996 was based on general humanitarian considerations rather than on the circular. As described in Chapter 2, the Presidential Decree (No. 38/1979) relating to Vietnamese asylum-seekers in Indonesia ruled that the Minister of Defence was in charge of coordinating the settlement of the Indochinese refugees in Indonesia and the Department of Defence and Security was responsible for their administration, handling, processing and security. Although the Minister of Defence and his department carried most of the responsibility for the refugees, the Minister of Foreign Affairs had the task of arranging contact with the UNHCR and with the third countries willing to accept refugees. The establishment of camps for the Indochinese refugees was mainly left to the Minister of Home Affairs. Despite having to handle tens of thousands of applications for international protection, Indonesia refrained from establishing a domestic protection framework.

During the last few years of the Soeharto regime, no regulations on handling of asylum seekers were issued, but Law 1/1979 on Extradition (Chapter 2, Article 14) stated that: "Requests for extradition will be rejected if the relevant authorities have well-founded suspicions that the person who is requested for extradition will be prosecuted, convicted or become subject to other punitive actions because of this person's religion, political beliefs, nationality, ethnic or minority status." In 1985, Indonesia signed the CAT, but it was only ratified under Soeharto's successor, President Bacharuddin

Jusuf Habibie in 1998, through Law No. 5/1998. The ratification of CAT effectively confirmed Indonesia's legal obligation against *refoulement* (forced return) of those who faced torture in their countries of origin.

It was not until 1999 that Law 39/1999 on Human Rights was implemented, which reiterated the right to seek asylum in Article 28. Article 7 of the Law on Human Rights provides for due process of law to be accorded to all those in Indonesia who have suffered from human rights abuse and reiterates that instruments of international law ratified by Indonesia are legally binding. Also passed in 1999, Law 37/1999 on Foreign Relations mentions the right to apply for asylum in Indonesia. In particular, Chapter 6 (Paragraphs 25–27), entitled "On granting asylum and the issue of refugees", places authority to grant asylum in the president's hands, with advice from the minister of foreign affairs, and restates that it is granted in accordance with Indonesian law with due regard to international practice and that the president will enact a policy on refugees on the recommendation of the minister of foreign affairs. None of these provisions have been properly implemented. There is no legislation that specifies procedures for granting asylum to refugees in Indonesia. The long-awaited Presidential Decree mentioned in Law 37/1999 is still in the making. It was alleged that a draft for the Presidential Decree to implement the provisions of Articles 25–27 of Law 37/1999 on Foreign Relations had been provided to President Susilo Bambang Yudhoyono, but he did not sign this decree before his presidency ended in October 2014.

With no legislation to regulate the presence of asylum seekers and refugees in Indonesia, the only authoritative device is a Department of Justice and Human Rights Directive from the Directorate General of Immigration, the "Procedures regarding aliens expressing their desire to seek asylum or refugee status" (F-IL.01.10-1297, dated 30 September 2002).[6] Although the directive set out that aliens will be prohibited from entering Indonesian territory under existing immigration regulations, it also states that measures such as their deportation to countries where their lives and freedom are threatened will not be taken. The directive's main stipulation is that asylum seekers in Indonesia be referred to the UNHCR in Indonesia to determine refugee status.[7] Particularly significant is Point 5 of the directive, which demands that the status and presence of those holding UNHCR-issued documentation be respected by Indonesian authorities. Although the Indonesian immigration authorities are not responsible for the care of asylum seekers, the directive requires them to register their presence for monitoring purposes. Similar to the 1979 Presidential Decree, the directive rules that none of the costs related to those of concern to UNHCR will be covered by Indonesian authorities.

In the persistent absence of relevant legislation, the Directorate-General of Immigration released Regulation No. IMI-1489.UM.08.05 on the Processing of Illegal Immigrants in September 2010. In its prelude, the regulation notes the increase in the numbers of foreigners arriving and their presence as illegal immigrants claiming to be asylum seekers and refugees, which has had an impact on ideology, politics, economics, culture, national security and immigration in Indonesia. The prelude further notes a need for coordinated handling and treatment of the illegal immigrants to minimize the impact. The regulation restates the responsibilities of the UNHCR for asylum seekers and refugees, as defined in the 1996 Memorandum of Mutual Understanding between the UNHCR and the Indonesian government, and that illegal immigrants in Indonesia are subject to Indonesian immigration law, although it also notes that those who wish to apply for asylum are exempt from deportation. It does not state that people of concern are to be held in immigration detention centres, but provides for their placement in facilities run by international organizations and the UNHCR, so long as the UNHCR reports their presence to the director general of immigration and they are under the purview of a local head of immigration. Asylum seekers whose claims for protection are rejected and closed by the UNHCR must be reported to the director general of immigration by the UNHCR, so that legal proceedings against them, as set out in immigration legislation, can commence.

In May 2011, Indonesia enacted a long-overdue Law on Immigration (No. 6/2011). Making no mention of "asylum seekers" or "refugees", the new law uses terminology that paints such migrants in a negative light, referring to them with phrases such as *imigran gelap* (illegal migrants), *orang asing* (foreigners), and *korban perdagangan orang dan penyelundupan manusia* (victims of trafficking and people-smuggling). Furthermore, the new law provides no new regulation for the protection of asylum seekers and refugees, but restates a number of exemptions for "victims of trafficking and people-smuggling" (that is, transit migrants). Article 86 stipulates that immigration sanctions do not apply to "victims of trafficking and human smuggling".[8] Article 87 rules that "victims of trafficking and human smuggling" be placed in immigration detention or elsewhere, and given special treatment that differs from other immigration detainees.[9] Article 88 rules that the minister of immigration or a designated immigration officer make arrangements for victims of trafficking and human smuggling to be immediately returned to their home country and to be given travel documents if they do not have them.

Calls for the revision of the Law on Immigration have demanded, amongst other issues, that more emphasis be placed on issues relating to asylum seekers and refugees residing in Indonesia and that human rights are strengthened over citizen rights. Other critics, such as Ali Akbar Tanjung from the Human Rights Working Group, have demanded that a completely new law be introduced instead, arguing that a law that addresses specifically issues relating to asylum seekers and refugees would improve and standardize handling of immigrants and shift the burden of responsibility for them from the Justice and Human Rights Ministry's Directorate General of Immigration to other government agencies, such as the Foreign Ministry and the Social Affairs Ministry (Amelia 2013). It is unlikely, however, that the Law on Immigration will be revised in the near future.

The Criminalization of People-Smuggling

Bearing in mind the general lack of interest in refugee protection in Indonesia, one of the main purposes of the new Law No. 6/2011 on Immigration was to criminalize people-smuggling, which was not deemed a criminal offence. The absence of people-smuggling as an offence in the earlier Law No. 9/1992 on Immigration was not exceptional as, until recently, many other countries also lacked legal provisions that made people-smuggling a crime (Missbach and Crouch 2013). Because Indonesia lacks the capacity to host or monitor transit migrants as required by law,[10] it seeks to at least limit some of the worst effects. The increasing numbers of Indonesian nationals involved in people-smuggling, as they seek to benefit financially from the transit migrants' demand for irregular passage to Australia, make their limitation all the more urgent. Although it is not illegal for the migrants to seek asylum and request protection, doing so often involves the use of illicit methods of transportation and border crossing, facilitated by the unlawful actions of the captains and crews of boats transporting asylum seekers.

The passage of the new Law on Immigration was also intended to fulfil Indonesia's international obligations and responsibilities under the Protocol against the Smuggling of Migrants by Land, Sea and Air, supplementing the United Nations Convention against Transnational Organized Crime, which Indonesia ratified in 2009 (Missbach and Crouch 2013). Under the new Law on Immigration the offence of *penyelundupan manusia* (people-smuggling) is defined in Article 1(32):

> People smuggling is an act that aims to make a profit, either directly or indirectly, for him or herself or for another person who takes a person or group of people, whether organised or unorganised, or instructs others to take a person or group of people, either organised or unorganised, who have no legal right to enter or exit the territory of Indonesia or outside the territory of Indonesia and/or into another country and the person mentioned does not have a right to enter the territory legally, either by using legal documents and false documents, or without a Travel Document, with or without undergoing immigration checks.

The Law on Immigration sets out several offences, some of a general nature and others specific to people-smuggling. The main provision regarding offences specific to people-smuggling, including attempts to smuggle people, is Article 120, which specifies that the offence carries a penalty of between five and fifteen years prison and a minimum fine of Rp500 million (AU$50,000), up to a maximum of Rp1,500 million (AU$150,000). Article 124 on assisting illegal migrants carries a prison term of up to two years and a fine of up to Rp200 million (AU$20,000). Both these articles give clear guidelines for sentencing those found guilty of the offences.

When samples of verdicts handed down after the Law on Immigration was introduced in May 2011 are analysed, it becomes apparent that judges have on a number of occasions imposed sentences below the minimum required by Article 120 (Crouch and Missbach 2013). Their leniency reflects the general perception that Indonesians are being victimized and exploited by irregular migrants (Missbach and Crouch 2013, p. 15). Among those found guilty, a number were from society's lower strata, such as self-employed or casual drivers, fishermen and manual labourers. Rather than being the organizers and recruiters, most of them had relatively minor roles in smuggling networks, acting as helpers, transporters and facilitators who organized food, travel and accommodation for the clients (Missbach 2013). Despite the deficiencies in the legal system that are apparent in the prosecution of people smugglers, migration issues in Indonesia have been drastically securitized, especially in immigration law enforcement and border protection.

LAW ENFORCEMENT

Formally initiated in January 2013, the Coordinating Desk for Handling People-Smuggling, Refugees and Asylum Seekers (Desk Penanganan Penyelundupan Manusia, Pengungsi dan Pencari Suaka, P2MP2S) is the most senior body to date involved in the coordination of all law enforcement measures addressing people-smuggling and asylum seekers.[11] Its members include the Coordinating Minister for Politics, the Ministries of Justice and Human Rights, Foreign Affairs, Internal Affairs, Finance, and Transportation, as well as the national police, the navy, the State Intelligence Agency (Badan Intelijen Negara, BIN) and the National Search and Rescue Agency (Basarnas). Its main tasks comprise the "monitoring, synchronisation and coordination of the implementing policies to prevent and handle people-smuggling". However, the P2MP2S desk has been rather inactive and has left the enforcement of anti-people-smuggling laws to the police and the courts.

As mentioned in Chapter 3, Indonesia established a special anti-people-smuggling taskforce (SATGAS) with sixteen local branches (SATGASDA) in 2009, of which twelve were still operating in 2012. The role of the SATGAS includes the prevention of people-smuggling, investigation of people-smuggling networks and the arrest of people smugglers. The taskforce consists of staff seconded from the police and the maritime police, intelligence officers and others, many of whom complain about the additional burden SATGAS activities place on top of their regular work.[12] The SATGAS works closely with the Australian Federal Police (AFP), which provides technical equipment, telecommunications and surveillance devices, and interpreters to assist in the investigation of suspected smugglers and witnesses. State funding for the basic operations of SATGAS appears, however, to be insufficient. Formerly, AFP funding went directly to the SATGASDA, the local branches of the SATGAS, but since 2012 it has gone to the national police headquarters in Jakarta, resulting in numerous complaints and a suspicion that some of the funding is not reaching its intended destinations.[13] Despite the problems of funding and staff shortages, SATGAS special units have been fairly active in Indonesia, as the increasing numbers of arrests of suspected people smugglers in Indonesia, presented in Table 6.1, indicate.

There are many problems associated with the apprehension of people smugglers, including organizers, facilitators, drivers and boat crew. The facilitators involved at the delivery end of smuggling networks usually have never seen or met their bosses; many may not even work for a particular boss on a regular basis and are recruited only for one-off jobs. This makes it difficult for the police to monitor or observe smuggling networks. Their work is made even harder by the fact that the main organizers make no appearance and participate in everyday transactions by phone and through middlemen. The smugglers make the strategic choice of employing casual, disposable smuggling facilitators for the more visible parts of their operations, such as transportation and accommodation on land. The law does not, however, differentiate between the main organizers, who derive the greatest benefit from people-smuggling operations, and the facilitators at the delivery end of operations, who face the greatest risks but receive the smallest share of the profits.

In order to prosecute someone suspected of people-smuggling, the police are required to present two forms of evidence, which may be witness statements, confessions, or material evidence. Police take witness statements after they have made an arrest, when they have some guarantee, albeit often minimal, of communication with witnesses with the help of interpreters, but it is often impossible to organize interpreters in time (IOM Indonesia 2012b, p. 36). Asylum seekers might not be able to appear in court to repeat or clarify their witness statements, as they may have been sent to distant immigration detention centres.[14] Boat crew and drivers will seize any opportunity to evade punishment by running away. For example, when a boat breaks down during a journey, its crew absconds (Pitakasari 2012;

Table 6.1
Suspected People Smugglers Arrested in Indonesia, 2007–13

	2007	2008	2009	2010	2011	2012	2013 (Jan– Sept)
Indonesian smugglers arrested	0	2	23	51	44	103	90
Non-Indonesian smugglers arrested	1	2	9	8	6	6	14

Source: Unpublished data provided by Indonesian Police Headquarters.

Assifa and Pati 2013). Some people smugglers have adopted a strategy of shadowing an asylum seeker boat with a smaller boat on which the captain and navigator can escape should Australian forces intercept them (Fox 2013). If they can prevent their arrest and imprisonment, they can make use of their navigational skill and experience in future smuggling operations. As many transactions are cash-based and a ship's documents are issued where it has been sold, material evidence, such as receipts for financial transactions relating to the purchase of boats and their documents, is often hard to find. Unless the captain of an arrested asylum seeker boat has these documents, the investigating police must fly to the place of the boat's purchase to get the documents, which costs both time and money.[15] The police can only hold suspects for twenty days in custody while they investigate their crimes.[16]

Law enforcement and the prosecution of people smugglers have been severely impeded by corruption and the involvement of Indonesian *oknum* (dishonest law enforcement officers) in people-smuggling operations (Missbach and Crouch 2013). The suspected, but hard-to-prove, involvement of the senior officials is an especially serious obstacle in preventing people-smuggling. As prices for irregular boat voyages to Australia have increased substantially over the last decade, people-smuggling has become an increasingly lucrative business that lures underpaid and corrupt law enforcement officers. Five cases have been selected here to demonstrate the collusion between people-smuggling networks and law enforcement authorities.

In December 2011, after a maritime incident near the coast of Trenggalek (East Java) in which about 200 asylum seekers drowned, five military officers from the Brawijaya Command in East Java who were involved in the smuggling operation and their civilian counterparts were arrested (Harsaputra 2011).[17] The case of the accused military officers was heard in the Military Courts and they were found guilty under Article 120(1) of the Law on Immigration. Despite the severity of the incident and the fact that 200 people had died, they received little more than the minimum sentence prescribed by the law — prison terms of between five and six years and fines of Rp500 million (AU$50,000) for organizing the operation.[18] All were dismissed from the military. In interviews with the press, they pointed to other senior officers who were involved.

Whereas only low-ranking police or military officers are usually arrested, the case of Amin Rukmakmur, who served as a presidential bodyguard, was somewhat of an exception. For his involvement in October 2012, which included renting several vehicles to transport asylum seekers to the beach and his escort services, he was sentenced to five years imprisonment and a fine of Rp500 million (AU$50,000), plus an additional three months in prison if he did not pay the fine.[19] Amin lost two appeals but the Supreme Court suppressed the judgment until all his options for appeal had expired (Roberts 2014).

In July 2012, five soldiers were arrested for escorting asylum seekers to a boat set to leave from West Java (Arnaz 2012). All the accused were low-ranking officers, whose task in the smuggling operation had been to provide security on the trip to the departure location. The five soldiers were tried under Article 120 in two separate cases in the Military Court in Bandung and received very lenient prison sentences of between eleven and sixteen months and were fined Rp500 million (AU$50,000).[20] The prosecution appealed the lenient sentences, resulting in the five soldiers receiving the minimum of five years imprisonment for their involvement, although their fines were not adjusted.[21] The request for cassation was rejected by the Supreme Court.[22]

In mid-April 2012, a boat carrying thirty-four asylum seekers from Somalia, including Ali who was introduced in Chapter 1, ran aground in Sumbawa. Among the organizers of their voyage were two police officers from Lombok, who were later apprehended and prosecuted ("Dua polisi NTB" 2012; Kusmayadi 2012). Both were sentenced to five years and six months imprisonment and fined Rp500 million (AU$50,000).[23]

In late November 2013, three naval officers were caught red-handed escorting 106 Rohingya to Cipangikis, a beach in West Java ("Sebanyak 106 warga" 2013). According to the court documents of Malikus Soleh, a civilian member of the smuggling team, the naval officers only faced disciplinary measures and were transferred to other posts.[24] Like many other members of the military, police or immigration authorities who facilitate people-smuggling by, for example, acting as middlemen who arrange accommodation and transport for a commission, they will not be held responsible for their criminal activity because their cases have not reached the courts.

Earlier research into the prosecution of people smugglers in Indonesia has shown that people smugglers whose cases have gone to court have rarely been acquitted; it has also shown that many people smugglers who are arrested never go to court for a variety of reasons, many of which arise from corruption in the arresting and prosecuting authorities (Missbach and Crouch 2013). One example is the case of Imanuel Pulungan, a former immigration officer who was arrested, together with nine Afghans, at the airport in Kupang in 2010. Although he had retired, the fact that he was still wearing his old uniform suggested he was making use of his former status as an immigration official to smuggle people ("Bekingi Imigran Gelap" 2010). Local police launched an investigation but Pulungan never stood trial. Repeated inquiries of the police investigators of his case and the public prosecutor elicited differing explanations. The police claimed that the file had gone missing because the main investigator had died and that the computer on which case documents were stored had broken down rendering the documents irrecoverable.[25] The public prosecutor claimed that he had received an incomplete file from the police and that his request for additional information was never fulfilled.[26] He also mentioned that a medical assessment had allegedly determined that Pulungan suffered from health conditions that prevented him from standing trial, although no evidence of this was provided.

Although the numbers of convictions of people smugglers have steadily increased since the enactment of the new Law on Immigration in May 2011, people-smuggling networks have remained widespread and intact in Indonesia. Given that judges are more inclined to hand down the minimum sentence of five years and a Rp500 million (AU$50,000) fine to people found guilty of people-smuggling or even stay below the minimum sentence, rather than use their discretion to hand down longer prison terms and higher fines, the possibility of tougher sentences has not yet proven to be a serious deterrent for people smugglers. While high-end organizers residing outside Indonesia continue to avoid arrest and prosecution, middlemen, facilitators and drivers are easily recruited and replaced if they are arrested. Moreover, some smuggling coordinators who have been arrested and charged are believed to have continued to conduct their business during their incarceration (see Chapter 8). Overcrowding in Indonesian prisons has further lightened the sentences of people smugglers by guaranteeing reduction in their prison terms through remission and early release.

BORDER CONTROL

No longer simply "hallmarks of modern nation states" (Kimball 2007, p. 16) or the "skin of the living state" (Friedrich Ratzel, quoted in Eigmüller

2006, p. 4128), borders have become politicized boundaries (Pickering and Weber 2006). The twin phenomena of the securitization of borders and the criminalization of irregular border-crossing are highly visible all around the globe. Border control does not take place only at official entry and departure checkpoints, but has permeated way beyond actual borderlines and includes the monitoring of land and sea that is close to borders. Unlike Western countries in recent decades, Indonesia lacks sophisticated high-tech equipment for border surveillance, such as radar, infrared sensors and heartbeat detectors. Even in countries with highly developed systems for border control, people smugglers are often able fairly quickly to bypass them, casting their effectiveness in stemming migration flows into doubt (Papadopoulou-Kourkoula 2008, p. 108). People smugglers are always seeking remote spots and "they know that our patrol boats are inadequate to master the high seas".[27] It is, therefore, hardly surprising that roaming transit migrants have been seen in extremely remote spots they had previously avoided, such as Merauke in West Papua (Somba 2013).

Indonesia and Australia share a maritime border in the Indian Ocean. Unlike land borders with their wired fences, walls and traps, crossings of sea borders are less easily detected. Generally, the edge of the territorial sea is taken as the ultimate state border. With regard to the Java–Christmas Island boundary, however, the "boundary is a weighted median boundary reflecting in part the different coastal lengths of the two Islands" (Australia–Indonesia Maritime Delimitation Treaty 1997, p. 17).

Unlike other countries that rely on specialized coastguards to protect their borders, Indonesia has no single law-enforcement institution to monitor the sea and the maritime borders. Several departments, including immigration, fisheries and customs as well as the maritime police, the navy and the Maritime Security Coordination Board (Badan Koordinasi Keamanan Laut, Bakorkamla), handle aspects of maritime affairs, and all operate with inadequate funding and staff.

Indonesia's exceptional topography poses a perpetual challenge to its ability to exercise full control over its borders. The lack of control over those who enter or leave the country not only enables the undetected movement of transit migrants and Indonesian labour migrants but also jeopardizes the legal trade of natural resources, such as timber and sand (Obidzinski, Andrianto and Wijaya 2006; Basuki 2012). Monitoring and preventing illegal trade, especially in timber, generally takes precedence among Indonesian law enforcement officials over controlling the movement of migrants in Indonesian territory. As Dewi Fortuna Anwar (2012, p. 2), a prominent public commentator and advisor to the vice-president in Indonesia, has acknowledged, "The capacity of Indonesian agencies to tackle transnational threats to security such as people smuggling and the plunder of fishery resources is something that needs to be built up and will take time to become effective. Corruption among officials has also made law enforcement more difficult."

Because the interception of transit migrants at sea is costly, dangerous and beyond the technical means of the Indonesian authorities, the majority of arrests of transit migrants take place on land rather than at sea.[28] Given that many of the patrol boats are small, old-fashioned and not ocean-going, Indonesian authorities concentrate their efforts on preventing transit migrants from reaching the "watery borderlands" (Weber 2006, p. 32) where, unless their boats have broken down, it is often too late to intercept them. Boats are rarely intercepted, as illustrated by the case reported by the head of the operational section within the maritime police in Indonesia's southernmost province:

> Back in 2009 we were on a routine patrol between Rote and Ndao. That day there were three boats carrying out this patrol, one large boat from the National Police Headquarters and two smaller speedboats. Around noon, our radar was suddenly indicating a boat that was going south. We issued a warning, but the boat did not stop. By the time we had reached the boat we realised that it was loaded with people from the Middle East. We kept following the boat, but it still refused to stop. Thus, we tried to apply the standard operation procedures in order to stop that boat. It kept moving. As it then turned out, the passengers had taken the captain hostage. When they threw the captain into the water, we had to save him.[29]

In late 2011, the AFP gave three high-speed patrol boats to the Indonesian maritime police as part of a new policy initiative to enhance regional law-enforcement capacity in a package worth AU$7.1 million, which included AU$1 million for the vessels' operational costs until November 2012 ("Federal Police Provide" 2012, p. 3), but lack of funding for fuel now prevents the use of those boats in regular patrols. For example, the maritime police in Pelabuhan Ratu (West Java) have only two boats to patrol 117 km of coastline. They have funding for 800 litres of fuel a month, which is enough for only two hours' patrol a week (Powell 2012). A senior maritime police officer explained that his office would often receive phone calls from the AFP about suspected vessels carrying transit migrants, but "if we do not have money for BBM [fuel], we cannot put to sea, we can do nothing (*ya sudah — kita diam saja*)".[30] Another obstacle often mentioned in conversation with maritime police officers was the uneven concentration of border protection. Indonesia's limited resources tended to be located at frequent exit points, such as those in West Java, Bali, Lombok, and further east, rather than along the common entry points, such as in the Riau Archipelago and along the Sumatran coast.

Instead of the militarization of border control, as practised at the United States–Mexico border, Indonesian border control has been outsourced to the general public (Missbach 2014*a*). Civilians are not only employed as spies and moles in exchange for a small payment, but even as manipulators. For example, a senior police officer on Rote explained that the police would sometimes "hire" young boat crews to sabotage the asylum seeker boats, using such techniques as placing sugar in motors to disable them.[31] Generally, Indonesian police officers and special taskforce members have found that educating the coastal populations, especially impoverished fishermen, about the legal consequences of people-smuggling is a more promising alternative to intercepting boats at sea.[32] In collaboration with the IOM, hundreds of public information campaigns aimed at preventing local fishermen from becoming involved with people smugglers have been staged over the last five years, and continue in many parts of Indonesia to this day. However, even though financial and material incentives for state–civilian collaboration in border protection are offered, not all segments of society support stricter impediments on the movement of transit migrants. Popular sentiments I encountered in the field were often along the lines of "if they [asylum seekers] want to reach Australia, why would we block or impede that?" and "it is better if Indonesia does not hold them, let them go, don't arrest them and don't bring them back here".

A second cost-effective means of border control is the acceptance of extraterritorial control measures and advances carried out by Australian authorities. For example, there are strong indications that Indonesia has tolerated the campaigns of Australian intelligence agencies to disrupt and sabotage asylum seeker boats before they leave Indonesia (Balint 2005, p. 132; Pickering and Weber 2006, p. 59; Crock and Ghezelbash 2010, pp. 265, 267).[33] The controversial forced returns and tow-backs of asylum seeker boats in 2001 began again in late 2013 and will be described in more detail in Chapter 7. At this point it is sufficient to note that "Australia manages the movement of non-citizens across its border by, in effect, pushing the border offshore" (Karlsen, Phillips and Koleth 2011, p. 14).

SEARCH AND RESCUE

Over the last three years many voyages by transit migrants have ended in tragedy; unseaworthy boats and unpredictable weather have led to the loss of hundreds of lives. Some boats were stricken in the middle of the ocean; others were still quite close to the Indonesian mainland or had almost reached Christmas Island. Many disasters at sea, such as the SIEV X incident, in which about 353 people drowned, would have had less tragic outcomes if help had arrived earlier or at all (Kevin 2004). Many lives were lost in the waters between Indonesia and Australia before the search and rescue organizations of the two countries began to cooperate effectively after Indonesia became a party to the 1979 International Convention on Maritime Search and Rescue in August 2012, when it was finally able to guarantee that it could meet all of its binding responsibilities.[34] Prior to this, Australia and Indonesia had agreed on an arrangement for the coordination of search and rescue services (2004), which provided for less formality for each state to enter the other's territorial waters to respond to incidents.

Usually when a boat experiences engine failure or other sorts of distress, passengers on board with access to emergency telephone numbers try to get in contact with the Australian Maritime Safety Authority (AMSA). However, in extreme situations, or where there is no phone coverage, they are not always able to make contact. According to Indonesian Search and Rescue Services, asylum seekers do not ring the Indonesian authorities, as they "want to be rescued by Australia" (Haryadi 2013). In some instances, asylum seekers not in immediate danger have contacted the AMSA in order to speed up their pick-up by Australia. When Australian search and rescue services receive emergency calls from asylum seekers in distress, they usually inform their Indonesian counterparts, especially when the boat is still in Indonesian waters. However, Basarnas can only carry out search and rescue operations when they have received instructions from the Coordinating Minister for Political, Legal and Security Affairs (Kemenko Polhukam), and the full protocol required by the chain of command can take up valuable time in the rescue of those in distress.

In the last two years the number of maritime search and rescue operations involving transit migrants in Indonesia has increased from forty-seven in 2012 to eighty between January and November of 2013 (Haryadi 2013). Not only have rescue operations been impeded by Basarnas's limited access to resources such as aircraft and boats, but, in some cases, coordination between Australian and Indonesian institutions has also proved problematic. It is needless to stress that, if more border protection and detention funding were to be used for rescues, many more lives could be saved.

As signatories of the 1979 International Convention on Maritime Search and Rescue, both countries are obliged to help people in distress at sea and extend aid, regardless of the nationality, status, and circumstances of whoever is in distress. The convention does not, however, spell out which country has to accept the rescued people (Bateman 2013). Australia and Indonesia have repeatedly disagreed about disembarkation locations and responsibility for those on boats rescued or intercepted outside the territorial waters of the rescuing nation. In several incidents, rescued asylum seekers have refused to disembark in Indonesia. One such incident took place in April 2012, when a group of more than 120 Afghans and Tamil asylum seekers were rescued by a Singapore-registered tanker from a sinking boat in waters near Panaitan Island in the Sunda Strait and brought back to Merak in Banten province (Bachelard 2012a). The asylum seekers refused to disembark because they did not want to be assessed in Indonesia or to be detained in immigration detention centres, where some had already spent time. For several days they demanded a meeting with representatives from the Australian Embassy, but were eventually convinced by Indonesian authorities and the representatives of the UNHCR and IOM to leave the Singaporean ship after their demands had been repeatedly rejected ("Java Asylum-Seekers Refuse" 2012). They disembarked without violence.[35]

In another incident in Merak in November 2013, sixty-three asylum seekers were rescued by an Australian customs vessel about 120 nautical miles north-northwest of Christmas Island, outside Indonesia's territorial waters and within Australia's search-and-rescue zone (Salna 2013; Alford 2013d). Not wanting Indonesia to become "a dumping ground" for unwanted asylum seekers, Indonesian politicians argued that the asylum seekers had not been in immediate danger when they were first approached by an Australian Navy vessel, HMAS *Ballarat*.[36] The Indonesian co-ordinating minister for political, legal and security affairs, Djoko Suyanto, was quoted as saying "Australia already has its own 'detention centres' in Nauru and PNG.... That's where the asylum-seekers should be sent, not to Indonesia" (Alford 2013e). The stand-off between Jakarta and Canberra arose from the growing tensions sparked by Australia's "turn-back-the boats" intentions driven by the newly elected Australian prime minister, Tony Abbott. Having moved from its initial concessionary attitude, Indonesia now refuses to be Australia's accomplice in border protection and to serve as a buffer or filter for Australia's unwanted asylum seekers. The reasons for the growing bilateral tensions and the end of cooperation in the prevention of people-smuggling will be the main focus of the following chapter.

SUMMARY

When measured against Kimball's determinants of a transit country, Indonesia is a typical transit country in many respects. This chapter has demonstrated Indonesia's half-hearted stance in providing protection to asylum seekers and refugees. Although it has failed to become a signatory to the Refugee Convention and its protocol, Indonesia has used other international conventions it has ratified as a hedge, and has guaranteed the basic rights of transit migrants, such as the prevention of *refoulement* (Juanda 2012). More importantly, Indonesia exercises de facto toleration of transit migrants, even though it has failed to either codify their rights in national legislation or provide a legal framework for asylum seeker and refugee protection.[37]

As in other typical transit countries, the failure to provide proper protection for transit migrants results from subsuming questions of asylum under the logic of immigration control, which in turn has been accompanied by an increase in attention to border protection. In the last five years there has been an unprecedented degree of securitization of migration in Indonesia, which has been driven by fears that transit migrants are a threat to national security (Yonesta 2013). The securitization of migration is reflected in the many arrests of transit migrants who tried to leave the archipelago irregularly, amongst other things. However, lack of funding and resources has meant that Indonesia has not only relied on cost-efficient state–civilian collaboration in its borderlands but has also absorbed a lot of Australian funding and thinking. An increase in the number of transit migrants arrested and detained without due process has accompanied the increase in the number of suspected people smugglers arrested. But, as already stressed in previous chapters, Indonesia lacks the capacity to host all of the transit migrants arrested and, more generally, does not know what to do with them. With regard to the prosecution of those involved in people-smuggling, intensification of law enforcement has not brought about the desired outcomes. The prosecution and sentencing of those involved at the lower end of the people-smuggling chain promises little for ending the irregular departure of transit migrants for Australia.

The politically half-hearted approach towards providing proper protection for asylum seekers and the indecision of politicians in coming up with any strategy on what to do with their growing numbers carry many risks. As Asep Kurnia (2011, p. vii) has warned, "the issue of illegal immigrants is a very sensitive and multidimensional issue that can easily be politicised". More conservative commentators have already paved the way for increasingly xenophobic sentiment in Indonesia by making statements along the lines of Meliala's repeated assertion that "issues surrounding human smuggling will, sooner or later, disturb Indonesian national security" (Meliala 2011, p. 107) and "illegal migrants will disrupt the national unity (*persatuan dan kesatuan bangsa*)" (Meliala 2011, p. 48). Anti-asylum-seeker propaganda could easily be used by any nationalistic politician to win votes in future elections, just as it has been used in Europe. Without a firm political line, the Indonesian government will continue to meander between providing half-hearted, ad hoc protection whenever it seems suitable and increasing securitization of migration issues whenever protection does not seem suitable. Its response to the presence of transit migrants in its territory will be shaped by the politics of the day rather than by any carefully considered strategy. Without new policy initiatives, Indonesia — as a transit country — could soon turn into a dead end.

Notes

1. Interview with Tariq, 28 February 2012, Cisarua.
2. For example, Rafendi Djamin, executive director of the Human Rights Working Group, a coalition of Indonesian NGOs, made this point on ABC TV's Q&A panel discussion on 4 July 2013, entitled "More Than Beef, Boats and Bali".
3. Kimball does not specify whether she includes both sea and land borders.
4. Articles 3 and 4 fail to elaborate on exactly what constitutes a "political crime". The Circular Letter also fails to establish any process for determining whether the precondition has been met.
5. According to Tri Nuke Pudjiastuti and Enny Suprapto, there was no case in which the provisions were applied directly. At the time, Indonesia was

very responsive towards refugees from communist countries and tried to demonstrate its concern for human rights to the international community (personal communication, 2 January 2014).

6. The directive cites Letters of the Director General of Immigration No. F4.IL.01.10-2.198 dated 7 February 2001 on Illegal Migrants/Asylum Seekers and the Letter of the Director General of Immigration No. F.IL.01.10.562 dated 14 May 2001 concerning the handling of illegal migrants from South Asia.

7. Or, in cases where the alien who is seeking asylum at immigration entry points far away from the UNHCR office, immigration officials shall contact the UNHCR and coordinate arrangements with the airline concerned until the arrival of the UNHCR official (Point 4).

8. Punishment for aliens who enter Indonesia without legitimate travel documents and valid visas is given in Article 119(1) as five years' imprisonment and a fine of up to Rp500 million (AU$50,000). It is also an offence for a foreigner to knowingly use a false travel document (Article 119[2]).

9. In the elucidation of the law, "special treatment" means that, unlike other detainees, "victims of trafficking and human smuggling" are not fully subjected to the regulations imposed at the detention centres.

10. See, for example, Regulation by the Minister of Home Affairs No. 49/2010 on Guidelines for Monitoring Foreigners and Foreign Community Organisations in the Region.

11. Decree of the Coordinating Minister for Political, Legal and Security Affairs No. KEP-10/MENKO/POLHUKAM/1/2013 on the [Establishment of a] Desk for Handling People-Smuggling, Refugees and Asylum Seekers.

12. Interview with the head of the Provincial Anti-People-Smuggling Taskforce, 17 October 2012, Batam.

13. Interview with a senior provincial intelligence officer, 2 May 2012, Kupang.

14. Interview with prosecutor of the Provincial Prosecution in West Java, 9 November 2012, Bandung.

15. Interview with the head of investigation at the Provincial Maritime Police, 26 November 2013, Merak.

16. Prosecutors and judges can order a suspect to be remanded for a further twenty days, but, if the evidence against the suspect is not yet complete within that time, the suspect must be released.

17. For a detailed analysis of the Trenggalek case, see Crouch and Missbach (2013).

18. Supreme Court Decision No. 42-K/PM.III-13/AD/VIII/2012, 27 September 2012 (Kornelius Nama and others); Supreme Court Decision No. 86-K/PMT.III/BDG/AD/XI/2012, 11 December 2012 (Kornelius Nama and others); Military High Court III Surabaya (East Java) Decision No. 86-K/PMT.III/BDG/AD/XI/2012, 11 December 2012 (Kornelius Nama); Military High Court III Surabaya

(East Java) Decision No. 79-K/PMT.III/BDG/AD/XI/2012, 11 December 2012 (Ilmun Abdul Said); Military Court III Madiun (East Java) Decision No. 38-K/PM.III-13/AD/VII/2012, 24 September 2012 (Ilmun Abdul Said).

19. Military Court II of Yogyakarta Decision No. 49-K/PM.II-11/AD/V/2012, 5 December 2012 (Amin Rukmakmur); Military High Court of Jakarta Decision No. 10-K/BDG/PMT-II/AD/I/2013, 12 February 2013 (Amin Rukmakmur) and Supreme Court Decision No. 105-K/MIL/2013, 18 June 2013 (Amin Rukmakmur).

20. Military Court of Bandung Decision No. 203-K/PM.II-09/AD/X/2012, 20 December 2012 (Rustam Mamulaty) and Military Court of Bandung Decision No. 215-K/PM.II09/AD/X/2012, 3 January 2013 (Rahman Tuasalamony).

21. Military High Court of East Jakarta Decision No. 34-K/BDG/PMT-II/AD/III/2013, 5 April 2013 (Rustam Mamulaty et al.) and Military High Court of East Jakarta Decision No. 35-K/BDG/PMT-II/AD/III/2013, 5 April 2013 (Rahman Tuasalamony).

22. Supreme Court Decision No. 171K/MIL/2013, 17 September 2013 (Rahman Tuasalamony).

23. District Court of Selong Decision No. 150/Pid.B/2012/PN.Sel, 27 November 2012 (Eka Gusmansyah and Mahyun) and High Court of Mataram Decision No. 10/PID/2013/PT.MTR, 11 February 2013 (Eka Gusmansyah and Mahyun).

24. District Court of Garut Decision No. 21/Pid.Sus/2014/PN.Grt, 26 March 2014 (Malikus Soleh).

25. Interviews with members of the Special Unit for the Surveillance of Foreigners at the District Police Office, 27 April and 22 May 2012, Kupang.

26. Interview with prosecutor at District Prosecution Office, 18 June 2012, Kupang.

27. Interview with the head of investigation at the Provincial Maritime Police, 26 November 2013, Merak.

28. Interviews with the head of investigation at the Provincial Maritime Police, 26 November 2013, Merak, and members of the District Maritime Police, 22 March 2012, Sekupang.

29. Interview, 18 June 2012, Kupang.

30. Interview, 18 June 2012, Kupang.

31. Interview, 30 April 2012, Rote.

32. Interview with the head of investigation at the Provincial Maritime Police, 26 November 2013, Merak.

33. Tony Kevin (2012, p. 61) mentions that the AFP and the Indonesian police cooperated in disruption campaigns from 1999 to 2001 and again from 2009 to 2011.

34. Search and rescue on the high seas is regulated by international conventions

as well as by agreements between individual countries. Conventions relevant to the waters between Australia and Indonesia include the 1982 United Nations Convention on the Law of the Sea (UNCLOS), the 1974 International Convention for the Safety of Life at Sea (SOLAS) and the 1979 International Convention on Maritime Search and Rescue (SAR).

35. Personal observation in Merak, 12 April 2012.
36. Contradictory media releases from Indonesian and Australian sources obscure the details of this group of asylum seekers. Indonesian Basarnas officers claimed that Australia had towed the asylum seekers' boat closer to the Indonesian coast before informing Basarnas, but these claims were denied by the Australian Minister of Immigration (Hamer 2013).
37. Interview with the head of the Research Section for International Law and Regulations, Komnas HAM, 10 January 2012, Jakarta.

7

TIDAL EBB AND FLOW: THE INDONESIA–AUSTRALIA RELATIONSHIP

> The Indonesian government needs to be wary of Australia's measures
> and policies, which are turning Indonesia into a fortress that
> fences off refugees and asylum seekers so that they cannot get to
> Australia. Eventually, Indonesia itself will be "flooded" with
> refugees and asylum seekers.
> (Komnas HAM 2012, p. 10)

Relations between Indonesia and Australia are often marked by extreme ups and downs (Brown 2013; Bhakti 2013). Even though Australia has at times been Indonesia's largest aid donor, rapid changes in political mood and underlying mutual mistrust have affected their relationship during the last fifteen years. The issues that have dominated the political agenda, and at times caused serious misunderstanding, have mostly been connected to Islamic terrorism and threats to Indonesia's sovereignty from both local separatism and irregular migration. Since 2009, when the number of asylum seekers coming to Australia by boat started to increase dramatically, the primary objective of Australian politicians has been to put an end to their movement, using a number of different battle cries, such as "stopping the people-smuggler business model" and just "stopping the boats", which ignore the plight of the people in "the boats".

Aware that stopping the movement of asylum seekers could not be achieved without the support of Indonesia, Australian politicians tried hard to win concessions from Indonesia by offering substantial incentives, while exerting constant political pressure but often ignoring issues that were important to successive Indonesian governments. As Meidyatama Suryodiningrat, the *Jakarta Post*'s editor-in-chief, noted during a TV panel discussion in July 2013, Australia should not have "unreasonable expectations" when it comes to dealing with irregular migration,[1] given that Indonesia faces many more serious problems with the regular and irregular labour migration of its national workforce and the frequent abuse of labour migrants, especially in Malaysia and Saudi Arabia. Although Indonesia agreed to join Australia-driven anti-people-smuggling initiatives, extended its border control and detention facilities for irregular travellers, and changed laws regulating immigration issues (as outlined in Chapter 6), it has at times complied only reluctantly with Australia's requests. Australia's continuing failure to acknowledge Indonesia's priorities and its repeated overstepping of the boundaries of its authority have caused extreme frustration in Indonesian government circles.

This chapter directs attention to the influence that the issue of transit migrants has had on relations between the Indonesian and Australian governments over the last fifteen years. It seeks to provide, first of all, an overview of how Indonesia–Australia relations have dealt with transiting asylum seekers and people-smuggling under several administrations in order to explain the downward spiral that culminated in the freezing of collaboration in the apprehension of people smugglers in November 2013. It then discusses a selection of topics that are particularly telling of the current unease in the bilateral relationship. These include detention and maltreatment of underage Indonesian people smugglers in Australia, failed attempts to establish an offshore processing centre in Indonesia, unsuccessful requests for the extradition of non-Indonesian people smugglers from Indonesia to Australia, and interference in Indonesian sovereignty, especially the violation of maritime borders during tow-back operations.

During the first few years after the fall of Soeharto, Indonesia was rather inward-looking but soon developed more interest and, more significantly, gained more confidence in foreign affairs, which was demonstrated by a new international activism and by several attempts to contribute to conflict resolution in the Middle East (McIntyre and Ramage 2008, p. 40). As the largest member state of ASEAN, Indonesia has made claims for leadership in the region. Australia has not, so far, given due acknowledgement of these trends, but has often revealed a rather condescending and patronizing attitude in its treatment of Indonesia, smoothed by the provision of very substantial amounts of aid. Australia's persistent courtship of Indonesia to win (or purchase) its favour culminated in a nasty relationship break-up.

BILATERAL RELATIONS: PRESSURE AND RELUCTANT COMPLIANCE

The increasingly restrictive migration and border policies of Western destination countries are intended to contain asylum seekers in transit countries. Just as the EU has created containment and buffer zones at its external supranational borders, Australia wishes to shield itself from unwanted asylum seekers, even though Australia lacks the gravity in the Asia-Pacific region of the EU member states within Europe and beyond because of their economic and political significance. Australia has spent very large amounts on reinforcing its border protection measures and deterring unwanted asylum seekers. For example, in the 2009–10 federal budget the Australian government provided AU$654 million to fund a comprehensive, whole-of-government strategy to combat people-smuggling and address the problem of unauthorized boat arrivals (Phillips and Spinks 2013). Expenditure estimates in the 2013–14 budget for the Australian Customs and Border Protection Service amounted to a total of AU$1,424,385,000 (Australian Government 2013, p. 78).

In order to achieve desired outcomes, "transit states are being courted [by destination countries], financially enticed and diplomatically pressured to control their borders and detain transit migrants" (Kimball 2007, p. 39). Rutvica Andrijasevic and William Walters (2010, p. 984) have remarked that "some 'choices' made by governments in the global South are going to be more 'voluntary' than others. But it is important to note the extent to which international government today operates and is legitimated not by direct coercion but by its elicitation of the active involvement of the states of the global South." Consistent with their comments, Australia has used diplomatic pressure to win Indonesia's support for Australian government objectives. It has pressured Indonesia to, first and foremost, criminalize people-smuggling and make other changes, such as in its policies relating to issuing visas on arrival for certain nationalities (as outlined in Chapter 3). More significantly, Australian diplomatic pressure has been cushioned by generous incentives, mostly in the form of cash distribution, aid programmes, training programmes, and capacity-building equipment (Taylor 2008; Kuncara 2010; Nethery and Gordyn 2014; Nethery, Rafferty-Brown and Taylor 2013). In 2008 Australia contributed AU$7.9 million to develop further Indonesia's border movement alert system (CEKAL) to improve the detection of people of concern and to help prevent people-smuggling and irregular migration (Bowen 2008). A year later, Australia helped implement the computerization of the main border-crossing warning system in five of Indonesia's major ports, which cost more than AU$10 million ("Australia–Indonesia Border" 2009).

Without doubt, "Australia needs Indonesia to cope with and reduce the number of illegal arrivals and people smuggling" (Kuncara 2010, p. 94). While Australia was clearly putting its own national security and public safety first, it wrapped the financial incentives and cooperation it offered in the language of "burden-sharing" to obscure the reality of the burden-shifting that was going on. Mochamad Tatra Kuncara remarked that these financial contributions "reflect Australia's national interests in Indonesia" (Kuncara 2010, p. 92). Relying on the collaboration it had bought at considerable cost through diplomatic pressure and incentives, Australia extended its presence in the region. Since 2001 the presence in Jakarta, Kuala Lumpur and Colombo of Australian Customs and Border Protection Service, the AFP, ASIO and immigration officials have increased significantly (Wesley 2007). The AFP has also received funding for more officers to support the Indonesian National Police and for the establishment of a new liaison post in Sri Lanka. Although the AFP can neither carry out anti-people-smuggling operations on its own nor be involved in interceptions outside Australian territorial waters, the extent to which it has exercised indirect influence has been extraordinary (Hoffman 2010*a*, p. 10; Marr and Wilkinson 2003, p. 42*f*). Australian activities in Indonesia have included collecting intelligence on upcoming voyages, offering cash and other incentives to cooperative Indonesian officials to help prevent voyages from leaving, and disrupting people-smuggling operations (Kevin 2012, p. 12). By moving its mobility and migration barriers offshore, Australia has succeeded, at least sometimes, in reducing the number of asylum seekers arriving in Australia by boat (Mares 2001; Phillips and Spinks 2013).

While the complexities of irregular migration and life in transit are often hard to comprehend, governments have shown that they are much more ready to comply with measures to stop or at least combat irregular migration than they are to accept the need to improve measures for handling asylum seekers. Similar to their counterparts in the EU, Australia and Indonesia have focused in their policymaking on how to prevent irregular migration and not on how to provide options for more regular alternatives. Indonesia is, after all, no more willing to deal with transit migrants for any length of time than is Australia, which has invested much in ensuring Indonesian cooperation in their exclusion from Australian territory. The current dominant perception in Indonesia is encapsulated in the words of Dewi Anwar Fortuna, a senior adviser to the Indonesian vice president, who said that "both Indonesia and Australia are victims [of smuggling]" (Alberici 2013). Indonesia's perception of itself as "victim" and its victim mentality do not stop here. According to Hassan Wirajuda, former foreign minister, "Indonesia is actually a victim of Australia's attractiveness" (Busyra 2014). The dominance of such a perception must not, however, be allowed to obscure the fact that any success the Australian–Indonesian collaboration may have in abolishing people-smuggling will have significant negative repercussions for the ability of asylum seekers to achieve effective protection in the Asia-Pacific region (Nethery and Gordyn 2014).

The Howard Years (1996–2006): Megaphone Diplomacy and Cartoon Wars

Indonesia and Australia drew up agreements for its police forces to cooperate in the investigation and prosecution of transnational crime as early as 1991 (Anwar 2002). However, in the course of the so-called Timor crisis following the East Timorese independence referendum of 30 August 1999, Indonesia abrogated the 1995 Australia–Indonesia Agreement on Maintaining Security and the Australia–Indonesia defence cooperation (Wesley 2007, p. 84). The reason for the abrogation was the deployment of Australian troops as part of the International Force for East Timor (INTERFET) in Indonesian territory shortly after the referendum that cemented East Timor's secession from Indonesia. Although the Indonesian government had accepted the international peacekeeping force, the decision was unpopular. Indonesia was puzzled by the Australian intervention, as it was not consistent with Australia's previous stance towards East Timor, which had been in full support of the Indonesian annexation (McDougall 2011). According to Michael Wesley (2007, p. 100), "the East Timor crisis left lingering suspicions among Indonesian elites and the public that Australia's ultimate intention was to break up Indonesia into several lesser units". When violent separatist conflicts emerged in other parts of Indonesia, such as in Aceh, West Papua, the Moluccas and Kalimantan, it was suspected that Australia might also have been involved in instigating these upheavals (Wesley 2007, p. 179). Once Indonesia had withdrawn from military cooperation with Australia, including from the exchange of intelligence data and from joint patrols after the East Timor crisis, the resulting vacuum allowed more asylum seekers to enter Indonesia (Anwar 2002, p. 71).

The state of the relationship between Indonesia and Australia deteriorated to the extent that both President Habibie and General Wiranto, then supreme commander of the Indonesian Armed Forces and minister of defence and security, refused to take phone calls from Prime Minister Howard (Wesley 2007, p. 178). Abdurrahman Wahid, before he became Indonesia's fourth president in October 1999, referred to Australia's pressure on Indonesia to fulfil its international obligations in East Timor as "pissing in our face" (Tanter 2000). Nevertheless, relations improved surprisingly quickly and in 2000 both countries agreed on a Regional Cooperation Model, aimed at disrupting people-smuggling operations but containing no guarantee of protection of refugees. Their agreement also promoted Indonesia's toleration of Australia's externalization of its border-control practices and its disruption programmes within Indonesian territory. The Indonesian government temporarily suspended this agreement on 12 September 2001, as a result of diplomatic tension over the *Tampa* incident, when the Norwegian freighter, MV *Tampa* rescued 438 people, mainly Hazaras, from a sinking Indonesian fishing vessel en route to Australia (summarized in Chapter 2). The *Tampa* incident destroyed the newly recovered bilateral relationship because Australia's conservative government under Prime Minister Howard insisted that the Indonesian government take back the *Tampa* passengers, all the while ignoring Australia's obligations as a signatory of the Refugee Convention. Howard even accused Indonesia of not fulfilling its international obligations by refusing to take back the rescued asylum seekers. Indonesians felt that they had become Australia's scapegoat, because Australia alleged that Indonesia was allowing migrants who wished to reach Australia to use

Indonesia as a place of transit, where their presence not only disturbed Indonesian–Australian relations but was also a burden on Indonesia (Sitohang 2002, p. 41).

Disappointed by the Australian government's "megaphone diplomacy", in which sensitive issues were always shared with the media before they were exchanged with Indonesian officials, President Megawati Sukarnoputri, who became president of Indonesia in July 2001, also refused to talk to Howard over the phone or meet any visiting Australian statesmen (Metcalfe 2010, p. 28; Wesley 2007, p. 181). Several visits to Jakarta made by Howard, Minister for Immigration Philip Ruddock and Foreign Minister Alexander Downer between 2000 and 2001 to convince Indonesia to accept more responsibility for transiting asylum seekers failed. In particular, Indonesia rejected a plan for an Australian-funded refugee-processing centre within its territory. Given that in the early 2000s Indonesia was coping with more than 1.3 million internally displaced people because of political unrest in its own territory and that the memories of the Galang experience (outlined in Chapter 2) were still fresh, Indonesia had no interest at all in such proposals, not least because there was such a stark absence of any shared position between the two governments on the asylum-seeker issue. Relations between Australia and Indonesia, under both Abdurrahman Wahid and Megawati, remained difficult through 2001, and it was not until after the sinking of SIEV X near Java on 19 October 2001, when 353 people lost their lives, that Indonesia became more open to finding a multilateral solution for transit migrants.

In late February 2002, Indonesia and Australia agreed to be the co-chairs of a Regional Ministerial Conference on People Smuggling, Trafficking in Persons and Related Transnational Crime in Bali, which was followed by many similar meetings, workshops and annual conferences, thus instituting what has become known as the Bali Process, which some have hailed as a significant Australian success in transnational diplomacy. The Bali Process aims to increase regional awareness of the consequences of people-smuggling, trafficking in persons and transnational crime and to improve coordination and cooperation on these issues. Representatives of thirty-eight countries and of the UNHCR and IOM attended the initial conference in Bali. The Australian participants planned the conference meetings in "minute detail", from the speaking order to the supposedly spontaneous comments, leaving nothing to chance (Wesley 2007, p. 196). In June 2002, Indonesia signed an agreement with Australia that focused solely on combatting people smugglers and transnational crime and on developing police cooperation, but left out any consideration of the protection and human rights of transit migrants (HRW 2002). In particular, the People Smuggling Disruption Program, a very secretive joint initiative of the AFP and the Indonesian police, was viewed with scepticism because of its lack of transparency. Former diplomat Tony Kevin made a string of allegations about the involvement of newly trained Indonesian police officers in the sinking of the SIEV X; they had just been taught disruption techniques by their Australian counterparts (Kevin 2004).

Further dissonance occurred in the bilateral relationship in November 2003, when the Australian Navy forced the *Mimosa Bone*, with fourteen Kurdish asylum seekers on board, back into Indonesian waters after they had landed on Melville Island. Despite the fact that they landed on Australian territory that was yet to be excised from the Australian migration zone, their claims for asylum were not heard. Although Indonesia had not protested previous tow-backs when they had first occurred in 2001, mainly because the Indonesian government had not been given any information about the operations (see Chapter 2), this time Indonesian authorities were informed and the government was able to protest. Yusril Ihza Mahendra, Indonesian minister for justice, stated that the deportation of these fourteen Kurdish Turks was possible and was Indonesia's preference (Petersen, Banham and Riley 2003; Osborne 2013), but in the end Indonesia did not follow through on this threat (Taylor 2013).

Although the reactions of Australia and Indonesia to the terrorist attacks of 11 September 2001 differed, with Indonesia condemning the United States' invasion of Afghanistan and Iraq and criticizing Australia's participation (McDougall 2006, p. 117), acts of religious terrorism in Indonesia affecting both Indonesian and Australian citizens brought the two countries closer together. In the aftermath of the Bali bombings on 12 October 2002 in the tourist district of Kuta, which killed 202 people, including eighty-eight Australians and thirty-four Indonesians, anti-terrorism police collaboration and intelligence were intensified in the investigation of the bombings and the prevention of future attacks, forging closer ties between Australian and Indonesian agencies. For example, in February 2004 the Indonesian and Australian governments announced the establishment of the Jakarta Centre for Law Enforcement Cooperation (JCLEC) in Semarang. Its development and operations attracted AU$36.8 million of Australian funding from 2004 to 2009 (JCLEC 2005). Inaugurated by President Megawati Sukarnoputri in July 2004, JCLEC offers training and workshops for police and law enforcement officers on transnational criminal activities, such as the narcotics trade, maritime crime, people-smuggling, child sex tourism and cybercrime.

Indonesian–Australian relations further improved when Susilo Bambang Yudhoyono became president in October 2004 (McDougall 2011). Not only was development aid to Indonesia boosted, but Australia also contributed generously to the post-tsunami reconstruction in Aceh and the post-earthquake recovery in Yogyakarta (together more than AU$1 billion) (Lindsey 2010). In 2005, both countries adopted a Joint Declaration on Comprehensive Partnership, which states their wish to "increase our cooperation in combating other forms of transnational crime and non-traditional security threats, especially in areas such as people smuggling, narcotics, outbreaks of disease and money laundering" (Joint Declaration 2005). The intention of forging closer partnerships between police forces, immigration and customs officials, and security and intelligence agencies, was further cemented by the 2006 Agreement on the Framework for Security Cooperation (the Lombok Treaty). However, before the Lombok Treaty was signed, a few more sensitive political challenges needed to be endured.

Although the number of boats carrying Middle-Eastern asylum seekers from Indonesia to Australia had sharply declined with the initiation of the Pacific Solution (Phillips and Spinks 2013), a different kind of boat people made their way to Australia in January 2006 and their requests for asylum reignited diplomatic tensions. This group included thirty-six adults and seven children from West Papua, Indonesia's easternmost province where separatist conflict has long persisted. They landed on Cape York in a traditional outrigger boat after five days at sea. Although President Yudhoyono asked Prime Minister Howard not to grant them refugee status, forty-two of the forty-three applicants were issued temporary protection visas in March 2006. Australia, taking into account the Indonesian government sentiment, had up to this point taken an accommodating stance towards asylum seekers from Papua (Palmer 2006), but the Indonesian government interpreted this decision as Australian support for Papua's secession from Indonesia. Protesting the decision, the Indonesian government withdrew its ambassador from Canberra and placed all cooperative activities on hold (Neumann and Taylor 2010).

Anger at Australia's decision was shared by the Indonesian media. One popular newspaper, *Rakyat Merdeka*, published a cartoon depicting Prime

Minister Howard mounting his foreign minister, Alexander Downer, for a spot of buggery and saying "I want Papua!! Alex! Try to make it happen." The reply to this cartoon came swiftly in the *Weekend Australian*, which published a cartoon depicting President Yudhoyono as a dog mounting a Papuan and declaring "Don't take this the wrong way", with the caption "no offence intended". The cartoon war certainly had a bad effect on the relationship between Indonesia and Australia, but less emotive politicians tried to smooth ruffled feathers behind the scenes.

The Lombok Treaty, signed in November 2006, brought an end to the crisis (Mackie 2007). Not only did the treaty state the two countries' intention to intensify bilateral relations and to engage more in dialogue and consultation, but it also spelled out a closer "cooperation between relevant institutions and agencies, including prosecuting authorities, in preventing and combating transnational crimes, in particular crimes related to a) people smuggling and trafficking in persons" ("Agreement between the Republic" 2006).

Labor Governments in Search of "Solutions"

Although one of the first policy changes ushered in by newly elected Prime Minister Kevin Rudd (December 2007–June 2010) was to end the expensive Pacific Solution by closing down the camps in Manus and Nauru (Metcalfe 2010; Grewcock 2013), the approach of the incoming Labor government towards maritime asylum seekers did not differ fundamentally from that of its conservative predecessors, and such things as mandatory and indefinite detention of unauthorized arrivals continued. The new Australian government was strongly committed to preventing asylum seekers from coming to Australia by boat, and the foreign policies it pursued in relation to Indonesia continued to be shaped by national interest and domestic issues (McDougall 2011). Whereas Australia was able to implement successfully what Michael Grewcock (2014, p. 75) has labelled "a more direct neocolonial relationship" in Nauru and Papua New Guinea by providing generous aid and cash contributions, Indonesia was less inclined to comply with Australia's demands for the establishment of facilities for detaining and processing asylum seekers outside Australian territory. Soon the issue of transiting asylum seekers became a "*kerikil* (pebble) in the shoe" of Australian–Indonesian relations (Kuncara 2010, p. 77).[2]

The capacity of the detention centre opened in 2008 to hold 800 newly arrived asylum seekers on Christmas Island was soon found to be inadequate; upgrading the centre to accommodate 1,400 proceeded too slowly. Two events of October 2009, in particular, affected Indonesian–Australian relations and marked the failure of Prime Minister Rudd's search for an "Indonesian Solution".

On 10 October 2009, Prime Minister Rudd telephoned President Yudhoyono to request the Indonesian interception of the *Jaya Lestari*, a boat with 254 asylum seekers on board bound for Australia. With the support of the Australian Navy, the boat was returned to an industrial harbour in Merak, Banten province, where it was stuck for the next six months, as its passengers refused to disembark (Ford, Lyons and Palmer 2010). Even though the Australian government pledged AU$50 million to fund policing and the processing of the asylum seekers in Indonesia in the hope that this would induce Indonesia to become more proactive in restricting the mobility of transit migrants, Rudd's request was rebuffed. The unwillingness of the passengers, fearing indefinite detention in Indonesia, to leave the boat caused Sujatmiko, the Indonesian Foreign Ministry's director for diplomatic security, to warn Australia that "an issue this small could damage the relationship between the two countries" (Fitzpatrick 2009*b*). In the same month, another boat with seventy-eight asylum seekers on board was turned back to Indonesia after the Australian customs vessel *Oceanic Viking* had responded to distress calls and rescued the passengers. At first, these passengers were also supposed to be taken to Merak, but, to prevent the two groups of rescued asylum seekers from forming an alliance, they were eventually taken to an Australian-funded detention centre on Bintan in the Riau Archipelago, where their arrival was strenuously resisted by the provincial government (Allard and Coorey 2009). Once more, Indonesia raised objections to the passengers' refusal to disembark, their hunger strike, and Australia's broken promises to resettle all those passengers found to be genuine refugees within twelve weeks (Grewcock 2013). Teuku Faizasyah, a senior Foreign Ministry spokesman summarized them in his question, "why is there not an Australian solution" instead of an Indonesian solution (Allard 2009)?

Despite the irritation caused by the *Oceanic Viking* and *Jaya Lestari* incidents, which once more revealed the dilemma of transit migrants in transit countries where they had neither formal right of residence nor effective protection, the relationship between Australia and Indonesia soon improved, in part because of the personal amity between Rudd and Yudhoyono, but more because of a series of high-level meetings and visits that culminated in the signing of the "Implementation Framework for Cooperation to Combat People Smuggling and Trafficking in Persons" in March 2010 when the Indonesian president visited Canberra. During his visit, Yudhoyono addressed a joint sitting of the House of Representatives and the Senate, the first Indonesian president ever to do so. In his address he spoke of a "love-hate relationship" and a "fair dinkum relationship" between Australia and Indonesia, which had evolved into a model partnership that, although not without its challenges, was attracting the envy of other countries. Yudhoyono also noted that government-to-government ties had never been better and announced that a new law would make people-smuggling a crime in Indonesia (Dodd 2010). It was not long, however, before the next mood swing.

The Australian government soon returned to its search for new regional solutions, but without Prime Minister Rudd. Under the leadership of Julia Gillard, who replaced Rudd in June 2010, the government renewed the search for "solutions" anywhere but in Australia. After approaching Papua New Guinea, the Australian government made advances in early July in an attempt to convince East Timor to establish a regional processing centre so that processing of maritime arrivals in Australia could be eliminated. The East Timor Solution did not win the support of the East Timorese government and did not proceed (Grewcock 2013).

Throughout the term of the governments of Rudd and Gillard, regional conferences, workshops and meetings under the Bali Process continued and the importance of reducing "irregular migration in the Asia and Pacific region" through greater bilateral and multilateral cooperation between source, transit and destination countries was repeatedly stressed. From the Bali Process emerged an inclusive and non-binding Regional Cooperation Framework (RCF), endorsed in 2011 (Regional Cooperation Framework 2011). It was hoped that the RCF would encourage Bali Process members to establish practical arrangements to ensure consistent processing of asylum claims, durable solutions for refugees, the sustainable repatriation of those not deemed to be in need of protection and the targeting of people-smuggling networks. Nevertheless, a further embarrassing episode was looming for Australia as the Bali Process proceeded. In July 2011 Australia convinced the Malaysian government to sign an agreement similar to the readmission agreements that the EU had forced upon its neighbours in order to remove unwanted asylum seekers. It allowed for the transfer of 800 unauthorized arrivals in Australian territory to Malaysia, in exchange for resettlement in Australia of 4,000 refugees who went through "proper procedures" in Malaysia over the next four years. The "Malaysian solution" was stopped on 31 August 2011 by the Australian High Court, which declared the agreement unlawful on two grounds. First, Malaysia was not a signatory of the Refugee Convention and reports of inhumane treatment of asylum seekers, refugees and irregular labour migrants in Malaysia indicated that it was not a suitable destination country (Grewcock 2013). Secondly, the Australian immigration minister had intended to return unaccompanied minors in this deal, but it was found that he, as the legal guardian of these children, would be violating their right to protection and safety if they were sent to Malaysia (Wood and McAdam 2012).

After two fatal incidents at sea, in which more than ninety asylum seekers lost their lives, the exasperated Labor government established the Expert Panel on Asylum Seekers in June 2012, led by retired air chief marshal Angus Houston, to advise the government on "how best to prevent asylum seekers risking their lives by travelling to Australia by boat" (Expert Panel 2012, p. 9).[3] In its recommendations, the panel advised the government to increase the annual humanitarian intake to 20,000 refugees and to draft new legislation that would enable the forced transfer of maritime arrivals to Nauru and Papua New Guinea so that they could be processed there. It also proposed reopening the camps on Nauru and Manus Island. By stressing that maritime asylum seekers would gain no advantage if they arrived by boat, the government tried to deter future asylum seekers from getting on the boats. The recommendations of the Houston Panel were welcomed in Indonesia. Johnny Hutauruk, the deputy head of Indonesia's Human Trafficking, Refugees and Asylum Seekers Desk, stated that "it would be good if Australia could take many of them [registered asylum seekers], all of them if possible" (Bachelard 2012c). Before the Houston Panel had made its recommendations, Indonesian officials had urged Australia to accept a larger number of the refugees who were stuck in the Southeast Asian region for permanent resettlement (Bachelard 2012b).

Despite its fierce warnings, the Australian government's approach had little effect, and more asylum seekers arrived on Australian territory. Newly arrived maritime arrivals underwent a pre-transfer assessment conducted by the Department of Immigration and Citizenship to determine whether it was "reasonably practicable" for them to be transferred and, by the end of 2012, 155 people had been transferred to Manus Island and 414 to Nauru where their claims for protection were to be assessed by the governments of Papua New Guinea and Nauru respectively (Phillips and Spinks 2013). If found to be genuine refugees, they would be eligible for resettlement in Australia within an unspecified period of time, as the Gillard government insisted on a "no advantage" principle that required those deemed to be genuine refugees to wait as long as refugees elsewhere to be resettled, which could be many years.

Even though Indonesia had made domestic changes which were intended to deter asylum seekers from coming into its territory, Australia kept making further demands for Indonesia to play a greater role in preventing people-smuggling, but Indonesia's concessions came at a price. For example, Indonesia expected Australia to release underage Indonesian people smugglers, some of whom were held in adult prisons (most of them have now been released). Indonesia, under pressure from Australia, did not hesitate to express its disappointment, as it did when it became common knowledge that some people smugglers were refugees now living in Australia and managing people-smuggling operations from there. Foreign Minister Marty Natalegawa asked in June 2012: "How can such alleged major people smugglers receive permits to live in Australia while others, including children, are put in detention despite being victims themselves of the people-smuggling rings?" (Saragih 2012a).

While more restrictions were being imposed on asylum seekers and refugees in Australia, such as those affecting their right to work and earn income (Grewcock 2013), on 27 June 2013, just a few weeks before the Australian federal election, Kevin Rudd was reinstated as prime minister. During Rudd's visit to Indonesia nine days later, President Yudhoyono announced a summit on people-smuggling to be held in mid-August, on the grounds that it was "not fair that Australia and Indonesia bore the burden for what had become a regional problem" (Alford and Maley 2013a). In advance of the summit, Rudd launched what is commonly referred to as "Pacific Solution II", largely in response to the federal Opposition's proposals for dealing with asylum seekers, which included tow-backs and other extreme measures that won the support of a very large number of Australian voters. Under the Pacific Solution II, every asylum seeker who arrived in Australia by boat after 19 July 2013 without a valid visa was refused settlement in Australia and taken to Papua New Guinea for their refugee status to be determined. If found to be genuine refugees, they were to be resettled permanently there or in any country other than Australia. On 3 August 2013 a similar agreement was signed with impoverished Nauru.

While the Australian government kept pushing for more bilateral collaboration, the Indonesian government expressed its preference for multilateral talks in order to find regional solutions. Foreign Minister Marty Natalegawa stated that:

> In the history of the issue, we have seen Australia considering numerous options, such as the so-called Pacific solution, Malaysia solution, Timor Leste solution and so on. But Indonesia will always be adamant that this issue should not only be a burden for certain countries. This needs cooperation between the destination countries, the countries of origin and transit countries such as Indonesia. (Saragih 2013)

The outcome of the summit held in Jakarta on 20 August 2013 was the Jakarta Declaration on Addressing Irregular Movement of Persons, a non-binding commitment by the thirteen countries attending to change visa policies that were being abused for people-smuggling purposes. It also acknowledged the need to replace voluntary repatriation of those found not to need protection with involuntary repatriation (Alford and Maley 2013a; Saragih and Ririhena 2013). Indonesia's concession was to end visa-on-arrival status for Iranian visitors, as more and more Iranians were found on the boats heading for Australia. As the representatives of the thirteen countries met, another boat with asylum seekers sank 220 kilometres north of Christmas Island, from which 106 were rescued and five presumed dead.

The Abbott Regime: From Bad to Worse

Three weeks after his election win on 7 September 2013, Prime Minister Tony Abbott made a trip to Indonesia to calm the rising tension across the Arafura Sea. As leader of the Opposition, Abbott had not only described asylum seekers as entering through "the back door rather than the front door" (Nicholson and Dodd 2012), but had also pledged on many occasions that he would "stop the boats" if he was elected, by which he meant that he would put in place a comprehensive regional deterrence framework to physically prevent asylum seekers from reaching Australia (Grewcock 2014). To achieve this Abbott would have to rely on the goodwill of the Indonesian government, because a number of his plans involved direct action within Indonesian territory. Amongst other propositions, many of which were of rather dubious merit and effectiveness, Abbott pledged funds to buy old Indonesian fishing boats to reduce the number available for smugglers to transport their clients ("Australia's Abbott Proposes" 2013). Another plan he announced was one that involved Australian intelligence agencies buying information from Indonesian informants in coastal areas where people smugglers operated. A third proposal was for intercepted boats to be towed back to Indonesia.

None of Abbott's plans were welcomed in Indonesia, whose politicians and commentators began to voice their concern before the Australian federal election and continued to do so afterwards ("Abbott dinilai perumit" 2013). Mahfudz Siddiq, the head of Indonesia's parliamentary commission for foreign affairs, for example, said the plan to buy unseaworthy fishing boats was "a crazy idea … degrading and offensive to the dignity of Indonesians" and warned that these policies would have broader implications for the relationship between Indonesia and Australia ("Tony Abbott's Boat Buy-back Plan" 2013). He criticized Abbott's "cowboy style" and the new Australian government's chauvinism that threatened Indonesian sovereignty (Bachelard and Wroe 2013). In reply Foreign Affairs Minister Julie Bishop said, "we're not seeking Indonesia's permission [to carry out our policies], we're seeking their understanding" (Nicholson and Maley 2013). Outraged by her lack of diplomatic tact, Indonesia responded in a similar fashion a few days later when Foreign Minister Marty Natalegawa met Bishop in New York, shortly before Abbott visited Jakarta on 30 September. Natalegawa made it clear that Indonesia "cannot accept any Australian policy that would, in nature, violate Indonesia's sovereignty" (Connolly 2013). Although the meeting between Natalegawa and Bishop in New York was supposedly a private conversation, the content of the discussion, in which Bishop tried to win Indonesia's support for a "quiet" and "behind the scenes" approach, was leaked by the Indonesians to the press as payback for Australia's earlier lack of decorum (Norman 2013).

While the diplomatic exchanges proceeded, two more boats with asylum seekers on board faced emergencies at sea. The first was escorted back to Indonesia, while the second waited so long for help that only twenty-eight of more than eighty passengers could be rescued. Immigration Minister Scott Morrison denied allegations made by survivors that Australian authorities did not react quickly enough to distress calls from the vessel (Wilson 2013). Little was achieved by Abbott's first visit to Jakarta as Australian prime minister. Aware of the offence caused by his plans to forcibly return boats to Indonesia, Abbott avoided raising the topic at all during his talks. The only concession he could elicit from President Yudhoyono was an agreement to begin looking for a bilateral solution, rather than relying on a multilateral approach, which Yudhoyono had already floated in previous talks. Technical details for a bilateral approach were left for ministers to sort out afterwards.

Pressure to find timely solutions on what to do with asylum seeker boats increased when, in early November, a boat with fifty-six asylum seekers on board issued a distress call (Bachelard 2013c). The call was first received by the Australian authorities, who intended to take the passengers back to Indonesia. The Indonesian refusal to receive this boat back in Indonesian territory resulted in a three-day stand-off in the middle of the ocean, at the end of which Australia took the asylum seekers. Despite this "failure", Tony Abbott remained confident, saying: "We have good relations with Indonesia. But we will stop these boats." ("Australia Accepts Boat People" 2013).

Abbott's optimistic confidence was soon to be undermined and the negotiation of more Indonesian concessions was suspended when it became public knowledge, late in November 2013, that Australia had engaged in espionage in Indonesia, including wiretapping the phone of the president, his wife and a number of very eminent political figures (Bachelard 2013d; Bhakti 2013). President Yudhoyono was outraged and announced: "For me personally, and for Indonesia, the wiretapping conducted by Australia toward some officials, including me, is really hard to comprehend…. It's not the Cold War–era anymore." ("Indonesia Suspends People Smuggling Cooperation" 2013). Once more, public opinion was inflamed by satirical cartoons. This time the cartoon on the front page of *Rakyat Merdeka* of 23 November depicted Prime Minister Abbott half-naked and masturbating while peeping into a room labelled "Indonesia" and groaning "Ssst! Oh my God Indo … So Sexy."

Outraged by the revelations of espionage, Indonesia not only recalled its ambassador from Canberra but also suspended all military and intelligence collaboration, including programmes aimed at preventing asylum seekers from reaching Australia. While bilateral cooperation between the Indonesian and Australian governments had been put on hold, Indonesian police intercepted only very few Australia-bound asylum seekers. The chief of the National Police, General Sutarman, said "[s]urely we will investigate all violations that take place within Indonesia's jurisdiction, but if anyone wants to head there [Australia]; it is not part of our authority. There is no more cooperation [in the area]" (Arnaz 2013*b*). Despite suspending all anti-people-smuggling collaboration, Australian funding for the IOM to provide care and support (including housing, food and medical assistance) to transit migrants intercepted in Indonesia continued. Some Indonesian politicians demanded that pressure on Australia be increased by the release of all asylum seekers from detention so that they could slip through to Australia, but this did not happen.

Although Tony Abbott has since written to the Indonesian president, an official apology for the offence caused by the Australian espionage and an assurance to refrain from espionage, as demanded by Indonesia, has not been offered. Initially Australia showed little interest in the six-step "road map" drawn up by President Yudhoyono on 26 November 2013, which Indonesia saw as essential for restoring the bilateral relationship and which proposed the drafting of a new "code of ethical conduct" and intelligence protocol. In February 2014 Prime Minister Abbott had to admit that progress in repairing the relationship has been slow ("Tony Abbott Wants Faster Progress" 2014). New allegations emerged in February 2014 that an Australian intelligence agency had spied on an American law firm representing Indonesia in a trade dispute with the United States during 2013 and had passed the information it gathered to the United States (Nicholson 2014). Further angered by these allegations, Foreign Minister Marty Natalegawa stated that it was about time that Australia decided whether it sees Indonesia as friend or foe ("Menlu RI" 2014).

Australia's tough new approach in dealing with asylum seekers, which relies on forced tow-backs, is a further major irritant in the relations between Australia and Indonesia. On at least five occasions (12, 22 and 25 December 2013 and 1 and 6 January 2014) the Australian Navy violated Indonesia's twelve-nautical-mile territorial zone when pushing asylum-seeker boats back (Belford 2014). On 17 January 2014 Foreign Minister Julie Bishop conveyed to her Indonesian counterpart, Marty Natalegawa, an apology from the Australian government for "inadvertently" breaching its sovereignty several times during the tow-back operations ("How

Australia Trespassed" 2014). In reaction, Coordinating Political, Legal and Security Affairs Minister Djoko Suyanto announced on 22 January that Indonesia would increase maritime patrols to prevent the recurrence of such incidents ("Australia Must Understand" 2014). One Australian newspaper has reported that the Indonesian Navy has added three small warships to its southern patrols to intercept people-smuggling boats, but not to deter Australian incursions (Alford and Nathalia 2014). However, an Indonesian Air Force spokesman was reported as having said that, in the event of a confrontation, "Australia is reachable" by the sixteen Sukhoi warplanes that Indonesia has based in Makassar (Bachelard 2014b).

In late March 2014, Tony Abbott celebrated the hundredth day of his government without any maritime arrivals of asylum seekers. The political, economic and human costs of this "success" are enormous, as critics in Australia and beyond have remarked. Hassan Wirajuda, former long-time Indonesian foreign minister dismissed the slowdown of maritime arrivals as "a temporary phenomenon". He said that potential asylum seekers might postpone crossing over to Australia for a limited period of time, but warned that "root causes, like conflicts, war, poverty, push people to migrate" (Alford and Nicholson 2014). Despite Australia's harsh border measures, at least two asylum-seeker boats tried to reach Australia in early May 2014; both were apprehended and forcibly returned to Indonesia (Bachelard 2014e).

Even though relations between Australia and Indonesia continued to be tense, Abbott declined an invitation from the Indonesian government to attend the Open Government Partnership conference in Bali in May 2014, which might have offered an opportunity to start mending the strained relations. Nonetheless, after a six-month absence, the Indonesian ambassador Nadjib Riphat Kesoema returned to Canberra later that month (Bachelard 2014f). Although Indonesia had not been able to elicit any meaningful concessions from Australia, his return was widely seen as a step towards the normalization of bilateral relations (McRae 2014, p. 12). Moreover, according to the federal government budget released in the same month, Indonesia was to receive AU$86.8 million over three years as part of the regional cooperation agreement to manage asylum seekers living in the archipelago (Martin 2014).

In June 2014, Prime Minister Abbott visited Indonesia for the first time since the breakdown of the bilateral relationship. During his visit Abbott declared that the boat issue which had troubled the Indonesian–Australian relationship had been resolved. Both President Yudhoyono and Foreign Minister Natalegawa, however, refrained from commenting on this topic. The main purpose of this meeting was to accelerate the signing of a code of conduct, as proposed earlier by Indonesia. Natalegawa stated that although the "resolution of a code of conduct was 'not directly linked' to [the] tensions over [the asylum-seeker] boats, but ... 'addressing one issue will help the other as well'" (Bachelard 2014*f*).

Yudhoyono's appeasing approach was not surprising, given that he had almost reached the end of his second term as Indonesian president. While he endeavoured to achieve the code of conduct, his potential successors were more critical towards the Australian government. In the lead-up to the presidential elections of July 2014, the two main competitors disclosed less conciliatory views for the future relationship between the two countries. During a nationally broadcast TV debate, former army general Prabowo Subianto claimed that Australia had a "phobia" about Indonesia and was to blame for the poor relationship (Bachelard 2014*h*). Joko Widodo, who went on to win the presidential election, not only lamented the absence of trust between Indonesia and Australia, but also even proposed to take Australia to an international court over asylum seekers if future diplomacy should fail to solve the disagreement (Bachelard 2014*h*).

On 28 August 2014, Julie Bishop and Marty Natalegawa eventually signed a joint understanding on a code of conduct, which, in essence, reaffirms the 2006 Lombok Treaty. The main novelties of this agreement were a two-point addendum:

1. The Parties [Indonesia and Australia] will not use any of their intelligence, including surveillance capacities, or other sources, in ways that would harm the interests of the Parties.
2. The Parties will promote intelligence cooperation between relevant institutions and agencies in accordance with their respective national laws and regulations.

Although hailed by the Australian government as a great success, the joint understanding on a code of conduct is nothing more than a face-saving measure for Indonesia, as Australia has conceded to none of the demands Indonesia had previously stated clearly (Bachelard 2014*i*). Australia can continue to spy on Indonesia, as long as Indonesia's interests are not harmed. The agreement, however, does not spell out how "harm" is to be defined. More significantly, in retrospect, it appears that the nine months deemed necessary to produce the mere two-point addendum served Australia very well. While relations with Indonesia were suspended, the Australian Navy was able to return nine asylum-seeker vessels to Indonesia and, thereby, convey a message to transit migrants waiting there that they had no chance at all of being received in Australia (Bachelard 2014*i*).

The diplomatic issues relating to asylum-seeker boats and sovereignty remain far from resolution. Two days before Joko Widodo was inaugurated as Indonesia's seventh president, he issued a blunt warning to Tony Abbott, stating, "it is unacceptable for the Australian Navy to enter Indonesian waters uninvited while turning back asylum seeker boats" (Garnaut and Bachelard 2014).

ISSUES OF CONTENTION

Thus far this chapter has provided a chronology of events that shaped Indonesian–Australian relations in the last decade. I now turn to a selection of points of contention for Indonesia in its collaboration with Australia in anti-people-smuggling initiatives and in dealing with transiting asylum seekers.

Detention and Maltreatment of Underage People Smugglers in Australia

In order to deter Indonesian boat crews from becoming engaged in transporting asylum seekers from Indonesia to Australia, Australian courts have been rigorous in their application of immigration law to detain those arrested, most of whom are impoverished Indonesian fishermen and farmers (Hunyor 2001; Schloenhardt and Martin 2012; Trotter and Garozzo 2012; Schloenhardt and Davies 2013). Mandatory sentencing requirements in Australian immigration law have meant that many convicted smugglers, even those who have played only minor roles, as cooks or helpers on the vessels carrying asylum seekers, have faced prison terms of at least five years. Many of the detained and convicted smugglers from Indonesia have claimed that they are under the age of eighteen and, therefore, entitled to lenient sentences. It has, however, often proved difficult to determine the ages of those charged, as they have not possessed birth certificates and X-ray determination is often found to be inaccurate (Australian Human

Rights Commission 2012). Hafid Abbas, former director general of human rights in the Indonesian Ministry of Justice and Human Rights, has warned against the re-victimization of already disadvantaged and innocent children (Abbas 2011). In July 2011 the Australian government commenced a policy of proactively giving alleged underage people smugglers the benefit of the doubt and many alleged minors were returned to Indonesia before their cases were examined by the AFP.

According to the Indonesian Foreign Ministry (2013, p. 17), between September 2008 and September 2013, 1,440 Indonesian boat crew were released from Australian prisons and returned to Indonesia; of these 1,440 crew members, 1,124 were adults and 316 were minors.[4] The majority of the minors were released without charge; some were freed after their cases had been heard in Australian courts; many minors, however, served their sentences before they were released (Saragih 2012c). Some of the minors were detained in adult prisons. Two Indonesian minors detained for more than a year in the Silverwater Correctional Centre in New South Wales claimed that they were drugged and sexually harassed by fellow inmates ("Minors Tell of Abuse" 2012). At first, despite the outcry of Indonesian rights groups and Australian media, the Indonesian government took no action after receiving reports of the alleged sexual harassment of the two boys ("Indonesia Approaches Alleged" 2012). The detention of Indonesian minors was, however, raised eventually in the bilateral talks (Saragih 2012b) and was also mentioned in the Houston Report (Expert Panel 2012, p. 43), which recommended:

> Changes to Australian law in relation to Indonesian minors and others crewing unlawful boat voyages from Indonesia to Australia should be pursued with options including crew members being dealt with in Australian courts with their sentences to be served in Indonesia, discretion being restored to Australian courts in relation to sentencing, or returning those crews to the jurisdiction of Indonesia.

In early 2013 a group of Australian lawyers prepared to sue the federal government on behalf of and seek compensation for as many as twenty-three out of forty-eight Indonesian youths who were held in adult prisons from 2008 until 2011, following their arrest for being among the crew of asylum boats ("Tahan ABK Muda" 2013). They did so with the support of Komnas HAM and other Indonesian government human rights and security bodies (Alford 2013a). In March 2014 the compensation lawsuit was about to return to the Supreme Court, where the Crown was applying to strike out the claim.

Offshore Refugee-Processing Centre

For many years, subsequent Australian governments have sought to persuade Indonesia to establish a refugee-processing centre, similar to that established on Galang in the late 1970s (described in Chapter 2). Indonesia has, however, persistently resisted this idea for several reasons. As Teuku Faizasyah, Foreign Ministry spokesman, has put it: "We are living in a different era … that was the Cold War. And opening a processing centre now would be like a pull factor for those coming to our region, expecting that they would be processed and find the best country as a final destination" (Fitzpatrick 2009*a*).

While the Australian proposals for a refugee-processing centre under Australian auspices within Indonesia were dismissed, Indonesian immigration officials developed a plan to accommodate more than 10,000 recognized refugees and asylum seekers on the eastern Indonesian island of Sumba while they awaited resettlement in a third country. Australia viewed this plan with suspicion, given that Sumba, one of the poorest and most isolated areas in Indonesia, is less than 700 kilometres from the Australian coast. The Australian government feared that Sumba would develop into a honeypot for people smugglers. Its preference was for a centre to be established on an island on the other side of the archipelago.[5] The Indonesian plan was set aside, only to re-emerge after Australia had adopted its Pacific Solution II in July 2013, which Indonesia feared would result in a trail of transit migrants returning to and remaining in its territory. Driven by the fear of public disorder and of the rise of anti-foreign sentiment in local communities, already evident in parts of West Java during 2012 where it had resulted in the relocation and eviction of several thousand asylum seekers and refugees (see Chapter 4), the Indonesian immigration authorities were seeking alternative arrangements for transit migrants. Although the Ministry for Justice and Human Rights approved this proposal, the co-ordinating minister for politics, security and the law, Djoko Suyanto, once again put the plan on hold, allegedly because of budgetary constraints (Alford and Nathalia 2013*b*). Nevertheless, according to officers of the Kupang immigration office, the regional immigration office possesses the certificate of ownership for and has prepared 5,000 square metres of land on Sumba for potential development as a temporary shelter for transit migrants (Kellen 2014).

Extradition of Non-Indonesian People Smugglers to Australia

The extradition of people smugglers from Indonesia to Australia to stand trial has been controversial in the Indonesian–Australian relationship. As one commentator has put it, using the pebble-in-the-shoe metaphor once again, "people smuggling is the pebble in relations between the two countries" ("Pengalaman membuktikan proses" 2009). Although Australia has requested the extradition of several people smugglers, Indonesia has so far only granted one — that of Hadi Ahmadi in 2009. Regardless of the legal aspects of conducting extraditions, which are bound by the extradition laws of Indonesia and Australia and by the 1992 Extradition Treaty between the two countries,[6] the decision that a person is to be extradited from Indonesia is an executive decision of the Indonesian president. In making a decision, the president takes into account the determination of a court and the considerations of the Ministry of Justice and Human Rights, Ministry of Foreign Affairs, the attorney general and the chief of the Indonesian police.

The first people smuggler whose extradition was considered, but never formally requested, was Egyptian Abu Quassey, alias Moataz Attia Mohamed Hassan. Abu Quassey was deemed responsible for the tragic voyage of SIEV X, which sank en route to Christmas Island on 19 October 2001. The lives of at least 353 people, mostly Iraqis, but also Iranians, Afghans, Palestinians and Algerians, were lost and only forty-four survived. Along with two Indonesian police officers suspected of involvement in organizing the boat, the Police Intelligence Service arrested Abu Quassey on 4 November in Bandung (Fitri 2001). Abu Quassey served six months in an Indonesian prison for a visa violation ("Egyptian Envoy" 2003). During 2002, Australia issued at least four international warrants for his arrest. After his release in January 2003, Abu Quassey was deported on 24 April 2003 to Egypt, having been deported from Indonesia twice before. An Egyptian court found him guilty of manslaughter and aiding illegal migration and sentenced him to seven years in prison. On appeal, Abu Quassey's sentence was reduced to five years and three months (Australian Senate 2005, p. 234).

The reasons why Indonesia might have refrained from extraditing Abu Quassey to Australia, if requested, would have been manifold. First, Indonesia argued that the boat sank in international waters, where neither Australian nor Indonesian law had any force; this meant that Quassey could not be charged with murder in Australia. Second, Indonesia argued that, because Abu Quassey was an Egyptian citizen, he could only be sent to Egypt to face justice — a view supported by Egypt's ambassador to Indonesia, Ezzat Saad (Moore 2003). Third, and most importantly, Minister of Justice and Human Rights Yusril Ihza Mahendra pointed out that the extradition treaty between Indonesia and Australia did not cover people-smuggling. He also indicated that Abu Quassey could not be charged in Indonesia because people-smuggling was not considered a crime under the Indonesian Criminal Code, which meant that the requirement of double criminality could not be stated (Unidjaja 2003). Fourth, Indonesia was reluctant to extradite Abu Quassey because of its pending request for the extradition from Australia of Hendra Rahardja, who was suspected to have committed banking offences relating to the mismanagement of Rp2.6 trillion (AU$260 million) of Bank Indonesia Liquidity Support funds ("Indonesia Rejects" 2001).

According to Julie Taylor (2011) of the International Crime Cooperation Central Authority at the Australian Attorney-General's Office, six people have been extradited to Australia to face prosecution for people-smuggling offences since 2000 — four from Thailand, one from Sweden and one from Indonesia. All of those extradited from Thailand were involved in people-smuggling operations in Indonesia. Iraqi Ali Al Jenabi, for example, operated as a people smuggler in Indonesia but was arrested in Thailand and extradited in February 2003 to Australia, where he was sentenced to eight years in prison; Pakistani Hasan Ayoub was extradited in July 2003 and sentenced to twelve years imprisonment (Ellison 2004; Downer and Ellison 2003); and another Pakistani, Masood Ahmed Chaudhry, was extradited and sentenced to eight years in prison.

The only successful extradition from Indonesia was of Hadi Ahmadi, an alleged people-smuggling organizer. Hadi Ahmadi, holding both Iraqi and Iranian citizenship, was extradited to Australia in May 2009, having been arrested by Interpol upon his arrival in Indonesia on 27 June 2008 for people-smuggling operations he had carried out mainly in 2000 and 2001. He had already been arrested once in 2007, when he was deported to Iraq. He was involved mostly in the day-to-day activities of people-smuggling, such as organizing food, transport and accommodation and worked for several other smugglers, including Sayed Omeid, who was later arrested in Malaysia for carrying forged identity documents and extradited to Australia from there (Callinan and Alford 2011; "Iraqi Man Extradited" 2013). Hadi's albinism made him stand out among the many other smugglers and facilitators.

On 29 July 2008 Australia handed the request for his extradition to Indonesia. In order to grant the request, a Presidential Decree (10/2009) had to be issued. After his extradition, Hadi stood trial in Perth and was sentenced to seven years and six months in prison ("Hadi Ahmadi Loses" 2011).[7] Hadi's case was the first successful extradition of a non-Indonesian people smuggler from Indonesia. In a press statement on 21 April 2009, Prime Minister Kevin Rudd not only expressed his gratitude for Indonesia's assistance and thanked President Yudhoyono for approving the extradition, but also used the success as a demonstration of Australian–Indonesian cooperation in the fight against people-smuggling and of the fact that people smugglers cannot escape justice. The request for Hadi's extradition may have had a satisfactory outcome for the Australian government, but an Indonesian commentator stated that the experience proved the need for more dialogue between the two countries so that extradition processes for people involved in human smuggling can be flawless (*mulus*) ("Pengalaman membuktikan proses" 2009).

Another case, erroneously reported in the press as a successful extradition from Indonesia ("Man to Stand Trial" 2011), is that of Iranian-born Ali Khorram Heydarkhani, who was arrested upon his "voluntary" return to Australia. An Australian citizen from 2004, he was arrested in Indonesia in January 2011. It remains unclear why he was not prosecuted in Indonesia. In Australia he faced eighty charges, including organizing four asylum seeker boats between November 2010 and January 2011, one of which smashed into rocks on Christmas Island in December 2010, causing the death of at least fifty asylum seekers. He was tried and sentenced in Perth to fourteen years imprisonment (Perpitch 2012).

While Australia has had to abandon some requests for extraction due to administrative shortcomings, others are still pending. An unsuccessful Australian request was for the extradition of Sajjad Hussain Noor, whom Indonesian authorities deported to Pakistan after Australia abandoned its request for Sajjad's extradition on advice from the Commonwealth Director of Public Prosecutions that the case was not strong enough for "reasonable prospects of success of the prosecution" (Alford and Nathalia 2013*a*). However, some sources claimed in early 2013 that he was back in business in Indonesia (Alford and Nathalia 2013*a*). The Indonesians also returned Zamin Ali (aka Haji Sakhi) to Pakistan in January 2012, after Australia had withdrawn its request for his extradition (Schloenhardt and Ezzy 2012, p. 144).

After Indonesia criminalized people-smuggling in May 2011, Australia mostly refrained from making further extradition requests, on the understanding that people smugglers would be held accountable in Indonesia. One extradition case still pending is that of Sayeed Abbas Azad bin Sayed Abdul Hamid, an ethnic Hazara from Afghanistan. Because of close media coverage of his case, his activities have had considerable exposure in Indonesia and Australia. Sayeed was born in 1982 and arrived in Indonesia in December 1999. After the UNHCR rejected his claims for protection multiple times, he avoided deportation and repatriation and remained in Indonesia.[8]

Sayeed became involved in people-smuggling, at first working for other smugglers and later developing his own business. In November 2008 he was arrested in Banten for people-smuggling. The court initially acquitted him,[9] but the prosecution appealed his acquittal and he was found guilty and sentenced to two years and six months in prison and ordered to pay a fine of Rp5 million (AU$500).[10] Although he was due to be released in September 2011, he was still in prison when interviewed in April 2012, while investigation of his suspected involvement in other people-smuggling cases proceeded.

In October 2009 Interpol issued a Red Notice (No A-4055/10-2009), in November 2009 Australia requested the temporary arrest of Sayeed, and in June 2010 Australia made an official request for Sayeed's extradition. He was sought for his suspected involvement in thirteen crimes that violated Australian immigration law. A diplomatic note issued on 19 February 2013, mentioning fourteen additional charges, strengthened the extradition call. In July 2013, however, Sayeed's extradition was suspended by an order (*penetapan*) of the District Court in South Jakarta, which stated that Sayeed was not extraditable. The court order gave a number of reasons for stopping the extradition, including claims that the extradition request did not have all the required documents, so did not fulfil the formal extradition requirements. The District Court's order, which created somewhat of a precedent, also stated that the embassy of Sayeed's country of origin had not consented to the request for his extradition and gave humanitarian reasons for stalling the extradition process.[11] In February 2014, the order was appealed and overruled in the Jakarta High Court.[12] The final decision on his extradition rests with the Indonesian President. Although Sayeed was released from prison, he is now detained in the immigration detention centre in Jakarta. According to senior members from the central authority in Jakarta, Sayeed is more likely to be extradited to Australia eventually than deported to Afghanistan.[13]

Forced Returns and Tow-back Operations

Although Australia has not concluded readmission agreements with any of its neighbouring countries, as the European Union has done, twelve SIEVs were intercepted by the Australian Navy during Operation Relex, the operation aimed at turning back the boats. In accordance with Operation Relex's turn-back policy, attempts were made to turn ten of these twelve boats back. Of those ten boats, only five were successfully returned to Indonesian waters. At least two passengers lost their lives in these turn-back attempts.

In August 2012 the Houston Panel suggested that irregular vessels heading with asylum seekers on board for Australia could be turned back to Indonesia "in the future, in particular if appropriate regional and bilateral arrangements are in place" and when it was safe to do so (Expert Panel 2012, p. 54). Forced returns and tow-backs have been criticized by many, however, as "inconsistent with decent safety-of-life-at-sea practice in border protection" (Kevin 2012, p. 101). Indonesians have also raised concerns about endangering the lives of people on boats by turning them back (Anwar 2012). Ikrar Nusa Bhakti, of the Indonesian Institute of Sciences, warned in 2012 that if a turn-back policy was imposed on boats carrying asylum seekers, "it's not only going to put the Australia–Indonesia relationship in bad condition, it will also give Australia a bad name as an international citizen" (Nicholson and Alford 2012). Indonesian Foreign Minister Marty Natalegawa reinforced his country's discomfort with the Australian plan to "turn back the boats" during a visit to Canberra in March 2012, when he said that a regional approach was needed to solve the rise in people-smuggling vessels travelling between Indonesia and Australia, rather than Australia passing the buck to Indonesia (Kevin 2012, p. 98). As Pierre Marthinus (2014) has noted, Indonesian senior diplomats and academics are infuriated by Australian arrogance and insistence on "flipping over the boats".

Despite ongoing protest, within one year of launching Operation Sovereign Borders on 18 September 2013, the Australian government had successfully stopped a total of forty-five ventures before they even set sail, through disruption operations with Australia's partner countries, and turned, towed, or sent back twelve boats carrying 383 asylum seekers, in most cases to Indonesia (Morrison 2014). For this purpose Australia has purchased eleven lifeboats, each equipped with an air conditioner, television and other facilities ("Australia Sends Back" 2014). Some of the asylum seekers returned to Indonesia have claimed they were duped by sailors who told them they were being taken to Darwin or Christmas Island, only to find that they had been taken back to Indonesia (Bachelard 2014*a*). In the first year of Operation Sovereign Borders, the Australian government under Tony Abbott has returned more boats than the government of his mentor John Howard returned in just over two years between October 2001 and November 2003 (Bachelard 2014*c*). Because the boats turned back during the Howard years were bigger and carried more people, the numbers of people forcibly returned were higher — 614 under Howard's leadership compared to 383 since Abbott was elected prime minister, with many more likely to be returned in the near future. Relations between Indonesia and Australia have been severely strained by the tow-backs; Vice-Chairman of the Indonesian Parliament, Priyo Budi Santoso, has characterized Australia's actions as "toying with Indonesia" (Akuntono 2014). A further consequence of tow-backs and forced returns, which has heightened the frustration of Australia's northern neighbours, is the increasing accumulation of asylum seekers in other transit countries such as Malaysia (Berkovic and Alford 2014).

Australia's actions in forcing the return of asylum seekers are in grave violation of the Refugee Convention. Adding to Australia's questionable record are serious allegations of verbal and physical mistreatment when the Australian Navy returned forty-five asylum seekers, including nine women, from Sudan, Eritrea, Somali, Ghana, Egypt, Yemen and Lebanon to Rote Island in early January 2014 ("Asylum Seekers Allege" 2014). According to the reports of the returned asylum seekers, which were not investigated further by the Indonesian police in Rote once it had been determined that they related to events that occurred outside Indonesian territory, Australian Navy personnel forced some of them to put their hands on hot pipes, causing burns (Bachelard 2014d). In the face of repeated denials by the Australian prime minister, the immigration minister and the Australian Navy, an Australian investigation was not launched either, even though Australia is obliged under international law to investigate impartially allegations of torture or other cruel, inhumane or degrading treatment, to punish perpetrators, and to provide effective remedies (including compensation) to victims. The Australian government has also refused to release video recordings made during the interception.

SUMMARY

Every year opinion polls are conducted to find out what comes into the minds of Australians when they think about Indonesia. Among the few positive thoughts Australians are found to have is the view of Bali as a popular holiday destination. Negative images clearly predominate, especially of asylum seekers, terrorism, religious extremism and drugs. The Newspoll report, commissioned by the Department of Foreign Affairs and Trade, found that the issue of greatest concern to Australians is people-smuggling to Australia through Indonesia; eighty-five per cent of those interviewed expressed concern about this issue, fifty-six per cent of whom are "very" concerned (Newspoll 2013, p. 11). Given current Australian foreign policy on Indonesia, it is hardly surprising that many ordinary Australians remain "lukewarm" about Indonesia (Oliver 2013, p. 12). On the other side of the Arafura Sea it is also hard to find positive feelings for Australia and Australians. According to Tim Lindsey (2010), many Indonesians suffer from "Australiaphobia" and see Australians as white neocolonial intruders without any decency. With such negative attitudes prevalent on both sides of the sea, what future can there be for the bilateral relationship?

Although the Indonesian–Australian relationship has never been without complications, and is even referred to by some in discussions of diplomatic relations between the two governments as a love-hate relationship, the current state of affairs seems to be particularly worrisome and to offer no guarantee that relations between Australia and Indonesia will not regress even further. As this chapter has shown, once East Timor had gained its independence from Indonesia through a process in which

Australia intervened heavily, transit migrants "became the major issue in Indonesian–Australian relations" (Anwar 2002, p. 63). Australia's arrogant megaphone diplomacy did no favours for the relationship (Lindsey 2010). An opportunity to make a new start and bring fresh air to the stalled relationship emerged when Joko Widodo assumed the presidency in October 2014. Any improvement will, however, require a lot of goodwill from Australia.

Notes

1. ABC TV's Q&A panel discussion on 4 July 2013, entitled "More Than Beef, Boats & Bali".
2. This expression harks back to the infamous comment of Ali Alatas, who, as Indonesian foreign minister, said after the massacre of more than 200 East Timorese at the Santa Cruz cemetery on 12 November 1991 that the East Timor issue was just "a pebble in Indonesia's shoe"; as it turned out, that "pebble" did, in fact, cause considerable inconvenience.
3. Many observers criticized this expression because it focused on safety issues, thus obscuring the government's real intention, which was to stop boats coming once and for all.
4. It was difficult to find firm and consistent figures at all, as sources promulgating the figures, even those within the same ministry, varied substantially.
5. Interview with head of the Research Section for International Law and Regulations, Komnas HAM, 10 January 2012, Jakarta.
6. In the preamble of Law 8/1994 which basically served to ratify the Extradition Treaty, the good political relations between the two countries are accentuated: "d) the cooperation between the Republic of Indonesia and Australia has developed well, in order to strengthen and enhance the effectiveness and efficiency of this cooperation further, particularly in the fields of law enforcement and the administration of justice, on April 22, 1992 the Extradition Treaty was signed between the Republic of Indonesia and Australia".
7. During his trial Hadi claimed that the AFP had tried to hire him to spy on Sayed Omeid, but that he had refused. One of his former associates, however, had accepted a similar offer from the AFP and testified against Hadi in court (Schloenhardt and Ezzy 2012).
8. Interview with Sayeed Abbas, 11 April 2012, Jakarta.
9. District Court of Serang Decision No. 17/Pid.B/2009/PN.Srg, 1 July 2009 (Sayeed Abbas).
10. Supreme Court Decision No. 2422K/Pid.Sus/2009, 26 February 2011 (Sayeed Abbas).

11. District Court of South Jakarta Decision No. 01/Pid.C/Ekts/2013/PN.Jkt.Sel, 11 July 2013 (Sayeed Abbas).
12. High Court of Jakarta Decision No. 16/PID/Plw/2014/PT.DKI, 25 February 2014 (Sayeed Abbas).
13. Interview with Director of International Law and Central Authority, 2 April 2014, Jakarta.

8

SELLING HOPE

> They create (*menciptakan*) people like me;
> at first, I was not a smuggler.
> (Interview with convicted people smuggler,
> 14 June 2012, Sukabumi)

THE SMUGGLING "INDUSTRY" IN INDONESIA

In this chapter the focus shifts back to the transit migrants in order to explore the correlation between protracted transit and people-smuggling. Through the portrayal of three convicted non-Indonesian people smugglers, it gives an insight into how people-smuggling networks evolved in Indonesia and how they adjusted in response both to increased demand and to intensified enforcement of anti-people-smuggling regulations. It retraces their paths, from rejected asylum seekers to middlemen, recruiters and organizers of people-smuggling ventures. Thus the chapter demonstrates how an extended and more professionalized people-smuggling "industry" is an unintended outcome of Australia's restrictive policies for asylum seekers, of intensified bilateral border control, and of Indonesia's determinedly passive approach to its handling of transit migration.

The hopelessness engendered by spending protracted periods of time in transit has pushed many transit migrants not only to accept higher risks to their own lives during unsafe voyages (Kevin 2012) but also, more significantly, to become actively involved in the irregular transport of transit migrants to Australia. From this perspective transit migrants are not just the clients of smugglers; some of them may also benefit financially from the irregular migration industry as it seeks to satisfy increasing demand among both documented and undocumented asylum seekers and "impatient" refugees. The increase in people-smuggling is, therefore, a result of the absence of legal and timely migration channels; this view is also held by members of the Indonesian police, one of whom stated, "in fact, their decision to create a [people-smuggling] network is based on their despair that they cannot get there [Australia]".[1] There is also little dispute among scholars of irregular migration that the growth of the smuggling industry is an unintended side effect of stricter visa regulations and increasingly restrictive migration. As George Borjas and Jeff Crisp (2005, p. 3) claim, "there is now good reason to believe that the imposition of restrictive asylum practices has had the effect of diverting migrants to alternative destinations and of prompting them to resort to clandestine forms of movement". It is also worth noting that between thirty and eighty per cent of all illegal entries into Europe are facilitated by smugglers (Papadopoulou-Kourkoula 2008, p. 71) and that experts estimate that there are between 400,000 and 600,000 illegal entries into the European Union every year (Jandl 2007).

If research into people-smuggling is to provide more conclusive, rather than simply indicative, insights into the motivations of and outcomes for those involved in and serviced by the industry, it must move beyond some of the methodological, and possibly ideological, constraints that persist in limiting its investigations at present. Smuggling operations from Indonesia need to be studied in their own right, as they differ notably from operations in northern Africa and in states bordering the European Union, where individuals seem to organize their own illegal entry and where smuggling operations are more spontaneous and demand-driven and generally less professional (Jandl 2004; Heckmann 2004; Papadopoulou 2004; Liempt and Doomernik 2006, pp. 174–76). In other words, whereas smuggling along the borders of European countries is a crime that may be organized but cannot really be considered to be organized crime (Papadopoulou-Kourkoula 2008, p. 73), smuggling people from Indonesia to Australia requires much greater planning and preparation (Munro 2011; Missbach and Sinanu 2011).

"People-smuggling" is a rather imprecise term used to cover many different activities, including transporting, directing, accommodating, sheltering, or hiding people who are willing to rely on a third person to enter or leave a country by crossing state borders clandestinely. Services offered by people smugglers to transit migrants can range from simple one-off services to more comprehensive packages that cover air, land or sea travel and the provision of falsified or fraudulent documents to enable entry into transit countries and destinations, such as Australia (Expert Panel 2012, p. 73; Hoffman 2010a, p. 220). In contrast to the predominant image of heinous criminal and exploitative networks, people-smuggling is a "transnational service industry" (Bilger, Hofmann and Jandl 2006), that simply exploits weak law enforcement and relies on corruption.

Depending on their financial situation and their range of social contacts, transit migrants in Indonesia can choose from a wide range of offers and services provided by several different ethnic and diasporic networks. According to the Indonesian anti-people-smuggling taskforce (SATGAS), in 2012 three main smuggling networks operated in Indonesia — the Sri Lankan, the Iranian–Iraqi and the Afghan–Pakistani networks (Meliala et al. 2011, p. 52). There was competition within these ethnic groups, but rarely across them.[2] By late 2013, the anti-people-smuggling taskforce had identified at least six major regional networks.[3] Most of those involved in the business of people-smuggling are men, with only one woman — a low-level transport arranger — identified in a study of people-smuggling convictions in Indonesia that covered forty-five cases between 2007 and 2012 (Crouch and Missbach 2013, p. 15).

People-smuggling flourishes under certain conditions, such as weak state control of the informal economy and unregistered businesses, an unlimited supply of poor and desperate helpers and clients, together with the involvement and active support of "agents of collusion" (Expert Panel 2012, p. 10), such as corrupt state officials who accept bribes in return for not obstructing or reporting people-smuggling operations (noted in Chapter 6). Rejected asylum seekers are at risk of being drawn into people-smuggling or criminal activity, as they have very few alternatives for generating an income while they linger in transit. They are, however, not the only wheelers and dealers; many resettled former refugees are also known to have become organizers of people-smuggling operations (Schloenhardt and Ezzy 2012, p. 143; Skelton 2011).[4] Rejected asylum seekers stuck in Indonesia play a significant role in paving the way for transit migrants within Indonesia, but they rely on the support of former refugees in destination countries and of suppliers in the countries of origin and in other transit countries along the way. This chapter directs most attention to the phase of the smuggling operation from the arrival of asylum seekers in Indonesia to the point that they seek to leave Indonesia.

Transnational people-smuggling networks are not centrally organized; they rely on kinship, ethnic, and national networks that operate across borders. They are not necessarily steered by mafia-like leaders and their clans and families, as drug trafficking networks are, for example (Içduygu and Toktas 2002; Danis 2006; Triandafyllidou and Maroukis 2012; UNODC 2011, p. 17; Bilger, Hofmann and Jandl 2006). The networks are often polycentric and some parts of a network may operate independently from others (Triandafyllidou and Maroukis 2012). Consequently, internal rivalry and constantly changing structures are not uncommon. Snitching and whistleblowing seem to be part of the overall business strategy and to enhance fierce competition (Amiri 2014). For example, some transit migrants who are involved with smugglers and may even work for them might at the same time collaborate with Indonesian or Australian police, providing them with information about boats that are soon to depart; after all, according to one transit migrant, "they just want to make money to buy drugs, women and go clubbing".[5]

Ahmet Içduygu and Sule Toktas (2002, p. 36) have distinguished ten different roles in the process of people-smuggling, in addition to that of the main organizers, who are often wrongly referred to as kingpins or masterminds. Australian and Indonesian laws generally do not differentiate amongst these roles, as blanket penalties for all people-smuggling activities are applied. On an average journey from their home country to their final destination, an asylum seeker is likely to have contact with a series of people: arrangers, who also oversee the operation; transporters, who arrange the land, air or sea journey, and their crew; support staff, who arrange such things as food and accommodation; and, of course, debt collectors and money movers, who complete the financial transactions. Other crucial actors in the process in Indonesia are protectors — the corrupt government officials in immigration, the military, the police and the public prosecutor's office, who ensure smuggling operations remain undetected. These protectors have the greatest potential to undermine the legal prosecution of people smugglers and are rarely prosecuted for their involvement.

This chapter focuses first and foremost on non-Indonesian middlemen, recruiters and organizers, who have been in transit in Indonesia for a long time and have collaborated with suppliers in countries of origin and in other transit countries. In the three case studies presented, attention is directed at the language and networking skills of people smugglers and their intimate knowledge of how to conduct business informally in Indonesia, thus confirming what one young Hazara has said about these rejected asylum seekers — that they were "compelled" to become involved in people-smuggling.

MAKING BIG BUCKS?

When Australian Prime Minister Kevin Rudd described people smugglers as "the absolute scum of the earth" who "are engaged in the world's most evil trade" (Rodgers 2009), he encouraged a public understanding of people smugglers as irresponsibly exposing their clients to serious risk and as being extremely greedy people. Given that people-smuggling does involve large sums of money, it is hard not to think of the Indonesian proverb, "where there is sugar, there are ants". The notion that people smugglers make lots of money from the misery of people who are stuck in Indonesia has persisted in public debate ever since (Schloenhardt and Ezzy 2012, p. 121). Although it is known that there is a substantial financial turnover in people-smuggling operations, there are many questions about who profits most from the operations, such as whether the money ends up in the pockets of people smugglers or whether it ends up in the pockets of others as increased border control and immigration law enforcement forces smugglers to pay off more people along the way (de Haas 2005). According to Friedrich Heckmann (2004, p. 1117), "the entrepreneurial core person(s) clearly dominate and profit the most from the [human smugglers'] network or even exploit the helpers". It is probably safe to assume that organizers who are involved at the very beginning of arranging irregular journeys stand to earn the most, simply because their clients have the most money at that point of their journey. But what is in it for the arrangers further along their path in Indonesia?

A hypothetical calculation of potential earnings, provided by an Indonesian maritime police officer in Kupang, takes into account a number of expenses that have to be met by the smuggling operator:

> Let's say, one smuggler charges seventy clients Rp70 million (US$7000) for a trip to Australia. That makes altogether Rp4.9 billion (US$490,000). But if he buys a boat in Sulawesi, where they are much cheaper than

here in Kupang, he can get one that is big enough for Rp190 million (US$19,000). All the operational costs, like food and petrol and the salaries for the crew won't cost him more than Rp400 million (US$40,000). This leaves the organiser with at least Rp4 billion (US$400,000). If he has four accomplices, it still leaves him Rp800 million (US$80,000).[6]

For a number of reasons, I question aspects of this calculation. According to informants, boat journeys from Indonesia to Australia cost anything between US$2,000 and US$10,000 per person. Former clients of people smugglers who have made the trip, when asked about how much they had paid, often provide amounts that include the entire trip and not just the journey from Indonesia. As payments are not always made in a single transaction, it is difficult to calculate overall fees and profits (UNODC 2011, p. 26). Clients from Iran, Pakistan and Afghanistan usually arrange payment before they leave their home country. They pay a certain amount at the very beginning of their journey directly to the organizer and deposit another amount with a middleman, who only releases this payment at the end of a successful journey (for example, when the client has reached Australia) (*Tempo* 2012, p. 61). These upfront payments and instalments are made to spare clients having to carry a lot of cash on their journeys, as that increases their risk of being robbed. If clients decide to change their smuggler rather than continue to rely on the network that brought them into Indonesia, they will have to pay a higher amount for the last leg to Australia. If the actual journey deviates from the original plan of quick transit through Indonesia, which is the case more often than not, clients usually face many extra payments and unexpected charges, especially when they are held up by interceptions and other delays that prevent them from leaving Indonesia. The longer they stay in transit, the more they must pay their smuggler for food, accommodation and protection.

Children often travel for free and families usually get special deals. People-smuggling organizers also offer free trips to clients who recruit a certain number of paying clients (Missbach and Sinanu 2011, p. 75), as was the case with the young Somali refugee Ali, introduced in Chapter 1. Prices are never fixed, with passengers on the same boat paying different sums; transit migrants who are assumed to be well off are generally charged higher fees (Rintoul 2012). So, if the smuggler in the calculation quoted above had seventy passengers, only fifty of those passengers, at most, would be paying customers and the amounts each paid might vary.

Assuming that most of these people would have purchased trips from their country of origin to Indonesia, the smuggler in Indonesia would only get about US$2,000 for each paying passenger, which would give him US$100,000. A boat to carry seventy passengers would probably cost more than the US$19,000 of the calculation above; prices of boats depend on their quality and on the conditions on board, as well as on where it is bought and the number of intermediaries in the purchasing process, all of whom would demand a fee for their services. For example, an Indonesian middleman whom a smuggling operator has given the task of organizing a boat might subcontract it to another Indonesian in order to deflect the attention of state authorities from his involvement.

Another consideration that has to be taken into account when reflecting on the profit-making of people smugglers is that some smugglers offer guarantees; for example, if the first smuggling attempt falls through, the second attempt is usually free. Some smugglers even promise to "help" with release from police arrest if their clients are intercepted. In one rather exceptional case, I heard of a smuggler who sent along a second boat to rescue clients on a boat with a broken engine so that they could continue their journey.[7] If guarantees are offered, the smuggler has to meet all expenses, so there is considerable financial risk in his provision of services. Newcomers face additional difficulties when they try to break into the smuggling industry as they lack the most important thing, a reputation of being trustworthy. The better the reputation of a smuggling organizer, which can only be established by his recent successes, the more money he can charge from future clients.[8] News of sunken ships and arrested clients has a bad effect on his reputation and, consequently, his income. In this regard, clients can exercise some choice among a wide range of prices.

Finally, and most significantly, in his calculations the maritime police officer probably underestimated fees that need to be paid to a number of corrupt people. Potential recipients of bribes and hush money may include members of the local population, but they are more likely to be police, immigration, and military officers whose tolerance of people-smuggling operations and silence about them needs to be bought (Fitri 2012b). There is also evidence of more active involvement of these government officials; for example, smugglers have hired members of the military as security in order to make sure their operations run smoothly (as noted in Chapter 6). One informant explained how payments are made: "nowadays you do not bribe in Rupiah but in US Dollars", and to avoid detectable transfers to bank accounts, "a smuggler would, for example, buy the daughter of a police officer a new car or something else that is demanded".[9]

Prices for people-smuggling have gone up over the last decade, not least because networks had to become more professionalized. What used to be a rather amateur opportunity-based delinquency has now become a more sophisticated crime (Munro 2011, p. 43; Balint 2005, p. 144). A heightened awareness of law enforcement bodies has pushed the smugglers into remote areas, thereby increasing operative risks as well as operational costs, such as of petrol, transport, hush money for locals, and bribes for authorities. When statements made in court by people smugglers and witnesses are compared, accounts of prices paid are often found to differ quite substantially. This could be, as already mentioned, because clients summarize the total cost of their journey to Australia, whereas mid-level organizers can only account for what they receive for their work in Indonesia. It is also possible that some former clients exaggerate the amounts they paid, especially if they hold a grudge against their former smuggler or have experienced a traumatic journey; this, in turn, would feed the discourse of the greedy smuggler. It is difficult, if not entirely impossible, to find reliable information on how much people smugglers spend on the actual voyage and on bribes and how much profit they make. Judging from the accounts of some of the mid-level organizers and facilitators, who may have participated in only a few operations before they were arrested and tried in court, it would seem that their "profits" were just enough to cover their living costs while they were in transit (Amiri 2014). Given the increase in the implementation of anti-people-smuggling policies, it is to be expected that people-smuggling will shift further from a "low-risk high-profit" to a "high-risk low-profit" business (Koser 2008).

Exploiting the Desperate?

The relationship between people-smuggling organizers, recruiters, and their clients can be simultaneously sympathetic and exploitative. Some smugglers look back at their own history of persecution and develop an altruistic stance of wanting to help people; they would provide their clients with Indonesian SIM cards in advance and give them instructions on what to say and what not to say in case of interception and on what information to give when applying for protection under the UNHCR. Other smugglers do not care at all what happens to their clients after they have received their payments. Some smugglers show little reluctance in acknowledging that they are mainly interested in making money, or at least enough to make the great risks they are taking worthwhile. One convicted people smuggler, who worked mostly as a recruiter, explained that he was paid US$2,000 for every fifty clients he could gather. Altogether he recruited about 500 asylum seekers for boat trips to Australia in less than one year. Payments he received for his efforts allowed him to rent an apartment for himself and his Indonesian wife in Casablanca (East Jakarta), a very popular location for the not-so-poor asylum seekers.[10] There were rumours that he had also bought a nice house back in his homeland, but, given the short period of his involvement and the relatively small profit he could have made, it is difficult to substantiate those rumours.

Stricter enforcement of border control has boosted the reliance of transit migrants on smugglers and has increased both the fees and the potential for abuse (Papadoloupou-Kourkoula 2008, p. 71). Although people-smuggling is often conceptualized as a crime without victims (Schloenhardt 2003, p. 139), this view is misleading. Clients of smugglers enter into a relationship of unequal power, as they face exploitation, coercion and negligence during their journeys (Missbach and Sinanu 2014; Koser 2010a, p. 189). Smugglers have often provided unseaworthy boats, have overloaded boats with too many passengers and have failed to arrange for adequate safety equipment on board. Their negligence has cost hundreds of lives. Some scholars claim that the more professionally organized the smuggling network the more brutal the behaviour of individual smugglers (Triandafyllidou and Maroukis 2012, p. 62). From this perspective, people smugglers have become viewed as modern folk "devils" and scapegoats who are blamed for all the deaths at sea, with no regard for the causal effects of the politics that have made the dangerous border crossings a necessary option for desperate asylum seekers (Weber and Pickering 2011; Khosravi 2010).

The absence of accurate and verifiable information, together with the purposeful misinformation regarding entry regulations, migration laws and general living conditions in the transit country, leaves some potential clients in the hands of greedy and irresponsible smugglers. People who pretend to be smugglers also take advantage of this lack of knowledge and information in order to steal money from potential clients, offering no services in return (Grewcock 2009, p. 182; Marr and Wilkinson 2003, pp. 41–43). Newcomers to Indonesia are often easy prey for people smugglers. Michael Leach and Fethi Mansouri (2004) claimed that sometimes smugglers even take their clients hostage in order to extort more money from them and their relatives. Misdeeds that I heard about during my fieldwork included the abandonment of clients by smugglers or their transporters halfway into their journey and leaving them stranded in remote areas. For example, one smuggler took a group of clients from Puncak to Solo, a city in central Java, which is relatively far from the sea. He checked them into a hotel and demanded that they wait until the next day to continue their trip, but he absconded, taking with him all the clients' mobile phones, which he had confiscated from them for alleged security reasons.[11] Other clients were stripped of their money, passports and belongings. A common deception by smugglers is to present their potential customers pictures of beautiful boats and superb equipment on board. Once the journey starts most transit migrants are shocked to see the poor quality of the boats, but some choose to believe that a better and bigger boat awaits them at sea. More often than not their hope is once again blighted. Nevertheless, although these forms of deception and exploitation add to the vulnerability of the transit migrants, they cannot simply be regarded as victims, because they do have a few options to pursue risk-reducing strategies. The exploitation and deception of the clients should not, however, deflect from the fact that the helpers and the foot soldiers of the smuggling organizers are also prone to exploitation and deception (Heckmann 2004; de Haas 2005), as the following sections reveal.

Recruitment of Clients and Assistants

According to one former refugee, "given that providing information on how to find a smuggler is considered a crime, at least ninety per cent of all asylum seekers and refugees were somehow involved, because we all passed on information, introduced people and established contacts for the purpose of moving people".[12] Usually recruitment is proactive, in that potential clients initiate the search for a smuggler, especially if transit migrants have only paid to get to Indonesia or if they decide to change to a new smuggler because they were not satisfied with the services of one they had used. Finding a smuggler in Puncak was not hard at all; contact could be made at many public meeting points, such as coffee shops, restaurants, supermarkets or post offices.

Recruiting also happened passively, with recruiters pursuing potential clients. One informant said that "locals came looking for business, so they knock at our doors".[13] Smuggling recruiters even went to the shelters for the underage asylum seekers and refugees in Puncak.[14] Recruiters and agents are not always affiliated with just one particular smuggler and use promises and "special offers" as enticements (Missbach and Sinanu 2011, p. 75). For example, recruiters would say, "you find the people and I take US$2,000 per person, I don't care how much you charge them". With incentives such as this, more than a few of the recruiters' clients were ready to become "smugglers" themselves. The larger a smuggling network grew in Indonesia, the more it attracted "foreign investors", such as former refugees and migrants residing in Australia, Canada and the United States (Skelton 2011). As holders of passports of their new countries, they faced few problems travelling back and forth between the countries of origin, transit countries and the destination countries, which was helpful for additional recruitment in the homelands and for financial transfers. Once trust was established, everything else became "a matter of arranging".[15]

Matters of arranging can at times include rather extraordinary tasks. For example, in January 2010 forty-three transit migrants from Afghanistan and Turkey became stranded on Sabu Island in East Nusa Tenggara and were taken into custody by the local police. When the district police chief received a fake phone call from a man who claimed to be with the national police and demanded the immediate release of the forty-three people, the local police followed these "orders". Upon release, the transit migrants got on a boat that awaited them and sailed off (Poke 2010).

People-smuggling operations rarely repeat the same patterns, as that would make them more detectable by intelligence and law enforcement authorities. Groups of operatives change with almost every smuggling operation; different drivers and boat crews are hired, boats are bought from different suppliers, and routes might be changed as well. By regularly changing communication lines, such as through buying new SIM cards for phones, or avoiding the use of phones altogether and communicating through Internet chat programs, which are more difficult to trace, people smugglers try to limit risk.

Despite the ever-changing modus operandi, there is one constant factor that turns out to be very supportive of people-smuggling ventures in Indonesia. People smugglers in Indonesia have integrated the services of the IOM and the UNHCR into their smuggling schemes as a kind of interim solution until the final departure to Australia, partly as a bolster against potential failure.[16] What this means in practice is that some smugglers suggest to their clients to register as asylum seekers with the UNHCR and start the process of determining refugee status in order to reduce their risk of arrest and deportation. They not only give them the address of the UNHCR head office and tell them how to get there, but may also even give advice on how to align their stories with accounts of asylum seekers whose requests for protection have been accepted. Other smugglers promote the services of the IOM by suggesting that fully paid-for housing and financial support are readily available to transit migrants. The fact that the IOM provides monthly funding to asylum seekers released from detention reduces the smugglers' expenses as they do not have to cater for their clients' needs while waiting for a favourable moment for departure.

Modus Operandi of Boat Voyages

Once they have recruited enough clients, the operators of the well-organized transnational smuggling networks purchase the services of local fishermen to navigate their mostly poorly maintained boats towards Australia. Smugglers have increasingly relied on underage boat crews for cooks and deckhands (as mentioned in Chapter 6), not only because they cost less to hire but also because they have on occasion been afforded more leniency in Australian courts for their involvement in people-smuggling (Warton 2002). Generally, over the last decade the size of the boats and the numbers of passengers on board seem to have increased, making the risk-taking worthwhile and probably also resulting in more profit for people smugglers. By putting more passengers on a boat, smugglers can also use fewer crew members, especially valued captains and crew members with navigational skills, who face long prison sentences in Australia if their boats are intercepted.

Boats are often bought in Sulawesi, the centre of the boat-building industry in Indonesia, where there is plenty of choice for new and old boats and where prices are usually a lot lower than elsewhere in the archipelago.[17] Boats purchased by smugglers are often not seaworthy (*tidak layak*) and most are designed to carry fishermen and fish and not for transporting large numbers of people. In order to make the passage to Australia, the boats are often equipped with extra engines designed to function on land and pumps unsuitable for salt water, some of which break down during the journey.[18] Smugglers know that they can use each boat just once, as the Australian Navy burns any boat that is confiscated when it arrives (Balint 2005; Stacey 2007; Trotter and Garozzo 2012).

Usually, after a boat has been purchased, it is brought by a local crew to a place that is not an authorized port to take on the passengers. There may also be an exchange of crew and deckhands, as these helpers are only auxiliary, often one-off members of networks. As observed in a number of court documents, many convicted captains and crew members were from Eastern Indonesia, especially from Rote, known for its extremely impoverished fishing communities and for the daredevil attitudes of its young men. It was no coincidence that the smuggling networks made use of Rote, given that smuggling was the only alternative for fishermen in debt whose boats had been confiscated and burned by Australian Customs when they had fished in the "wrong" areas — that is, within Australia's exclusive economic zone (Balint 2005; Stacey 2007; HRW 2002, p. 30 fn115). Given the intensive anti-people-smuggling campaigning among fishing communities, especially in the provinces of Nusa Tenggara Timur, Banten and West Java, smugglers now have to recruit their crews from urban slums (Fox 2013, p. 4; Lutfia 2012). As well as facing the greatest risks in the whole people-smuggling operation, crews and captains of the boats are often financially exploited. They usually receive an advance payment (*uang persekot*) of only twenty to fifty per cent of the amount promised to them, which is usually the equivalent of several months' of their average salary, so they are easily tempted (*tergiur*). If they are arrested and jailed, however, they will never receive the rest of what was promised to them. Given that the crew and captains, who are at the low end of the people-smuggling hierarchy, actually move the passengers across the borders, it is them who are at the greatest risk of apprehension. However, their loss does not weaken the functionality of the smuggling network (Bilger, Hofmann and Jandl 2006). In fact, smuggling network operators factor the potential loss of their boats' crews into their operations, knowing full well that there is a plentiful supply of willing workers in Indonesia's most impoverished regions (Kebon 2011).

In order to avoid too much attention, the boat often awaits its passengers a few miles offshore and they are ferried to the boat in dinghies. The boat, which probably does not meet its passengers' expectations, then sets course towards Christmas Island, or Ashmore Reef (the closest Australian territory to Indonesia, comprising three small islands: West Island, Middle Island and East Island; Warton 2002). Although Christmas Island is further away from Indonesia, making the journey more difficult, it has attracted more arrivals, not only because Eastern Indonesian routes were under greater surveillance, but also because of the magnetic effect of the opening of a processing centre there in 2008.[19] Given that captains and crew members with navigational skills are valued in smuggling operations, some smugglers send along a smaller boat to pick up the captain shortly before the boat and its cargo of transit migrants are about to enter Australian waters in order to ensure that he avoids arrest (Warton 2002; Fox 2013). The passengers on board are often unaware that their boat has been shadowed by another boat and react with confusion when they find that their captain has gone. One young passenger who survived the tragic incident near Trenggalek in December 2011 showed the level of deception in his naïve account: "On our boat there were six Indonesians, the captain, two mechanics and three helpers. They all survived the storm. They swam back the fifty kilometres to the beach, you know, they swim like sharks."[20]

Captains are recruited from various places in the archipelago, especially from the famous port cities, such as Makassar, and from the Eastern Indonesian islands where poverty is prevalent, such as Flores, Sumba and Lombok. Police investigators reported that the captains are often deceived by the smuggling organizers, who tell them they are to transport timber and other materials but not people. Having accepted an advance payment, it is often too late for them to refuse to continue with the transporting of people. One police investigator added: "among the many cases [of boats carrying the clients of people smugglers] I handle, the captains jumped ship and left everybody behind, but I came across one who had enough of a conscience (*hati nurani*) to swim back to the boat".[21] In a few cases the crew, once they became aware of where the journey was headed, decided to sabotage the engine in order to put the journey on hold. For example, in December 2011 a boat with more than fifty asylum seekers on board departed from the island of Bima, but became stranded near the island of Rote, because the two crew had sabotaged the engine ("Pengangkut imigran gelap divonis" 2012). Local residents alerted the police and both crew and captain were arrested and prosecuted for people-smuggling.[22] The judge ignored the fact that the crew had actually tried to stop the journey and sentenced them to five years in prison and fined them Rp500 million (AU$50,000). An appeal confirmed the sentence.[23]

As already noted, the transporters and boat crew are at greatest risk of apprehension, while "the masterminds behind the whole activity are difficult to bring to court" (Ashari 2012). A number of people have argued in favour of introducing a specific law on people-smuggling rather than just relying on the relevant paragraphs on people-smuggling under the Law on Immigration (6/2011) (quoted in Chapter 6). Those paragraphs are insufficient to address the complexity of the issue, and, as proponents of a new law argue, a multidimensional approach is required that not only considers migration-related aspects of people-smuggling but also pays attention to the protection of asylum seekers and refugees as well as maritime and border security (Ashari 2012). Such legislation is, however, unlikely to be drawn up, passed, and implemented any time soon.

BECOMING A PEOPLE SMUGGLER: PROFILES AND PROSECUTIONS

Research into people-smuggling suffers a number of serious methodological limitations, as most of it is undertaken from a criminological perspective and relies solely on police files and records of court proceedings (Liempt and Doomernik 2006; Koser 2008).[24] The three accounts of formerly active non-Indonesian people smugglers given in this chapter are constructed from court documents, supplemented by interviews with the smugglers while they were in prison, which allows for a limited extent of triangulation. The incarceration of my informants of course imposed a number of limitations on what could be asked and answered. Visiting time was often short and some interviews had to be conducted in the presence of an Indonesian guard. One of the informants stressed several times that these limitations prevented him from being able to tell the whole story. I did, however, try to locate people away from the prison who knew each of the three imprisoned smugglers and could help to verify some aspects of their accounts.

During fieldwork, I came across cases of other non-Indonesian people smugglers operating within Indonesia, but I did not attempt to contact them for an interview while they were still in business. Often they were rather shadowy characters stalking potential clients rather than identifiable individuals. More of the activities of the smugglers I interviewed became known only after their arrest and prosecution. I have chosen the three examples because they depict most faithfully the transformation from asylum seeker to people smuggler, thus reinforcing the central point of this chapter. In my portraits of the three smugglers, I do not intend to expose them as "criminals" but to present them as "indispensable service providers" (Liempt and Doornernik 2006, p. 174) whose activities are the direct outcome of current international and domestic migration and asylum policies, first and foremost of Australia's *non-entrée* policies.

Sayeed Abbas Azad

Sayeed Abbas Azad bin Sayed Abdul Hamid, an ethnic Hazara from Afghanistan was born in Ghazni in 1982 and arrived in Indonesia in December 1999 on his own, leaving behind his mother and younger siblings.[25] As already sketched in Chapter 7, he travelled via Malaysia and took a boat to Tanjung Asahan (North Sumatra), from where he eventually made his way to Jakarta. At first he was housed with a number of other clients of the same smuggling ring in a villa in Puncak, but as time went by and the cost of their accommodation became too expensive, his smuggler abandoned him. After several failed attempts to leave by boat in 2000 and 2001, his chances of escaping Indonesia diminished when the Pacific Solution was implemented. While waiting in Indonesia, Sayeed was exploited by another Afghan who left him stranded in Surabaya for eight months, where he was eventually arrested by the police and detained in the Kalideres detention centre for three months.

Although his claims for protection were rejected three times by the UNHCR in Jakarta, he stayed on in Indonesia, receiving monthly payments from the IOM. Instead of being deported or repatriated, Sayeed remained in Indonesia and married an Indonesian woman named Dewi Susanti, with whom he had a daughter. In early 2005, after he failed three times to report his whereabouts to the IOM, he lost his entitlement to monthly support payments and was forced to seek his own means of support. Back in Afghanistan he had trained as a tailor. In order to make some money he started selling bread to other transit migrants and to the Afghan embassy staff in Jakarta. While in Puncak he had learned some rudimentary Arabic from Iraqi transit migrants, which allowed him to work as a translator for Saudi tourists, of whom there are many in Puncak.

Sayeed became involved in people-smuggling, working at first for other smugglers and later developing his own business. Together with his Pakistani accomplice named Asadullah bin Khuda Nazar, in October 2008 he ordered an Indonesian man named Firman Kelana to buy two boats.[26] In November 2008, he was arrested in Banten when trying to transport nineteen clients, five of whom were escapees from the detention centre in Kalideres (Jakarta). At this time, people-smuggling was not yet considered a crime in Indonesia, so the charges against him related to the lack of valid immigration documents for the people he was trying to transport out of the country. Sayeed went to court, but in the first instance the local district court in Serang acquitted him, on 1 July 2009.[27] He remained, however, in prison until early 2011. On 26 February 2011 the High Court overruled the decision of the district court. Sayeed was found guilty of violating the old Law on Immigration (Art. 52 and 54b and c of 9/1992) and he was sentenced to two years and six months in prison and fined Rp5 million (AU$500), or an additional three months in prison if he did not pay the fine.[28] By that time he had already served his punishment. In August 2011 he was again arrested because of an earlier Interpol Red Notice for his arrest.

As early as June 2010, Australia requested Sayeed's extradition for people-smuggling offences (see Chapter 7). After the District Court in South Jakarta ruled in July 2013 that he could not be extradited to Australia,[29] Sayeed was placed in immigration detention in Jakarta. In February 2014 the High Court in Jakarta overruled the decision and Sayeed's extradition seemed more likely than ever.[30]

Because of widespread media exposure of his case, Sayeed Abbas became something of a trademark for people-smuggling in Indonesia. Many rumours sprang up around his persona. For example, when I interviewed young Afghan refugees in Puncak, they were convinced that Sayeed had become a direct victim of Australia's Pacific Solution. According to their information, he had been one of the many unsuccessful passengers sent from Ashmore Reef to Nauru, and from there back to Afghanistan, after accepting a repatriation package. These rumours were never verified by Sayeed. Nonetheless, my young Afghan interviewees also believed that he was one of the protesters in Nauru who had sewn their lips together for four days to protest their incarceration on a remote island and the rejection of their protection claims. The young Afghans also claimed that "if Australia had not sent him back, he would not have become a smuggler, but maybe a good citizen, so it is Australia's fault that he became so broken-hearted",[31] and that he had suffered permanent health damage, especially to his digestive system, which helped them explain why he looked so emaciated.

Other informants who knew Sayeed or had befriended him, when asked would claim that he was no mastermind but that "he was just a simple man without money". One informant said that "we were in the same situation" but made different decisions.[32] However, these evaluations were contradicted by reports about the expensive lawyer who helped Sayeed avoid extradition to Australia, and by comments some of the prison guards made to me about the privileges Sayeed enjoyed behind bars because he could afford them. When I asked Sayeed, he acknowledged that he received remittances, stating that a Saudi Arabian man he had met while working as a freelance translator in Puncak would send him Rp4–5 million (AU$400–500) each month.[33]

Timotius Omid Hussein Ali Jilarry

Timotius Omid Hussein Ali Jilarry, alias Amir Kecil, alias Omid bin Majid, was born on 15 June 1976, in Tehran, Iran,[34] where he had studied mathematics. As an adherent of the Baha'i faith he faced religious persecution in Iran. He decided as a young man to leave Iran for Australia, but only made it to Indonesia, where he got stuck for more than thirteen years. At first, in 2001, he tried to reach Australia by boat, but the Australian Navy forcibly returned his boat to Indonesia. He and the other passengers on board were held for twenty days at sea before they were allowed to disembark in Kupang. From Kupang he was taken to Java and there he applied twice for international protection under the UNHCR but was rejected both times. It is unclear whether Timotius, too, married an Indonesian woman.

During these early years in Indonesia, he decided to convert to Christianity, hoping that this would benefit him somehow. Later, he converted to Islam (or at least his religion was noted as Islam in the court files). Until 2010 he was under the care of IOM, as he could neither be repatriated nor resettled.[35] As he had almost reached the maximum time for IOM support, he decided to become self-reliant. Timotius started working for a smuggler referred to as "Amir Besar". His tasks included organizing accommodation, mostly in Jakarta, and checking out new routes to transport the clients of the smuggler to the beach from which they would then depart.[36] He received either a bonus from every client, usually Rp2,000,000 (AU$200), or some sort of a monthly payment from Amir Besar.

On 3 October 2011 he was en route to Pelabuhan Ratu with ten cars and forty-four passengers who had been collected from different hotels in Jakarta, when at about eleven o'clock at night one of the cars was stopped by the police who had been tipped off. Timotius was charged as one of the first people smugglers under the new Law on Immigration (6/2011). Although the prosecutor demanded seven years imprisonment, he was eventually sentenced to five years prison and a fine of Rp500,000,000 (AU$50,000). During his court case a number of puzzling allegations came up about a member of the local maritime police, who was said to have been involved in setting up this and previous people-smuggling operations and in buying a boat.[37] His boss, Amir Besar, was not arrested or charged as he had managed to stay "beneath the radar". Timotius did not appeal his verdict, as he could neither afford a lawyer nor see much sense in doing so. Wearily, he said that he "preferred to be in prison in Indonesia than to go back to Iran" because "in Iran, they would hang me".[38] Asked why he did not try to get to Australia by boat during the years when it was still possible, he explained that he had been traumatized by his earlier experience on the boat that was turned back in 2001. Looking back, he regretted not having made use of this opportunity.[39]

Dawood Amiri

Dawood Amiri, alias Irfan, born in 1993 in Shashpar (Afghanistan), is one of the youngest people smugglers to have been arrested and prosecuted. Unlike other arrested smugglers who tried to avoid any kind of media attention, Dawood chose a very public approach and published his memoirs as a smuggler while still in prison (Amiri 2014). Travelling from Pakistan via Thailand and Malaysia, he arrived in Jakarta on the 17 May 2010 and shortly after that registered with the UNHCR, as advised by his friends. At the same time, he started to look out for possible smugglers to organize his trip to Australia. By collecting information on several smugglers who were active at that time, Dawood gained his first insight into the networks. He decided for a smuggling network under Abdul Sindi (Allard 2010). In August 2010 Dawood attempted to leave Indonesia by boat but was arrested by immigration officers in Serang and, on 25 August 2010, put in immigration detention in Pekanbaru for fourteen months.[40] During his stay in prison he was interviewed by the UNHCR. His application for protection was rejected. In his words, "apparently, I could not be certified as a refugee, according to their rules" (Amiri 2014, p. 53). In October 2011, together with six other detainees, Dawood managed to run away from the detention centre.[41] Dawood organized the breakout and acted as guide and translator for the group during their journey to Jakarta, for which he charged each of them US$100 (Amiri 2014, p. 53).

In November 2011 Dawood married Sri Hartati, an Indonesian woman twelve years his senior, but the marriage was never officially registered. Together they had a son. According to his own statements, he did not pursue the process to claim international protection any further "because the UNHCR requested all sorts of documents from Afghanistan, which I could not provide". As an escapee, he never received financial support from the IOM, so to support himself and later his family Dawood became involved in people-smuggling. From his previous attempt to leave by boat he had gained some knowledge about different smuggling networks operating in Indonesia. At first, he worked for Mohammad Ali Chotay, alias Reza Wakili, and later for a Pakistani smuggler named Javaid Mahmood, alias Billu, alias Hasan Ayub. He saw himself as "the servant of many different agents" (Amiri 2014, p. 59). In his memoirs, he explains: "My job was to explain the system and procedures and expenses ... to his Afghan customers, and to make sure that their money was deposited in cash with a third party in Pakistan" (Amiri 2014, p. 56). For his tasks recruiting new clients and collecting money, he received a commission of US$100 per person from the agent. In a good month he could earn up to US$1,500. With the money he made, Dawood covered his daily expenses, supported his relatives in Pakistan and also paid off debts he had accumulated while in transit.

Dawood helped send at least four boats to Australia (Bachelard 2013a), knowing that people-smuggling was considered a crime in Indonesia. Instead of leaving for Australia, he decided to remain in Indonesia as part of a smuggling network. He insisted that his main motivation was to help asylum seekers "because the UNHCR and the IOM do not care about asylum seekers".[42] Again, in his memoirs, Dawood explained that he "spent most of [his] time helping newcomers (asylum seekers) to settle temporarily in Indonesia" (Amiri 2014, p. 58). His "help" included renting villas for newly arrived potential passengers and accompanying them to the UNHCR office in Jakarta. Dawood remains convinced that his work served his clients well, stating in his memoirs that "the people-smugglers were the real saviours of those asylum-seekers. We offered them survival and peace of mind for only $4,000, saving them and their families years — a big proportion of their lifetime — of grief and torment" (Amiri 2014, p. 63).

One of the boats Dawood helped organize was overcrowded when it left Indonesia on 17 June 2012. During its journey, Dawood tried to follow the boat's passage on his laptop, using the real-time computer program Google Earth and coordinates sent to him from a passenger's satellite phone.[43] He lost contact after the boat was hit by bad weather. Amidst time-consuming confusion between Australian and Indonesian rescue agencies about which organization was in charge of carrying out the rescue operation, the boat sank north of Christmas Island on 21 June 2012; only 110 out of 204 passengers on board survived (Roberts 2013b). Among the dead were a few of Dawood's good friends (Amiri 2014, p. 70).

The Indonesian police arrested Dawood in late June 2012 in his apartment in Jakarta, after they had received information from their Australian counterparts who had interviewed the surviving passengers. They testified that they paid Dawood between US$4,200 and US$5,500 for the trip, but Dawood usually only collected a down payment of US$200 in cash, with the rest to be transferred only after the passengers had arrived in Australia. During the trial it was uncovered that Dawood worked for a network stretching from the Middle East to Australia. One of the more senior figures, Javaid Mahmood, alias Billu, was arrested in May 2013, after he had continued to smuggle more asylum seekers to Australia by boat. Javaid was sentenced to seven years imprisonment and a fine of Rp800 million (AU$80,000) in January 2014.[44] Dawood insisted that he only played a minor role, saying "[i]f I made a lot of money, I wouldn't be here" (Sheehy and Salna 2013). In his memoirs Dawood mentioned that after his initial arrest he was encouraged to pay a bribe of US$24,000 to have the evidence of his case made to disappear, but he could not afford to so (Amiri 2014, p. 81). During his trial, Dawood made allegations of corruption against members of the Indonesian police, customs and immigration officials, and Indonesian Navy officers, claiming that many were directly profiting from the people-smuggling trade (Wright 2014). The East Jakarta District Court sentenced Dawood to a six-year jail term and a fine of Rp750 million (AU$75,000) and a further six months if he was unable to pay the fine.[45]

A young Hazara who knew Dawood in Pakistan and in Indonesia described him as a "good boy, a really nice guy" who came from a very poor background and "never ate anything other than roti and onions".[46] When Dawood first started to recruit potential clients, nobody wanted to believe that he might be capable of organizing boat trips to Australia. After he had sent two dozen people, "he became instantly famous". A fellow Hazara in Indonesia knew that Dawood had no money after he ran away from the detention centre. In his view, "he was compelled to do that kind of work and become involved with gangsters, such as Billu [Javaid Mahmood]". He also blamed "the UNHCR and the IOM and Australia. Because of them he became a smuggler."

At the beginning of his prison term, Dawood remained involved in organizing people-smuggling operations (Amiri 2014, p. 92). According to him, the main reason for continuing in the risky business at that point was to earn money in order to make life in jail more bearable and provide for his wife and child. Later on, he decided to stop, not only because he had lost contact with many collaborators, but also because there were fewer clients interested in taking a boat to Australia after the Australian government had launched Operation Sovereign Borders in September 2013, which resulted in a decline in boat departures from Indonesia. Dawood claimed in his memoirs that he now lives off donations, which he receives from former clients (Amiri 2014, p. 174).

REMAINING QUESTIONS

Although only a limited selection of case studies is given above, there are some notable similarities in the reasons why and how these three asylum seekers became involved in smuggling. Sayeed and Timotius had experienced protracted stays in Indonesia as asylum seekers before they were eventually rejected; they made the decision to become smugglers after several years. In contrast, having spent less than three years in limbo in Indonesia, Dawood could still be considered a newcomer. His path to people-smuggling was accelerated by his financial problems after he escaped from detention and was unable to receive support from the IOM.

From what we know of the activities of these three convicted smugglers, it is difficult to characterize them as kingpins; in fact, this term can be applied to very few people smugglers. Within the large transnational smuggling networks, which often react spontaneously to general trends in demand and supply, the three men acted in roles of arrangers and facilitators. They depended on multiple suppliers from overseas. Other smuggling arrangers based in the home countries of asylum seekers or in other transit countries offered to collaborate with them for the purpose of receiving clients, accommodating them and organizing boats to take them to Australia. When the offer of collaboration was made, some of the clients were still in their home country, while others were already on their way. It is unlikely, however, that the suppliers from the home countries would have communicated directly with the three men; they would have done so through other middlemen. Initially, Sayeed, Timotius and Dawood worked for more senior and more experienced facilitators, of whom many escaped detection by law enforcement agencies. Only Sayeed "climbed up" the career ladder and almost certainly earned more money than the other two, who were only paid a small share of what they helped to collect.

One of the greatest risks for the three men was the irregularity of their presence in Indonesia. They held no valid passports or visas, nor had they achieved asylum seeker or refugee status, which would have meant that their presence was tolerated. It would appear, however, that smuggling networks have developed resilience in managing such risks, as facilitators, recruiters and middlemen can be relatively easily replaced, just as drivers and transporters can. Willing beginners are not very hard to find in the pool of impoverished asylum seekers in Indonesia, many of whom have the required skills and abilities. No seed money is needed to join a smuggling network, and those who become involved can learn on the job.

People-smuggling networks in Indonesia often operate along ethnic and linguistic lines, as that ensures mutual trust among and control over the clients. Every network, however, relies substantially on collaboration with Indonesians. All three men described above speak Indonesian fluently and could, therefore, perform well as brokers. In this regard, smuggling networks are examples of very successful cross-cultural enterprises. While non-Indonesians take care of recruiting clients, collecting money, and the overall coordination of the journeys, their Indonesian counterparts provide temporary accommodation, pick up and transport the clients from scattered locations and are in charge of purchasing the boats and finding suitable crews to steer the boats to Australia. One well-known serial smuggler from Indonesia is Abraham Lauhenapessy, alias Captain Bram, who has continued to be involved in smuggling even though he had served prison sentences previously (Crouch and Missbach 2013, p. 26). Another infamous Indonesian smuggler is a former policeman, known to his business associates as "Freddy Ambon"; he worked for Javaid Mahmood alias Billu and others (Bachelard 2013b).

When it comes to collaboration between Indonesians and non-Indonesians within people-smuggling networks, it appears that the Indonesian wives and girlfriends play an essential role. Both Sayeed and Dawood had Indonesian wives and children. Timotius had an Indonesian girlfriend, but the relationship ended while he was in prison. Sayeed's marriage was registered, so he had a marriage certificate, but more often than not transit migrants engage in customary Muslim marriages, as it is very difficult for them to register their marriages at a civil registry if they lack legal residency documents. Customary marriage requires a short and inexpensive ceremony by an ulama and, usually, the consent of the bride's parents, which can be given over the phone.

With the help of Indonesian wives and girlfriends, asylum seekers and smugglers often find it much easier to acquire sufficient language skills in a short time. More importantly, having an Indonesian wife will help them be more readily accepted by other Indonesians, especially when it comes to making money. Last but not least, having an Indonesian wife by their side gives them access to more secure ways of storing money and of buying property in Indonesia. The bank accounts of a wife's siblings and parents are useful places to hide the money from the police.[47]

From my general observations of the social background of the Indonesian wives of asylum seekers, women who become involved with asylum seekers, especially in Jakarta and Puncak, are not necessarily poor. A member of the people-smuggling taskforce explained that some of the smugglers live off their wives and girlfriends (*jadi mereka numpang hidup*). A number of the Indonesian wives are widows or divorcees with children from previous marriages, who generally enjoy more social freedom in everyday life. Although they usually denied any knowledge of their husbands' involvement in people-smuggling, police claim to have observed some of them serving as contact persons for their husbands while they were detained.

Given the acceptance of polygamy in certain parts of Indonesian society, it is not surprising that some smugglers have more than one wife. Javaid Mahmood, for example, had a wife in Sukabumi (a popular embarkation point for asylum seekers' boats) whom he married in 2000. She then introduced him to the Pakistani community in Tanah Abang (Jakarta) and helped him get a job in a carpet shop there. Later Javaid took another wife in Kalimantan, as he was trying to get a foot in a palm oil business there.[48] The social and economic dimensions of these marriages, and the risk that some of these Indonesian women might be drawn into criminal activities, helps explain the moral panic about relationships between transit migrants and local women in the local community, discussed in Chapter 4.

SUMMARY

An initial consideration of people smugglers might lead one to understand their involvement in people-smuggling as a personal career choice, made only by people who are greedy, opportunistic and of a criminal nature. Closer investigation has revealed a number of social conditions and global forces that drive asylum seekers to follow this career option, especially those whose applications for refugee status have been rejected and those who have fallen through the international protection net. The case studies of the three men convicted for people-smuggling reveal that they are all "victim-offenders", to use a label suggested by Karen Block, Elisha Riggs and Nick Haslam (2013, p. 13). When I discussed similarities in the life stories of smuggling offenders with members of the Indonesian anti-people-smuggling taskforce, an officer confirmed that "most of them failed to leave, hence they became smugglers".[49] Those most likely to become involved in smuggling are rejected asylum seekers without a regular income, as they have no alternative means of making a living. They are stuck. Smugglers are victims of failed migration, unable to move forward or return home. In the words of a Hazara refugee who knew two of the three smugglers presented in this chapter: "They invested so much money to get here, but they gained nothing. It really hurts them."

Aspasia Papadopoulou-Kourkoula (2008, p. 95) has supported the view that smugglers can be "agents for exploitation and salvation" at the same time. Although the spectrum between opportunity and necessity is wide and cannot always be definitely determined, this chapter has demonstrated that people-smuggling is an outcome of national and international policies that try to restrict mobility and impose stasis. In a way, it is a necessary evil. The pressure that transit migrants feel to move on irregularly increases when they cannot receive the protection they require in transit states, which avoid or are incapable of caring for mobile people who are not their citizens and, therefore, outsource their responsibilities to non-government actors. The lack of state control and weak law enforcement in transit states serve people smugglers well, as they can take advantage of ambiguous migration regulations, liberal visa regimes and, more generally, an absence of the rule of law. The currency of smuggling is trust, and it is establishing trust that is perhaps the most important factor that distinguishes people-smuggling from other exploitative activities, especially from more deceptive and involuntarily organized activities such as trafficking. Through the process of building good contacts with the organizers, facilitators, and arrangers in people-smuggling networks, the clients of their services may gather much of the information that they need, but, as Veronika Bilger, Martin Hofmann and Michael Jandl (2006, p. 65) have noted, the people-smuggling industry and those involved in it will inevitably be dominated by "imperfect information".

Transit migrants often turn to smugglers when they perceive that they have exhausted all options available to them. Khalid Koser (2010a, p. 188) has proposed that the services of smugglers might no longer be required if more opportunities for legal migration were made available. Given the current political conditions in countries that asylum seekers continue to flee, it is likely that the services of people smugglers will be in high demand in the years to come. As Gil Loescher and James Milner (2003) noted a decade ago, instability and insecurity in the regions that asylum seekers leave, feed the demand for people-smuggling as they attempt to reach safer places where they can build better lives. The increase in the sophistication of people-smuggling operations will not only fuel the international criminal economy, but will also push many asylum seekers to the margins of social and economic life while they are in transit.

Notes

1. Interview with director of Investigation and Immigration Enforcement, Criminal Investigation Police Headquarters, 13 November 2013, Jakarta.
2. Interview with director of Investigation and Immigration Enforcement, Criminal Investigation Police Headquarters, 10 February 2012, Jakarta.
3. Interview with director of Investigation and Immigration Enforcement, Criminal Investigation Police Headquarters, 13 November 2013, Jakarta.
4. The case that has received the most media attention is that of an Iraqi man, "Captain Emad", also known as Abu Kalid and Ali Al Abassi, who came to Australia as a refugee in 2010 and subsequently set up a smuggling operation in Canberra (Packham 2012; "People Smugglers Set Up Business" 2013). My

investigations have revealed several further cases of former refugees who had taken up Australian citizenship, including Saadhat Ali and Heidar Ali bin Ali Muhammad. See District Court of Pandeglang Decision No. 23/PID/B/2013/PN.Pdg, 7 May 2013 (Saadhat Ali), High Court of Banten Decision No. 84/PID/2012/PT.BTN, 10 June 2013 (Saadhat Ali), and District Court of Cibadak Decision No. 365/Pid.B/2011/PN.Cbd, 3 October 2011 (Heidar Ali).

5. Interview with refugee, 28 February 2012, Cisarua.
6. Interview with head of the Operational Section at the Provincial Maritime Police, 18 June 2012, Kupang.
7. Interview with asylum seeker, Jakarta, 31 March 2014.
8. Interviews with several asylum seekers in Cisarua, March and April 2012.
9. Interview with Iraqi refugee, 18 May 2013, Sydney.
10. Interview with Dawood Amiri, 24 March 2014, Purwakerta.
11. Interview with asylum seeker, 23 June 2010, Cisarua.
12. Interview with Iraqi refugee, 18 May 2013, Sydney.
13. Interview with asylum seeker, 24 June 2010, Cipayung.
14. Interview with asylum seeker, 28 February 2012, Cipayung.
15. Interview with Iraqi refugee, 18 May 2013, Sydney.
16. Interviews with director of Investigation and Immigration Enforcement, Criminal Investigation Police Headquarters, 10 February 2012 and 13 November 2013, Jakarta.
17. Interview with head of the Operational Section at the Provincial Maritime Police, 18 June 2012, Kupang.
18. Interview with director of Investigation and Immigration Enforcement, Criminal Investigation Police Headquarters, 10 February 2012, Jakarta.
19. Critics of Australia's asylum policies and border politics have stressed repeatedly that "Australian policies helped to make these journeys progressively more dangerous for passengers" (Kevin 2012, p. 12).
20. Interview, 13 January 2012, Cipayung.
21. Interview with head of investigation at the Provincial Maritime Police, 26 November 2013, Merak.
22. District Court of Rote Ndao Decision No. 16/Pid.Sus/2012/PN.RND, 19 June 2012 (Husni and Hamka).
23. High Court of Kupang Decision No. 105/PID/2012/PTK, 26 July 2012 (Husni and Hamka).
24. Welcome exceptions are the auto-ethnographic account of Shahram Khosravi (2010) and the work of Gabriella Sanchez (2015).
25. Interview with Sayeed Abbas, 11 April 2012, Jakarta.
26. District Court of Serang Decision No. 18/Pid.B/2009/PN.SRG, 1 July 2009 (Asadullah) and High Court of Banten Decision No. 129/PID/2009/PT.BTN, 6 January 2010 (Asadullah) and also Supreme Court Decision No. 1260 K/Pid.Sus/2010, 21 December 2011 (Asadullah).

27. District Court of Serang Decision No. 17/Pid.B/2009/PN.Srg, 1 July 2009 (Sayed Abbas).

28. Supreme Court Decision No. 2422K/Pid.Sus/2009, 26 February 2011 (Sayeed Abbas).

29. District Court of South Jakarta Decision No. 01/Pid.C/Ekts/2013/PN.Jkt.Sel, 11 July 2013 (Sayeed Abbas).

30. High Court of Jakarta Decision No. 16/PID/Plw/2014/PT.DKI, 25 February 2014 (Sayeed Abbas).

31. Interview, 13 January 2012, Cipayung.

32. Interview, 18 May 2013, Sydney.

33. Interview with Sayeed Abbas, 11 April 2012, Jakarta.

34. District Court of Cibadak Decision No. 15/Pid.B/2012/Pn.CBD, 2 May 2012 (Timotius).

35. Interview with Timotius, 14 June 2012, Sukabumi.

36. District Court of Cibadak Decision No. 15/Pid.B/2012/Pn.CBD, 2 May 2012 (Timotius).

37. District Court of Cibadak Decision No. 15/Pid.B/2012/Pn.CBD, 2 May 2012 (Timotius).

38. Interview with Timotius, 14 June 2012, Sukabumi.

39. Interview with Timotius, 26 March 2014, Cibinong.

40. Interview with Dawood Amiri, 24 March 2014, Purwakerta.

41. Breakouts from the detention centre in Pekanbaru happened rather frequently (such as that reported by Tanjung [2010]).

42. Interview with Dawood Amiri, 24 March 2014, Purwakerta.

43. District Court of East Jakarta Decision No. 1374/PID.B/2012/PN.JKT.TIM, 16 January 2013 (Dawood Amiri).

44. District Court of East Jakarta Decision No. 1128/PID.SUS/2013/PN.JKT.TIM, 21 January 2014 (Javaid Mahmood).

45. District Court of East Jakarta Decision No1374/PID.B/2012/PN.JKT.TIM, 16 January 2013 (Dawood Amiri).

46. Interview, 31 April 2014, Jakarta.

47. Interview with director of Investigation and Immigration Enforcement, Criminal Investigation Police Headquarters, 14 March 2014, Jakarta.

48. District Court of East Jakarta Decision No. 1128/PID.SUS/2013/PN.JKT.TIM, 21 January 2014 (Javaid Mahmood).

49. Interview with director of Investigation and Immigration Enforcement, Criminal Investigation Police Headquarters, 13 November 2013, Jakarta.

9

CONCLUSION

> ... in 25 march 2013 i left from indonesia
> by ilegal boat and i have been in torture five days
> in the oceon between kindari sulewesi
> and to darwin, then australian navy caught us and servived us,
> at the moment iam ... still in camp
> i hope that next month to come to Sydney.
> (message forwarded by Ali through Facebook, 16 April 2013)

STUCK AGAIN

On a balmy autumn afternoon in 2014 in a not so cosy suburb in Western Sydney I am about to meet Ali, whose story this book begins with, again. A few weeks earlier, I received notice that he had finally been released from immigration detention in Darwin. Despite a number of failed attempts earlier on and "many litres of swallowed salt water", as Ali put it, he had kept trying to reach Australia by boat. In April 2013, just a few months before the Australian government sealed its borders to maritime arrivals, Ali had eventually made it. The decision to risk his life, once again, on a tiny boat to cross the sea was anything but an easy one. Ali had spent years waiting for his proper resettlement as a recognized refugee. At times, when waiting became unbearable and he was about to lose hope, he had even contemplated returning voluntarily to Somalia, but the UNHCR would not approve this plan, leaving him stuck in Indonesia.

Having faced death once before on a sinking boat near Sumba, Ali was fully aware of the risks involved. When the prices charged by people smugglers dropped in early 2013 because of the very high demand for their services and a sort of "end-of-season sale", Ali wanted to try his luck once more. He called a number of friends in Europe to lend him money and managed to scrape together AU$2,000. Just after he had paid the money collector, he got notice from the United States Embassy that he was invited for an interview to determine whether or not he could be resettled in the United States. Ali was torn: should he opt to continue the proper process, knowing that in the preceding four years only one Somali person had been approved for resettlement by any destination country? Or should he just get on a boat straight away, anticipating a likely change of government in Australia that would cement Australia's *non-entrée* policies even further and make it more difficult in the future to enter the country irregularly?

Ali opted for the latter. The price he had to pay was not just another near-death experience when a storm hit, the engine of the boat failed, and the boat sank. After his rescue by the Australian Navy he was further punished with mandatory immigration detention for a year, first on Christmas Island and then in Darwin. Even after his release, the punishment seemed not quite over, as he was given only a bridging visa which did not grant him any rights to work or study. Had he arrived a few weeks earlier, his chance for fast integration would have been much greater. In a way, the endless waiting for an unclear outcome, to which he had become accustomed while in Indonesia, now seemed to continue in Australia as well. While Ali had coped with the uncertainty in Indonesia by daydreaming about his future life in Australia, now, while waiting in Australia, he reminisced about Indonesia. Many of the small details of his everyday life in Puncak, to which he had paid little attention back then, suddenly appeared memorable, even cherished.[1]

This book has attempted to describe the time-intensive migration processes and to provide a detailed account of the conditions for transit migrants in Indonesia, a hub for the irregular movement of people that had previously been widely ignored. At a time that Shahram Khosravi (2010, p. 1) has described as "an epoch of border fetishism", critical scholars have drawn attention to the phenomenon of "crimmigration" (Stumpf 2006, quoted in Moran, Gill and Conlon 2013, p. 1), which captures the portrayal by governments of irregular migrants as criminals. Irregular or unmanaged migration has become the new nightmare for which states have to prepare. No matter how small the numbers of uninvited guests might be in reality, their unwanted presence serves government and anti-immigration lobbyists well as they construct new concepts of threat and, consequently, the need to erect more barriers to protect long-term established residents from anticipated "invasion". A comparison of the political agendas of destination countries reveals that the rights and privileges of their citizens are to be protected before the human rights of non-citizens are to be fully considered and respected. Leanne Weber and Sharon Pickering (2011, p. 15) have noted that "the withdrawal of legal rights from irregular travellers coincides with the granting of extra-legal powers for agents of the state". Even though there are several conventions and laws in place that should protect mobile populations in search of protection, legal measures available to those needy populations often remain far too abstract for them to access (Khosravi 2010, p. 36). Access to protection is frequently compromised and fundamental rights for transiting asylum seekers and refugees are often not safeguarded (Papadopoulou-Kourkoula 2008).

By giving a current and historical overview of how Indonesia has tried to immobilize illegalized travellers and how unwanted mobility has been increasingly criminalized and punished through the detention of transit migrants in response to pressure and incentives from Australia, this book not only challenges the usefulness of detention regimes, but also questions the value of immobilization and detention, as they cause more damage to the transit migrants rather than constitute an effective deterrent to the increased movement of people. Although community detention is much preferred by transit migrants while they are in Indonesia, recent violence and raids in Puncak, as well as the evictions from Puncak, where asylum seekers, refugees and undocumented migrants had found temporary homes for more than a decade, have signalled the limits of community toleration in Indonesia. As Leanne Weber and Sharon Pickering (2011, p. 28) have warned, immobilizing illegalized travellers in transit puts them at risk of hostility and violence from local populations and of confinement in detention centres.

Being stuck in transit for an undetermined period of time becomes a state of permanent temporariness, marked by great uncertainty, desultoriness and the constant need for improvization. Thus, being stuck in transit has been described as "purgatory of waiting" (Hiemstra 2013, p. 70) and as "a state between life and death, a limbo between here and there" (Khosravi 2010, p. 74). Nevertheless, what makes transit migration different from other types of migration and migratory decision-making is the voluntary nature of the making of certain decisions before and during the journeys (Koser 2010a, p. 189). Transit migrants usually retain a degree of agency with which they engage in the migration process to negotiate hurdles (Schuster 2005a, p. 758). However, the voluntariness of irregular modes of mobility more often than not brings its own risks, as was confirmed by an Iraqi refugee who had tried several times to reach Australia by boat: "We didn't come to Indonesia to stay here, but we wanted to go to Australia. I was forced to risk my life, but when already under threat another risk doesn't really matter."[2]

Where there are borders, it would seem that there is also the crossing of those borders, both regularly and clandestinely. Despite the increased walling-off by destination countries that spend enormous amounts on the securitization of their borders, transit migrants and those who benefit financially from providing them with smuggling services find ways to outmanoeuvre the strict surveillance of the borders and make their way into these countries even at an often extremely high personal cost. New border policies and technologies, referred to by some as border-necropolitics, often only manage to stop the flows temporarily.

By definition, transit migrants have no desire to settle in transit (Vachudova 2000, p. 160); yet, in Indonesia, thanks to the Australian government's latest relaunch of Pacific Solution II, they are stuck in a "carceral archipelago". Even those transit migrants who were not in immigration detention while in Indonesia felt restricted and constrained by prohibitions on work and study. The restrictions on everyday life and the lack of opportunities are often experienced as punishment; as an Iraqi refugee who spent more than ten years in Indonesia before he was resettled has put it: "Every country has its own method of torture. In Iraq they use bullets, in Indonesia it is the discrimination by organizations and their regulations. Night and day they say we are criminals, illegals, this was more painful than a bullet in your head."[3]

Aspasia Papadopoulou-Kourkoula (2008, p. 141) has succinctly and accurately argued that, for transit migrants, "emotions, preferences and physical condition can have as much of an impact as policy frameworks and decisions". For many transit migrants who spend any considerable time in Indonesia, the humiliating treatment they experience there is unforgettable; some even claim that they "lost their dignity, identity and confidence". Even if eventually resettled, they find it hard to move on, as the experiences in transit weighs heavily on their minds. In the words of a former transit migrant, "We were like a dead person, out of energy and power and when we come here [i.e., Australia] we are expected to function and fit in and work and contribute to society."[4]

Those who are not resettled from Indonesia through formal legal processes, but come by boat, face even greater disappointment, trauma and humiliation in Australian detention centres or, more recently, in the Australian-funded detention camps on Manus Island and Nauru. Given the dangers at sea, the numbers who have vanished into maritime graveyards and, particularly, what awaits these transit migrants once they manage to reach the "lucky country", the question of whether the boat trips are worth taking must be asked. Sailing into a seemingly unknown future, many of these people who are fleeing war and conflict in their homelands may not have had the chance to consider their options sufficiently and make an informed decision at the start of their journey. Weighing up the pros and cons of onward migration when stuck in a hostile transit environment is also likely to inhibit deliberate and informed decision-making about the next leg of their journey.

In avoiding overemphasis on the agency that transit migrants have over their own destinies or the migration policies in the destination country that affect their destinies, this book has aimed to provide a comprehensive analysis that takes into account the attitudes of the Indonesian government and parts of Indonesian society, offering a perspective that has for a long time been entirely ignored. Indonesia's attitude towards transit migrants has never been particularly welcoming; nevertheless, Indonesia has again and again tolerated their presence and allowed them to reside in its territory temporarily. In years when many thousands were stranded on its shores, the Indonesian government decided to host them in peripheral, largely uninhabited islands. In years when only a few hundred came, Indonesia had a rather laissez-faire attitude towards their movement. Indonesian state authorities only started to turn towards more proactive immobilization of transit migrants once it was guaranteed that it needed to make no major contribution from its domestic budget for their care in detention. Without the very generous Australian funding channelled through the IOM, it is unlikely that Indonesia would detain thousands of transit migrants. Moreover, Indonesia only began to combat people-smuggling once lucrative funding and collaboration was offered from Australian and other sources. While the issues of transit migrants and people-smuggling are not considered to be of high priority in Indonesia's domestic affairs, they have become increasingly important pawns in shaping its diplomatic relations with Australia.

A driving question of this research has been whether the securitization of migration in Indonesia, which received a serious boost when the new Law of Immigration came into force in 2011, has trumped aspects of protection for mobile populations. Despite persistently paying lip service to an interest in protecting asylum seekers and refugees, Indonesia has not really substantiated this interest. Not only is Indonesia still not a signatory to the 1951 Refugee Convention and the 1967 Protocol, it also still lacks a basic legislative framework for the protection of refugees, which is generally understood as protection from persecution, non-*refoulement*, access to a legal procedure for claiming asylum and the possibility for adequate survival. Because Indonesian immigration authorities would not disclose any data on forced returns and denied entry, it was impossible to reach a final conclusion about whether *refoulement* takes place. However, there is some ground for suspicion that potential asylum seekers are occasionally turned away at border entry points. So far, a small number of asylum seekers who had managed to enter Indonesia reported that their relatives were rejected by immigration at the airport in Jakarta and forced to get on a return flight, despite possessing valid visas and legal documents.

Asylum seekers and refugees in Indonesia do not have any rights of lawful residence in the country; they are only tolerated by the authorities and there is no legal pathway for them to gain citizenship. If found outside certain designated areas or attempting to enter or leave the country anywhere other than at official border posts, they risk arbitrary detention by local law enforcement agencies. Transit migrants have no lawful access to the labour market and, thus, they are not able to work legally, which leaves them with no adequate or dignified means of existence. Extremely few manage to enter the informal employment sector and work illegally. There are no durable solutions available for recognized refugees, other than to be resettled in another country. Those who have been recognized as refugees but have repeatedly been rejected by potential resettlement countries are left in a legal, social, political and economic limbo.

In late 2004 the UNHCR published its views on the concept of effective protection as it relates to Indonesia and found that "the protection situation in Indonesia cannot be characterized as affording effective protection" (UNHCR Canberra 2004). Over the last decade, numerous attempts have been made to improve the material welfare of transit migrants, both in detention and outside, through the provision of medical care, housing and other services, but many aforementioned protection challenges remain in place. Thus, the nature of protection in Indonesia can at best be labelled as semi-protection only. Nevertheless, even without a proper legal protection framework, Indonesia treats transit migrants better than its neighbours do. The de facto protection on offer in Indonesia has in fact attracted thousands of transit migrants who were previously in Malaysia.

Governments and state authorities are not the only institutions responsible for handling transit migrants and granting effective protection. As has become very clear in the case of Indonesia, international organizations such as the UNHCR and the IOM play a vital role, offering the services that the Indonesian government refuses to provide. Even though, as this book has demonstrated, the UNHCR remains too understaffed and under-resourced to deal with the many asylum applications it receives in a timely manner, the organization has managed to extend its reach beyond Jakarta. The organization that clearly benefitted the most from the presence of transit migrants in Indonesia is the IOM, as it has received very generous funding from Australia, its main funding provider, to cater for unwanted asylum seekers inside and outside of immigration detention centres and thereby to try to keep them at bay. Whether providing training for Indonesian law enforcement officers with methods of combatting people-smuggling, running anti-people-smuggling workshops in the communities of coastal hotspots, or distributing anti-people-smuggling propaganda, the IOM has been in the midst of the action and has expanded its organizational reach within Indonesia.

Quintessentially, as Aspasia Papadopoulou-Kourkoula (2008, p. 141) has argued, it is challenging to develop effective policy responses for the management of transit migration, because it is difficult to predict the outcome of policymaking, as transit migrants rarely follow set plans. Enhancing protection for asylum seekers and refugees in the Asia–Pacific region warrants greater attention than combatting people-smuggling and controlling borders, which are at present the main focus of policymaking. After all, when the lives and livelihoods of people are effectively protected wherever they happen to be, the need for building barriers to limit and control their movement will diminish.

Notes

1. During our last meeting in Indonesia I had given Ali a little digital camera so that he could preserve scenes from Puncak, his Indonesian friends and things he held dear while in transit. Unfortunately, the camera and all his documents were lost at sea.
2. Interview, 18 May 2013, Sydney.
3. Interview, 18 May 2013, Sydney.
4. Interview, 18 May 2013, Sydney.

BIBLIOGRAPHY

"16 Imigran Kabur dari Kantor Imigrasi, Satu Tewas". *Metro Pagi*, 15 November 2011 <http://metrotvnews.com/read/newsvideo/2011/11/15/139767/16-Imigran-Kabur-dari-Kantor-Imigrasi-Satu-Tewas/6> (accessed 4 June 2013).

"47 Imigran Gelap Ditangkap di Pelabuhan Ratu". *Pos Kota*, 3 June 2012.

"55 Imigran Kabur, Jebol Jeruji Besi Rudenim Tanjung Pinang". *Batam Post*, 17 July 2012.

"80 Orang Pengungsi di Rudenim Belawan Masih Mogok Makan". *Tribun Medan*, 7 April 2013.

"160 Afghan Asylum Seekers Launch Hunger Strike in Indonesian Detention Centre". *Jakarta Globe*, 4 May 2012.

"4,000 Imigran Ilegal Berkeliaran". Kepolisian Negara Republik Indonesia, Daerah Jawa Barat, 14 December 2012 <http://www.lodaya.web.id/?p=15330> (accessed 9 August 2013).

Abbas, Hafid. "Cycle of Victimization: RI Children in Prisons". *Jakarta Post*, 5 December 2011.

"Abbott Dinilai Perumit Hubungan Dengan Indonesia". *Suara Pembaruan*, 10 September 2013.

Abdurrahman, Muhammad Nur. "Pengungsi Somalia Demo Kantor Perwakilan UNHCR Makassar". *Detik News*, 24 October 2012.

Adam, Asvi Warman. "Kontroversi Soeharto". *Tempo Interactive*, 28 November 2005.

Adamrah, Mustaqim. "Refugees Make Money from Farming". *Jakarta Post*, 7 June 2011.

Adepoju, Aderanti. "Emigration Dynamics in Sub-Saharan Africa". *International Migration* 33 (1995): 315–90.

———. "Trends in International Migration in and from Africa". In *International Migration: Prospects and Policies in a Global Market*, edited by Douglas Massey and Edward Taylor. New York: Oxford University Press, 2004.

"Agreement between the Republic of Indonesia and Australia on the Framework for Security Cooperation". 2006 <http://www.dfat.gov.au/geo/indonesia/ind-aus-sec06.html> (accessed 7 March 2014).

Akuntono, Indra. "Pencari Suaka Dikembalikan, Priyo Sebut Australia Ledek Indonesia". *Kompas*, 7 February 2014.

Alberici, Emma. "Indonesia Australia Relations Could Be Closer". *ABC News*, 1 October 2013 <http://www.abc.net.au/news/2013-10-01/indonesia-australia-relations-could-be-closer/4990212> (accessed 7 May 2014).

Alford, Peter. "Indonesian Boat Crew Youths to Sue over Prison". *The Australian*, 23 January 2013*a*.

———. "Rohingyas the Next Wave to Seek Australian Refuge". *The Australian*, 13 April 2013*b*.

———. "Jakarta's Visas Let Iranians Flow Free". *The Australian*, 19 July 2013*c*.

———. "Tony Abbott's Policy Under Pressure as Jakarta Puts Limits on Turn-backs". *The Australian*, 9 November 2013*d*.

———. "New Stand-off with Indonesia over Asylum Seekers". *The Australian*, 11 November 2013*e*.

Alford, Peter and Paul Maley. "Asylum Tide Swamping Solution". *The Australian*, 21 August 2013*a*.

———. "Last Hopes of Asylum Evaporate with Election Win". *The Australian*, 12 September 2013*b*.

Alford, Peter and Telly Nathalia. "People-Smuggler Let Go by Australia is 'Back in Business'". *The Australian*, 16 May 2013*a*.

———. "Indonesia's Bid to Put 10,000 Refugees on Isle". *The Australian*, 21 September 2013*b*.

———. "Jakarta's Warships to Target Refugees". *The Australian*, 29 January 2014.

Alford, Peter and Brendan Nicholson. "Asylum Flow to Indonesia Slashed, Says UN". *The Australian*, 20 February 2014.

Allard, Tom. "Indonesia Wants to Find the 'Australian Solution'". *Sydney Morning Herald*, 3 November 2009.

———. "Key Suspect Traffics Iranians, Kurds". *The Age*, 17 December 2010.

Allard, Tom and Phillip Coorey. "Indonesia Governor Rebels on Refugees". *Sydney Morning Herald*, 27 October 2009.

Al-Wafa, Ahmad Abu. *Hak-hak Pencarian Suaka Dalam Syaruat Islam dan Hukum International*. Jakarta: UNHCR Indonesia and the Law Faculty of UIN Syarif Hidayatullah, 2011.

Amelia, Rizky. "Activist Calls for Updated Laws on Immigrants Passing Through Indonesia". *Jakarta Globe*, 23 April 2013.

Amiri, Dawood. *Confessions of a People-Smuggler*. Melbourne: Scribe, 2014.

Andreas, Peter. *Border Games: Policing the U.S.–Mexico Divide*. New York: Cornell University Press, 2000.

Andrijasevic, Rutvica and William Walters. "The International Organization for Migration and the International Government of Borders". *Environment and Planning D: Society and Space* 28 (2010): 977–99.

Anwar, Dewi Fortuna. "Aspek Imigran Illegal Dalam Hubungan Indonesia–Australia". In *Indonesia Dalam Strategi Keamanan Australia: Persoalan Migrasi Illegal*, edited by M. Muna and M. Riefqi. Jakarta: Pusat Penelitian Politik, 2002.

———. "A Problem of Mixed Messages". *The AsiaLink Essays* 4, no. 6 (2012) <http://asialink.unimelb.edu.au/research_and_policy/the_asialink_essays/past/a_problem_of_mixed_messages> (accessed 7 May 2014).

Arnaz, Farouk. "Two More Suspects Named in TNI People Smuggling Case: Police". *Jakarta Globe*, 19 July 2012.

———. "BNN Discovers '2–3 Hectares' of Khat Drug in Bogor". *Jakarta Globe*, 4 February 2013*a*.

———. "Indonesia to Turn a Blind Eye to Australia-Bound Boats". *Jakarta Globe*, 25 November 2013*b*.

Ashari, Khasan. "Why We Need a Law on People Smuggling". *Jakarta Post*, 16 January 2012.

Ashutosh, Ishan and Alison Mountz. "Migration Management for the Benefit of Whom? Interrogating the Work of the International Organization for Migration". *Citizenship Studies* 15 (2011): 21–38.

Assifa, Farid and Kiki Andi Pati. "Mesin Kapal Mati, 210 Imigran Gelap Terdampar di Kendari". *Kompas*, 21 May 2013.

"Asylum Seekers Allege Mistreatment by Australian Navy". Agence France-Presse, 8 January 2014.

"Australia Accepts Boat People in Stand-off with Indonesia". News.com, 9 November 2013 <http://www.news.com.au/national/australia-accepts-boat-people-in-standoff-with-indonesia/story-fncynjr2-1226756370551> (accessed 7 May 2014).

"Australia–Indonesia Border Computerized Value". Press statement by Coordinating Minister for Political, Legal and Security Affairs, 11 December 2009 <http://www.indonesia.go.id/en/ministries/minister-of-coordinator/coordinating-minister-for-political-legal-and-security-affairs/342-provinsi-jawa-barat-pertahanan-dan-keamanan/1538-australia-indonesia-nilai-komputerisasi-perbatasan> (accessed 7 May 2014).

"Australia Must Understand RI Sovereignty: Minister". *Jakarta Post*, 22 January 2014.

"Australia Sends Back Another Asylum-Seeker Boat". *Jakarta Globe*, 25 February 2014.

Australian Department of Immigration and Border Protection. "Country Profile Indonesia". 2013 <http://www.immi.gov.au/media/statistics/country-profiles/_files/indonesia.pdf> (accessed 7 May 2014).

Australian Department of Immigration and Citizenship. *East Timor-born: Community Information Summary*. Canberra, 2007.

———. *Asylum Statistics–Australia, Quarterly Tables, March Quarter*. Belconnen, 2012*a*

<http://www.immi.gov.au/media/publications/statistics/asylum/_files/ asylum-stats-march-quarter-2012.pdf> (accessed 7 May 2014).

———. *Asylum Trends, Australia: 2011–12, Annual Publication.* Canberra, 2012*b* <http://www.immi.gov.au/media/publications/statistics/asylum/_files/ asylum-trends-aus-annual-2011-12.pdf> (accessed 7 May 2014).

———. "Administered Item: Management and Care of Irregular Immigrants in Indonesia". 2012*c* <http://www.immi.gov.au/about/reports/annual/2011-12/ html/performance/outcome_4/program_4.3/administered_items.htm> (accessed 7 May 2014).

Australian Government. "Immigration and Citizenship", in *Budget Paper no. 2, part 2.* 2011 <http://www.budget.gov.au/2011-12/content/bp2/html/ bp2_expense-14.htm> (accessed 7 May 2014).

———. "Agency Resourcing: Attorney-General's", in *Budget Paper no. 4.* 2013 <http://www.budget.gov.au/2013-14/content/bp4/html/bp4_ar-02.htm> (accessed 7 May 2014).

Australian Government and UNHCR. *Partnership Framework between Australian Agency for International Development and the Department of Immigration and Citizenship on behalf of the Commonwealth of Australia and The Office of the United Nations High Commissioner for Refugees 2013–2016.* 2013 <http://www.ausaid. gov.au/makediff/humanitarian/policy-partnerships/Documents/ausaid- unhcr-partnership-framework-summary.pdf> (accessed 7 May 2014).

Australian Human Rights Commission. *An Age of Uncertainty: Inquiry into the Treatment of Individuals Suspected of People Smuggling Offences Who Say That They Are Children.* Sydney, 2012.

Australian Senate. *Official Hansard No. 4.* 8 February 2005 <http://www.aph.gov. au/binaries/hansard/senate/dailys/ds080205.pdf> (accessed 12 March 2014).

———. "Question Taken on Notice: Additional Budget Estimates Hearing, Immigration and Border Protection Portfolio, 25 February 2014" <http://www. aph.gov.au/~/media/Estimates/Live/legcon_ctte/estimates/add_1314/ DIBP/AE14-283.pdf> (accessed 25 October 2014).

Australian Senate Standing Committee on Legal and Constitutional Affairs. "Australian Customs and Border Protection Service: Question 115 ... 14 February 2012" <http://www.aph.gov.au/~/media/Estimates/Live/ legcon_ctte/estimates/add_1112/ag/QoN115_ACBPS.ashx> (accessed 7 May 2014).

"Australia's Abbott Proposes Buying 'Smuggler' Boats". Agence France-Presse, 23 August 2013.

Azam, Suhaini and Michael Vatikiotis. "For Those in Peril: Malaysia, Indonesia at Centre of Boat People Row". *Far Eastern Economic Review* 148, no. 18 (1990): 8–9.

Bachelard, Michael. "Boat People Refuse to Leave Rescue Ship". *Sydney Morning Herald*, 10 April 2012*a*.

———. "Indonesia Calls on Australia to Lift Refugee Intake". *Sydney Morning Herald*, 14 July 2012*b*.

———. "Indonesia Welcomes Asylum-Seeker Report". *Sydney Morning Herald*, 13 August 2012*c*.

———. "'Sacrificial Lamb' Reveals All While People-Smuggling Kingpins Go Free". *Sydney Morning Herald*, 23 February 2013*a*.

———. "The Man Who Trades on Tragedy". *Sydney Morning Herald*, 25 June 2013*b*.

———. "Australia, Indonesia in Asylum-Seeker 'Stand-off'". *The Age*, 7 November 2013*c*.

———. "Indonesia Spy Row: Talks Have Stalled, Say Indonesians". *Sydney Morning Herald*, 26 November 2013*d*.

———. "Asylum Seekers Say They Were Tricked by Navy". *Sydney Morning Herald*, 17 January 2014*a*.

———. "Indonesians Think Prime Minister Tony Abbott is Inflaming Tensions for Political Gain Over Asylum Seekers". *Sydney Morning Herald*, 24 January 2014*b*.

———. "Australia Turns Back Sixth Boat Carrying Asylum Seekers". *Sydney Morning Herald*, 6 February 2014*c*.

———. "Investigation: 'Burned Hands' on the High Seas". *Sydney Morning Herald*, 6 February 2014*d*.

———. "Tony Abbott's Policy a Failure as Boats Keep Coming, Says Indonesian Foreign Minister Marty Natalegawa". *Sydney Morning Herald*, 6 May 2014*e*.

———. "Indonesian Ambassador Quietly Returns to Canberra". *Sydney Morning Herald*, 26 May 2014*f*.

———. "Tony Abbott Declares Boats Issue with Indonesia Resolved following Meeting with Susilo Bambang Yudhoyono". *Sydney Morning Herald*, 4 June 2014*g*.

———. "Australia has Indonesia 'Phobia', Says Presidential Candidate". *Sydney Morning Herald*, 23 June 2014*h*.

———. "Australia Wins the Spy War with Indonesia". *Sydney Morning Herald*, 28 August 2014*i*.

Bachelard, Michael and David Wroe. "Abbott's 'Cowboy' Tack Riles Indonesian MPs". *Sydney Morning Herald*, 20 September 2013.

Baldwin-Edwards, Martin. "'Between a Rock and a Hard Place': North Africa as a Region of Emigration, Immigration & Transit Migration". *Review of African Political Economy* 108 (2006): 311–24.

Balfour, Frederik. "Home Again: Repatriation Money Turns Returnees into Nouveau Riche". *Far Eastern Economic Review* 156, no. 9 (1993): 28.

Balint, Ruth. *Troubled Waters: Borders, Boundaries and the Possession in the Timor Sea*. Crows Nest, NSW: Allen & Unwin, 2005.

Ball, Rochelle, Laura Beacroft and Jade Lindley. *Australia's Pacific Seasonal Worker Pilot Scheme: Managing Vulnerabilities to Exploitation* (Trends & Issues in Crime and Criminal Justice no. 432). Canberra: Australian Institute of Criminology, 2011.

Bari, Shamsul. "Refugee Status Determination under the Comprehensive Plan of Action (CPA): A Personal Account". *International Journal of Refugee Law* 4 (1992): 487–513.

Barker, Cat. "The People Smugglers' Business Model" (research paper no. 2). Canberra: Parliamentary Library, 2013 <http://www.aph.gov.au/About_Parliament/Parliamentary_Departments/Parliamentary_Library/pubs/rp/rp1213/13rp02> (accessed 7 May 2014).

Barnett, Michael and Martha Finnemore. *Rules for the World: International Organizations in Global Politics*. Ithaca, NY: Cornell University Press, 2004.

Basuki, Orin. "Penyelundupan Pasir Masih Terjadi". *Kompas*, 2 February 2012.

Bateman, Sam. "Explainer: The Law of the Sea and Asylum Seekers". *The Conversation*, 13 November 2013.

Batoor, Barat Ali and Aubrey Belford. "In Between Persecution and Asylum". *The Global Mail*, 5 April 2013 <http://www.theglobalmail.org/feature/in-between-persecution-and-asylum/586/> (accessed 7 May 2014).

"Bekingi Imigran Gelap: Staf Imigrasi Jadi Tersangka". *Timor Express*, 17 April 2010.

Belford, Aubrey. "Resort of Last Resort". *Global Mail*, 5 April 2013 <http://www.theglobalmail.org/feature/resort-of-last-resort/585/> (accessed 7 May 2014).

———. "Jakarta Sees Chilly Ties with Australia until October: Indonesian Govt Document". *Jakarta Globe*, 17 February 2014.

Berkovic, Nicola and Peter Alford. "Failed Asylum-Seekers in U-turn to Malaysia". *The Australian*, 21 February 2014.

Bertrand, Jacques. "Legacies of the Authoritarian Past: Religious Violence in Indonesia's Moluccan Islands". *Pacific Affairs* 75, no. 1 (2002): 57–85.

Betts, Alexander. *Comprehensive Plans of Action: Insights from CIREFCA and the Indochinese CPA* (New Issues in Refugees Research Working Paper 120). Geneva: UNHCR, 2006.

Betts, Alexander, Gil Loescher and James Milner. *The United Nations High Commissioner for Refugees (UNHCR): The Politics and Practice of Refugee Protection into the 21st Century*. New York: Routledge, 2012.

Bhakti, Ikrar Nusa. "Jika Garuda Murka". *Kompas*, 22 November 2013.

Bilger, Veronika, Martin Hofmann and Michael Jandl. "Human Smuggling as a Transnational Service Industry: Evidence from Austria". *International Migration* 44, no. 4 (2006): 59–93.

Block, Karen, Elisha Riggs and Nick Haslam, eds. *Values and Vulnerabilities: The Ethics of Research with Refugees and Asylum Seekers*. Toowong: Australian Academic Press, 2013.

"Boats Carrying Fleeing Rohingya Muslims Capsize". *Jakarta Post*, 14 May 2013.

Borjas, J. George and Jeff Crisp, eds. *Poverty, International Migration and Asylum.* Basingstoke: Palgrave Macmillan, 2005.

Bowen, Chris. "Australia and Indonesia Improve Immigration Cooperation", press statement, 13 November 2008 <http://archive-au.com/page/518/2012-05-08/http://www.minister.immi.gov.au/media/media-releases/2008/ce08107.htm> (accessed 7 May 2014).

Bräuchler, Birgit. "Religions Online: Christian and Muslim (Re)presentations in the Moluccan Conflict". In *Christianity in Indonesia*, edited by Susanne Schröter. Berlin: LIT-Verlag, 2010.

Bredeloup Sylvie and Olivier Pliez. *The Libyan Migration Corridor.* San Domenico di Fiesole: Robert Schuman Centre for Advanced Studies, European University Institute, 2011.

Brown, Colin. "Spying 'Scandal': Another Challenge to the Australia–Indonesia Relationship?" *The Conversation*, 7 November 2013.

Brown, Matt. "Asylum Seekers Tunnel to Freedom". *ABC News*, 19 January 2012 <http://www.abc.net.au/news/2012-01-18/asylum-seekers-escape-detention-centre-in-indonesia/3781496> (accessed 7 May 2014).

"Buddhist Vihara in Jakarta Bombed, 3 Injured". *Jakarta Post*, 5 August 2013.

Busyra, Vita A.D. "On Matter of Asylum Boats, an Ocean of Differences". *Jakarta Globe*, 21 February 2014.

Callinan, Rory and Peter Alford. "People-Smugglers Sent to Prison; Fines Not Imposed Since Introduction". *The Australian*, 5 July 2011.

Carling, Jorgen. "Unauthorised Migration from Africa to Spain". *International Migration* 45, no. 4 (2007): 3–37.

Carrick, Damien. "Hazara People in Indonesian Legal Limbo". *Radio National Law Report*, 26 March 2013 <http://www.abc.net.au/radionational/programs/lawreport/hazaras-in-indonesia/4589070#transcript> (accessed 10 January 2014).

Cassrels, Deborah. "Asylum-Seekers Out of Sight, Out of Mind", *The Australian*, 16 March 2013.

Castles, Stephen. "What Role Does Australia Play in Accepting the World's Refugees?" *The Conversation*, 26 July 2012.

Chatelard, Géraldine. "Iraqi Asylum Migrants in Jordan: Conditions, Religious Networks and the Smuggling Process". In *Poverty, International Migration and Asylum*, edited by J. George Borjas and Jeff Crisp. Basingstoke: Palgrave Macmillan, 2005.

Church World Service (CWS). *Accessing Services in the City: The Significance of Urban Refugee–Host Relations in Cameroon, Indonesia and Pakistan.* New York, 2013.

Cohen, Margot. "Home from the Sea: Jakarta Mulls Plans to Close People Island Camp". *Far Eastern Economic Review* 156, no. 33 (1993): 15.

Collyer, Michael. *States of Insecurity: Consequences of Saharan Transit Migration*

(WP-07-31). Oxford: Centre on Migration, Policy and Society, University of Oxford, 2006.

————. "In-between Places: Trans-Saharan Transit Migrants in Morocco and the Fragmented Journey to Europe". *Antipode* 394 (2007): 668–90.

Collyer, Michael and Hein de Haas. "Developing Dynamic Categorisation of Transit Migration". *Population, Space and Place* 18 (2012): 468–81.

Collyer, Michael, Franck Düvell and Hein de Haas. "Critical Approaches to Transit Migration". *Population, Space and Place* 18 (2012): 407–14.

Conboy, Kenneth J. *INTEL: Inside Indonesia's Intelligence Service*. Jakarta: Equinox, 2004.

Connolly, Ellen. "Indonesia Voices Concerns about Coalition's Boats Policy 'Loud and Clear'". *Sydney Morning Herald*, 25 September 2013.

Corlett, David. *Following Them Home: The Fate of Returned Asylum Seekers*. Melbourne: Black, 2005.

Crespigny, Robin de. *The People Smuggler: The True Story of Ali Al Jenabi, the "Oskar Schindler of Asia"*. Camberwell, Vic: Penguin, 2012.

Crock, Mary and Daniel Ghezelbash. "Do Loose Lips Bring Ships? The Role of Policy, Politics and Human Rights in Managing Unauthorised Boat Arrivals". *Griffith Law Review* 19 (2010): 238–87.

Crouch, Melissa and Antje Missbach. *Trials of People Smugglers in Indonesia: 2007–2012* (policy paper no. 1). Melbourne: Centre for Indonesian Law, Islam and Society, 2013.

Dani , Didem A. *Waiting on the Purgatory: Religious Networks of Iraqi Christian Transit Migrants in Istanbul* (Working Paper RSCAS no. 25). Florence: European University Institute, 2006.

"Depresi, Imigran Afghanistan Coba Bunuh Diri di Rudenim Tanjungpinang". *Batam Today*, 15 June 2012.

Dodd, Mark. "Susilo Bambang Yudhoyono to Jail People-Smugglers for Five Years". *The Australian*, 11 March 2010.

Dowd, Rebecca. *Trapped in Transit: The Plight and Human Rights of Stranded Migrants* (New Issues in Refugees Research, research paper no. 156). Geneva: UNHCR, 2008.

Downer, Alexander and Chris Ellison. "Another People Smuggler to Face Australian Courts". Joint Media Release, 18 July 2003 <http://www.foreignminister.gov.au/releases/2003/fa_joint_peoplesmuggling.html> (accessed 8 May 2014).

Downer, Alexander and Amanda Vanstone. "Minasa Bone Returns to Indonesia". Joint Media Release, 9 November 2003 <http://www.foreignminister.gov.au/releases/2003/joint_Minasa_Bone.html> (accessed 20 May 2014).

"Dua Polisi NTB Terlibat Penyelundupan Imigran". Antara News, 28 April 2012 <http://www.antaranews.com/berita/308181/pelatih-persita-waspadai-kepemimpinan-wasit> (accessed 8 May 2014).

Dunn, Kevin M., Natascha Klocker and Tanya Salabay. "Contemporary Racism and Islamaphobia in Australia". *Ethnicities* 7 (2007): 564–89.

Düvell, Franck. "The Globalisation of Migration Control". *Open Democracy: Free Thinking for the World*, 11 June 2003 <http://www.opendemocracy.net/people-migrationeurope/article_1274.jsp> (accessed 8 May 2014).

———. *Crossing the Fringes of Europe: Transit Migration in the EU's Neighbourhood* (working paper no. 33). Oxford: Centre on Migration, Policy and Society, University of Oxford, 2006.

———. "Transit Migration: A Blurred and Politicised Concept". *Population, Space and Place* 18 (2012): 415–27.

Düvell, Franck, Anna Triandafyllidou and Bastian Vollmer. "Ethical Issues in Irregular Migration Research in Europe". *Population, Space and Place* 16 (2010): 227–39.

Edwards, Alice. "Tampering with Refugee Protection: The Case of Australia". *International Journal for Refugee Law* 15 (2003): 192–211.

"Egyptian Envoy Asks Indonesia to Hand Over Alleged People Smuggler to Egypt". *Jakarta Post*, 7 February 2003.

Eigmüller, Monika. "Soziologische Grenzbeobachtungen: Die Markierung von Differenzen durch Staatsgrenzen". In *Soziale Ungleichheit, Kulturelle Unterschiede*, Verhandlungen des 32. Kongresses der Deutschen Gesellschaft für Soziologie in München 2004, edited by Karl-Siegbert Rehberg. Frankfurt: Campus, 2006.

Ellison, Christopher. "Alleged People Smuggler Extradited to Australia". Media Release, E153/04, 12 November 2004 <http://sievx.com/articles/defending/2004/20041112Ellison.html> (accessed 20 May 2014).

European Commission. "EU Member States Granted Protection to More than 100,000 Asylum Seekers in 2012. Brussels: 2013 <http://epp.eurostat.ec.europa.eu> (accessed 27 May 2014).

Every, Danielle and Martha Augoustinos. "Constructions of Racism in the Australian Parliamentary Debates on Asylum Seekers". *Discourse & Society* 18 (2007): 411–36.

Expert Panel on Asylum Seekers. *Report* (commonly known as Houston Report). Canberra: Australian Government, 2012 <http://expertpanelonasylumseekers.dpmc.gov.au/sites/default/files/report/expert_panel_on_asylum_seekers_full_report.pdf> (accessed 8 May 2014).

Fandik, Mohammad. "Penampungan orang Vietnam di Pulau Galang 1975–1979". *Avatara* 1, no. 1 (2013): 164–72.

Fardah. "Sri Lankan Immigrants in Despair, Finally Surrender". Antara News, 27 August 2011 <http://www.antaranews.com/en/news/75206/sri-lankan-immigrants-in-despair-finally-surrender> (accessed 8 May 2014).

Fassin, Didier. "The Precarious Truth of Asylum". *Public Culture* 25, no. 1 (2013): 39-63.

"Federal Police Provide Three New Patrol Boats to Indonesia". *Australian Maritime Digest*, 1 February 2012: 3–4.

Field, Ophelia and Alice Edwards. "Alternatives to Detention of Asylum Seekers and Refugees" (POLAS/2006/03). Geneva: UNHCR Division of International Protection Services, 2006.

Fields, Rona M. "Life and Death on a Small Island: Vietnamese and Cambodian Refugees in Indonesia". *Migration World* 20, no. 5 (1992): 16–20.

Fitri, Emmy. "'Chief' People-Smuggler Arrested". *Jakarta Post*, 8 November 2001.

Fitri R. "Possible Asylum Seekers' Boat Found in Waters off Lombok". *Jakarta Globe*, 14 April 2012a.

———. "Military to Probe Claims Officers Extorted Cash from Asylum-Seekers". *Jakarta Globe*, 30 August 2012b.

Fitzpatrick, Stephen. "Galang's Refugee Hell". *The Australian*, 5 November 2009a.

———. "Jakarta Fearful of Asylum-Seeker Fallout". *The Australian*, 7 November 2009b.

Ford, Michele, Lenore Lyons and Wayne Palmer. "Stopping the Hordes: A Critical Account of the Labor Government's Regional Approach to the Management of Asylum Seekers". *Local–Global: Identity, Security, Community* 8 (2010): 28–35.

Fourth Bali Regional Ministerial Conference on People Smuggling, Trafficking in Persons and Related Transnational Crime. *Co-Chairs' Statement*, 29–30 March 2011 <http://www.unodc.org/documents/southeastasiaandpacific/2011/04/som-indonesia/110330_FINAL_Ministerial_Co-chairs_statement_BRMC_IV.pdf> (accessed 14 January 2014).

Fox, James J. "People-smugglers and the Crews They Recruit: Changing Patterns". Paper presented at annual conference of the Australian Anthropological Society, 5–8 November 2013, Canberra.

Freudenstein, Roland. "Rio Odra, Rio Buh: Poland, Germany, and the Borders of Twenty-First-Century Europe". In *The Wall around the West: State Borders and Immigration Controls in North America and Europe*, edited by Peter Andreas and Timothy Snyder. Lanham, MD: Rowman and Littlefield, 2000.

Gallagher, Heather. "Asylum Seekers on Lombok Complain of Long Limbo". *Epoch Times*, 29 October 2005.

Gammeltoft-Hansen, Thomas. *The Refugee, the Sovereign and the Sea: EU Interdiction Policies in the Mediterranean* (working paper no. 6). Copenhagen: Danish Institute for International Studies, 2008.

Garnaut, John and Michael Bachelard. "Joko Widodo's Blunt Warning to Prime Minister Tony Abbott". *Sydney Morning Herald*, 18 October 2014.

Genova, Nicholas de. "Theoretical Overview". In *The Deportation Regime: Sovereignty, Space, and the Freedom of Movement*, edited by Nicholas de Genova and Nathalie Peutz. Durham, NC: Duke University Press, 2010.

Georgi, Fabian. "For the Benefit of Some: The International Organization for

Migration and its Global Migration Management". In *The Politics of International Migration Management*, edited by Martin Geiger and Antoine Pécoud. Basingstoke: Palgrave Macmillan, 2010.

Georgi, Fabian and Susanne Schatral. "Towards a Critical Theory of Migration Control: The Case of the International Organization for Migration (IOM)". In *The New Politics of International Mobility: Migration Management and its Discontents*, edited by Martin Geiger and Antoine Pécoud. Osnabrück: Institut für Migrationsforschung und Interkulturelle Studien, 2012.

Ghulam, Hassan. "Afghani Asylum Seekers and Refugees in the Republic of Indonesia: First Report". Project Safecom Inc, 2004 <http://www.safecom.org.au/pdfs/hassan-report.pdf> (accessed 8 May 2014).

Gilley, Bruce. "The Final Stretch: Detention Centres are Being Cleared across the Region". *Far Eastern Economic Review* 159, no. 29 (1996): 19.

Green, Penny. "State Crime Beyond Borders". In *Borders, Mobility and Technologies of Control*, edited by Sharon Pickering and Leanne Weber. Dordrecht: Springer, 2006.

Grewcock, Michael. "Shooting the Passenger: Australia's War on Illicit Migrants". In *Human Trafficking*, edited by Maggy Lee. Uffculme, Devon: Willan, 2007.

———. *Border Crimes: Australia's War on Illicit Migrants*. Sydney: Institute of Criminology Press, 2009.

———. "Australia's Ongoing Border Wars". *Race and Class* 54, no. 3 (2013): 10–32.

———. "Australian Border Policing: Regional 'Solution' and Neocolonialsm". *Race and Class* 55, no. 3 (2014): 71–78.

Guest, Debbie. "Merak Boat Protesters from 2009 'Left Languishing' in Indonesia". *The Australian*, 8 March 2012.

Gultom, Silvester. "Stop Detention of Children!" *Refuge* (March 2013): 5–6.

Gunawan, Apriadi. "8 Myanmar Detainees Die in Medan Brawl". *Jakarta Post*, 6 April 2013.

Haas, Hein de. "Morocco: From Emigration Country to Africa's Migration Passage to Europe". *Migration Information Source*, 1 October 2005 <http://www.migrationpolicy.org/article/morocco-emigration-country-africas-migration-passage-europe> (accessed 8 May 2014).

———. *Irregular Migration from Africa to Europe: Questioning the Transit Hypothesis*. Oxford: International Migration Institute, University of Oxford, 2007.

"Hadi Ahmadi Loses Application to Appeal People-Smuggling Conviction". *The Australian*, 1 November 2011.

Hage, Ghassan. "Waiting Out the Crisis: On Stuckedness and Governmentality". In *Waiting*, edited by Ghassan Hage. Carlton, Vic: Melbourne University Press, 2009.

Hamer, Alex. "Australia Evades Basarnas Claims". *Jakarta Globe*, 16 November 2013.

Harsaputra, Indra. "200 Missing in Boat Tragedy". *Jakarta Post*, 19 December 2011.

Haryadi, Yopi. "SAR Operation in Illegal Movement of People (IMP)". Presentation by Head of Search-and-Rescue Operation Evaluation at Basarnas at Jakarta Foreign Correspondents Club, 13 November 2013, Jakarta.

Hasan, Nurdin. "Aceh Fishermen Rescue 76 Stranded Rohingya Asylum Seekers". *Jakarta Globe*, 8 April 2013*a*.

———. "Aceh Fishermen Rescue 68 Rohingya Asylum Seekers from Indian Ocean". *Jakarta Globe*, 28 July 2013*b*.

Hasibuan M.S. *Prajurit TNI Dalam Tugas Kemanusiaan Galang 96*. Jakarta: Markas Besar Tentara Nasional Indonesia, Pusat Sejarah, 2007.

Hathaway, James C. "Labelling the 'Boat People': The Failure of the Human Rights Mandate of the Comprehensive Action Plan for Indochinese Refugees". *Human Rights Quarterly* 15 (1993): 686–702.

Hayaze, Nabiel. Presentation by IOM staff member at Joint Seminar on Optimizing the Handling of Human Trafficking, Refugees and Asylum Seekers, Jakarta, 21 November 2012.

"Heartbreaking Protest". *Jakarta Post*, 6 November 2012.

Heckmann, Friedrich. "Illegal Migration: What Can We Know and What Can We Explain? The Case of Germany". *International Migration Review* 38 (2004): 1103–25.

Hedman, Eva-Lotta. "World Refugee Day in One Country: Celebrating Refugees and UNHCR in Malaysia". *Journal of Refugee Studies* 22 (2009): 283–301.

Helton, Arthur C. "The Comprehensive Plan of Action for Indo-Chinese Refugees: An Experiment in Refugee Protection and Control". *New York Law School Journal of Human Rights* 8 (1990/1): 111–48.

———. "Refugee Determination under the Comprehensive Plan of Action: Overview and Assessment". *International Journal for Refugee Law* 5 (1993): 544–58.

Hess, Sabine. "De-naturalising Transit Migration: Theory and Methods of an Ethnographic Analysis". *Population, Space and Place* 18 (2012): 428–40.

Hiemstra, Nancy. "'You Don't Even Know Where You Are': Chaotic Geographies of US Migrant Detention and Deportation". In *Carceral Spaces: Mobility and Agency in Imprisonment and Migrant Detention*, edited by Dominique Moran, Nick Gill and Deirdre Conlon. Farnham: Ashgate, 2013.

Hoffman, Sue. "Fear, Insecurity and Risk: Refugee Journeys from Iraq to Australia". PhD thesis, Murdoch University, Perth, 2010*a*.

———. "Looking Back, Looking Forward: Australia, Indonesia and Asylum Seekers 1999–2009". In *Enter at Own Risk? Australia's Population Questions for the 21st Century*, edited by Suvendrini Perera, Graham Seal and Sue Summers. Perth: Black Swan Press, 2010*b*.

Hope, Alastair Neil. "Record of Investigation into Death" (Western Australia State Coroner's report no. 29), 2002 <http://humanrights.gov.au/legal/submissions_court/intervention/husseini.htm> (accessed 9 May 2014).

Horn, Eva. "Partisan, Siedler, Asylant: Zur politischen Anthropologie des Grenzgängers". In *Grenzsoziologie: Die politische Strukturierung des Raumes*, edited by Monika Eigmüller and Georg Vobruba. Wiesbaden: Verlag für Sozialwissenschaften, 2006.

"How Australia Trespassed into Indonesia's Waters, Had Wrong Information". News.com.au, 18 January 2014 <http://www.news.com.au/national/how-australia-trespassed-into-indonesias-waters-had-wrong-information/story-fncynjr2-1226804452006> (accessed 9 May 2014).

Howard, Jessica. "To Deter and Deny: Australia and the Interdiction for Asylum Seekers". *Refuge* 21, no. 4 (2003): 35–50.

Human Rights Watch (HRW). *"By Invitation Only": Australian Asylum Policy*. Washington, DC, 2002 <http://www.hrw.org/reports/2002/australia/australia1202.pdf> (accessed 9 May 2014).

⸻. "The International Organization for Migration (IOM) and Human Rights Protection in the Field: Current Concerns". Paper submitted by HRW to IOM Governing Council Meeting, 86th session, 18 November 2003.

⸻. *Barely Surviving: Detention, Abuse and Neglect of Migrant Children in Indonesia*. New York, 2013.

"Hundreds of Vietnamese Refugees Go on Hunger Strike". Agence France-Presse, 25 April 1994.

Hunter, Cynthia. "The 'People in Between': Indonesia and the Failed Asylum Seekers to Australia". *Review of Indonesian and Malaysian Affairs* 38 (2004): 101–27.

⸻. "People in Between: There is No Home and No Justice for Failed Asylum Seekers". *Inside Indonesia* 88 (2006).

Hunyor, Jonathon. "Don't Jail the Ferryman: The Sentencing of Indonesian 'People Movers'". *Alternative Law Journal* 26 (2001): 223–28.

Hutton, Marg. *Drownings on the Public Record of People Attempting to Enter Australia Irregularly by Boat 1998–2011*, updated 6 February 2013 <http://sievx.com/articles/background/DrowningsTable.pdf> (accessed 26 May 2014).

Hyndman, Jennifer and Alison Mountz. "Another Brick in the Wall? Neo-*refoulement* and the Externalization of Asylum by Australia and Europe". *Government and Opposition* 43 (2008): 249–69.

Içduygu, Ahmet. "The Politics of International Migratory Regimes: Transit Migration Flows in Turkey". *International Social Science Journal* 52 (2000): 357–67.

Içduygu, Ahmet and Sule Toktas. "How Do Smuggling and Trafficking Operate via Irregular Border Crossings in the Middle East? Evidence from Fieldwork in Turkey". *International Migration* 40, no. 6 (2002): 25–54.

"Imigran Afghanistan Setop Mogok Makan". *MetroTV News*, 5 May 2012 <www.metrotvnews.com/metromain/news/2012/05/05/90359/Imigran-Afghanistan-Setop-Mogok-Makan> (accessed 9 May 2014).

"Imigran Mabok di Masjid, Nyaris Tewas Dikromas Warga". *Detak*, 8 November

2013 <http://detak.co.id/home/bogor/item/400-imigran-mabok-di-masjid-nyaris-tewas-dikromas-warga/400-imigran-mabok-di-masjid-nyaris-tewas-dikromas-warga> (accessed 27 May 2014).

"Imigrasi Perketat Pengawasan di Puncak". Antara News, 20 June 2012 <http://bogor.antaranews.com/print/1956/imigrasi-bogor-perketat-pengawasan-di-puncak> (accessed 9 May 2014).

"Immigration Detains Four Afghans for Illegal Entry". *Jakarta Post*, 30 April 2010.

Index Mundi. "Indonesia Net Migration Rate". 2013 <http://www.indexmundi.com/indonesia/net_migration_rate.html> (accessed 9 May 2014).

"Indonesia: Aceh Embraces Rohingya Refugees". *IRIN*, 24 February 2009 <http://www.irinnews.org/report/83120/indonesia-aceh-embraces-rohingya-refugees> (accessed 9 May 2014).

"Indonesia Approaches Alleged Teen Abuse in Australian Prison with Caution". *Jakarta Globe*, 21 July 2012.

"Indonesia Rejects Australia's Request to Extradite Abu Quassey". *Jakarta Post*, 9 November 2001.

"Indonesia Suspends People Smuggling Cooperation following Australia Spy Scandal". *Jakarta Globe*, 20 November 2013.

Indonesian Air Force. "Pelibatan Dalam Operasi Latihan". 2009 <http://tni-au.mil.id/content/pelibatan-dalam-operasi-dan-latihan> (accessed 13 November 2014).

Indonesian Department of Foreign Affairs. *Meeting on the Establishment of a Processing Centre for Indochinese Refugees*, 15–16 May 1979, Jakarta.

Indonesian Department of Information. *Galang Island for Processing Centre of Vietnamese Refugees*. Jakarta: Proyek Pusat Publikasi Pemerintah, 1979.

———. *Pulau Galang, Pusat Pemrosesan Pengungsi Indocina di Indonesia*. Jakarta, 1980.

Indonesian Foreign Ministry. *Diplomasi Indonesia 2013: Fakta dan Angka*. Jakarta, 2013 <http://www.kemlu.go.id/Documents/Diplomasi%202013%20Fakta%20dan%20Angka/Facts%20and%20Figures%202013.pdf> (accessed 7 May 2014).

Indonesian Government. *Program Legislasi Nasional tahun 2005–2009*. 2005 <http://www.jdihukum.bantenprov.go.id/hukum/PROLEGNAS%20DPR.pdf> (accessed 28 January 2014).

Indonesian Ministry of Maritime Affairs and Fisheries. *The Establishment of MMAF*. 2008 <http://www.kkp.go.id/en/index.php/archives/c/2072/MMAF-History/?category_id=53> (accessed 22 October 2014).

International Centre for Migration Policy Development (ICMPD). *Irregular Transit Migration in the Mediterranean: Some Facts, Futures and Insights*. Vienna, 2004.

International Organization for Migration (IOM). *Transit Migration in Poland*. Geneva, 1994.

———. "Indonesia". 2011a <http://www.iom.int/cms/en/sites/iom/home/where-we-work/asia-and-the-pacific/indonesia.html> (accessed 9 May 2014).

———. "IOM, Indonesia Train Police to Combat People Smuggling", 6 May 2011*b* <http://www.iom.ch/cms/en/sites/iom/home/news-and-views/press-briefing-notes/pbn-2011/pbn-listing/iom-indonesia-train-police-to-combat-pe.html> (accessed 9 May 2014).

———. *Assisted Voluntary Return and Reintegration: Annual Report of Activities 2011.* Geneva, 2012*a*.

———. *Programme and Budget for 2013.* Geneva, 2012*b* <http://www.iom.int/files/live/sites/iom/files/About-IOM/governing-bodies/en/council/101/MC_2349.pdf> (accessed 9 May 2014).

International Organization for Migration (IOM) Indonesia. *Buku Petunjuk Bagi Petugas Dalam Rangka Penanganan Kegiatan Penyelundupan Manusia dan Tindak Pidana Yang Berkaitan Dengan Penyelundupan Manusia* [User guide for officers handling human smuggling and criminal offences related to human smuggling]. Jakarta, 2009.

———. *Buku Khotbah: Kumpulan Khotbah Nasrani Tentang Penyelundupan Imigran Illegal.* Jakarta, *c.*2010.

———. *Annual Report 2009.* Jakarta, 2010*a*.

———. *Irregular Migrant People Smuggling: Public Information Campaign, Market Research Report.* Jakarta, 2010*b*.

———. *Labour Migration from Indonesia: An Overview of Indonesian Migration to Selected Destinations in Asia and the Middle East.* Jakarta, 2010*c*.

———. *Public Information Campaign to Curb Irregular Migration and People Smuggling in Indonesia, Final Activities Report.* Jakarta, 2010*d*.

———. *RMIM-Newsletter* 4 (September) 2010*e*.

———. *RMIM-Newsletter* 22 (November) 2011.

———. "Irregular Migrant Statistics under IOM Indonesia Programme as per 30 November 2012" (unpublished report). 2012*a*.

———. *Operational Booklet for the Coordinated Handling of People Smuggling: Interceptions, Investigations and Prosecutions in Indonesia.* Jakarta, 2012*b*.

———. *Petunjuk Penanganan Tindak Pidana Penyelundupan Manusia: Pencegatan, Penyidikan, Penuntutan dan Koordinasi di Indonesia* [Manual for the coordinated handling of people smuggling: interceptions, investigations and prosecutions in Indonesia]. Jakarta, 2012*c*.

———. *Pocketbook on the Handling of People Smuggling Interceptions.* Jakarta, 2012*d*.

———. *RMIM-Newsletter* 24 (April) 2012*e*.

———. "Irregular Migrant Statistics under IOM Indonesia Programme as per 30 June 2013" (unpublished report). 2013*a*.

———. *RMIM-Newsletter* 28 (June) 2013*b*.

———. "Irregular Migrant Statistics under IOM Indonesia Programme as per 28 February 2014" (unpublished report). 2014.

Interpol Indonesia. "Said Mir Bahrami", 13 June 2011 <http://www.interpol.go.id/id/dpo/red-notice/413-said-mir-bahrami> (accessed 9 May 2014).

"Iraqi Man Extradited to Face People Smuggling Charges in Australia". *ABC News*, 1 November 2013 <http://www.abc.net.au/news/2013-11-01/iraqi-man-faces-people-smuggling-charges-in-australia/5064612> (accessed 9 May 2014).

Ismayawati, Isye. *Manusia Perahu: Tragedi Kemanusiaan di Pulau Galang*. Jakarta: Kompas, 2013.

Jakarta Centre for Law Enforcement Cooperation (JCLEC). "About JLEC". 2005 <http://www.jclec.com/index.php?option=com_content&task=view&id=14&Itemid=28> (accessed 6 March 2014).

Jandl, Michael. "The Relationship between Human Smuggling and the Asylum System in Austria". *Journal for Ethnic and Migration Studies* 30 (2004): 799–806.

———. "Irregular Migration, Human Smuggling, and the Eastern Enlargement of the European Union". *International Migration Review* 41 (2007): 291–315.

"Java Asylum-Seekers Refuse to Disembark, Despite Earlier Deal". *The Australian*, 10 April 2012.

Jesuit Refugee Service (JRS). "Indonesia: Finding Ways to Release Stress in Immigration Detention", 18 July 2011 <http://www.jrsap.org/news_detail?TN=NEWS-20110719010058> (accessed 7 June 2012).

"Joint Declaration on Comprehensive Partnership between Australia and the Republic of Indonesia". 2005 <http://www.dfat.gov.au/geo/indonesia/comprehensive_partnership_1105.html> (accessed 7 March 2014).

Jordão, Manuel. Presentation by the UNHCR Country Representative in Indonesia, Joint Seminar on Optimizing the Handling of Human Trafficking, Refugees and Asylum Seekers, Jakarta, 21 November 2012.

"Jual Roti, Imigran Gelap Ditangkap", *Radar Bogor*, 22 October 2010 <http://www.radar-bogor.co.id/index.php?rbi=berita.detail&id=63031> (accessed 1 June 2011).

Juanda, Hongky. "Penananan Imigran Illegal Berstatus Pencari Suaka dan Pengungsi di Wilayah Indonesia". Paper presented at Joint Seminar on Optimizing the Handling of Human Trafficking, Refugees and Asylum Seekers, Jakarta, 21 November 2012.

Kabir, Nahid Afrose. *Muslims in Australia: Immigration, Race Relations and Cultural History*. London: Kegan Paul, 2005.

Karlsen, Elibritt, Janet Phillips and Elsa Koleth. "Seeking Asylum: Australia's Humanitarian Program" (background note). Canberra: Parliamentary Library, 2011 <http://www.aph.gov.au/binaries/library/pubs/bn/sp/seekingasylum.pdf> (accessed 9 May 2014).

Kebon, Asriana. "Of Fishers and Men: Indonesians Held in Detention in Australia for People Smuggling are There Because of Poverty". *Inside Indonesia* 103 (2011).

Kellen, Yoseph. "Plan to House Asylum Seekers in Sumba Stirs Controversy". *Jakarta Globe*, 25 February 2014.

Kevin, Tony. *A Certain Maritime Accident: The Sinking of SIEV X*. Melbourne: Scribe, 2004.

———. *Reluctant Rescuers: An Exploration of the Australian Border Protection System's Safety Record in Detecting and Intercepting Asylum-Seeker Boats, 1998–2011*. Manuka, ACT: T. Kevin, 2012.

Khosravi, Shahram. *"Illegal" Traveller: An Autoethnography of Borders*. Basingstoke: Palgrave Macmillan, 2010.

Kimball, Ann. *The Transit State: A Comparative Analysis of Mexican and Moroccan Immigration Policies* (working paper no. 150). San Diego: Center for Comparative Immigration Studies, University of California, 2007.

Kistyarini. "Bikin Tali Handuk, 13 Tahanan Kabur". *Kompas*, 28 June 2011*a*.

———. "Imigran Gelap Demo Tuntut Status". *Kompas*, 25 July 2011*b*.

Kneebone, Susan. "The Legal and Ethical Implications of Extra-Territorial Processing of Asylum Seekers: Europe Follows Australia". In *Seeking Asylum in Australia 1995–2005: Experiences and Policies*, edited by Susan Aykut and Jessie Taylor. Clayton, Vic: Institute of Public History, Monash University, 2006.

———. "Controlling Migration by Sea: The Australian Case". In *Extraterritorial Immigration Control: Legal Challenges*, edited by Bernard Ryan and Valsamis Mitsilegas. Leiden: Koninklijke Brill NV, 2010.

Komisi Nasional Hak Asasi Manusia (Komnas HAM). *Penelitian Tentang Pengungsi (Refugee) dan Pencari Suaka (Asylum Seeker) di Indonesia*. Bagian Pengkajian dan Penelitian, 2012.

Koser, Khalid. "Why Migrant Smuggling Pays". *International Migration* 46, no. 2 (2008): 3–26.

———. "Dimensions and Dynamics of Irregular Migration". *Population, Space and Place* 16 (2010*a*): 181–93.

———. *Responding to Boat Arrivals in Australia: Time for a Reality Check*. Sydney: Lowy Institute, 2010*b*.

Krismantari, Ika. "Displaced People Big Spenders in Puncak". *Jakarta Post*, 24 June 2010.

Kuncara, Mochamad Tatra. "Upaya-upaya Diplomasi Australia Terhadap Indonesia Dalam Menghadapi Imigrasi Illegal dan Penyelundupan Imigran ke Australia". *Jurnal Ilmiah Hubungan Internasional* 6, no. 2 (2010): 72–97.

Kurnia, Asep. *Imigran Ilegal: Potret Penanganan dan Pencegahan dalam Perspektif Sistem Manajemen Nasional*. Jakarta: IOM Indonesia, 2011.

Kusmayadi. "2 Polisi Ditangkap, Diduga Bekingi Penyelundupan Imigran ke Australia". *detikNews*, 25 April 2012 <http://news.detik.com/read/2012/04/25/144925/1901259/10/2-polisi-ditangkap-diduga-bekingi-penyelundupan-imigran-ke-australia> (accessed 9 May 2014).

"Lampung Menjadi Jalur Favorit Para Imigran". *Radar Lampung*, 19 January 2012.

Lander, Brian. "Indonesia: Far from Paradise". *Refugees Magazine* 104 (1996).

Leach, Michael and Fethi Mansouri. *Lives in Limbo: Voices of Refugees under Temporary Protection*. Sydney: University of New South Wales Press, 2004.

Leribun, Joe. "Minta Suaka, Warga Somalia Demo Kantor UNHCR". *Kompas*, 6 November 2012.

Liempt, Ilse van and Jeroen Doomernik. "Migrant's Agency in the Smuggling Process: the Perspectives of Smuggled Migrants in the Netherlands". *International Migration* 44, no. 4 (2006): 166–90.

Lindsey, Tim. "Australia, Indonesia and the Boat People". *The Diplomat* 1, no. 1 (2002): 20–3.

———. "'Preposterous Caricatures': Fear, Tokenism, Denial and the Australia–Indonesia Relationship". *Dialogue* 29, no. 2 (2010): 31–43.

Lloyd K., S. Suchet-Pearson, S. Wright and L. Burarrwanga. "Stories of Crossings and Connections from Bawaka, North East Arnhem Land, Australia". *Social & Cultural Geography* 11 (2010): 701–17.

Loescher, Gil and James Milner. "The Missing Link: The Need for Comprehensive Engagement in Regions of Refugee Origin". *International Affairs* 79 (2003): 595–617.

Lutfia, Ismira. "Jakarta Man Tell his Story of Being Conned into Smuggling". *Jakarta Globe*, 16 July 2012.

Mackie, Jamie. *Australia and Indonesia: Current Problems, Future Prospects*. Sydney: Lowy Institute for International Policy, 2007.

Magner, Tara. "A Less than 'Pacific' Solution for Asylum Seekers in Australia". *International Journal of Refugee Law* 16 (2004): 53–90.

Mainwaring, Cetta. "Constructing a Crisis: The Role of Immigration Detention in Malta". *Population, Space and Place* 18 (2012): 687–700.

"Malaysia to Extradite Alleged People Smuggler". *Express Tribune*, 15 August 2012.

Malaysian Immigration Department. "Visa Requirements by Country". 2013 <http://www.imi.gov.my/index.php/en/main-services/visa/visa-requirement-by-country/7-perkhidmatan-utama/286-visa-requirement-by-country> (accessed 14 November 2014).

"Man to Stand Trial over Christmas Island Boat Tragedy". *ABC News*, 4 November 2011 <http://www.abc.net.au/news/2011-11-04/people-smuggler-pleads-not-guilty/3629590> (accessed 12 March 2014).

Mansouri, Fethi. "Middle Eastern Refugees in 'Fortress' Australia". In *Australia and the Middle East: A Front-Line Relationship*, edited by Fethi Mansouri. London, New York: Tauris Academic Studies, 2006.

Mares, Peter. "Moving the Barriers Offshore: Cooperation with Indonesia Reduces the Number of 'Boat People' Arriving on Australia's Shores". *Rantau* 2 (2001): 11.

————. *Borderline: Australia's Response to Refugees and Asylum Seekers in the Wake of the Tampa*. Kensington: UNSW Press, 2002.

Marr, David and Marian Wilkinson. *Dark Victory: How a Government Lied its Way to Political Triumph*. Crows Nest, NSW: Allen and Unwin, 2003.

Marthinus, Pierre. "Flipping over the Boats: Restoring RI-Oz Ties". *Jakarta Post*, 18 February 2014.

Martin, Lisa. "Indonesia to Get Asylum Seeker Cash", *The Australian*, 13 May 2014.

Masanauskas, John. "Make Way for 'Jetset' Asylum Seekers". *Herald Sun*, 22 September 2011.

Mason, Jana. "Paying the Price: Australia, Indonesia Try to Stop Asylum Seekers". *Refugee Reports* 22, no. 8 (2001).

Maulia, Erwida. "Children Remain Hopeful for the Future while in Refuge". *Jakarta Post*, 1 February 2012.

McBeth, John. "Long Goodbye: Vietnamese Asylum Seekers Revolt on Island Camp". *Far Eastern Economic Review* 158, no. 28 (1994): 16.

McCormack, Terri. "East Timorese". *Dictionary of Sydney*. 2008 <http://www.dictionaryofsydney.org/entry/east_timorese> (accessed 12 May 2014).

McDougall, Derek. "Australia and the 'War on Terrorism': A Preliminary Assessment". In *Australian Security after 9/11: New and Old Agendas*, edited by Derek McDougall and Peter Shearman. Burlington, VT: Ashgate, 2006.

————. "Australia's Engagement with its 'Near Broad': A Change of Direction under the Labor Government, 2007–2010". *Commonwealth & Comparative Politics* 49 (2011): 318–41.

McIntyre, Andrew and Douglas Ramage. *Seeing Indonesia as a Normal Country: Implications for Australia*. Barton, ACT: Australian Strategic Policy Institute, 2008.

McRae, Dave. *A Few Poorly Organized Men: Interreligious Violence in Poso, Indonesia*. Leiden: Brill, 2013.

————. *More Talk Than Walk: Indonesia as a Foreign Policy Actor*. Sydney: Lowy Institute, 2014.

Meliala, Adrianus. *Pemantapan Legalitas dan Kebijakan Menyangkut Penyelundupan Manusia*. Jakarta: Fakultas Ilmu Sosial dan Ilmu Politik, Universitas Indonesia, 2011.

Meliala, Adrianus, Herlina Permata Sari, et al. *Critical Assessment on People Smuggling in Indonesia and its Various Impacts, Research Report*. Jakarta: Department of Criminology, University of Indonesia in collaboration with Jakarta Centre for Law Enforcement Cooperation, 2011.

"Menlu RI: Australia Harus Tentukan Jadi Teman Atau Lawan Indonesia". *Kompas*, 17 February 2014.

Metcalfe, Susan. *The Pacific Solution*. Melbourne: Australian Scholarly Publishing, 2010.

"Minors Tell of Abuse in Australian Prison". *Jakarta Post*, 20 July 2012.

Missbach, Antje. *Politics and Conflict in Indonesia: The Role of the Acehnese Diaspora*. New York: Routledge, 2011.

———. "Easy Pickings: The Plight of Asylum Seekers in Indonesia". *Asian Currents*, June/July 2012.

———. "People Smuggling Trials in RI". *Jakarta Post*, 28 May 2013.

———. "Doors and Fences: Controlling Indonesia's Porous Borders and Policing Asylum Seekers". *Singapore Journal for Tropical Geography* 35, no. 2 (2014*a*): 228–44.

———. "Indonesia's Treatment of Transit Migrants: Everyday Life Realities between Human Rights Protection and Criminalisation". In *Migration Flows and Regional Integration in Europe, Southeast Asia and Australia: A Comparative Perspective*, edited by Juliet Pietsch and Marshall Clark. Amsterdam: Amsterdam University Press, 2014*b*.

Missbach, Antje and Melissa Crouch. "The Criminalisation of People Smuggling: Legal Insights from Indonesia". *Australian Journal of Asian Law* 14, no. 2 (2013): 1–19.

Missbach, Antje and Anne McNevin. "Anti-people Smuggling Campaigns in Indonesia: Using Religion for Deterrence". *Inside Story*, 5 November 2014.

Missbach, Antje and Frieda Sinanu. "'The Scum of the Earth'? Foreign People Smugglers and Their Local Counterparts in Indonesia". *Journal of Current Southeast Asian Affairs* 30, no. 4 (2011): 57–87.

———. "Life and Death in Detention". *Inside Indonesia* 113 (2013).

———. "People Smuggling in Indonesia: Dependency, Exploitation and Other Vulnerabilities". In *Human Trafficking in Asia: Forcing Issues*, edited by Sallie Yea and Pattana Kitiarsa. New York: Routledge, 2014.

Mohari, Henky. "Ratusan Imigran Desak UNHCR Tentukan Status". Antara News, Kepulauan Riau, 25 July 2011 <http://kepri.antaranews.com/berita/17868/ratusan-imigran-desak-unhcr-tentukan-status> (accessed 6 June 2013).

Moore, Matthew. "Australia 'Has No Right' to Smuggler". *The Age*, 11 February 2003.

Moran, Dominique, Nick Gill and Deirdre Conlon, eds. *Carceral Spaces: Mobility and Agency in Imprisonment and Migrant Detention*. Farnham: Ashgate, 2013.

Morrison, Scott. "A Year of Stronger Borders". Press Statement, 18 September 2014 <http://www.minister.immi.gov.au/media/sm/2014/sm217927.htm> (accessed 23 October 2014).

Morrison, Scott, Angus Campbell and Steve Lancaster. "Operation Sovereign Borders Update". Press Conference, Sydney, 25 October 2013 <http://www.minister.immi.gov.au/media/sm/2013/sm209107.htm> (accessed 12 May 2014).

Moulin, Carolina and Peter Nyers. "'We Live in a Country of UNHCR': Refugee

Protest and Global Political Society". *International Political Sociology* 1 (2007): 356–72.

Mountz, Alison. "The Enforcement Archipelago: Detention, Haunting, and Asylum on Islands". *Political Geography* 30 (2011a): 118–28.

———. "Where Asylum-Seekers Wait: Feminist Counter-Topographies of Sites between States". *Gender, Place & Culture* 18 (2011b): 381–99.

Munro, Peter. "People Smuggling and the Resilience of Criminal Networks in Indonesia". *Journal of Policing, Intelligence and Counter Terrorism* 6, no. 1 (2011): 40–50.

Museum Pulau Galang, Galang Kota, *c*.2010.

Nabbs-Keller, Greta. "Indonesia as ASEAN Chair: A Test of Democracy". *The Interpreter*, 29 June 2010.

Nassery, Ramezan Ali. "Questions". Interview conducted on 7 February 2004 in Mataram <http://www.hazara.net/refugees/indonesia/interview.pdf> (accessed 10 July 2011).

Nethery, Amy, Brynna Rafferty-Brown and Savitri Taylor. "Exporting Detention: Australian-Funded Immigration Detention in Indonesia". *Journal of Refugee Studies* 26, no. 1 (2013): 88–109.

Nethery, Amy and Carly Gordyn. "Australia-Indonesia Cooperation on Asylum-Seekers: A Case of 'Incentivised Policy Transfer'". *Australian Journal of International Affairs* 68, no. 2 (2014): 177–93.

Neumann, Klaus and Savitri Taylor. "Australia, Indonesia, and West Papuan Refugees, 1962–2009". *International Relations of the Asia-Pacific* 10, no. 1 (2009): 1–31.

Newspoll. *Australian Attitudes towards Indonesia: Report*. Canberra, 2013.

Nicholson, Brendan. "New Indonesian Spy Claims Put Jakarta Relationship Back in Spotlight". *The Australian*, 17 February 2014.

Nicholson, Brendan and Mark Dodd. "Abbott Slams Boatpeople as Un-Christian". *The Australian*, 10 July 2012.

Nicholson, Brendan and Paul Maley. "Julie Bishop Says Coalition's Policies Would Not Breach Indonesia's Sovereignty". *The Australian*, 17 September 2013.

Nicholson, Brendan and Peter Alford. "Boat Plan Could Spark Navy Deaths, Indonesia Backlash". *The Australian*, 23 January 2012.

Norman, Jane. "Indonesia Says Email about Talks between Marty Natalegawa and Julie Bishop Sent to Media by Mistake". *ABC News*, 27 September 2013 <http://www.abc.net.au/news/2013-09-27/indonesia-says-bishop-talks-email-sent-in-error/4984416> (accessed 23 October 2014).

Nugroho, Bambang Hartadi. "Challenges for Indonesia as ASEAN Chair". *Jakarta Post*, 6 January 2011.

Nyers, Peter and Kim Rygiel, eds. *Citizenship, Migrant Activism and the Politics of Movement*. London: Routledge, 2012.

Obidzinski, Krystof, Agus Andrianto and Chandra Wijaya. *Timber Smuggling in Indonesia Critical or Overstated Problem? Forest Governance Lessons from Kalimantan*. Bogor: Center for International Forestry Research, 2006.

O'Brien, Natalie. "Teen Refugees Excluded Until Adulthood". *The Age*, 11 August 2013.

Oelgemoller, Christina. "'Transit' and 'Suspension': Migration Management or the Metamorphosis of Asylum-Seekers into 'Illegal' Immigrants". *Migration Studies* 37, no. 3 (2011): 407–24.

Oliver, Alex. *Australia and the World: The 2013 Lowy Institute Poll Report*. Sydney: Lowy Institute, 2013.

Osborne, Paul. "Behind Howard's Last Boat Tow-back". *The Australian*, 28 March 2013.

Packham, Ben. "People-Smuggling Suspect Captain Emad's Australian Visa Cancelled". *The Australian*, 3 August 2012.

Palang Merah Indoneisa (PMI) "Kerja Sama PMI Kota Makassar dan UNHCR". 2005 <http://www.pmi.or.id/ina/publication/?act=detail&p_id=483> (accessed 20 May 2014).

Palmer, David. "Between a Rock and a Hard Place: The Case of Papuan Asylum Seekers". *Australian Journal of Politics and History* 52 (2006): 576–603.

Papadopoulou, Aspasia. "Smuggling into Europe: Transit Migrants in Greece". *Journal of Refugee Studies* 17 (2004): 167–84.

———. *Exploring the Asylum-Migration Nexus: A Case Study of Transit Migrants in Europe* (Working Paper 23). Geneva: Global Commission on International Migration (GCIM), 2005.

Papadopoulou-Kourkoula, Aspasia. *Transit Migration: The Missing Link between Emigration and Settlement*. New York: Palgrave Macmillan, 2008.

"Pengalaman Membuktikan Proses Persidangan Terpidana Warga Negara Indonesia di Australia Bisa Bertahun-Tahun. Ekstradisinya Tidak Gampang". Hukum Online.com, 5 March 2009 <http://www.hukumonline.com/berita/baca/hol21365/penyelundupan-orang-dan-ekstradisi-kerikil-dalam-hubungan-indonesia--australia> (accessed 20 May 2014).

"Pengangkut Imigran Gelap Divonis Tujuh Tahun". *Timor Express*, 22 June 2012.

"People Smugglers Set Up Business in Australia". *ABC Four Corners*, 4 June 2012 <http://www.abc.net.au/news/2012-06-04/powerful-people-smugglers-caught-living-in-australia/4050506> (accessed 20 May 2014).

Perpitch, Nicolas. "People-Smuggler Ali Khorram Heydarkhani Jailed 14 Years over Christmas Island Tragedy". *The Australian*, 22 October 2012.

Pertiwi, Ni Luh Made. "Kamp Vietnam di Batam Jadi Hotel?" *Kompas*, 20 July 2012.

Petersen, Freya, Cynthia Banham and Mark Riley. "Judge Rejects Bid to Return Kurdish Boat People". *Sydney Morning Herald*, 15 November 2003.

Phillips, Janet. *Asylum Seekers and Refugees: What Are the Facts?* Canberra: Parliamentary Library, 2011 <https://www.aph.gov.au/binaries/library/pubs/bn/sp/asylumfacts.pdf> (accessed 23 May 2014).

Phillips, Janet and Harriet Spinks. *Boat Arrivals in Australia since 1976.* Canberra: Parliamentary Library, 2013 <http://www.aph.gov.au/About_Parliament/Parliamentary_Departments/Parliamentary_Library/pubs/rp/rp1314/BoatArrivals#_Toc347230718> (accessed 22 May 2014).

Phillips, Melissa Anne. "Re-visualising New Arrivals in Australia: Journey Narratives of Pre-Migration and Settlement". PhD thesis, University of Melbourne, 2012.

Pickering, Sharon and Leanne Weber, eds. *Borders, Mobility and Technologies of Control.* Dordrecht: Springer, 2006.

Pitakasari, Ajeng Ritzki. "Kapal Pengangkut Imigran Terdampar, Nahkoda Diduga Kabur". *Republika*, 26 July 2012.

Poke, Eras. "43 Illegal Immigrants Freed from Indonesian Detention by Fake Phone Call". *Jakarta Globe*, 27 February 2010.

"Polda Banten Tangkap Pelaku Penyelundupan Imigran Gelap". *Suara Pembaruan*, 21 May 2013.

Powell, Sian. "Welcome to the People-Smuggler Frontline: Two Runabouts, Two Hours of Fuel and 117km to Patrol". *The Australian*, 6 July 2012.

Prasetyo, Aris. "Mengabadikan Kisah Kemanusiaan di Pulau Galang". *Kompas*, 30 August 2010.

Prima, Dian: "Cabuli Gadis Lokal, Imigran Pakistan Babak Belur". *Inilahcom*, 27 April 2012 <http://m.inilah.com/read/detail/1855510/cabuli-gadis-lokal-imigran-pakistan-babak-belur> (accessed 23 May 2014).

Refugee Action Collective. "Howard's Forgotten People: Ninety-two Asylum Seekers Left to Rot on Lombok". Media release, 10 October 2005 <http://rac-vic.org/archive/media-releases/media_05_10_10.htm> (accessed 23 April 2012).

Refugee Council of Australia. "Global Refugee Statistics". Surry Hills, NSW, 2013 <http://www.refugeecouncil.org.au/r/stat-int.php> (accessed 23 May 2014).

"Regional Cooperation Framework". Bali Process, 2011 <http://www.baliprocess.net/regional-cooperation-framework> (accessed 10 March 2014).

Rintoul, Stuart. "Refugees' Cut-price Ticket to Death". *The Australian*, 29 June 2012.

Roberts, Anita. *Asylum Seekers dari Timur Tengah di Indonesia: dari Perspektif Republik Indonesia.* Malang: Australian Consortium for In-Country Indonesian Studies (ACICIS), *c.*2001.

Roberts, George. "Indonesian Uni Grants Scholarships to Asylum Seekers". *ABC News*, 14 August 2013a <http://www.abc.net.au/news/2013-08-14/

indonesian-uni-grants-scholarships-to-asylum-seekers/4885170> (accessed 23 May 2014).

———. "Court Hears Jailed Smuggler Had Australian Links". *ABC News*, 21 February 2013*b* <http://www.abc.net.au/news/2013-02-21/court-hears-of-australian-links-to-jailed-people-smuggler/4530982> (accessed 23 May 2014).

———. "Indonesian President Susilo Bambang Yudhoyono's Bodyguard Involved in People Smuggling, Court Judgment Shows". *ABC News*, 21 May 2014 <http://www.abc.net.au/news/2014-05-21/indonesian-president-bodyguard-involved-in-people-smuggling/5466530> (accessed 24 October 2014).

Robinson, Courtland. "The Comprehensive Plan of Action for Indochinese Refugees, 1989–1997: Sharing the Burden and Passing the Buck". *Journal of Refugees Studies* 17, no. 3 (2004): 319–33.

Rodgers, Emma. "Rudd Wants People Smugglers to 'Rot in Hell'". ABC News, 17 April 2009 <http://www.abc.net.au/news/2009-04-17/rudd-wants-people-smugglers-to-rot-in-hell/1653814> (accessed 23 May 2014)

Roggeveen, Sam. "Diplomatic Fallout from the Latest Snowden Revelations". *The Interpreter*, 18 November 2013.

"Rumah Detensi Imigrasi Dianggap Tidak Perlu Ditambah". Pencaru Suaka di Indonesia, 7 March 2011 <http://pencarisuakaindonesia.blogspot.com.au/2011/03/rumah-detensi-imigrasi-dianggap-tidak.html> (accessed 23 May 2014).

Salna, Karlis. "Indonesia Refuses to Take Asylum Seekers". *The Australian*, 8 November 2013.

Sanchez, Gabriella. "Human Smuggling Facilitators in the US Southwest". In *The Routledge Handbook on Crime and International Migration*, edited by Sharon Pickering and Julie Ham. Abingdon, Oxfordshire: Routledge, 2015.

Saragih, Bagus BT. "RI Disappointed over People Smuggling Report". *Jakarta Post*, 7 June 2012*a*.

———. "RI, Aussie Discuss People Smuggling, Detained Minors". *Jakarta Post*, 17 July 2012*b*.

———. "RI–Australia Relations: SBY, Abbott Omit Talk on Minors". *Jakarta Post*, 16 October 2012*c*.

———. "SBY Braces for Asylum, Cattle Talks with Rudd". *Jakarta Post*, 4 July 2013.

Saragih, Bagus BT and Yohanna Ririhena. "Australia Gets Pledges from Boat People Homelands". *Jakarta Post*, 21 August 2013.

Sassen, Saskia. *Guest and Aliens*. New York: New Press, 1999.

Schiller, Nina Glick, Linda Basch and Christina Szanton Blanc. *Nations Unbound: Transnational Projects, Postcolonial Predicaments and Deterritorialized Nation-States*. Amsterdam: Gordon and Breach, 1994.

Schloenhardt, Andreas. *Migrant Smuggling: Illegal Migration and Organised Crime in Australia and the Asia Pacific Region*. Leidenn: Nijhoff, 2003.

Schloenhardt, Andreas and Charles Martin. "Prosecution and Punishment of People Smugglers in Australia 2008–2011". *Federal Law Review* 40, no. 1 (2012): 111–40.

Schloenhardt, Andreas and Linley Ezzy. "Hadi Ahmadi – and the Myth of the 'People Smugglers' Business Model'". *Monash University Law Review* 38, no. 3 (2012): 120–47.

Schloenhardt, Andreas and Connor Davies. "Smugglers and Samaritans: Defences to People Smuggling in Australia". *University of New South Wales Law Journal* 36, no. 3 (2013): 954–84.

Schuster, Liza. "The Continuing Mobility of Migrants in Italy: Shifting between Places and Statuses". *Journal of Ethnic and Migration Studies* 31, no. 4 (2005a): 757–74.

―――. *The Realities of a New Asylum Paradigm* (working paper no. 20). Oxford: Centre on Migration, Policy and Society, University of Oxford, 2005b.

Schuster, Liza and Nassim Majidi. "What Happens Post-Deportation? The Experience of Deported Afghans". *Migration Studies* 1, no. 2 (2013): 221–40.

"Sebanyak 106 Warga Etnis Rohingya Diamankan Polisi Garut". *Pos Kota*, 17 November 2013.

Sen, Krishna. "Beef, Boats and Elections: What's in Store for the Australia–Indonesia Relationship". *The Conversation*, 20 September 2013.

Seo, Yohanes. "Polisi Sita Uang Imigran Afganistan". *Tempo Interaktif*, 19 March 2010.

Sheehy, Alexandra and Karlis Salna. "Man behind Deadly Voyages Faces 7 years". *The Australian*, 13 February 2013.

Simanjuntak, Hotli. "'Boat People' Stranded in Aceh". *Jakarta Post*, 3 February 2012.

Sitohang, Japanton. "Masalah Imigrasi Illegal: Dari dan Melalui Indonesia". In *Indonesia Dalam Strategi Keamanan Australia: Persoalan Migrasi Illegal*, edited by M. Riefqi Muna. Jakarta: Pusat Penelitian Politik, 2002.

Skelton, Russell. "People Smugglers Operate on Streets of Dandenong". *The Age*, 29 January 2011.

Soeprapto, Enny. "Indonesia Must Ratify 1951 UN Convention". *Jakarta Post*, 28 July 2001.

Somba, Nethy Dharma. "Asylum Seekers Detained in Merauke". *Jakarta Post*, 20 August 2013.

Spinks, Harriet, Elibritt Karlsen, Nigel Brew, Marty Harris and David Watt. *Australian Government Spending on Irregular Maritime Arrivals and Counter-People Smuggling Activity*. Canberra: Parliamentary Library, 2011.

Stacey, Natasha. *Boats to Burn: Bajo Fishing Activity in the Australian Fishing Zone*. Canberra: ANU E-Press, 2007.

Stevens, Dallal. *What Do We Mean by Protection?* Warwick School of Law, research paper no. 20. Warwick: University of Warwick, 2013.

Suminar, Ilmi. "Seorang Ibu Rumah Tangga Yang Menjadi Perempuan Pebisnis". CWS Indonesia, 8 March 2011 <http://www.cwsindonesia.or.id/id/news/103_Seorang+ibu+rumah+tangga+yang+menjadi+perempuan+pebisnisn> (accessed 23 May 2014).

"Tahan ABK Muda, Australia Diharapkan Beri Pemberdayaan Sosial". *Liputan 6*, 11 February 2013 <http:// news.liputan6.com/read/509460/tahan-abk-muda-australia-diharapkan-beri-pemberdayaan-sosial> (accessed 23 May 2014).

Tanjung, Banda Haruddin. "28 Imigran Gelap di Pekanbaru Kabur". Antara News, 5 December 2010.

Tanter, Richard. "After Fear, Before Justice: Indonesia and Australia over the Long Haul, as if Ethics Mattered". *Inside Indonesia* 61 (2000).

Taylor, Jessie. *Behind Australian Doors: Examining the Conditions of Detention of Asylum Seekers in Indonesia*. Asylum Seekers in Indonesia: Project, Findings & Recommendations. 2009 <http://www.law.monash.edu/castancentre/news/behind-australian-doors-report.pdf> (accessed 23 May 2014).

———. "Between the Devil and the Deep Blue Sea: A Reflection on What Turns a Person into a Boat Person". *Local–Global* 8 (2010): 22–27.

Taylor, Julie. "Extradition Issues Arising in People Smuggling Matters: Australia's Experience". Paper presented at Technical Expert Workshop on Mutual Legal Assistance (MLA) and Law Enforcement, Bangkok, May/June 2011.

Taylor, Savitri. "The Pacific Solution or a Pacific Nightmare: The Difference between Burden Shifting and Responsibility Sharing". *Asian-Pacific Law and Policy Journal* 6, no. 1 (2005): 1–43.

———. "From Border Control to Migration Management: The Case of a Paradigm Change in the Western Response to Transborder Population Movement". *Social Policy & Administration* 39, no. 6 (2006): 563–86.

———. "Australia's Border Control and Refugee Protection Capacity Building Activities in the Asia-Pacific Region". In *Asylum Seekers: International Perspective on Interdiction and Deterrence*, edited by A. Babacan and L. Briskman. Cambridge: Cambridge Scholars Publishing, 2008.

———. "Asylum Seekers and the Houston Report's 'Australian Solution'". *The Conversation*, 23 August 2012.

———. "Towing Back the Boats: Bad Policy Whatever Way You Look at It". *The Conversation*, 12 June 2013.

Taylor, Savitri and Brynna Rafferty-Brown. "Waiting for Life to Begin: The Plight of Asylum Seekers Caught by Australia's Indonesia Solution". *International Journal of Refugee Law* 22, no. 4 (2010*a*): 558–92.

———. "Difficult Journeys: Accessing Refugee Protection in Indonesia". *Monash University Law Review* 36, no. 3 (2010*b*): 1–32.

Tempo. Investigasi Sindikat Manusia Perahu, special issue, 11–17 June 2012.

Thom, Graham. "Houston Report a Major Setback for Refugee Rights". *The Drum*, 13 August 2012.

"Tony Abbott Wants Faster Progress on Code of Conduct with Jakarta". *The Australian*, 17 February 2014.

"Tony Abbott's Boat Buy-back Plan an 'Insult to Indonesia'". *The Australian*, 26 August 2013.

Toohey, Paul. "That Sinking Feeling: Asylum Seekers and the Search for an Indonesian Solution", *Quarterly Essay* 53, March 2014.

Tran, Quan Tue. "Remembering the Boat People Exodus: A Tale of Two Memorials". *Journal of Vietnamese Studies* 7, no. 3 (2012): 80–121.

Tran, Yen. "The Closing of the Saga of the Vietnamese Asylum Seekers: The Implications on International Refugees and Human Rights Laws". *Houston Journal of International Law* 17, no. 3 (1995): 463–517.

Triandafyllidou, Anna and Thanos Maroukis. *Migrant Smuggling: Irregular Migration from Asia and Africa to Europe*. New York: Palgrave Macmillan, 2012.

Trotter, Andrew and Matt Garozzo. "Mandatory Sentencing for People Smuggling: Issues of Law and Policy". *Melbourne University Law Review* 36 no. 2 (2012): 553–617.

Türk, Volker. *Statement by the Director of International Protection*, UNHCR Headquarters, at the Special Conference on Irregular Movement of Persons, Jakarta, 20 August 2013.

UNHCR. *The 1951 Refugee Convention*. Geneva, 1951 <http://www.unhcr.org/pages/49da0e466.html> (accessed 25 May 2014).

———. *The State of the World's Refugees: Fifty Years of Humanitarian Action*. Oxford: Oxford University Press, 2000.

———. *Statistical Yearbook 2002*. Geneva, 2003 <http://www.unhcr.org/414ad5af7.pdf> (accessed 27 May 2014)

———. *Statistical Yearbook 2006*. Geneva, 2007 <http://www.unhcr.org/478cda572.html> (accessed 27 May 2014).

———. *Input Provided by the United Nations High Commissioner for Refugees into the Office of the High Commissioner for Human Rights' Compilation and Stakeholders Reports for the Universal Periodic Review of Indonesia*. Geneva, 2007.

———. *Frequently Asked Questions About Resettlement*. September 2009 <http://www.unhcr.org/refworld/docid/4ac0d7e52.html> (accessed 24 May 2014).

———. *Frequently Asked Questions About Resettlement*. Geneva, 2010 <https://www.unhcr.org.hk/files/news/faq/News%20and%20Updates_FAQ%20about%20Resettlement.pdf> (accessed 26 May 2014).

———. *Asylum Levels and Trends in Industrialized Countries 2010*. Geneva: Division of Programme Support and Management, 2011a <http://www.unhcr.org/4d8c5b109.html> (accessed 25 May 2014).

————. *Refugee Protection and Mixed Migration: The 10-Point Plan in Action*. Geneva, 2011*b* <http://www.refworld.org/docid/4d9430ea2.html> (accessed 25 May 2014).

————. *Global Trends 2011*. Geneva, 2012*a* <http://www.unhcr.org/4fd6f87f9.html> (accessed 25 May 2014).

————. *Guidelines on the Applicable Criteria and Standards Relating to the Detention of Asylum-seekers and Alternatives to Detention*. Geneva, 2012*b* <http://www. refworld.org/docid/503489533b8.html> (accessed 25 May 2014).

————. "UNHCR Releases New Guidelines on Detention of Asylum-seekers". Briefing Notes. Geneva, 21 September 2012*c* <http://www.unhcr.org/ 505c461f9.html> (accessed 25 May 2014).

————. "2013 UNHCR Country Operations Profile — Malaysia". Geneva, 2013*a* <http://www.unhcr.org/pages/49e4884c6.html> (accessed 31 July 2013).

————. "2013 UNHCR Country Operations Profile — Thailand". Geneva, 2013*b* <http://www.unhcr.org/cgi-bin/texis/vtx/page?page=49e489646> (accessed 31 July 2013).

————. *Global Appeal 2013 Update*. Geneva, 2013*c* <http://www.unhcr.org/ga13/ index.xml> (accessed 25 May 2014).

————. "UNHCR Calls for Urgent Action to Prevent Rohingya Boat Tragedies". Briefing Notes. Geneva, 22 February 2013*d* <http://www.unhcr.org/cgi-bin/ texis/vtx/search?page=search&docid=512756df9&query=rohingya> (accessed 25 May 2014).

————. "UNHCR Saddened by Loss of Life in Indonesia Detention Centre Incident". Briefing Notes. Geneva, 5 April 2013*e* <http://www.unhcr.org/515eae199. html> (accessed 25 May 2014).

————. "Indonesia: 2014 UNHCR Regional Operations Profile — South-East Asia". Geneva, 2014 <http://www.unhcr.org/cgi-bin/texis/vtx/ page?page=49e488116> (accessed 26 May 2014).

————. Statistical Online Population Database <http://www.unhcr.org/ pages/4a013eb06.html> (accessed 6 January 2014).

UNHCR Canberra. *UNHCR's Views on the Concept of Effective Protection as it Relates to Indonesia*. 2 December 2004 <http://www.unhcr.org.au/pdfs/EFFECT.pdf> (accessed 25 May 2014).

UNHCR Indonesia. "Relasi Dengan Pemerintah dan Peningkatan Kapasitas". Jakarta, 2011 <http://www.unhcr.or.id/id/relasi-pemerintah-dan-peningkatan-kapasitas> (accessed 25 May 2014).

————. "Durable Solutions". Jakarta, 2012*a* <http://www.unhcr.or.id/en/what-we-do/durable-solution> (accessed 25 May 2014).

————. *Fact Sheet & Statistical Information, February 2012*. Jakarta, 2012*b*.

————. *Fact Sheet & Statistical Information, October 2012*. Jakarta, 2012*c*.

————. *Fact Sheet & Statistical Information, December 2012*. Jakarta, 2012*d*.

———. *Fact Sheet & Statistical Information, February 2013*. Jakarta, 2013*a*.

———. *Fact Sheet, March 2013*. Jakarta, 2013*b*.

———. *Fact Sheet, July 2013*. Jakarta, 2013*c*.

———. *Fact Sheet, October 2013*. Jakarta, 2013*d*.

———. *Fact Sheet, November 2013*. Jakarta, 2013*e*.

———. *Fact Sheet, March 2014*. Jakarta, 2014.

UNHCR Malaysia. *Fact Sheet, March 2013*. Kuala Lumpur, 2013.

———. *Statistical Snapshots, January 2014*. Kuala Lumpur, 2014 <http://www.unhcr.org/pages/49e4884c6.html> (accessed 24 October 2014).

UNHCR Thailand. *Statistical Snapshots, January 2014*. Bangkok, 2014 <http://www.unhcr.org/pages/49e489646.html> (accessed 24 October 2014).

Unidjaja, Fabiola Desy. "RI Caught between Egypt and Australia". *Jakarta Post*, 7 February 2003.

United Nations Economic Commission for Europe (UN/ECE). *International Migration Bulletin* 3 (November 1993).

United Nations General Assembly. *Report of the Secretary-General on Meeting on Refugees and Displaced Persons in South-East Asia*, 20–21 July 1979. New York, 1979 <http://www.unhcr.org/refworld/docid/3ae68f420.html> (accessed 11 March 2013).

———. Note on International Protection (A/AC.96/830). New York, 1994 <http://www.refworld.org/docid/3f0a935f2.html> (accessed 5 November 2013).

United Nations Office on Drugs and Crime (UNODC). *Smuggling of Migrants: A Global Review and Annotated Bibliography of Recent Publications*. Vienna, 2011.

United States General Accounting Office. *Vietnamese Asylum Seekers: Refugee Screening Procedures under the Comprehensive Plan of Action: Report to the Chairman, Subcommittee on International Relations and Human Rights, Committee on International Relations, House of Representatives* (GAO/NSAID-97-12). Washington, DC, 1996 <http://www.gao.gov/archive/1997/ns97012.pdf> (accessed 25 May 2014).

Vachudova, Milada. "Eastern Europe as Gatekeeper: The Immigration and Asylum Policies of an Enlarging European Union". In *The Wall around the West: State Borders and Immigration Controls in North America and Europe*, edited by Peter Andreas and Timothy Snyder. Oxford: Rowman and Littlefield, 2000.

Wanandi, Jusuf. "Indonesia: A Failed State?" *Washington Quarterly* 25, no. 3 (2002): 135–46.

"Warga Cisarua Tolak Imigran Ilegal". wn.com, 20 September 2012 <http://article.wn.com/view/2012/09/19/Warga_Cisarua_Tolak_Imigran_Ilegal/> (accessed 23 May 2014).

Warton, Andrew. "The Changing Tide of People Smuggling". *Platypus* 75 (2002): 14–19.

Webber, Frances. "How Voluntary are Voluntary Returns?" *Race & Class* 52, no. 4 (2011): 98–107.

Weber, Leanne. "The Shifting Frontiers of Migration Control". In *Borders, Mobility and Technologies of Control*, edited by Sharon Pickering and Leanne Weber, 21–43. Dordrecht: Springer, 2006.

Weber, Leanne and Sharon Pickering, eds. *Globalization and Borders: Death at the Global Frontier*. London: Palgrave, 2011.

Wesley, Michael. *The Howard Paradox: Australian Diplomacy in Asia, 1996–2006*. Sydney: ABC Books, 2007.

White, Hugh. "What Indonesia's Rise Means for Australia: Northern Exposure". *The Monthly* 90 (June 2013) <http://www.themonthly.com.au/issue/2013/june/1370181600/hugh-white/what-indonesia-s-rise-means-australia> (accessed 13 November 2014).

Wilson, Dean. "Biometrics, Borders and the Ideal Suspect". In *Borders, Mobility and Technologies of Control*, edited by Sharon Pickering and Leanne Weber. Dordrecht: Springer, 2006.

Wilson, Dean and Leanne Weber. "Surveillance, Risk and Preemption on the Australian Border". *Surveillance & Society* 5, no. 2 (2008): 124–41.

Wilson, Lauren. "We Responded Appropriately to Asylum-seeker Distress: Scott Morrison". *The Australian*, 29 September 2013.

Wood, Tamara and Jane McAdam. "Australian Asylum Policy All at Sea: An Analysis of Plaintiff M70/2011 v Minister for Immigration and Citizenship and the Australia–Malaysia Arrangement". *International and Comparative Law Quarterly* 61, no. 1 (2012): 274–300.

World Bank. "Indonesia Overview". 2014 <http://www.worldbank.org/en/country/indonesia/overview> (accessed 23 May 2014).

Wright, Jessica. "Turn-back Policy 'Will Stop the Boats', Says People Smuggler". *Sydney Morning Herald*, 3 February 2014.

Wulandari, Melani. "Becoming Vulnerable in the Community". *Refuge* (Jesuit Refugee Service), March 2012.

Yonesta, Febi. "Situation of Refugee in Indonesia". Presentation by Director of LBH at Jakarta Foreign Correspondents Club, 13 November 2013, Jakarta.

Yursal, Aidi. "Detained for Years, Indonesia's Asylum Seekers Demand Resolution". *Jakarta Globe*, 8 March 2012.

Zaat, Kirsten. *The Protection of Forced Migrants in Islamic Law*. Research paper no. 146. Geneva: UNHCR, 2007.

Indonesian Laws and Regulations
Circular Letter of the Prime Minister on Political Refugees (No. 11/R.I./ of 1956), UNHCR refworld translation <http://www.refworld.org/docid/3ae6b4e918.html> (accessed 27 May 2014).

Law No. 1 of 1979 on Extradition.
Presidential Decree No. 38 of 1979 on the Coordination of the Vietnamese Refugees in Indonesia.
Law No. 9 of 1992 on Immigration.
Law No. 8 of 1994 on Ratification of Extradition Treaty between Indonesia and Australia of 1992.
Law No. 5 of 1998 on Ratification of the United Nations Convention against Transnational Organised Crime.
Law No. 37 of 1999 on Foreign Relations.
Law No. 39 of 1999 on Human Rights.
Directorate General of Immigration (under Department of Justice and Human Rights) Directive No. F-IL.01.10-1297 of 2002 on the procedures regarding aliens expressing their desire to seek asylum or refugees status.
Decree of the Minister of Justice and Human Rights of the Republic of Indonesia No. M.01.PR.07.04 of 2004 on the Organisation and Work Procedures of Immigration Detention Centres.
Presidential Decree No. 10 of 2009 on the Extradition of Hadi Ahmadi.
Regulation of Minister of Justice and Human Rights of the Republic of Indonesia No. M.HH-11.OT.01.01 of 2009 on the Organisation and Administration of Immigration Detention Centres.
Regulation of Minister of Home Affairs of the Republic of Indonesia, No. 49 of 2010 on Guidelines for Monitoring Foreigners and Foreign Community Organisations in the Region.
Regulation of the Director General of Immigration No. IMI-1489.UM.08.05 of 2010 on Processing of Illegal Migrants.
Law No. 6 of 2011 on Immigration.
Presidential Decree No. 23 of 2011 on the National Plan of Action Program on Indonesian Human Rights Year 2011–2014.
Decree of the Coordinating Minister for Political, Legal and Security Affairs No. KEP-10/MENKO/POLHUKAM/1/2013 of 2013 on the [Establishment of a] Desk for Handling People-Smuggling, Refugees and Asylum Seekers.

Decisions of Indonesian Courts
District Court of Serang Decision No. 17/Pid.B/2009/PN.Srg, 1 July 2009 (Sayeed Abbas).
Supreme Court Decision No. 2422K/Pid.Sus/2009, 26 February 2011 (Sayeed Abbas).
District Court of South Jakarta Decision No. 01/Pid.C/Ekts/2013/PN.Jkt.Sel, 11 July 2013 (Sayeed Abbas).
High Court of Jakarta Decision No. 16/PID/Plw/2014/PT.DKI, 25 February 2014 (Sayeed Abbas).

District Court of Cibadak Decision No. 365/Pid.B/2011/PN.Cbd, 3 October 2011 (Heidar Ali).

District Court of Pandeglang Decision No. 23/PID/B/2013/PN.Pdg, 7 May 2013 (Saadhat Ali).

High Court of Banten Decision No. 84/PID/2012/PT.BTN, 10 June 2013 (Saadhat Ali).

District Court of East Jakarta Decision No. 1374/PID.B/2012/PN.JKT.TIM, 16 January 2013 (Dawood Amiri).

District Court of Serang Decision No. 18/Pid.B/2009/PN.SRG, 1 July 2009 (Asadullah).

High Court of Banten Decision No. 129/PID/2009/PT.BTN, 6 January 2010 (Asadullah).

Supreme Court Decision No. 1260 K/Pid.Sus/2010, 21 December 2011 (Asadullah).

District Court of Negeri Praya Decision No. 125/PID.B/2012/PN.PRA, 28 January 2013 (Burhanuddin).

District Court of Selong Decision No. 150/Pid.B/2012/PN.Sel, 27 November 2012 (Eka Gusmansyah and Mahyun).

High Court of Mataram Decision No. 10/PID/2013/PT.MTR, 11 February 2013 (Eka Gusmansyah and Mahyun).

District Court of Mempawah Decision No. 92/Pid.B/2012/PN.MPW, 30 August 2012 (Andy Hermawan et al.).

District Court of Rote Ndao Decision No. 16/Pid.Sus/2012/PN.RND, 19 June 2012 (Husni and Hamka).

High Court of Kupang Decision No. 105/PID/2012/PTK, 26 July 2012 (Husni and Hamka).

District Court of East Jakarta Decision No. 1128/PID.SUS/2013/PN.JKT.TIM, 21 January 2014 (Javaid Mahmood).

Military High Court of East Jakarta Decision No. 34-K/BDG/PMT-II/AD/III/2013 5 April 2013 (Rustam Mamulaty et al.).

District Court of Mempawah Decision No. 94/Pid.B/2012/PN.MPW, 30 August 2012 (Muhammad).

Supreme Court Decision No. 42-K/PM.III-13/AD/VIII/2012, 27 September 2012 (Kornelius Nama and others).

Military High Court III Surabaya (East Java) Decision No. 86-K/PMT.III/BDG/AD/XI/2012, 11 December 2012 (Kornelius Nama).

Supreme Court Decision No. 86-K/PMT.III/BDG/AD/XI/2012, 11 December 2012 (Kornelius Nama and others).

District Court of Mempawah Decision No. 93/Pid.B/2012/PN.MPW, 30 August 2012 (Rio Ojahan et al.).

Military Court II of Yogyakarta Decision No. 49-K/PM.II-11/AD/V/2012, 5 December 2012 (Amin Rukmakmur).

Military High Court of Jakarta Decision No. 10-K/BDG/PMT-II/AD/I/2013, 12 February 2013 (Amin Rukmakmur).

Supreme Court Decision No. 105-K/MIL/2013, 18 June 2013 (Amin Rukmakmur).

Military Court III of Madiun (East Java) Decision No. 38-K/PM.III-13/AD/VII/2012, 24 September 2012 (Ilmun Abdul Said).

Military High Court III of Surabaya Decision (East Java) No. 79-K/PMT.III/BDG/AD/XI/2012, 11 December 2012 (Ilmun Abdul Said).

District Court of Garut Decision No. 21/Pid.Sus/2014/PN.Grt, 26 March 2014 (Malikus Soleh).

District Court of Cibadak Decision No. 15/Pid.B/2012/Pn.CBD, 2 May 2012 (Timotius).

Military High Court in East Jakarta Decision No. 35-K/BDG/PMT-II/AD/III/2013, 5 April 2013 (Rahman Tuasalamony).

Supreme Court Decision No. 171 K/MIL/2013, 17 September 2013 (Rahman Tuasalamony).

Treaties and Non-binding Commitments

Extradition Treaty between Australia and the Republic of Indonesia 1992.

Treaty between the Government of Australia and the Government of the Republic of Indonesia establishing an Exclusive Economic Zone Boundary and Certain Seabed Boundaries (commonly known as Australia–Indonesia Maritime Delimitation Treaty) 1997 <http://www.austlii.edu.au/au/other/dfat/treaties/notinforce/1997/4.html> (accessed 27 May 2014).

Agreement between the Republic of Indonesia and Australia on the Framework for Security Cooperation (commonly known as the Lombok Treaty) 2006 <https://www.dfat.gov.au/geo/indonesia/ind-aus-sec06.html> (accessed 27 May 2014).

Jakarta Declaration on Addressing Irregular Movement of Persons. Jakarta, 20 August 2013 <http://www.unhcr.org/5214ae709.html> (accessed 27 May 2014).

Index

ABOUT THE AUTHOR

Antje Missbach is a research fellow at the Department of Anthropology at Monash University in Melbourne. Living in Indonesia as a teenager sparked an ongoing interest in socio-political developments in Indonesia. She studied Southeast Asian studies and anthropology at Humboldt University in Berlin and obtained a PhD from the Australian National University in Canberra for a thesis about the long-distance politics of the Acehnese diaspora. Before taking up the McKenzie Postdoctoral Fellowship at the University of Melbourne, which allowed her to engage intensively with her research subjects in Indonesia, she taught at universities in Berlin and Heidelberg. Her research has been supported by the Australian Research Council, Fritz-Thyssen-Stiftung and the German Academic Exchange Service (DAAD). Her current research interests include transit migration, diaspora politics, as well as border and mobility studies.

www.ingramcontent.com/pod-product-compliance
Lightning Source LLC
Chambersburg PA
CBHW072053020426
42334CB00017B/1496